THE
EXPLORERS
OF
ARARAT

THE EXPLORERS OF ARARAT

AND THE SEARCH FOR NOAH'S ARK

B. J. Corbin, Editor

Web Site: http://noahsarksearch.com
Email: bjcorbin@noahsarksearch.com

Great Commission Illustrated Books
Long Beach, CA

Web Site: http://greatcommission.com
Email: books@greatcommission.com

THE EXPLORERS OF ARARAT

AND THE SEARCH FOR NOAH'S ARK

Published by Great Commission Illustrated Books

Printed in the United States of America

Second Edition
First Printing, July 1999

ISBN 0-9653469-8-6

Cover Photo by Bob Garbe
Helicopter Pilot Chuck Aaron
1989 Expedition to Mount Ararat, Turkey

Back Cover Background Photo by Robin Simmons
1990 Expedition to Mount Ararat, Turkey

B.J. Corbin Family Photo Copyright Release
Courtesy of Olan Mills

Cover layout by William To

DEDICATION

First, this book is dedicated to the memory of Eryl Cummings, Violet Cummings, Jim Irwin, George Hagopian, Jacob Chuchian, Arthur Chuchian Sr., David Fasold, and Ed Davis. They contributed so much to Ark research over the years and motivated many of us to join the quest for Noah's Ark.

Second, I would like to dedicate this project to everyone involved with the search for Noah's Ark. Though this book is not all-inclusive, it gives a good representation of what Ark researchers experience while searching for Noah's Ark.

Third, to my son Daniel, in the hope that he will grow up to be proud of his father's efforts in the search for the remains of Noah's Ark.

Last, I would like to dedicate this project to my father, Robert Gardner Corbin, Sr., who died February 23, 1999.

B.J. Corbin, 1999

Jim Irwin (far left) and Eryl Cummings (second from right)
Courtesy of John McIntosh

CONTENTS

PREFACE

As the publisher, I felt strongly that a preface was necessary for *The Explorers of Ararat*. Many readers of this book may not know the detailed history of the biblical "mountains of Ararat," of modern day "Mount Ararat," or of the search for Noah's Ark. Because of this, I highly recommend that those people who are not well versed with these topics first read the 1) Introduction, 2) Key Terms, and 3) "Noah's Ark Sources and Alleged Sightings" appendix. This will give the reader, whether novice or expert, a better overview of the history of Mount Ararat and why the explorers of Ararat search for Noah's Ark in that location in the first place. The more than 230 photographs and illustrations included in the book should also help the reader *get the feel* of Mount Ararat. After reading those sections, the reader will understand and enjoy the explorers' stories even more. *The Explorers of Ararat* will be updated to include subsequent expeditions, as new information becomes available.

The uniqueness of *The Explorers of Ararat* can be found in that B.J. Corbin (the initiator and editor of this multi-authored book) and the publisher went to many primary sources to garner the book's material, namely the exploration leaders (who have explored Mount Ararat on nearly 100 expeditions) and the alleged eyewitnesses. Rather than relying completely on secondary or tertiary sources, the writers discuss their own personal knowledge and experiences. In this way, the book avoids the sensationalism normally associated with this subject. For instance, even the title of the popular mass media book, *The Incredible Discovery of Noah's Ark*, should be regarded as misleading, sensationalized and at the very least premature. One may note that the title and cover of this book are purposely much less intriguing than they could be, which is in keeping with the premise of the book to be a more accurate, levelheaded view of the search for Noah's Ark.

As an acknowledgment, the publisher would like to especially thank Bill Crouse and his detailed research of the Noah's Ark historic sources. Bill's *Ararat Report* collection is an invaluable resource and this book's "Noah's Ark Sources and Alleged Sightings" appendix would be remiss to not include his studies. Even more important than the *Ararat Report*, Bill provides critical thought and objectivity that is rare in this subject and counterbalances the emotionalism and extreme interpretations of those who have caught "Ark Fever."

It should be noted that there is absolutely no convincing photographic or hard evidence to indicate that Noah's Ark has survived to the current date on modern day Mount Ararat or anywhere else. In fact, if it were not for the purported sightings and its name, Mount Ararat would have very little to link it with the biblical account.

The only major reason to consider Mount Ararat is because of the few documented eyewitnesses. I encourage the reader to approach this subject with an open mind and consider the evidence both for and against the original statements of the alleged eyewitnesses. In fact, since a number of locations still need to be researched and explored, it is premature to make any final conclusion either way at the present time about the current existence of the Ark. As time marches on, expeditions will continue to research and rule out proposed sites.

In regard to the purported eyewitnesses of Noah's Ark, in most cases their statements are provided directly from their own mouths to the reader rather than as secondhand testimony. However, the eyewitness testimonies are not the only statements provided. The reader is also provided with a critical analysis of each alleged eyewitness with pros and cons about their testimony as well as some comparisons between the eyewitnesses.

Remember that other than the biblical name of "Ararat," the only reason a person would look for Noah's Ark on modern day Mount Ararat is because of the alleged eyewitnesses so their statements need to be cautiously and critically examined. However, it should be stated that some of the so-called eyewitness accounts have been thoroughly disproved already. It is intellectually dishonest for Noah's Ark enthusiasts to propagate false eyewitnesses (such as the alleged eyewitness "Donald Liedmann" who turned out to be an outright fraud) or to perpetuate problematic stories as if they were accepted events in the historic record.

There are a number of problems with some of the eyewitnesses including: many of the witnesses are now older which reduces memory; many are now deceased so no further questioning can take place; and many were in the Armed Forces where information security is necessarily strict and difficult for the public sector to access for verification. Each alleged eyewitness should be treated separately, honestly critiqued and then evaluated. Just because several statements may be highly suspect, only one valid sighting of an object is enough to make the study worthwhile. These issues are discussed in more detail in the "Noah's Ark Sources and Alleged Sightings" appendix.

There is a number of intriguing statements from individuals who indicate that there may be a barge-like or boat-like structure high on modern day Mount Ararat. These statements are really the primary basis for the search on Mount Ararat. Although there are questions and concerns about each of these statements, some of the accounts come from somewhat credible people including the following. This is not an all-inclusive list but does relate some of the more credible statements.

Year	Author of Statement
1900-1908	Armenian shepherd George Hagopian
1921	Russian Colonel Alexander A. Koor
1942	U.S. Navy Machinist Mate 1st Class Ray Lubeck
1942	U.S. Seabees Dale Nice and Roy Tibbetts
1943	U.S. Army Corps of Engineers Sergeant Ed Davis
1943-1945	U.S. Air Force Technical Sergeant Vince Will
1945	U.S. Army Air Forces Corporal Lester Walton
1948	U.S. Air Force Personnel Andy Anderson
1953	U.S. Navy Photographer & Chief Petty Officer William Todd
1959	U.S. Air Force Captain Gregor Schwinghammer
1968	Smithsonian Institution Vertebrate Paleontology Section Volunteer David Duckworth
1969-1970	U.S. Air Force Lieutenant Colonel Walter D. Hunter
1973	U.S. Air Force Personnel Ed Behling
1974	U.S. Navy Lieutenant JG Al Shappell
1985	U.S./NATO Air Force Two-Star General Ralph Havens
1989	U.S. Military Satellite Remote Sensing Analyst & Photo Interpreter George Stephen III

The Explorers of Ararat is focused on the explorers of modern day Mount Ararat and the search for Noah's Ark, not on creation, evolution, the biblical flood, Noah, or antediluvian (pre-biblical flood) history. There are a number of helpful appendices which serve as wonderful reference sections for the book. These include:

1) Recommendations For Future Expeditions
2) Using Topography in the Search for Noah's Ark
3) High Resolution Remote Sensing Satellites
4) Another Iranian Location
5) Geologic Survey of Mount Ararat
6) Who Controlled Ararat When?
7) Noah's Ark Sources and Alleged Sightings
8) Historical Research Still Needed
9) The U.S. Government and Noah's Ark Evidence
10) What if Noah's Ark is Found or Not Found?

The publisher encourages the reader to not allow the religious language or personal beliefs of the explorers distract your attention from the overall historic facts detailed in the book. In the publisher's view, this book should be more of a historical reference document. If this were the case, the religious terminology would be out of place and removed. The religious views show the bias of the explorers which is natural since the origin of the search itself is an object discussed in the earliest chapters of the Bible. While some believers in the Bible debate the age of the earth, most of the Ark searchers tend to be young-earth creationists who believe the Ark could have survived in petrified and frozen conditions for thousands of years. Although the biblical structure was originally some unknown type of wood rather than flesh and bone, the creationists' belief may be supported by frozen, millennia-old examples such as the Swiss/Italian Alps iceman, the Andean Mountains children and the wooly mammoths. While their beliefs do bias their views, it also makes their research more detailed than others who do not even allow the possibility that portions of the Ark might still be found.

Although the publisher has deep personal convictions in regard to biblical and spiritual matters, the publisher does not recommend the sharing of religious viewpoints in this type of book nor does he agree with some of the views which are expressed. However, the primary author's desire was to let the explorers share their complete stories, part of which may include the reasons why they wanted to search for the Ark in the first place. On the one hand, the primary reason they search for Noah's Ark is because of a religious belief based on the Bible. On the other hand, in order to impact a skeptical scientific world, the "Arkeologists" must remove religious bias from any scientific assertion.

The publisher's favorite view of modern day Greater Mount Ararat
Courtesy of Robin Simmons 1990 Helicopter Flight

The irony of the search is that other than Genesis 6-9, the Ark of Noah is found in only four verses in the entire Bible, which shows that all the time, effort and money that has gone into the search is not biblically based.

However, professional archeologists of biblical sites have consistently unearthed ruins that show the Bible is an accurate historical record so the search for this relic continues.

There is also a temptation for Bible believers to apply every bit of scripture to their own time period, whether the verse is based in the book of Revelation, Daniel or elsewhere. There is no biblical reason that the Ark needs to be found at the current time or in the "end times." This concept is simply not in the Bible and should not be propagated as fact. For instance, the pitch inside and out of the Ark could have been simply because God wanted an extra sealing on the Ark to make it waterproof rather than to cause the Ark to survive throughout written history until the present day. Also, the Mount Ararat of today may not be the Mount Ararat of one millennia ago, let alone the same Mount Ararat as the biblical text's "mountains of Ararat" at the time of the flood or at the time of the writing of Genesis.

Other than the history of Mount Ararat and the search for Noah's Ark, an entire book could be written about the consistent desire by Ark explorers for excitement, glory, and money which has caused a tangled web of intrigue, deceit, and false or premature Ark "sightings." In regard to these human factors, scholar Dr. John Warwick Montgomery (former Division Chairman of Church History at Trinity Evangelical Divinity School) once stated, "The most fascinating thing about the search for Noah's Ark is the diversity and interaction of the explorers themselves."

In any type of religious-based research, there is a desperate need for an appeal to reason and objectivity rather than "Ark Fever," the discovery of lost treasure or the pot of gold at the end of the rainbow. In fact, "Ark Fever" can negatively impact one's own family and other personal relationships. Also, the modus operandi of the researchers should be to share information and discover the truth—which this book illustrates—rather than to gain fame or fortune. Too often people want to be involved in the "last great search" or the final frontier (as in Star Trek). The reader and researcher must constantly remember that there have been literally hundreds of individuals and nearly 100 expeditions that have gone to the "mountains of Ararat" and have failed to find Noah's Ark. What makes the reader and others any different from those failed expeditions?

Despite my warnings, after reading *The Explorers of Ararat* some people may be "inspired" and catch "Ark Fever." My advice to those individuals is to search for truth and to not re-invent the wheel. The search for Noah's Ark is entering an age where technology and experts are required. Infrared sensors mounted on a plane or helicopter could quickly find the answer to the mystery, one way or the other. The current explorers have updated search plans after decades of research and dozens of failures. Also, one should not simply decide to become an explorer because too many explorers in eastern Turkey, complicated by the Kurdish issue and the proximity of the Iranian and Armenian borders, could cause the Turkish government to shut down all research. Unless the reader is a Remote Sensing expert, has a plane or helicopter that can carry Ground Penetrating Radar (GPR) over a 17,000-foot mountain in Eastern Turkey, or is a gifted climber and excavator of lethal glacier-covered volcanic mountains, I recommend that the reader should not get involved in the search for Noah's Ark.

In conclusion, Dr. Grosvenor, the late editor of the National Geographic Magazine, stated, "If the Ark of Noah is discovered, it will be the greatest archaeological find in human history, the greatest event since the resurrection of Christ, and it would alter all the currents of scientific thought." Even if Noah's Ark is not found, the initiator of this project, B.J. Corbin, the explorers turned authors, and the publisher are pleased to present *The Explorers of Ararat: And the Search for Noah's Ark.*

Rex Geissler
Publisher

[Editor's Note]

When one thinks of the search for Noah's Ark, one immediately conjures up romantic, fanciful images similar to Spielberg's movie *Raiders of the Lost Ark.* Behind these glittering illusions lay biblical truth, however, and it is often difficult to distinguish or separate the two.

This book brings together a selection of men who have been, or are actively, searching for Noah's Ark. Yet I hope that readers of this book will distinguish fact from fancy in order to gain a more comprehensive understanding of Noah's Ark.

Tad Wakefield

Acknowledgments

I would like to thank the explorers of Ararat for taking the time to be a part of this project. Also, thanks to each explorer for their courage, contribution and sacrifice in the search for Noah's Ark.

To my wife, Jennifer; my son, Daniel; my parents and my family for their support and encouragement (especially my mom) for purchasing my first book about Noah's Ark.

I would like to thank Dr. Paul Meier for the Foreword, as well as for the musical opportunity he allowed my wife and me. Thanks to Charles Willis, Chuck Aaron, Bob Garbe, Don Shockey, Robert Michelson, and Jim Hall for allowing me to be a part of four historic expeditions to Mount Ararat.

To Dr. Salih Bayraktutan and the administration at Ataturk University, Erzurum, Turkey; the Ministry of Culture, the governor of Agri, mayor of Dogubayazit, and to all other Turkish government and military officials, and friends that have helped us with our research efforts.

A special thanks goes to Judy Walker for the initial proof reading, editing, typesetting and preparation of the draft. Also thanks go to editors Brian Craig and Tad Wakefield and to William To for the cover design. Thanks also go to Gary and Robbie Walker at Atlantic Printing in Tabor City, North Carolina.

Thanks to John Comber, Bill Crouse, Rex Geissler, Albert Groebli, Jim Hays, Matthew Kneisler, Elfred Lee, John McIntosh, Carl Nestor, David O'Neil, Angelo Palego, Robin Simmons, Dr. Charles Willis, and the Ark Research Team, for adding valuable information to the reference section of the book and or web site. To my other "virtual" Internet researchers, contributors, and past team members, all too numerous to mention. You know who you are! Thanks!

A very special thanks goes to Rex Geissler of Great Commission Illustrated Books, for publishing the book and for providing so much attention to detail, and for making *The Explorers of Ararat* even better.

B.J. Corbin south of Mount Ararat 1998
Courtesy of B.J. Corbin

FOREWORD

The search for Noah's Ark has fascinated me for years. I participated in an expedition to Mount Ararat in 1985. I was the doctor for the PROBE team organized by Bill Crouse and John McIntosh. Some incredible things happened to us on that particular trip, but I will let the explorers of Ararat give you the details later in this book. From then on, I decided to stay home and write books, because it is much safer.

B.J. Corbin has taken a valuable approach to the subject by making *The Explorers of Ararat—And the Search for Noah's Ark* a truly collaborative effort involving most of the top Ararat expedition leaders in the country. What you are about to read are the actual firsthand accounts written by the explorers. Never has there been a book on the subject of Noah's Ark with so much collective experience. The explorers in this book account for nearly one hundred expeditions to Turkey. B.J. himself was a team member with Dr. Charles Willis in 1988, with Chuck Aaron and Robert Garbe in 1989, with Dr. Don Shockey in 1990, and with Robert Michelson and Jim Hall in 1998. His twelve years of research and four trips to Mount Ararat give B.J. a unique and qualified perspective on the search for Noah's Ark.

The thing that I really appreciate about B.J. Corbin is that he does not jump to conclusions. He attempts to objectively weigh the evidence and demands conclusive proof before he will accept any premature announcement that Noah's Ark has been found. This ability to step back and analyze the data objectively before jumping forward to a conclusion is an extremely desirable quality for any reputable explorer.

I met B.J. when he and his wife were providing the music for one of my national book seminars. B.J. and Jennifer write and perform Christian music and were my special musical guests. I feel that it was no coincidence that we met under those circumstances, found we had both been to Mount Ararat and found that we both studied Bible prophecy.

I think you will enjoy the fact that each chapter is a separate story in itself. Having been to Mount Ararat, I respect the explorers who risk their lives in the search. Our hope is that a conclusive discovery would help stir the heart of the unbeliever to accept our modern day Ark of salvation, Jesus Christ.

Paul Meier, MD
1999

INTRODUCTION

The Explorers of Ararat—And the Search for Noah's Ark is a compilation of accounts written by experienced explorers who have searched for Noah's Ark since the 1960's. These individuals have been to Mount Ararat in Turkey many times in search of the elusive Ark. Each explorer conveys his unique experiences and insights regarding the search.

The potential for the Ark's discovery is greatly improved when there is sharing of information and unity among the various researchers. I am grateful for their cooperation and for the participation of each contributor to this book.

The biblical book of Genesis states that the Ark came to rest upon the mountains of Ararat. Ararat is translated as Armenia or Urartu. Bible scholars describe the mountains of Ararat as a mountain range within the ancient kingdom of Urartu. The NIV Study Bible states in the reference section that the Ark probably landed in southern Urartu. This conflicts with alleged eyewitness accounts of the Ark's location on what is today known as Mount Ararat, since it is located in northern Urartu. Mount Cudi (pronounced Mount Judi) is a mountain located in what was ancient southern Urartu. Mount Cudi also has a Noah's Ark tradition, which in ancient texts and references precedes the tradition of Mount Ararat. There are several other mountains outside the boundaries of the "mountains of Ararat" which have a Noah's Ark tradition. This book primarily focuses on the explorers of Ararat, some of who are also interested in becoming explorers of Mount Cudi (Cudi Dagh).

There are several researchers still interested in Durupinar, the boat-shaped formation near both Mount Ararat and the Turkish-Iranian border. This site received attention by the efforts of Ron Wyatt and the late David Fasold. There is actually a Turkish visitor's center above the site with signs stating that the formation is the remains of Noah's Ark. Professor Robert Michelson of Georgia Tech University and David Deal are interested in performing more in-depth research on the formation and areas surrounding the site before dismissing the area as natural. Michelson and Deal speculate that the formation may actually be a "footprint" of the remains of Noah's Ark. Michelson and Deal believe the majority of current reports debunking the site as natural (not a Noah's Ark footprint) are not based on good science, and want to conduct further study of the area.

If the Ark did land on Mount Ararat, where exactly did it land? Given the biblical account, in which it took over seventy days before the tops of other mountains became visible, one would expect a near-summit landing. Greater Ararat dominates the surrounding landscape and is the tallest mountain in the region at nearly 17,000 feet. Lesser Ararat to the southeast is approximately 13,500 feet high. Some consider these two peaks to meet the plural definition of mountains of Ararat. Mount Ararat's peak is permanently covered with ice and glaciers. The depth of the ice measures over two hundred feet in some areas of the mountain. I should mention that Mount Cudi is a considerably smaller mountain with an elevation of approximately seven thousand feet.

Most alleged sightings of Noah's Ark on Ararat are near the northeast and northwest glacier areas between 14,000 and 16,000 feet. If the Ark is

buried under the ice, and was constructed using pitch inside and out to waterproof it, this would lend credence to stories of its petrifaction and survival for thousands of years. There are many good books available giving evidences for a universal flood and comparing theories of

Scott Little and B.J. Corbin at Mihtepe preparing to climb the East Summit 1988
Courtesy of B.J. Corbin

special creation and evolution. I have personally found marine fossils at an elevation between 8,000 and 10,000 feet near Mount Ararat (in the foothills behind the old Simer Hotel).

Is there conclusive evidence that the remains of Noah's Ark still exist on Mount Ararat? A person may have read books or watched television programs that claim Noah's Ark has already been discovered. It is certainly possible that it has been rediscovered, but the significant problem has always been the validation of the discovery. Why is it so difficult to validate such a discovery? If the reader does not already know the difficulties faced by Ark researchers, they will become quite clear upon reading this book. The obstacles and frustrations are many.

What do these explorers of Ararat have in common? The explorers are joined by a bond created by incredible shared experiences searching for the remains of Noah's Ark on Mount Ararat. They have experienced a foreign culture very different from their own. They have traveled across a rugged, hostile terrain in an ancient land divided by ethnic war and barricaded borders. Most have spent many frustrating hours, days, and weeks wading through a maze of political and bureaucratic processes to obtain a special research permit. Even after special permission to climb Mount Ararat has been obtained, the local military police often restrict, delay or cancel permits to climb the desired, specific areas of the mountain. Many explorers have come across ferocious wolf-like dogs on their way up the mountain. While climbing there is the possibility of avalanches of snow or lava rocks, lack of water, high winds and bitter cold on top of glaciers with deep crevasses. Altitude sickness is another common problem high on the mountain. Sometimes the difficulties of Mount Ararat can inhibit the climber's critical thinking skills. An often overlooked hindrance is the fact that a Christian searching for evidences of the Bible in an Islamic country often faces stiff opposition. As an introduction to each explorer, I have given the reader a brief statement about the explorer at the beginning of each chapter.

Some ask if we should be searching for Noah's Ark at all. What is God's will concerning Noah's Ark? What should Noah's Ark and the flood story represent to our modern global community?

Some people question the efforts of the explorers who search for the remains of Noah's Ark. Christianity is typically accepted on faith rather than geology or scientific exploration, and to some, the search for evidences that prove the truth of the Bible is inappropriate. I obviously do not agree with that particular sentiment or I would not have gone to Mount Ararat four times. If we search the Bible we see the impact the great miracles (evidences) had on the people of their day, and still do today. The miracles of Jesus and the testimony of witnesses tremendously aided the spread of Christianity so that it eventually became a major world religion. If there were no evidences of God's divine power, where would Christianity be? Do not misunderstand. I believe that faith

Explorers hiking up Ararat - Metin Karadag and Rick Licata 1983
Courtesy of John McIntosh

comes from hearing the word of God (Romans 10:15). Trust in the Bible (the word of God) can be built through evidence of its authenticity and validity. These evidences can come through the study of history, archaeology, or fulfillment of prophecy, just as people became followers of Jesus after seeing the word of God confirmed by miracles in the New Testament (Hebrews 2:4 and a few examples from the church history book of Acts 2:1-47, 3:1-16, 5:12-16, 8:4-13, 9:1-19, 9:32-42). In the past, there has been some criticism of Ark research, as explorers have sometimes been viewed as glory-mongers, treasure-hunters, or just out to prove the Bible. To the contrary, most Ararat explorers view themselves as humble archaeologists (or in this case, "arkeologists"), painstakingly (time-wise, health-wise, and monetarily) trying to discover the truth about any possible remains of Noah's Ark. Most of those who search for the remains of Noah's Ark are not searching for proof or validation of the Bible. The majority of the explorers have a Christian background and they believe that the discovery of Noah's Ark would have a positive impact on many people from other backgrounds. There are some people who could take a guided tour through Noah's Ark and still not believe in God. The fact is that they believe the search for Noah's Ark is worth the risk, danger and sacrifice if only one person turns to the Bible. There are many people who have witnessed the power of God and Jesus, and unfortunately, still do not accept it. Evidences that support the Bible and creation can be presented as seeds for belief in the Bible and possibly more.

The heart and intent of the Ark researcher must remain true. The sensationalism of the possible discovery of Noah's Ark does tug on our temporal weaknesses. We must not let the desire to be important, significant, or even famous cloud our vision. I was initially lured by the mystery and adventure surrounding the search for Noah's Ark, but God has his ways of humbling and teaching us to seek his will in all things, even the discovery of Noah's Ark. Some attach the discovery of the Ark to end times Bible prophecy. This may be, but I find no basis for this assumption in Scripture. I understand the biblical references comparing the wicked generation of Noah's day to that of the last generation at the end times, which could possibly be the one we live in. If explorers are searching for the remains of Noah's Ark for any other reason than to help people trust in the Bible, they are *missing the boat!* Whatever the reader's views or opinions concerning the search for Noah's Ark, I hope that he or she will come away with a deeper understanding and a respect for the explorers of Ararat.

B. J. Corbin
May 1999
Delmar, MD

DEFINITION OF KEY TERMS AND LOCATION NAMES

Ark researchers at times seem to be talking in a secret coded language. To overcome this, there are pictures of Ararat throughout this section to familiarize oneself with most key terms. After the key terms, there is a photo section showing views as if one was literally flying a circle around Ararat.

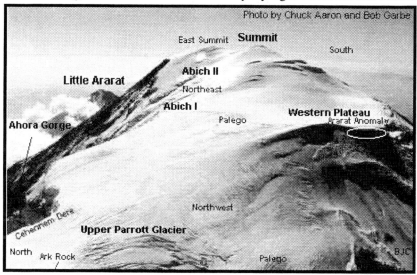

Northwest photo map of Mount Ararat by B.J. Corbin 1989
Helicopter Photo Courtesy of Chuck Aaron and Bob Garbe

Abich II and beginning of Abich I Glaciers 1986
Courtesy of Bob Garbe

Abich I and II Glaciers - were named after Herman von Abich who climbed the mountain. They are located between the main summit and eastern peaks on the northeast side of the mountain.

Upper Ahora Gorge with clouds moving in 1990
Courtesy of Robin Simmons

Ahora Gorge -is a large canyon or gorge on Mount Ararat. It was enhanced by an earthquake in 1840 and is located on the northeast side of the mountain. The Abich II glacier extends into

Ahora Gorge photomap
Courtesy of Bob Stuplich and B.J. Corbin

the gorge in two fingers, one of which continues into the Araxes or Black Glacier, which extends down through the gorge or gulch all the way past Jacob's Well. The Black Glacier is colored black or gray by the rock slides which constantly falls on it.

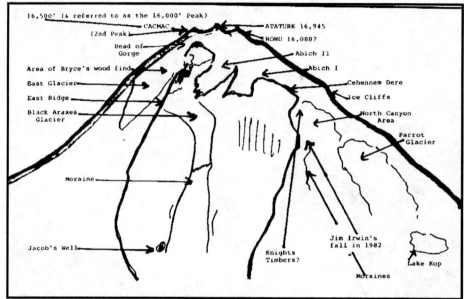

Map of Northeastern and Northwestern Ararat
Courtesy of Dick Bright

Ark Rock - a rock outcropping landmark on the northwest side on Ararat, with the Parrot Glacier flowing beside it to the northwest.

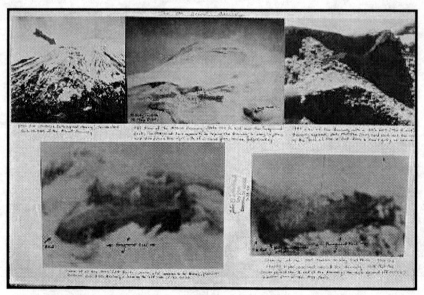

Ararat Anomaly photos on the northwestern side of Ararat
Courtesy of John McIntosh

Ararat Anomaly - an area usually associated with the object identified from declassified Defense Intelligence Agency photos. Ark researchers also use the term anomaly to refer to any interesting Ark-shaped object.

Cehennem Dere from the Ahora Gorge
with triangular "Doomsday Peak" in foreground 1983
Courtesy of Bob Stuplich

Cehennem Dere - a V-shaped canyon on the north side of Mount Ararat. A local transliteration is "Valley of Hell."

Dogubayazit with Ararat in the background 1985
Courtesy of Bill Crouse

Dogubayazit or Dogubeyasit - a small frontier town at the southern base of Mount Ararat, and a popular starting point for most expeditions.

Ground Penetrating Radar (GPR) - a unit which can be used to "view" or profile underneath the ice.

**Top of Ahora Gorge, Eastern Plateau, Eastern Summit, and
actual summit in right background 1990**
Courtesy of Chuck Aaron, Al Jenny and John McIntosh via B.J. Corbin

Eastern Plateau, Snowfields, Summit - a relatively large flat area of snow and ice located on the eastern summit area at approximately 16,800 feet. Some call the eastern summit the 16,000 or Cacmac peak, but it is actually more like 16,800 feet.

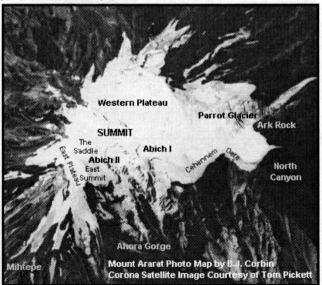

Ice Cap - the general term for the permanent seventeen square mile ice cap or covering on Mount Ararat.

Ice Cave or "Eye of the Bird" photo 1989
Courtesy of John McIntosh

Ice Cave or "Eye of the Bird" - a dominant landmark on the south / southwest side of the mountain at approximately 14,500 feet. From the town of Dogubayazit, you can see a large dark spot on the mountain that some believe may be a volcanic vent and has been mistaken in the past for Noah's Ark.

Jacob's Well - a popular landmark inside the northeast Ahora Gorge. There is also a lesser-known Jacob's Well on the southwest side of Mount Ararat which Arthur Chuchian was referring to. It was his father Jacob's personal well.

Lake Kop with Mike and SEARCH President John Bradley in 1982
Courtesy of John McIntosh

Lake Kop - a small lake on the northwest side of Mount Ararat.

Little Ararat viewed from Mihtepe Dog's Tooth
Courtesy of John McIntosh

Little Ararat - the smaller sister peak of Ararat at approximately 13,000 feet, located just southeast of Ararat. Some contend that by Ararat being composed of two mountain peaks, this meets the plural definition of "mountains of Ararat."

Snow Tiger Team at High Rock Camp 1986
Courtesy of Dr. Charles Willis

Mihtepe - a popular rocky base camp on the southeast side of Ararat at approximately 13,500 feet. The name means "dog's tooth."

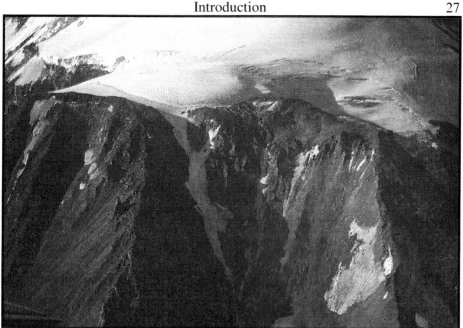

**North Canyon where Jim Irwin fell and nearly died and Dr. John Morris was
struck by lighting 1983**
Courtesy of Bob Stuplich

North Canyon - an area of steep cliffs and glacial ice fingers on the north side of Ararat, located between the Parrot Glacier and the Cehennem Dere.

Parrot Glacier on northwest Ararat - Navarra ice pack is left of photo
Courtesy of Dr. John Morris

Parrot Glacier - a glacier located on the northwest side of Mount Ararat named after Dr. J.J. Friedrich W. Parrot. This glacier was a prime target area for Fernand Navarra (1953, 1955) and the SEARCH Team (1968-1969).

**The Saddle is the area between the main peak and the Eastern summit.
Some like Colonel Koor, George Stephen III, and Robin Simmon's
grandfather claimed the Ark was just below the saddle on the Northeast**
Courtesy of Dr. Don Shockey 1990

Saddle, The - the area between the two main summit peaks of Greater Mount Ararat that seems to be shaped like a horse's saddle.

Ark Scale on Mount Ararat by B.J. Corbin
Photo by Chuck Aaron and Bob Garbe

**Summit peak in center with Ark scale drawn in for both the upper
Abich II and Western Plateau areas 1989**
Courtesy of B.J. Corbin, Chuck Aaron and Bob Garbe

Summit - the main or western peak of Mount Ararat. It is also called Ataturk peak. The summit is about 17,000 feet. Various measurements have been given above and below that height but it is consistently changing due to the ice depth also changing.

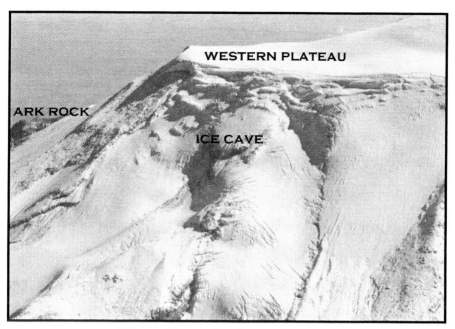

Western Plateau, Ice Cave, and Ark Rock
Courtesy of Bob Garbe

Western Plateau - large area of the western ice cap believed to be a caldera or sunken volcano cone at approximately 15,000 feet. In 1989, this area was measured using Ground-Penetrating Radar to an ice depth of over 250 feet.

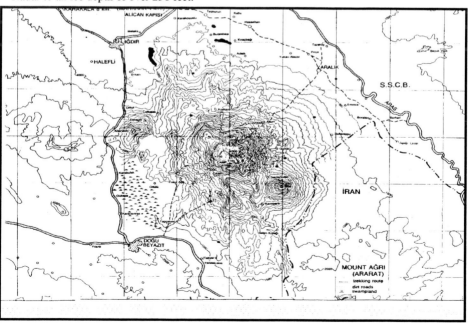

Mount Ararat Topographical Map
Courtesy of John McIntosh via B.J. Corbin

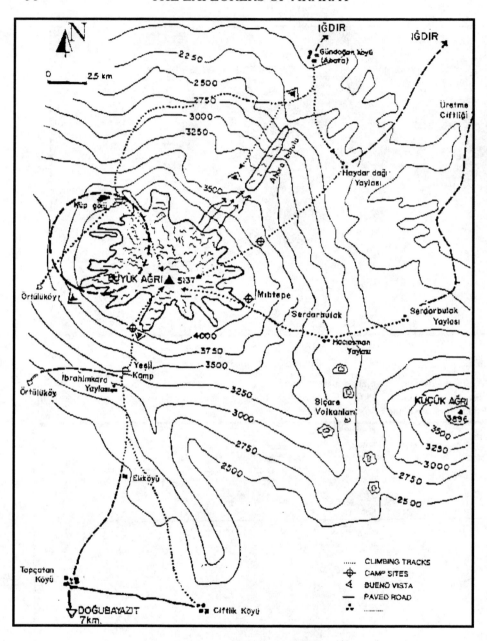

Mount Ararat Hiking Guide
Courtesy of John McIntosh via B.J. Corbin

East Glacier 1983
Courtesy of Bob Stuplich

East Glacier & Northeast Ahora Gorge 1983
Courtesy of Bob Stuplich

Ahora Gorge with East Wall Ridge 1983
Courtesy of Bob Stuplich

Ahora Gorge with eastern and western walls 1983
Courtesy of Bob Stuplich

Ahora Gorge with eastern and western walls 1983
Courtesy of Bob Stuplich

Ahora Gorge with lower Abich II and heart-shaped glacier 1983
Courtesy of Bob Stuplich

Gorge with Abich II, Abich I, Inverted Heart-Shape and Cehennem Dere 1983
Courtesy of Bob Stuplich

Ahora Gorge photomap and unmarked Inverted Heart-Shaped Glacier
Courtesy of Bob Stuplich and B.J. Corbin 1983

**North Canyon area where Jim Irwin fell and Dr. John Morris
was struck by lighting 1983**
Courtesy of Bob Stuplich

Northwest Ararat with Parrot Glacier snaking down the mountain 1983
Courtesy of Bob Stuplich

Northwest Ararat with Parrot Glacier snaking down the mountain 1983
Courtesy of Bob Stuplich

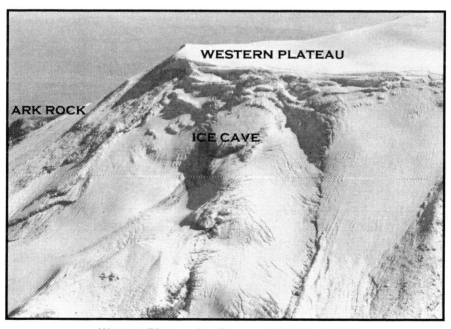

Western Plateau, Ice Cave, and Ark Rock 1989
Courtesy of Bob Garbe

Southwest Ararat 1983
Courtesy of Bob Stuplich

South Ararat 1984
Courtesy of Bob Stuplich

South Ararat 1983
Courtesy of Bob Stuplich

Southeast and east Ararat 1983
Courtesy of Bob Stuplich

John McIntosh is one of the most persistent, consistent, and respected Ark searchers in the modern era. Hardly a summer goes by without John at least thinking about a chance to get on Mount Ararat.

1

JOHN MCINTOSH

I am a teacher at the high school level and in 1999 completed my fourteenth year teaching in the physical sciences and geology at Colton High School in southern California. Originally from the Midwest, I grew up in Frankford, Indiana, and attended Indiana University. Although I started out as an astronomy major, I ended up majoring in physics and math, with side interests in earth science and geology. After obtaining my masters degree in the late sixties, I moved to California and accepted a teaching job at a junior high school. Four years of teaching General Science at the junior high level convinced me I was ready for a change, so I worked in industry for the next ten years before going back to teaching.

I first became interested in the Noah's Ark search around 1976 at a home Bible study in Riverside, California. One evening after a Bible study someone brought out a book about the search for Noah's Ark. I believe that was the first time I had heard about the search for the remains of the Ark. At the time I thought it was really a pretty ridiculous idea. I knew there had been an Ark at one time according to the Bible, but I wondered why people thought there could be anything left of it.

That initial curiosity began two years of research, after which I became convinced that there was a good possibility that there might have been something preserved. At that time in my life, God was working in a special way and really drawing me spiritually closer to him and I felt a calling to be involved in the search. I felt that the background I had in mountaineering, cave exploring and rope work could be useful in the Ark research. I began preparing for a possible trip to eastern Turkey and to Mount Ararat. This led to a solo trip to the mountain and what I call a spiritual odyssey in 1978.

Except for short trips into Mexico, I had never been out of the United States so going to Turkey was indeed a step of faith for me. As I prepared, and eventually headed east, I had a really deep spiritual peace that God was leading me. Basically, this was to be a trip to get acquainted with the mountain and the people of the region. I believed that God was in charge and calling the shots. This trip would lead to an open door for later research.

My 1978 trip to Mt. Ararat turned out to be one challenging experience after another. After spending a couple of days at Dogubayazit, the largest town at the southern base of the mountain, I checked with the local police authorities to see if I could get permission to hike around the mountain. I showed one of the policemen a sketch map I had made of Ortulu and Ahora villages and indicated I wanted to go around the west side of the mountain. He seemed to indicate that I would not be allowed to get up high on the mountain—he was putting his hands up above his head, but he seemed to indicate I could go to the mountain as long as I stayed at the lower elevations. Not being completely uninformed, I thought that I had been given some kind of verbal permission to hike around the lower parts of the mountain.

I was able to hire a taxi, which took me over some very primitive roads to Ortulu. After I was dropped off there in the little village, one of the older men of the village came out, greeted me and invited me into his home to meet his family. He treated me to some Kurdish

Northeast of Mount Ararat including Ahora Gorge 1977
Courtesy of Dennis Burchett via John McIntosh

food, took me around the village to show me some of the sites of the village, and then I indicated to him that I wanted to go up over the foothills north of the village and hike around the mountain. He made it very clear at that point that I couldn't go there. He shook his head, threw his hands up over his head and waved them back and forth, indicating that it was not permitted. I thought that perhaps I could go west on through the other villages and swing far around the western side of the mountain. He went through more motions indicating that I would be tied up and beaten if I went that way, so that it appeared God was closing the door. I was ready to be satisfied with that and to return to Dogubayazit.

At this point a younger Kurdish man grabbed me by the shoulder and yanked me towards the house, indicating that he really didn't want me to go anywhere. I began to feel a bit like a captive when both the older man and the younger man kept looking down the slope towards Dogubayazit, as if they were expecting someone to come up from the town. I sat on the stone steps of the home doing a lot of praying, occasionally pointing at my watch and indicating that it was time for me to leave. This action brought only a negative response from the two. Finally, toward evening the younger man left and I once again pointed at my watch. This time the old man threw his hands up over his head and waved me on, indicating I could get my backpack and leave, which I did very quickly.

John McIntosh and a gorgeous view of the Ahora Gorge 1978
Courtesy of John McIntosh

I headed up over the foothills behind his home, heading north along the western flank of Mt. Ararat. I camped that evening on top of the foothills and the next morning hiked around the western Kup Gol plain. Toward evening I heard some sheep coming down the hillside and some boys yelling. I hid behind a large boulder, hoping not to be seen, and the sheep passed on each side of me. Finally the boys passed off to one side, glancing back at me as they went. They were heading toward some campfires, and what I assumed was a Kurdish camp. At this point, I knew that I probably was going to get more company looking for me if I stayed around very long.

I continued up the western slope of Mt. Ararat and, having run out of water, stopped to get some at a very stagnant little pond. When I turned on the flashlight to do this, someone yelled at me from further down the slope, so the rest of the evening my hike was without light. I could see lights coming up the mountain behind me, but they disappeared as I entered into a dark canyon, stumbling along and asking God for a place to sleep. I found a large boulder with about a two-foot-wide crack in it and I decided this was the place. I camped there that night thinking that I should get up early and leave the area, heading north as early as possible in order to avoid any of the local inhabitants. I committed the situation to God and went to sleep. Later that evening I woke up, and as I sat up and looked around, a big full moon was coming over the mountain. I knew it was time to proceed north around the Kup Gol plain. I walked until I came to another valley that ended where the steep volcanic cone of Ararat continued upward, up around the 11,000-foot level, on up to the ice cap. I spent the day in this spot recuperating after throwing up from the stagnant water that I had attempted to purify. Later that day I rose to find a beautiful day ahead.

As I was about to proceed north along the base of the steep cone, I noticed three horses directly north of me right on my route. I decided the only way to avoid them was to go up the cone and try to drop back down behind them. So I began a very long slow hike up the western side of Mt. Ararat. This turned out to be a two-day hike up the side of the cone. I got up on the steep side of the mountain into an area

Southwestern foothills of Mount Ararat 1982
Courtesy of John McIntosh

of finger glaciers that dropped off very steeply. I couldn't cross them at their widest points and had to climb up the cone to where they narrowed. Basically I stair-stepped up the western side of the mountain. I spent the night on a very steep slope on a little two-foot-wide level area carved out of the steep terrain. The next morning, I continued north and up around the western face. I was carrying a pack that weighed approximately seventy pounds and some snow- and cold-weather gear, but I didn't have an ice ax or crampons. I had not really planned on being up on the ice cap, so I very carefully worked around these couloirs of ice. As I gingerly crept on, the terrain began to level out a little, but I found myself on a massive ice cap. I found out later that this was part of the western ice cap, and I had crossed over above the Parrot Glacier, crossed the Cehennem Dere (Hell's Valley) and ended up at the drop-off point of the Abich II Glacier (see maps).

At this point, I knew where I was—the gorge was directly below me and I was in one of the prime research areas for the Ark. I spent the night there, took some of the best photos of the gorge area that I have been privileged to take and then was faced with the task of finding a way back down the mountain. Re-crossing the northern ice cap across the Cehennem Dere area, I went down the northern slope, in the process spraining an ankle, and camped

Ahora Gorge snow and ice avalanche coming from the Abich II Glacier 1978
Courtesy of John McIntosh

at a lower elevation from the steep drop-off that I had climbed down previously.

The next day I continued northward down the slope, crossing over the western rim of the Ahora Gorge and spent the night on the west rim. This allowed me to take some very special pictures of the gorge, including one of an ice avalanche going over a 450-foot fall.

The next day I continued on down toward Ahora Village, hoping not to encounter any people. On approaching the village I did meet two young men with horses and guns, who became very curious about my backpack. When they were getting some water at a small stream I was able to part company with them. At another point on the trail to the village I had stopped to take off my mountaineering boots to put on some lighter boots, and as my back was turned to the trail, I noticed a hand in the side of my backpack—a little man had come along and was attempting to rob me of my goods. We straightened that encounter out and I had almost made it through the village, when three wolfhounds decided to get acquainted with me. Anyone who has seen one of these dogs knows they are very ferocious-looking, and with hackles raised and teeth bared, they came charging at me. I was walking backwards with rocks in my hands and praying when finally a peasant lady, who evidently, owned the dogs was able to call them off.

While I was in the process of getting through the village the people stopped me, brought out a chair and had me sit in it and about fifteen or twenty of them surrounded me. A gentleman I assumed to be the mayor of the town came out with an English dictionary and asked me "what-you-doing here?" We tried to have a little conversation but eventually it became clear to me that it was time to leave, although they wanted me to stay. After spending the night north of Ahora Village, as I made my way toward Arilik, I got a ride into the village with some of the peasant people in a truck. Arilik has a bus service, so I got a ticket about ten minutes before the bus was to leave.

A plain-clothes detective looked in the window of the bus, motioned for me to get off and for the next three or four hours I was the guest of the local police department, while they filled out a report and did a very gentle interrogation as to where I had been on the mountain. When they were done the police chief said "We are done, you go to army now." My escort took me to the army post west of town and as we arrived at the commander's quarters he was screaming and yelling at a Turkish enlisted man who evidently had done something wrong. He was hitting him across the face and motioning for him to leave the room. My guide went in next, and the commander began yelling again and throwing his hands up over his head, apparently indicating he didn't want anything to do with me. We went back to the police chief and he insisted that the army do something, so everybody went back to the army post and they finally had an English-speaking officer arrive. We had a nice discussion of the trip around Ararat. The officer explained that I had been in an off-limits area, that it was under martial law that I could have been killed, and that I was worth money dead or alive. Then, after telling me I should be held for a hearing, he said "You seem like a nice person, you're free to go." Needless to say, I was thanking God! I made quick preparations to head west to Igdir, spent the night there, and then headed back to the United States.

After this trip, communication with Eryl and Violet Cummings helped open the door for further research. I began corresponding with them, sharing some of the pictures from this trip. I actually prepared every summer after 1978 for a return to the mountain, but circumstances seemed to close the door. In 1982, I was contacted by Dr. Willis from Fresno, California,

John McIntosh, Violet and Eryl Cummings
Courtesy of John McIntosh 1979

and invited to be a part of his expedition. I prepared for that expedition but the permit did not arrive in time.

I felt led to go on my own as the finances and two-week period I needed were available and I had heard that Eryl Cummings was already in Turkey with Jim Irwin, the former Apollo 15 astronaut. I thought perhaps I could contact them and be of help. I began another solo trip began in 1982. I arrived in Dogubayazit and after inquiring, found that the team was already on the mountain. A local truck driver who spoke a little English tried to help me. He went to several military bases trying to get permission for me to go up on the mountain.

While he was doing this, one of the expedition guides had come down to

**(L-R) John McIntosh, Jim Irwin, Bob Stuplich,
Ahmet Arslan, Dick Bright 1986**
Courtesy of John McIntosh

Dogubayazit from the mountain for supplies. I was able to introduce myself to him, showed him a picture of myself and Eryl, and explained that I was trying to make contact with him. The guide and driver arranged for a meeting with the head military officer at the base east of town. I don't know all that went on there, but in my opinion, God worked another miracle. After they talked with the commanding officer for some time, and showed him some pictures, he came out to meet me, nodded, and gave me his permission to go up the mountain.

The next day, up we went with the expedition guide and several pack animals. Upon arriving at the base camp, I introduced myself to Jim Irwin, told him I was a friend of Eryl Cummings, that I was interested in the search for the Ark and I would like to help them out. If this turned out to be impossible, well, this would be just a visit. Jim let me visit with Eryl while he talked with some of the team members and prayed about it.

Later he came back to me and told me that, while their original team had had twelve members, the twelfth team member had unexpectedly had to drop out. I could take his place! So, praise God, I was part of the Irwin expedition for 1982. We conducted some very interesting research that year, mostly on the northwestern part of the mountain. We established a base camp at Kup Gol at around 11,000 feet, then moved our higher camp up to 14,000 feet up on the ice cap. We explored around to the gorge, photographing and documenting the area. The expedition ended suddenly when Jim Irwin, the leader, had a very serious fall on North Canyon going down a very steep slope.

The experience I gained on the 1982 expedition opened more doors for me. Also, I received the nickname "KGB John." The team members were suspicious of this stranger who had suddenly arrived at the base camp. After they heard that the Russians knew the astronaut was on the mountain and that they were keeping track of him, the team began to wonder about me. The

Bob Stuplich warning Jim Irwin not to go down North Canyon alone just prior to Irwin's fall. Irwin spent the night where he fell and was lucky to survive. Mountain safety dictates that no hiking or climbing should be done without three individuals. Irwin liked to refer to hiking Ararat as walking on a mountain of bowling balls 1982
Courtesy of John McIntosh

Soviets had also jammed our walkie-talkie communications during our rescue operation for Jim. I found it rather humorous to later learn that the team leaders had thoroughly researched my background at the end of the expedition.

In 1982, I met one of the main expedition guides. He wrote me later and said if I wanted to come back next year he could get me a permit. I told him to go ahead and see what he could do. In the meantime, I made preparations to work with Dr. Willis as a member of his 1983 expedition. As time went on and I learned more about the area Willis planned to research, I felt led to seek an opportunity to research a different part of the mountain. When I was contacted and told I had a permit, I dropped off the Willis team.

Along with two other Americans, Doris Bowers, an outdoor education teacher from Cedar Glen, California, and Rick Licata, a Bible teacher at Calvary Chapel Bible College in Twin Peaks, I went to the southeastern part of Ararat where we researched what we call the pinnacle area on the side of the eastern plateau. We set up a base camp near Mihtepe, then proceeded from there up the East Glacier on to the eastern plateau where we set up another camp. There were only three of us at the high camp and the guide and Rick were both sick, so we were only able to spend a day up there. The guide and I did go to the summit, and we got to check out the pinnacle area, but we had to descend the same day to the lower base camp and the next day on down the mountain.

About this time Jim Irwin arrived in the area. We shared with him what we had been able to research on the southeast part of the mountain and asked if we could go back up with him, since he was getting into the northeast part of the mountain, a very difficult area for which to get a permit. Jim checked with authorities and Doris and I was able to join him. We spent another week on the northeast side of the mountain and explored the east face. The group we were with was very large and included some of Jim's immediate family as well as Eryl Cummings. Eryl was supposed to have stayed at a lower elevation. Eryl had gotten a ride on a donkey part way up the mountain and "just happened" to miss the military truck for the trip back down. So here he was, stuck with us, and of course, very happy.

We explored much of the eastern face from the east rim of the gorge around to Mihtepe. We also took a separate short trip down into Ahora Village and into the first part of the gorge. The military wouldn't let us take any pictures in this area, but we did get to see some of the village and the mouth of the gorge.

In 1984 I again obtained my own permit and, accompanied by Rick Hatch from San Bernardino, California, and Doris Bowers, was planning to explore what we were calling the "ice cave" about 14,500 feet up on the western side of the mountain. I had tried to get up to the cave at the end of the 1982 expedition but had run out of time, so we were hoping to get up there this year. We had also been told by one of the guides that there was a beam of wood sticking out of the ice cap near the summit.

Doris Bowers, with her blond hair, hard work and fair complexion, was especially interesting to the local Kurds. In less than one month, she received five marriage proposals from guys looking for another worker in their family. One of the offers was from a highly respected individual on the mountain and resulted in Doris being labeled the "Princess of Ararat."

In 1984 we went up the south face to the 13,500-foot camp and moved on up to the ice cap, with a three-man team. From there we went around to the ice cave and investigated it. We climbed between

Unexcavated Urartian ruins near Eli Village 1983
Courtesy of Doris Bowers

approximately five hundred to a thousand feet down-slope from it and we could see at that point it just looked like a big wall of rock with an overhang. The reported beam of wood that was supposedly in the ice cap turned out to be an old pair of Russian skis that had come to be a known landmark on the mountain.

We found out later that we had been accused of removing these skis and moving them to another location and were also accused of having anti-Turkish/pro-Armenian material in our possession. This led to a house arrest and our room being sealed up. I was taken to the local police headquarters, where they proceeded to

Eryl Cummings on Donkey 1983
Courtesy of John McIntosh

make telephone calls. They found out that the information we had in our rooms that they had noticed was a pro-Turkish/anti-Armenian publication put out by the Turkish government concerning the Armenian issue and that the claim about the skis was also false. It is very intriguing, this cloak-and-dagger mentality in eastern Turkey.

On that same trip we were shown some ruins near Eli Village that were very ancient. We kept this information confidential for fear that the ruins would be closed off from other researchers if the site became publicly known.

We also went out to visit another site to the south of Mt. Ararat. Ron Wyatt was there and there had been a lot of publicity generated about it. Ron had taken some samples from the site and left the country and Marv Steffins had made an announcement in either Istanbul or Ankara that they had found something of value. This resulted in a tense situation. All researchers were now suspected of stealing Ark artifacts, and our being able to leave the country was beginning to look questionable. Eventually, we were able to leave without incident and immediately began making plans for another year.

In 1985 I was asked by Bill Crouse to assist with an expedition he was putting together. The expedition was being sponsored by PROBE Ministries of Dallas, Texas. When we arrived in Turkey we heard that a mountaineering group had been attacked by some Kurdish rebels and that the military had moved in and was trying to make the mountain safe. After we arrived in Dogubayazit and waited a number of days it was announced that the mountain was now safe and that we would be allowed to go up the mountain.

**Probe team including Bill Crouse, John McIntosh, Dr. Paul Meier,
Chief who signed permit, Greg Cromartie, Gary Meoski 1985
Courtesy of Elfred Lee via John McIntosh**

We were given a military escort that continued with us from Eli Village up to around the 11,000 or 12,000-foot level. After that they stayed behind but kept in walkie-talkie contact with the mountaineering guide who was assigned to us as we proceeded up to the 13,500-foot camp on the south face. About midnight that night we heard noise, saw lights shining and next we saw the barrels of AK-47's being shoved through our tent openings. The next three hours were a nightmare as we were held at gunpoint by masked outlaws as they searched for money, photo equipment, and passports. After they got what they wanted, they threw gasoline on everything and torched thousands of dollars worth of equipment.

We were then forced to hike down to the 11,000-foot camp, in the early morning hours, carrying extra packs of material that they wanted to look at. Stumbling and falling, with guns being poked in our backs we descended the mountain. At the 11,000-foot camp there was a campfire and more people. The marauders laid out all the material that they had us carry down the mountain, looked it over and divided it up. Then they shoved us into a line and had their gunmen level their AK-47's at us. There were some desperate thoughts and prayers taking shape in the researchers' minds. Fortunately, God still wanted us around, because all they did was take flash pictures for publicity and release us.

Exhausted and dehydrated, we made our way on down to Eli Village and reported what had happened to the authorities. One or two other groups had been attacked on the mountain also, and had received much harsher treatment than had we. The mountain was surrounded for a week by five hundred troops. They went through villages, interrogated people, sent commandos up on the ice cap, and finally found the terrorist camp and had a gun battle. Six of the eight terrorists were killed, one escaped into Iran, and the other was captured.

Around this time Jim Irwin arrived in Dogubayazit with a large tour group. Of course, everything was shut down. There were a lot of very

Explorers including John Bradley, Eryl Cummings and John McIntosh
Courtesy of Doris Bowers via John McIntosh

disappointed people in that tour group, since they were not able to even set foot on the mountain. Jim finally got permission for a small research group to go back up and I was able to join that group. We went back up to the 13,500-foot camp and spent the evening, planning to climb on up to the northeast part of the ice cap the next day. Some of the team had gotten up to the ice cap when complications with the military made it necessary for only a few to go on, and the rest had to go back down. Jim Irwin was himself in the group that had to go back down. Later, the team on the ice cap was commanded to go back down also, as it was suspected that terrorists were coming up the north side of the mountain to try to capture the astronaut. That expedition ended with no one being able to reach the northeast peak.

In 1986 I was again in eastern Turkey, this time with my own five-person team. We were hoping to check out the Davis Canyon. This was the year the Ed Davis eyewitness account had become known, and we hoped to check out this reported sighting from the northern ice cap. Terrorist activity, however, shut down the mountain before we were able to get any permit for clearance into the northern part of the mountain.

Jim Irwin had succeeded in getting permission for a flight around the mountain in a fixed-wing aircraft, and we were able to visit with him in Erzurum the day of the planned flight. The day after the flight, the hotel that we had been staying in was surrounded by fifty armed Turkish security agents. Everybody was placed under house arrest for suspected American spy activity. Our permit was questioned, and so for the next ten hours none of us were allowed to leave the hotel. Eventually, things were clarified and apologies were given to the American team and I was able to join the Irwin team in a dinner celebration.

Also in 1986, we (Doris, myself and the group) got together with a couple other climbers from Norway who were cousins. The Norwegian climbers hired a Kurd and went up the mountain illegally. So that they would not attract attention, they disobeyed the mountaineering rule of having three

Paul Olav Jernæs before his disappearance on Ararat 1986 Courtesy of Norwegian newspaper via Dr. Ole Honningdalsnes via Doris Bowers

people together at all times and instead split up to meet at a certain point on the mountain. One of the cousins, Paul Olav Jernæs of Drammen, Norway, never arrived at the meeting place on the mountain. The Kurd made the other cousin, Leif Torkaas promise not to say anything until Torkaas left Turkey for fear both of them would be arrested and placed in jail. Meanwhile, the Kurd moved away from Ararat. Once the missing Norwegian became known, the Turkish Military reportedly sent a search party that looked on the mountain for a week but did not find anything. The official story, reported in a Norwegian newspaper and shown by explorer Dr. Ole Honningdalsnes, was that Paul, aged 28 in 1986 and who we had just spent time with, disappeared and was presumed dead somewhere on Mount Ararat. The paper stated that Paul was waiting alone at an elevation of 4500 meters located at the Cehennem Dere. They were going to climb on the glacier at the Cehennem Dere to search for the Ark. Hopefully, this will dissuade those who consider climbing illegally or who don't climb in groups of three or more.

In 1987 Richard "Dick" Bright and I teamed up and were hoping to get a permit to explore the northern part of the mountain. However, terrorist activity had shut down the mountain except for the southern route to the peak. Jim Irwin had arrived in the area with a research team and was hoping to get permission for a helicopter flight. The local authorities at Dogubayazit, however, denied them any kind of permit for the northern part of the mountain. They were limited to a brief aerial search of the southern and western parts of the mountain.

In 1988 I was asked by Al Jenny and Chuck Aaron to join them on a helicopter flight. We were able to do several flights around the mountain, over the gorge, taking hundreds of slides and some video footage. The ice cave, or "Eye of the Bird," as the locals call it, was photographed in shadow and did not seem impressive. Another linear feature was noticed on the northwest of the mountain that we later investigated and found not to be significant. It appeared from these investigations that if the Ark were still visible on Ararat, it was not obvious, and it surely must be partially or almost completely covered.

In 1989 I prepared for a trip to the mountain, but was told not to come by the advance team that was already there. Dick Bright's new Ark book had just been released and it included a picture of me baptizing a young man in the headwaters of the Euphrates. It had been seen in eastern Turkey and Jim Irwin told me that I would probably be arrested as soon as I got off the plane.

Due to terrorist activity, no permits were being granted to most of the researchers in 1990 (except the Dr. Don Shockey helicopter expedition), 1991 or 1992, but in 1993, Dick Bright was able to obtain a money grant for a possible expedition and received encouraging promises concerning a permit. So I teamed up with Dick in 1993 and we attempted to mount an expedition that would land a helicopter on the ice cap to check out the ice cap locations as possible burial sites of the Ark. We flew across Turkey by helicopter to Kars, about fifty miles

Ed Davis in Albuquerque, New Mexico
Photo Courtesy of Ken Long via John McIntosh

from the mountain, and at that point the authorities canceled our permits because of the military activity on the mountain. Later, after leaving Kars, we learned that three policemen had been shot and killed by terrorist on the street that runs past the hotel where we were staying. There was speculation that the terrorists were interested in capturing us and keeping us as American hostages. Each summer we continue to make tentative plans for a return trip to Ararat, but because of the military condition there it is never certain whether any permits will be granted. If the military condition improves in the near future, we hoped to get back to the mountain.

In 1996 I cautiously returned to Mt. Ararat with four other researchers to appraise the situation around the mountain. Larry Crews and his wife Sharon and Professor David Merling and his wife Stephanie were my research companions. Professor Merling is and archeologist with Andrews University and Curator at the Horn Archaeological Museum. We had been told that the mountain was off limits but were hoping that the area to the west of the mountain was accessible. There were large anchor stone like rocks and ancient rock carvings there that we wanted to examine.

We were able to examine many of the stones and carvings as well as the Durupinar site south of the mountain. The rural area surrounding Ararat was found to be relatively safe but the military maintained tight control of the mountain and no access to do research on Ararat was being permitted.

In 1997 Dick Bright and I returned to Ararat, having applied for a permit to do research with Dr. Salih Bayraktutan-head of the Ataturk University Earthquake Research Center and chief administrator for issuing research permits for the Ararat area. Unfortunately, the military situation on Ararat was still extremely sensitive and even Dr. Bayraktutan's permit request was denied.

Some interesting research was done, however, in Dogubayazit (a frontier city a few miles south of Ararat). We met and interviewed several local people who claimed that they had been to the Ark on the north side of the mountain—and even in it—within the last two years. They claimed that it was broken into several pieces and was mostly buried in the Gorge area. That was a surprising development since we had never found any local people, in 21 years of research, to make such a claim. Only future research in the Gorge area will be able to substantiate if these claims are true.

John McIntosh on 17,000-foot Summit 1983
Courtesy of John McIntosh

In 1998 Dick Bright, Dave Larsen and I again returned to see if our permit application with Dr. Bayraktutan would be approved. The military situation was still sensitive enough to not permit research. Local research contacts were visited in the Ararat area and some new information was gained that still indicated the Gorge area as the resting place of the Ark. Rumor has it that the military situation has improved significantly and that limited research access to the mountain might be permitted in 1999.

I am presently working with Professor James Hall from Virginia who has put together the Ark Research Project. We are in the process of submitting applications to the relevant Turkish authorities and attempting to raise funds for a 1999 expedition.

As I have studied the evidence for the preservation of the Ark on Ararat, it seems very likely that God might have preserved the Ark as an end-times witness. The Ark is symbolic of Christ. As we put our faith in him and receive salvation, in a similar way the people entering the Ark of Noah put their trust in God and were delivered from his wrath. The discovery of the Ark would be a very appropriate end-times sign of the nearness of God's return to an unbelieving world, that a time of judgment is again approaching and

Chuck Aaron, Al Jenny, John McIntosh Team 1988
Courtesy of John McIntosh

that people should reexamine the Bible and its claims and put their trust in God. The rediscovery of the Ark would also have a significant impact on the creation/evolution debate.

It is not a foregone conclusion that God has preserved the Ark. As we study and investigate the many reported sightings and accounts, it appears that many can be explained as mistakes. There are many "ark-like" structures on the mountain. Of special note in this regard is the southwest ice cave, the "eye of the bird." At the 14,500-foot elevation and in a north/south orientation, this looks very much like the Ark. There are eyewitness accounts,

however, of those who claimed to have actually walked on the Ark and entered it. I find it difficult to explain away eyewitness accounts. They are either true or they are deliberate lies, multiple mistakes or hoaxes. Time will tell.

Scientifically speaking, there is no problem with

Bottom of Abich II Glacier near Avalanche Canyon 1983
Courtesy of John McIntosh

the idea that the Ark could be preserved on a volcanic mountain; being buried under volcanic ash would naturally petrify it, preserve it, harden it, and turn it basically into rock. It is possible that there is a structure still on the mountain, but if it is there, it is most likely, if not completely, buried. As I study the various accounts and claimed sightings, the northeast part of the mountain seems like the most likely spot for it to be buried. The Ark could be under part of the ice cap or at the very edge of the ice cap, as most reported sightings claim, on the northeast. The sites that are up around 15,000 feet or higher have the difficulty of being contrary to the Ed Davis sighting, unless there was a very extreme melt-back. In my opinion there are six to seven possible burial sites on the northeast part of Ararat that need to be checked out. If these could be thoroughly explored, I think it is possible we could settle the question of the Ark's survival.

If the Ark is not on Ararat, I'm sure God has been using these trips and experiences for other good purposes. Spiritual seeds have been sown in eastern Turkey. There have been other types of good done but it is my hope that God's words in regard to the "Days of Noah" being likened to the days of his return, are an indirect reference to the fact that he has indeed preserved the Ark of Noah as that end-time witness.

John McIntosh in front of Ice Cave 1984
Southwest part of Mountain
Courtesy of John McIntosh

Armenian tradition relates that in the end times, God will allow the Ark to be rediscovered to be a witness to his truth. Time will tell. I plan to remain open to the leading of God to contribute to this work until he shows me to do otherwise. I believe the time is close when the question of the Ark's preservation will be resolved. Regardless of the outcome of the search efforts, I hope that each reader will thoroughly examine the claims and the historical facts surrounding the present day Ark of safety, Jesus Christ.

Elfred Lee has been involved with the Who's Who list of Ark researchers since 1960. He was involved with the SEARCH expeditions and Fernand Navarra, interviewed both George Hagopian and Ed Davis, and has worked with most of the top Ark researchers in the world. Did I mention he is a professional artist and archaeological illustrator?

2

ELFRED LEE

This is an edited transcription of an interview with Elfred Lee conducted by Dr. John Goley, Dr. Paul & Rosie Kuizinas, and Martha Lee at Montemorelos University of Mexico. Elfred and family have since moved to

1969 SEARCH Foundation explorers departing Dulles Airport for Ararat
Hugo Neuburg, Ralph Lenton, Fernand Navarra, Bud Crawford, Elfred Lee
Courtesy of Elfred Lee

the San Diego area.[1] The beginning statement below is by Elfred.

Since the first expedition of the SEARCH Foundation I have witnessed and experienced a desperate need for unity among Ark researchers. With this book, B.J. Corbin and Rex Geissler have provided a forum to fulfill that need. It's about time! It is time to unite and finish the search for Noah's Ark.

Each researcher and explorer must ask himself this question: Do I want to find Noah's Ark or do I want Noah's Ark to be found?

Who cares who finds Noah's Ark? The only thing that matters is that the Ark is found, not who finds the Ark! Unless we have this heart as researchers, we will never achieve the unity that we can.

As responsible researchers, we must also respect and obey the Turkish government. To obey the law of the land is also to obey God. Those who attempt to go around or question rules only hurt future attempts. And why should people act ungodly when they are attempting to find a Biblical artifact?

I am not a scholar but I do lecture all over the globe. Simply put a microphone in my face and I would love to share what I know with anyone. It may be a bit less polished than writing, but feel free to ask me whatever questions you have if it will aid the search for the Ark.

John: As an artist, how did you get involved with the search for Noah's Ark?

Elfred: My being an artist is probably what got me involved in the first place. I was contacted by an archeological research group from Washington, D.C., which needed an artist and photographer. They were working with Fernand Navarra, the explorer and author who claimed to have found Noah's Ark. They asked if I would come along as their photographer, illustrator and public relations person.

John: Who were these people getting you involved and why would you be interested?

Elfred: The people who invited me were a new group that became the SEARCH Foundation. SEARCH is an acronym for Scientific Exploration and Archeological Research. We wanted to be a responsible, scientific group that promoted the Word of God in an acceptable manner to a skeptical world.

Rosie: Elfred, if I'm understanding you correctly, you got involved because of your professional expertise. Do you also have a personal interest in this project?

Elfred: Yes. From a Christian background, I was born and raised knowing the Bible, creation and the story of the flood. I heard about a group that went to Turkey in 1960 and thought they might have discovered Noah's

---

[1] Elfred Lee's phone number is 619.216.0119.

Ark near Mt. Ararat at what is now know as the Durupinar site. I knew the men on the Durupinar expedition and they got me excited about the search for Ark. I had some exposure and personal interest in the search for Noah's Ark prior to my involvement with SEARCH.

John: How did you get involved in photography and art?

Elfred: I became interested in art at the age of four when I was in

Elfred Lee Painting of Mount Ararat 1970
Courtesy of Elfred Lee

Japanese prison camps in the Philippines during World War II. A Portuguese man named Pedro had some colored pencils and was drawing portraits. Watching Pedro hour after hour, I became fascinated with art. It was then that I decided I wanted to be an artist, especially one who could draw faces and figures. Ever since, art has been my main interest. I studied in Japan, Southern California at La Sierra, Newbold College in England, and finally at Pacific Union College, where I graduated with a bachelors degree. I later went to San Jose to the University of California and was pursuing a masters degree when I was drafted into the army during the Vietnam War.

John: What did you do in Vietnam?

Elfred: When I went into the army, I asked to be trained as a medical illustrator and was sent to Walter Reed Army Hospital in Washington, D.C. They were looking for volunteers to go to Vietnam on a photo mission. The training included working with a Hollywood movie producer. I thought this would be a great opportunity. Of the four hundred men who volunteered, I was fortunate to be one of twelve chosen. I went to Vietnam in 1967 as a motion picture photographer, a really great experience. They would strap me in hanging out the helicopter door while I would be photographing an area with guns right next to me. It was tough at times and I saw a lot of incredible things. The difficult conditions in which I had to photograph the action—including getting shot down in a helicopter during a night mission—helped to prepare me for Noah's Ark explorations. In 1985, I completed a Masters of Fine Arts (MFA) at Syracuse University after studying Archaeological Illustration at London University, Ankara University, and two universities in Israel, which later won me an honorary doctorate in Fine Art since the MFA is a terminal degree so a person cannot earn a doctorate in this field in school. All this study and practice I did for one reason, to find and properly document Noah's Ark or any artifact of importance. I have seen so much time and money be wasted because people do not share information. And I believe that the type of training I have received needs to be used for Ark research.

John: Would you say that your involvement in Ark research is from a standpoint of "this is something really exciting to do," or is there something deeper?

SEARCH Expedition mounting up 1969
Courtesy of Elfred Lee

Elfred: Searching for Noah's Ark is exciting, but I believe the bottom line is the validation of Holy Scripture, all of it. The discovery of Noah's Ark would help prove creation and the flood. I had to ask myself the question, do I want to find the Ark or do I want the Ark found? This is not my project. This is God's project, and He knows the best time and people to be involved. I've been fortunate to be at the right place, at the right time, with the right skills for certain opportunities. I've received information that no one else has and

I've tried to share it as best as I can. Rosie: Elfred, you've been involved in other Noah's Ark projects. How is this one different?

Elfred: For me they're all one project. I've been involved with many expeditions and groups. My first official involvement was in 1969, right after I returned from Vietnam. And I've been involved ever since, either officially or unofficially. We formed the SEARCH Foundation, which was really the first scientific group to go. After that, I was involved more or less on a freelance basis with many groups that have come and gone. But I consider them all one project.

Paul: How many trips have you made to Ararat?

Elfred: Four or five. But I've been involved with other expeditions while remaining here. This is where fundamental work is done to insure success in the field.

John: Could you tell us your story, beginning with your first expedition?

Elfred: My first expedition was in 1969, after much preparation and fund raising. We had a great team of internationally respected scientists and

Turkish Military commando in front of East Glacier 1983
Courtesy of Bob Stuplich

managers: Ralph Lenton, Hugo Neuberg, Ross Arnold, John Bradley, the Crawfords and many people from Takoma Park, Maryland. When we got our expedition to Turkey and mounted there were military escorts, extra food, transportation, donkeys, horses, porters and all this equipment that had to be hauled up. We had scientific equipment, coring augers and depth-sounding electronic equipment. It was a really elaborate set-up and my job was to document it all. I ate something at the hotel for breakfast. Perhaps it was rancid fried egg. As we climbed higher, I got so sick and filmed an vomited all day. It took us four days to get up to and established on the Parrot Glacier. We went up from Ortulu to Lake Kop, and then at about 11,000 feet our horses started falling and tripping. Horses cannot go beyond a certain altitude.

John: Where were you in relation to the Ahora Gorge?

Elfred: The Ahora Gorge lies north by northeast. We were on the southwest, making our way up and around. Fernand Navarra was leading us. He is a great guy and very charismatic. His son Coco Navarra could speak English and went along as a translator. By the fourth morning we had established our base camp in the rocky moraine at the base of the Parrot Glacier. It looked like a bulldozer had gone in the day before and cleared a spot out. There was a high wall all around us. The glacier came down and melted into a little pond from which we got our water. It was difficult to get water in the morning. It would take over thirty minutes every morning just to melt water on our cook stove at that altitude. We went up every day and worked, then came back down to the campsite by sliding down the glacier using our ice axes as rudders and breaks. What fun!

John: What detailed work were you trying to do? Digging core samples through the ice?

Elfred: Yes. With some difficulty, we took coring augers up. We started drilling where Navarra specified on the glacier. He claimed this was where he saw the wooden structure through the ice.

John: This took place almost 20 years after Navarra had seen the structure?

Elfred: It was 14 years later. He had seen it in 1955, and we were there in 1969.

Paul: When you first saw the area, what was your impression of it?

Elfred: Where is the Ark? We were disappointed. It must have been covered with many feet of ice. Navarra said the whole glacier had changed as he looked around for points of reference. There was a deep crevasse. We went down into it and started probing around. There was a big ice bridge that we had to go under for several days, not noticing that it was melting. One day, while I was filming, this huge ice bridge made up of tons of ice came crashing down right between us. It was quite a scary situation.

John: I understand that on this expedition your team found some wood?

Elfred: Yes. We dug for over a week, probing through the ice with the coring augers and all we brought up were rocks and moraine. It was starting to dull the little teeth of the coring augers. They were like hollow pipes with a corkscrew on the outside. As the auger is turned, it drills down and fills the center with ice. We were probing down in a crevasse, because it was at the level Fernand had been before. There was a pond of melt water and we started digging along it. I was up on the glacier filming Bud Crawford, who

SEARCH Wood from Ararat's Parrot Glacier 1969
Courtesy of Elfred Lee

was doing some work on top of the ice pack. Suddenly Hugo and Navarra were shouting and waving a piece of wood down below. To find wood on that mountain where there are no trees was very exciting. We all came running and started digging, and sure enough, we found more wood, smaller pieces and little splinters. We gathered around with our arms around each other and had a little prayer meeting. We were sure we had located Noah's Ark. Even the scientific, skeptical Hugo was convinced as tears filled his eyes. We all cried!

John: What did your team do after the discovery of the wood?

Elfred: The first thing we did was to clean the glacier. Then we covered our tracks and went down the mountain. An interesting thing occurred physiologically as we went lower and lower. The cuts and bruises we had obtained suddenly became infected at the lower altitude. The situation at the time with other groups also searching for Noah's Ark was highly competitive. We were all sworn to secrecy, and I was very uncomfortable with that. We met two or three other groups, which were very anxious to see us. We were not allowed to speak or talk to them. Eryl Cummings, who was a friend of mine, was leading one of the groups and asked me to go back up with them. They needed a photographer. I wasn't allowed and couldn't go. I was really frustrated. We went to Istanbul and checked into our hotel. Then we immediately contacted AP, NBC, ABC, CBS, BBC, and writers from other major news companies around the world. We called a press conference at the hotel and showed our wood. The next morning we were headline news all over the world. NOAH'S ARK FOUND BY SEARCH FOUNDATION. We saw all our pictures and names in print: Hugo Neuberg, Elfred Lee, Bud Crawford, Ralph Lenton, and so on. It was kind of an exciting time. It was my duty as the secretary of the foundation to see to it that the wood got home safely. I went home immediately by way of France with Navarra. It was in the homes of the Navarras where they showed me all kinds of evidence (wood, photos and discussions) that convinced me they had seen Noah's Ark..

Rosie: You said you held a press conference after coming off the mountain? Had any scientific testing been done on your wood yet?

Elfred: No. This was another thing that bothered me, and you have a very good point. We were too anxious to get in the news. The best thing would have been to stay quiet and get back to the United States to test the wood samples, have a debriefing, and come out with a scientific report. But no, most of the members toured around Europe and the Middle East using precious time and money. I came home immediately—alone with the wood.

John: So later when the wood was tested, what was found?

Elfred: I went to the University of Pennsylvania in Philadelphia, where there was a very good carbon dating lab, one of the best in the country at that time. I took two samples of wood. Remember that I went back to France with Fernand Navarra, and he gave me samples of his previously collected wood. I went to the University of Pennsylvania and marked these two samples, "N" and "O." "N" stood for Navarra and "O" stood for ours. I told them these were two different samples found at two different dates. That is all I told them. I wanted them to be objective about it. I didn't even want them to know whose it was. In a few days they had the reports and I drove back up to Pennsylvania. They had conducted carbon 14 dating and other tests. When we read the report, we were crushed. The dates of the wood samples were between 1300 and 1900 years of age, much too young to be Noah's Ark.

Lake Kop with SEARCH Pres. John Bradley 1982
Courtesy of John McIntosh

Paul: Both samples of wood?

Elfred: Yes. Both. There was no difference in the samples. They had taken it upon themselves to also have the U.S. Forestry Department come in and identify the wood. They said the wood is a species of white oak. So the dates and the wood were the same. To look at the weights and grain, you could not tell them apart. Later, the president of the SEARCH Foundation, Ralph Crawford, concealed this report, and would not allow it to be published. But at least we had proven that Navarra's wood was the same as our wood.

Paul: Hadn't Navarra already had his samples analyzed?

Elfred: Yes, but by different methods rather than Carbon-14 dating. Navarra had his wood tested in Bordeaux, Madrid and Cairo with well-accepted methods. They studied the lignite formation, the gain in density, the cell modification, growth rings and fossilization. On the strength of Navarra's earlier studies, we claimed that our wood was the same as his, with the same age of 5,000 years. We went on with our fundraising of serious money and all went well.

John: When you find a few pieces of wood that are out-of-place artifacts on Mt. Ararat, does that necessarily mean that they were from Noah's Ark, or that the Ark was found?

Elfred: No, and you make a good observation.

John: How did this make you feel, in terms of scientific validity, having said that the Ark had been found, based on the

1969 Photo of Navarra Wood from 1953 or 1955
Courtesy of Elfred Lee

discovery of a few pieces of wood? This wood might even have been found in a location different from where the Ark is supposed to be.

Elfred: I had a lot to learn. But my hands were also tied very securely by the president of SEARCH.

John: You said that you were basically on the southwest side, correct?

Elfred: As I look at the mountain, it was southwest, but we eventually worked our way towards the west-northwest area of the Parrot Glacier.

John: I have heard that the Ark may actually be somewhere near the Ahora Gorge, which you said was on the north side.

Elfred: Correct.

John: How is there a correlation with Navarra's wood and your wood being found on the west side of the mountain, while many Ark researchers think it may actually be on the north side of the mountain?

Elfred: I asked this very same question after talking with Navarra. He told me some things that he had not told anyone else. He had found wood elsewhere on the mountain. On a topographical map he pinpointed the places he had found wood. With the help of Eryl Cummings, we found that the wood our expedition found had come down from an upper area where Navarra had seen wood before, and where George Hagopian said he saw the Ark.

John: I'm still wondering how it is possible that a piece of wood was found in the Parrot Glacier area, when others claim the Ark may have been on the north side of the mountain.

Elfred: Navarra found other wood. He saw wood in three different locations on the mountain. Hagopian confirmed to me that the Ark landed above the Parrot Glacier. It is possible that wood from the Ark drifted down into the Ahora Gorge to the north, and also towards the Parrot Glacier to the west.

Rosie: Did Navarra actually see wood from the Ark in 1952? Did he excavate?

Elfred: He saw a shadow in the ice in 1952. In 1955, he was actually able to reach the site and dig with his son Rafael. They made a black and white movie, then had to hide for 13 hours in a cave during a snowstorm, where they nearly froze to death. They continued to dig and did find pieces of wood in 1955.

George Hagopian and Elfred Lee with Ararat Painting in Easton, Maryland 1970
Courtesy of Elfred Lee

John: What about George Hagopian? How did you find out about him?

Elfred: When I was working on fund raising for SEARCH, a letter came in from a Mrs. Mary Board of Annapolis, Maryland. I opened the letter and there was a hundred-dollar check and a note. In the note she described a man to whom she sold property some years earlier. He now lived on the Eastern Shore of Maryland and claimed to have seen Noah's Ark. She had been trying for 22 years to contact someone going to Mt. Ararat. Board said, "This man has seen it. He knows where it is, but nobody will pay any attention." I called Mary Board the next day to set up an appointment. We talked for quite a long time and she felt comfortable to share information with me. She took me to meet George Hagopian in July 1970. He was not in the best of health, but he was very alert mentally. He had been born and raised near Lake Van, in eastern Turkey and had a very thick Armenian accent. At that time, Mt.

Ararat or "Masis" was part of Armenia, which was a predominantly Christian country.

He told me his story and I have hours of tapes and pages of notes on our conversations. I called him "Uncle Georgie," and he called me "Freddie" or "Sonnie." He told me, "Freddie, I be glad to go with you and show you, but my health won't permit." I had just come back with movies and slides and wood in my hand, which I showed him. When George Hagopian started talking while I was drawing in front of him, his memory seemed to clear up and focus. He was able to give me details that you and I can't exchange with mere words, because he was visualizing the events.

John: What were the details of George Hagopian's experience with Noah's Ark? What happened when he and his uncle went up to see the Ark?

Elfred: Many people from Hagopian's village had seen Noah's Ark, and it was common knowledge. His grandfather had also seen it. His family were basically shepherds. He and his uncle would go every summer from Lake Van to Mt. Ararat where they would graze their sheep and goats. When George was eight years old there had been a three- or four-year drought in the region. Animals were dying. The glacial ice had melted way back on the mountain. His uncle suggested they go up toward the top of the mountain for water and grass and see if the holy Ark was visible. The ice might be melted back enough this year. So George and his uncle went up. They found the fully-exposed Ark resting there. They were in reverence and awe. It was a very holy experience for them. He said that the thing looked to him to be a thousand feet long.

Elfred Lee Drawing of Hagopian Ark 1972
Courtesy of Elfred Lee

He could remember that the Ark was of wood and he could see the grain, color, fitted joints and wooden dowels. It had something like shellac covering the wood. It appeared to have been covered with some kind of paint that was peeling. There was a green moss growing on it, and at the far end was a set of stairs coming down to within about ten feet of the ground. It looked like the stairs had been attached by someone else. He said Noah didn't put them there and they were not part of the original construction. Incidentally, Rene Noorbergen found a report in the Jerusalem library that told of early Christians going on pilgrimages up there and doing repairs on the Ark. There was a monastery called St. Jacob's near the base of the mountain which housed relics from the Ark.

John: Was this the monastery that was destroyed by the earthquake?

Elfred: Yes. It was destroyed by an eruption in 1840. It was common for pilgrims to go up there when the weather permitted, and they would stop at the monastery and then go up the mountain. The report said that they did some repairs, so they probably took pieces of wood up with them, or pieces that were lying around that had come off the Ark, and made a stairway so they could walk up on it. The reason the stairs came only within ten feet of the ground was probably because of the higher snow level at the time they were built. Hagopian and his uncle piled rocks to reach the stairs. His uncle then hoisted little Georgie up to the stairs, and he walked on the top where he saw openings all the way down the middle of the roof. The roof had a very slight pitch to it, but was almost flat. Down the middle of the roof was a small raised area running from stem to stern, and on each side of that raised area were openings. This would help prove a lot of other important things to us. Hagopian looked inside these openings and he

Elfred Lee Drawing of George Hagopian Account
Courtesy of Elfred Lee 1972

shouted. His voice echoed down inside. It was hollow and dark. On the top of the roof there was a hole. But the windows along the side in the center of the roof were well preserved.

He walked to the far end and looked down and saw that he was on an overhanging cliff. This may be another very important clue to the Ark's location. We believe that it is in part of the Ahora Gorge. He said he could not see the bottom. There was a lot of fog down below him. He could see the tops of clouds and it looked like the ocean to him. It looked like he could see the whole world. He was standing on top of the world. He was very excited as a little boy, but also became very scared. He said the Ark was not a rock construction or an earth formation, it was obviously hand-tooled, man-made wood. It was rectangular in shape, very long and was very high. He could not give the exact measurements, but to him it was huge. The Ark was covered with this green moss in patches, but he could still see the wood grain.

John: Did he see a fully intact Ark, or did it look like large pieces were missing from it?

Elfred: No, No. To him it appeared the Ark was fully intact. I told him others say that the Ark is broken into several pieces, and he almost cried at the thought of it.

John: I have a question in relation to Hagopian being eight years old when he first saw the Ark. An eight-year-old boy can be very impressionable. You spent many hours with him, do you really believe he saw the Ark?

Elfred: Yes. Absolutely. He was not one who would fabricate or lie. We checked him out as well. He had a very good reputation in town. We verified his bank accounts and income to make sure he was not making anything off of his statement. We also went to Lake Van in Turkey and specific sites he discussed to verify his authenticity.

Rosie: You said that Hagopian went up with his uncle. Was any information ever received from the uncle about what he saw or the other people who also frequented the mountain during that time?

Elfred: His grandfather had also seen it. He did not tell me anything more than to say his uncle and grandfather were very glad that George had able to see the Ark. Hagopian went up again two years later, and saw the same thing in the same place, but there was more ice and snow covering it.

John: He would have been about ten years old then?

Elfred: Yes. He and his uncle went home and

Elfred Lee Drawing Hagopian Climbing Stairs
Courtesy of Elfred Lee 1972

told his grandfather and others about it. His grandfather said, "Georgie you're going to be a hagi, a holy man, because you've walked on the holy Ark."

John: No one interested in the Ark at that time would have been searching out information about his family?

Elfred: No. There was very little international travel to that part of the world in those days. There were also growing racial tensions that isolated the Armenians.

Rosie: Did they leave any written record that might have been passed on?

Elfred: Just oral histories and traditions. But he said there were many others who had seen the Ark and knew about it. I wish Hagopian had lived long enough to meet Ed Davis.

Rosie: It would seem to me that the Turks must also have had an interest in discovering the Ark, and all the implications that go with it?

Elfred: Yes, you would think so. The government, the head of tourism especially. The increase in tourism would be a good way to help stabilize the economy of eastern Turkey. It has been so shaken with insurrections, the Kurdish problem, the Armenian problem. If that area could be economically developed, it could be a very stable part of the country.

Living here in Mexico helps one understand a little bit of what the Middle East is like. The bureaucracy is demanding. They don't have the American system of organization. They rely on us to do it for them. But they want our technology, and they also want all the credit and the money that would come with it.

Rosie: Are you saying that Turkey does not have a scientific interest in finding the Ark?

Elfred: Not really. Turkey is a secular state, and perhaps because Noah's Ark is so strongly associated with the Armenians, there may be a reticence on the part of some to have it discovered. At one time to be an Armenian in Turkey was like being a Jew in Nazi Germany. Germany is no longer Nazi and Turkey is no longer under the ancient system. There are few Armenians left or else they've changed their names. Once in awhile we'll talk to someone we think is from Turkish decent and he will quietly tell us he's Armenian, or a descendant of the Armenians. But times have changed and today you couldn't find nicer people than the Turks.

Rosie: In these past 12 years there was no further research?

Elfred: There was research, but nothing we could do on the mountain. Thanks to Colonel James Irwin, the astronaut who walked on the moon, with his political connections he was able to get eastern Turkey opened up again to expeditions. They were afraid of foreigners coming in on that border and they're under pressure from Soviet Russia. They didn't like anyone up on Mt. Ararat looking down on Soviet territory. I saw their tanks and their missile bases and all the hustle and bustle on the north side of the border.

I'm telling you it's well fortified and the Soviets brag that they could take Turkey in 24 hours with no problem. They had the biggest and best tanks in the world. It was a very sensitive thing for Americans to be there with electronic equipment, they just knew we were spies. I am against any such spying activity. I do admit to meeting with the CIA, along with Bud Crawford.

About the second day I was a member of the SEARCH Foundation Bud took me to Washington, DC. He invited me to a meeting with some friends who were interested in photography. As I sat in the room and looked around, I saw all these plaques with awards and honors given by the CIA to this "friend." All he wanted was for us to aim our cameras a certain way and bring back photographs. I was not about to get involved in that. I refused. But Bud did not and he took the money. He liked to brag about it. It got us into a lot of trouble. I don't blame the Turks for closing down the expeditions. We have no business spying while searching for this sacred object. On the way down the mountain in 1985, our guide Ahmet Turan and I had a chance to talk as I knew him from 1969. He asked many questions: Are you CIA? What are you

(Back) Ark-a-thon Don Shockey, Ed Davis, John McIntosh, Bob Stuplich, Elfred Lee, John Morris, Bill Crouse - June 1986
(Front) Larry Williams, Eryl Cummings, Violet Cummings, Ken Alexander
Courtesy of Elfred Lee

doing on our mountain? If you find Noah's Ark, what will you do with it? I said that we were not CIA. Spying is not our business at all. We are only looking for Noah's Ark for the glory of God. Turkey, also, will benefit as well: tourists, money, establishment of the east. Noah's Ark must stay here. It belongs to Turkey.

John: During this twelve-year period what was really going on? Where does Ed Davis fit into all this?

Elfred: He is another key eyewitness. We met him after the 1985 expeditions. I forget the exact dates that the expeditions began to be allowed in again, but the next main expedition was in the summer of 1985. I went on an expedition with a very fine group of men from the Dallas area. Bill Crouse was one of the main ones, Dr. Paul Meier of the Minirth-Meier Clinic was my roommate at the hotel at the foot of Mt. Ararat. He is a very fine psychiatrist and godly man.

While waiting for permits in Dogubayazit, we visited Ishak Pasa Palace nearby and some of us also explored an ancient Hittite cave. Since the permits for Dr. Meier and myself had not yet arrived, we decided to join the climbers later. In the meantime, Bert Sabo and I took off in his V.W. camper for Van, where George Hagopian was born and raised. This gave me some time to confirm details about Hagopian's life that he had told me. We took a boat to Aktamar Island in Lake Van where Hagopian had gone to church. Some of the details Hagopian gave me such as church cemetery under the tiles was confirmed. The place was completely desecrated and I am glad George was not with me to see it.

The war between Iran and Iraq kept us from going further south so we headed up the west side of the huge Lake Van north toward Ararat again. On the way we met Ian McDonald making his world record run from England to Tasmania

On Monday, Paul, Martin and I picked up our permits in Agri and prepared to climb the next morning. At midnight I was looking at the mountain wondering how our teammates were doing. Then I saw a light, then another. I got out my telescope. They were fires! What was burning? Were they cooking at midnight? They should be dog-tired and sleeping soundly. During the night, the Probe "A" Team was taken captive at AK-47 gunpoint. Kurdish terrorists burned them out and stole or destroyed everything.

While waiting in Ankara for another expedition (Jim Irwin's) to get permits, Jim Irwin, Bert Sabo and I met with the American Ambassador Robert Strausz-Hupé, who was most cordial. After describing out intent, I made the point that if we could get up the mountain and back before the terrorists do anything they would lose face (very important in the East) and lose political influence while showing that the Turkish government was in charge. He assured of his support and put us in touch with top military generals who could help us with the expedition.

He arranged a chauffeur in an Embassy car to the headquarters of the top U.S. and NATO military officials (I have to avoid some names and details). We were again warned of the hostage possibilities as the Soviets, Iran and Iraq benefited from destabilization in the eastern sector. Negotiations went on for three days and although we could not get a helicopter for our use, we were assured of military protection by a top Turkish General.

Here's another interesting thing verifying or confirming the stories of George Hagopian and Ed Davis. At the U.S. and NATO headquarters, I talked with U.S. Two-Star General Ralph Havens, the commanding General of the United States forces in Turkey. I went there on August 29, 1985, with Jim Irwin, John Bradley and Eryl Cummings. We interviewed this man and I showed him the paintings I had done of Hagopian's description, and General Ralph Havens said, "We've seen that. We have photos of that. Our pilots have photographed that very object. It looks just like that. It is on a ledge. In fact, I was shown two slides of this object at Fort Leavenworth in a presentation for people assigned to Turkey." The General actually told Irwin and I that his flyers had seen a similar structure on the north side of Mount Ararat. When the General checked on the two slides, they were missing from the presentation. Despite not having slides and after 40 years of Ark study, this confirmation from an American General caused Eryl Cummings to exclaim with tears in his eyes, "This is the greatest day in all the years of Ark research."

So there is confirmation of the structure on Ararat in modern times by a military authority. Also, the Russians had found it and photographed it in 1917.

John: Was it on this expedition or the following one?

Elfred: This expedition. When we came back, the "ark fever" was high. There was a lot of sensationalism again and interest in the Ark. They called an Ark-a-Thon in Farmington, New Mexico, in honor of Eryl Cummings, a pioneer Ark researcher. Eryl and his wife Violet have given their life's blood, and their daughter Phyllis has done a lot of the research and writing.

They invited all those interested in the Ark. We gave reports and showed slides of our various findings. They said there was a man there who had seen the Ark.

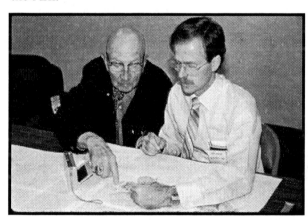

Ed Davis and Elfred Lee at Ark-a-Thon 1986
Courtesy of Elfred Lee

Dr. Don Shockey of Albuquerque had found him, quite by accident, in his office one day. Don Shockey will tell his story much better than I can, but he was the one who first met Ed Davis, and shared him with the rest of us, very much as I had done with George Hagopian. Ed then became seriously ill. It was something life threatening. He was flat on his back, just at the time we needed him to come to the Ark-a-Thon. The first evening we all prayed. We prayed for unity. I gave a special program at the opening appealing for unity, because I had seen such a lack of it through the years. And we all got together and prayed for Ed Davis.

Then the phone rang. It was Ed. "I'm feeling so good, come and get me." Someone went down and brought him up to Farmington. I had never met him but I had heard so many people claiming things, that I thought, Here's just another one. I was frankly not interested. Then in came Ed Davis wearing a cowboy hat, a big silver buckle, cowboy boots, silver and turquoise. I was really skeptical.

Rosie: So who is Ed Davis?

Elfred: I will tell you. He came walking in and started talking. As I listened my hair on my neck stood up. He sounded like George Hagopian. He started describing the mountain, his experiences, how long it took to go from point A to point B, the caves, the fog, the rock formations, describing the interior of the caves, and the stone steps and how they're carved. My goodness, I said, where did this guy hear this information? None of this information is published. I have George Hagopian on tape and in notes, but none of his information had been published yet, so I became very interested.

We came to find out that Ed Davis had been in the Army in 1943, stationed in Hamadan, Iran. He was in the Army Corps of Engineers. Of course, the story will be told in more detail by Don Shockey and in the appendix of this book. Ed Davis was building roads in northern Iran and helping to supply equipment to the Soviet Army during World War II. Mt. Ararat is the back door to Europe.

Ed befriended a group of Moslems, a family named Abas. He did some favors for this family and they felt very indebted to him. They asked if he would like to see Noah's Ark? Well, as any young GI would, he said, "Why not?" So one night they drove from Iran, between Big and Little Ararat, through the saddle, and around to the north side. They stopped in a village there, Abas-Abas Village. He described it, saying there's a tree there, it was at the foot of the Cehennem Dere, near the Ahora Gorge. He described the rock formations and everything. The village was between Arilik and Ahora [this is named Tarlabas' village in Ahmet Arslan's 1986 map in *The Lost Ship of Noah*] and they went up by Jacob's well and Jacob's graveyard, across the Cehennem Dere and up towards Doomsday Rock. He described all this to me.

I spent some quality time with Ed Davis that night. He wanted to work all night. By midnight I was tired out. He was feeling very good, providentially healed for that occasion. People suggested "that Elfred Lee do with Ed Davis what he had done with George Hagopian." So I got paper and pencil, turned on my tape recorder and started drawing. People were standing around flashing pictures and recording on tape and asking questions. It became a kind of circus. I forget who it was, I think Eryl Cummings or somebody, took it upon himself to get people out of the room and closed the door. So I was alone with my tape recorder and sketchpad and one or two others.

I think John McIntosh came in quite a bit. He asked some very good questions, and took some pictures, too. John has been a very good researcher and has helped very unselfishly. I kept having to send people out for more paper and cellophane tape as the drawing grew bigger and bigger. It became huge, and as Ed Davis talked and I drew, his memory sharpened and focused and he was able to describe rock formations and locations of cliffs, ledges, snow banks and moraine—everything. He would say, "I was standing here and saw that and went over here and saw that. From this point I could see the

Ark and the other broken part that was over here." The Ark had slid down from the Hagopian site and was now in two pieces.

Ed Davis has been able to describe Noah's Ark very well, though he didn't see it as well as Hagopian, because he went up only once and he went up at night and was in the fog a lot of the time. But he's given enough information to me and to Ahmet Arslan to confirm that he was there, and that he indeed was in the same place that Hagopian was. Hardwicke Knight of New Zealand also went through that region and he claims to have seen Noah's Ark and his descriptions are the same as Ed Davis and Hagopian. So he was in the same place.

Elfred Lee Drawing of the Hagopian Ark in 1900-1908 and the Davis Ark 1943
Courtesy of Elfred Lee

George Jefferson Greene also took photos of it. Haji Yearam describes it also, and Reshit in 1943 saw it the same year Ed Davis did. In 1945 the Soviet Air Force and US Air Force photographed it, so evidently in 1943 and 1945 it was visible. In 1955, George Jefferson Greene saw it and photographed it the same year Navarra did on his last expedition before he took us in 1969. These are interesting coincidences.

John: So you're saying that they saw it, like Navarra, who saw this shape under the ice as opposed to an exposed Ark.

Elfred: Right. In 1955, he could see it right through the ice. The ice was so melted, it was on a thaw cycle, there's a freeze and thaw cycle on Mt. Ararat that's approximately 20 years. Not exactly, but that was a thaw cycle year. In 1952, he saw it in the distance, in 1953 saw it better. In 1955, the ice was melted right down to the wood. He could walk on the ice of this lake and see the wood right under him, cut down through it and pull out pieces. He could actually see that the length of some of this wood was about 150 feet. That's hard to believe. . .

John: He was on the south side of the mountain when he found this, right?

Elfred: No. The west over above Lake Kop in the Parrot Glacier.

John: You are basically saying here would be sort of north where the Ahora Gorge is, the Parrot Glacier would be over here. (Pointing to map)

Elfred: That would be west.

John: So you were saying that it was coming down on this side, and this is the area where he was looking, kind of on the west-southwest side. Navarra was finding this?

Elfred: But he has also been up here.

John: So he's actually been up to the general site.

Elfred: Navarra has stood at a place looking right into the cove that Ed Davis went to. I have evidence of that and photographs of the area from other people. He led us to another place though, and we found wood there. But that's not the mother lode.

We want to find where this Navarra/SEARCH/Parrot Glacier wood came from. And I can show you where that is, because I have spent a lot of personal time, not only with Hagopian, but with Ed Davis and Navarra, and it's all together. All three of these men have seen Noah's Ark and lived to tell about it. As an artist and a personal friend of these men, they took me into their confidence and told me things. I waited to go back and follow up.

Rosie: How does the size of the boat as perceived by the different people compare?

Elfred: Most of them have not seen the full thing from stem to stern. It's covered at one end or broken now. Hagopian's the only one who's seen it whole. "Roskovitsky" (or his real life counterpart from Gurley's/Koor's story) and some other Russians went up in 1917 and he said they saw it, but didn't give any measurement. The Czar sent up a team to measure it, and they indeed would have that information. They measured it, walked inside it, and photographed it. I've talked to Col. Alexander Koor of the Russian Army who was in charge of that region at the time. Before World War I, it was still part of Russia. Mt. Ararat was his command post and he was there when the Czar sent 150 troops up the mountain to photograph the Ark and measure it. As you know, in 1917, the Bolshevik Revolution took place, and we're not sure where that information is. I heard one report it was somewhere in Leningrad, which is again called St. Petersburg. Maybe it will be released. Who knows? There are some Russians who know about it, but at that time they weren't willing to help us.

John: Okay. I have a couple questions in relation to some of things you've mentioned up to this point. One is about the carbon 14 dating method. The man who developed the dating method, Wilbur F. Libby, told you that obviously these samples, which were dated 1700 to 1900 years old, were contaminated by more recent organic material. What kind of contamination occurs at 14,000 feet? You've got to have contamination with organic material, because it contains carbon, which is organic.

Elfred: Okay. They also said there was carbon of a more recent vintage, that it had infiltrated the sample. Now there's organic material growing there. There's moss and lichens and little low bushes, and even goats climb up there. I saw goats up above us, over this very site. Goat droppings could come down into the water and the goats were up there eating something. They weren't eating just rocks.

John: Okay. So there is organic material of more recent vintage that could have infiltrated the sample and in that manner caused it to have a more recent date?

Elfred: Yes.

John: Another question. You said something about Hagopian, who saw it as an eight-year-old, saying he thought it was a thousand feet long. The Bible says the Ark was 300 cubits, the cubit being approximately 18 inches, usually considered to be from the elbow to the fingertips.

Elfred: So that would make Noah's Ark, using the conservative 18-inch cubit, 450 feet long, by 75 feet wide, by 45 feet high. Hagopian here is saying in effect, it's twice that size. Now he was a wide-eyed little boy, he was very excited, but he pointed to me from where we are now sitting, to that tree over there behind the house to indicate the length, and it was close to a thousand feet. But he was an eight-year-old boy who's about three feet tall, and he could stand up in the windows of the Ark.

There were about fifty of those windows, going all the way down the length of the Ark, forming a ventilation system. These openings were really part of one window, as the Bible says, one window in the roof. Doesn't say how long, but we know now, it was the full length of the ship, and since the window was right in the middle of the roof, the Ark would have to almost capsize before water would go in. He stood up, looking in these openings, so there is your cubit, approximately three feet high. He said a cow could walk through them. I would say a small cow or a heifer, and so that would make a 36-inch cubit.

John: Which would easily make it a thousand feet long.

Elfred: That's right. And I believe, speaking as a creationist, that we're inferior to what Adam and Eve were or what Noah was. I believe Noah was even bigger than Moses, who wrote the account, and so I believe men were much larger than men now living.

Ahora Gorge from the Foothills 1985
Courtesy of Elfred Lee

John: Therefore their forearm and hand length would be longer than 18 inches.

Elfred: That's right, but when we get in there and measure Noah's bed, that will help, you know, and see some of the furniture in the Ark, that will really help. And this will help verify not only Scripture, but creation. It will help prove we were created superior and that we are devolving, not evolving. We're inferior to what was originally created by God, and this would help verify creation science.

John: Any other questions related to George Hagopian, Davis, Cummings, Navarra?

Paul: The question about the wood type that they found. It was not of the area. What type of wood is it, and where is it from?

Elfred: It was white oak, Quercus species of white oak, which we are told is a common type of wood used by seagoing vessels, before the time of metal ships. The only area where it grows is way down the Euphrates River. As you know, the Euphrates begins at Mt. Ararat, and it's about 300 miles away. So this wood, these huge beams, this huge construction would certainly have to float by a huge flood to reach such an altitude, 300 miles to the north.

John: So that really brings us question number four. Do you personally believe that Noah's Ark is on Mt. Ararat? Did it land there? And is its remnants still there? If so, what, in your mind, is conclusive proof that it really is there?

Elfred: That's a long question. Yes, I do believe Noah's Ark is there to this day. On a spiritual note, because God does not waste things, even 12 baskets of food collected after he created it. He created Noah's Ark to last for centuries, and it had a useful life of only one year and 10 days.

It was made of very durable material and was made to last. He quick-froze it, so it's not only petrified, but frozen, the best form of preservation, and it's been seen by too many people. Even Marco Polo says the Ark of Noah is in the eternal snows of Mt. Ararat. There's another very important clue: Marco Polo. So this other site that some have been talking about at a lower elevation (Durupinar), is exposed every year most of the time. In regard to Durupinar, I would question the integrity of anyone claiming something is "Noah's Ark" before objective, scientific work can be done to check it out. Ron Wyatt told me, "God told me this is Noah's Ark and I don't need university Ph.D.'s to tell me otherwise." Sometimes we are too eager to make a public announcement. I have been guilty myself. I was quite convinced by Ron Wyatt while working with on the site until an incident in the Istanbul Airport. A few feet from the police check, Ron stuffed his rocks he had taken from Durupinar site into my luggage without talking to me about it. That type of planting evidence wherever and whenever it is convenient is a dangerous precedent for a "researcher." Noah's Ark is in the eternal snows. It's very rarely seen, very rarely uncovered. There's been a climatology study done that confirms the exact dates that

Durupinar village mayor handing Elfred Lee a rock which he alleged was a piece of Noah's Ark 1985
Courtesy of Elfred Lee

Hagopian said a four-year drought occurred, scientifically proving that Hagopian was right. As to his integrity, he had a PSE test, the lie detector test.

John: Hagopian did?

Elfred: Yes, Hagopian, and he passed the test. Also, his personal life, his reputation, his friends, and business acquaintances bore witness that he was an honest man who would not lie or fabricate. And he was not looking for any personal gain from it. The details that he and Ed Davis have given coincide with the others who have seen it, and it can't be coincidental. As for the seaworthiness of the Ark, the hydraulics lab in San Diego, where they study ship designs for the Navy, made a scale model from my drawings, as they were preparing for this Hollywood movie, and they found that Noah's Ark would not capsize. It could sustain tidal waves 200 feet high. A Coast Guard captain told me, "This is the most seaworthy design I've ever seen."

It's like a box, it's not very pretty, and artists have been painting Noah's Ark wrong for years. It's just a box. The word "ark" means a box or container. The Ark of Noah is not a boat, it's a box, so Noah's Ark was basically a kind of big old clumsy shoebox, with a window down the middle of the roof. That's all it was. Not very pretty, but very stable.

John: When you say clumsy, you mean in terms of a utilitarian boat to get from point A to point B?

Elfred: It could not cruise very well.

John: But its purpose wasn't to cruise.

Elfred: That's right. It was not to go anywhere; it was just to house and sustain life in the worst catastrophe the world has every known. Hagopian's authenticity is very clear to me, his knowledge of Ararat and the region, the geography and the history are all accurate. The dating, the climatology all prove out. His honesty, his reputation, his consistency, the basic facts and

details, he never varied. Even though people would make him angry by questioning and cross-questioning him, he would still hold to his facts. He would not waver for the sake of popularity or anything else.

Rosie: Earlier you mentioned that Hagopian was irritated or seemed to be irritated at some people who came to question him and he gave them misinformation. Could you tell us a little bit about that? And how does this tie in to what you just said?

Elfred: Yes. He told me that there were some people who were wanting him to tell them where to

SEARCH Expedition team 1969
Courtesy of Elfred Lee

go. He didn't trust them and he would not give them all the information that he could have. He let them be misinformed. He would not lie. But he could withhold information and let some people draw wrong conclusions and that's what he did. That's what he told me he did, because he said he didn't trust them.

Paul: On about how many occasions did you meet with George Hagopian?

Elfred: My goodness. It would be very hard to count how many. But over a period of a year and a half, it was very often. Sometimes several times a week, then sometimes, because of my duties, I couldn't go out for a few weeks, then I'd go again. I was on the phone with him quite often, and also with Mary Board until she died. She had implicit confidence and faith in him and gave a very good recommendation of him.

John: What about Ed Davis? Your first impression of him was that here was this cowboy who you might as well write off, he doesn't have anything to say.

Elfred: I'd been living in Washington, DC, too long. Gray suits and ties, briefcases, and here's this guy in jeans, shiny silver, and whatnot. He was in style in Albuquerque, and I let my first impressions kind of make me judgmental, but he very quickly proved that he knew what he was talking about.

John: When you say he proved, what do you mean he proved?

Elfred: He knew the mountain as nobody can unless he's been there. And when I got together with him and Arslan and my information from Hagopian—my goodness! Don Shockey was saying that this was the most historic moment in all of Ark research. Ed Davis said the very same thing.

Also, I have confidence that Ed Davis is a fine Christian man. He has not sought to be written up or to be photographed. He doesn't want money or fame. Don Shockey has been very kind and generous to share him with us and let us have free access to him. However, I have never gone to see Ed Davis without Don Shockey.

John: Did Ed Davis go through a lie-detector test as well?

Elfred: Yes. I think he has. And in my book he's an honest person, not seeking self-glory or anything. After the 1986 Ark-a-thon, I was able to meet David Duckworth at Eryl Cummings' house. Violet wanted to show Ed's sketch to David but I refused to let her since that could easily be leading questioning. First, I asked David to draw a sketch of the composite photo he saw in the Smithsonian Institution. Then we compared it to the Ed Davis broken structure. There was an uncanny resemblance beside it being broken.

John: What about Navarra? You said many people thought he had a big ego that he wanted to protect, that he's been to the Ark site itself, but he took your SEARCH Foundation to another place, down the glacier from where the

Ark would have been. How do you feel about Navarra? You spent a lot of time with him?

Elfred: Yes. That's a little more difficult. Personally, I consider him a friend. We had some problems, because I pushed him on a few points and he got a little upset. I was searching for truth, but overall, I believe Navarra has been there, and has also seen the Ark. There are questions about his personality, but people have questions about my personality, you know.

Ararat High Grasslands where Shepherds like George Hagopian
Grazed their Sheep 1985
Courtesy of Elfred Lee

John: Artists are a little different.

Elfred: Yes. We're sometimes accused of being prima donnas, but in my heart I know that I want God to receive the glory and I want the Ark to be found. So far, nobody has really been able to find it, and people have started coming to me more recently and saying, "Elfred, you have all this information, maybe you should go." The only way I can give all the information I know is to take my head off and hand it to you. It's like pieces of a jigsaw puzzle in a box. I have been given information over the years by Hagopian, and Ed Davis, and Navarra and there are a lot of pieces that fit, and there are a lot of pieces that don't fit.

If I could get my body on the location, on Mt. Ararat, I believe I could recognize places and a lot of these pieces would come together in my head.

John: Are there any other things that you would say in your own mind that make you sure and that are conclusive proofs that the Ark is there, other than the three men whom you've talked with?

Elfred: Jesus spoke about it. He's a good reference for me and He mentioned Noah and the Ark. Peter, in 2 Peter 3 talks about how there would be scoffers and mockers in the last days. People who walk after their own fleshly desires, saying, Where is the promise of his coming? And all things continue exactly as they did from the beginning. You know, that's the theory of evolution right there. That's uniformitarianism right there, and they deny the fact that the heavens were created by the word of God and that the earth was destroyed by water. They deny the existence of a flood. This is one of the signs of the last days, and we're right in it. It's right in our universities. You can hardly talk about creation now. Evolution is the thing that has led to much of the godlessness, crime and corruption that's bringing our country and

Ed Davis with Elfred Lee at Ark-a-thon 1986
Courtesy of John McIntosh via Elfred Lee

the world down. We need the Ark as a witness today!

In 1970, I went to the Islamic Center in Washington, D.C. to research the Quran issue. The curator of the center, Henry Youssef Ahmed Abadi, showed him a book which said that "Jebel Judi" was a peak of Masis, Mount Ararat. The curator also said that Judi results in Cudi which results in Kudi which results in Kurds. So there is a possibility that finding the Ark on Mount Ararat could substantiate Jewish, Christian and Muslim sources. This would be one area where Jews, Christians and Moslems actually agree.

John: So from a personal experience, as it relates to having been on the mountain, touched wood, dug it up; from your understanding of your discussions with people who have actually seen the entire Ark; and from biblical understanding and your personal faith in God, you are sure that the Ark is there?

Elfred: I am sure that the Ark is on Mount Ararat, in the eternal snows of Mount Ararat.

John: Okay. That brings us to the final question. You've really covered number seven in terms of a Christian perspective and the search for Noah's

Ark. Numbers five and six: Do you plan any future trips to Mt. Ararat? If so, when? Where is the Ark?

Elfred: People would love for me to take a map and point my finger or give a street address as to where Noah's Ark is. They pump me for information and the next thing I know, they're on the mountain and I'm still here. I'd be very happy to freely offer my services. They can have all the glory and the publicity. That's fine. I don't care. I've seen too many people with their own agendas come and go. Let's get together and get the job done.

The Parrot Glacier is not the mother lode. It's further up the mountain, above the Ahora Gorge. There are certain landmarks. If only I could actually get up there. It could fit what my picture in my mind is. I have a very vivid photographic memory as a trained illustrator and have heard many accounts.

John: Another question in relation to the satellite information that has been analyzed. In both the 1974 video *In Search of Noah's Ark* and also in the more recent CBS one in 1992 or '93, they both used supposed satellite information. They pinpointed a spot using specific pixels and computer animation and so forth. They have said, this is the site and we expect it to be right there. With that kind of precision, a person who has a GPS should be able to walk to that site and find the Ark in that moment.

Elfred: I wish they would. Why haven't they?

John: That's my question.

Elfred: That's my question, too. Just because there's a foreign object or shape doesn't necessarily prove it's Noah's Ark. It should be investigated. Everything should be investigated. But I believe there's another factor here and that is timing. Maybe God hasn't wanted it to be found yet. He knows better than I do when the history of the world is at a point where there's a crossroads and the world has got to make a decision. There are certain things in prophecy that have to be fulfilled before that happens and I don't know when it is. My appeal to all researchers is that we need to lay all on the altar and put aside all differences and egos. We need to unite and join talents and resources to finish this great project to God's glory.

Bob Stuplich was a lead climber for both Dr. John Warwick Montgomery in the 1970's and with Jim Irwin in the 1980's, and is considered by many ark researchers as one of the best climbers to explorer Mount Ararat.

3

BOB STUPLICH

Introduction

At the University of Wisconsin in Madison, one of my options for an archaeology class term paper was to find out if there was any evidence for the existence of Noah's Ark on Mt. Ararat. My professor had heard of possible sightings and was interested in learning more. I began my research. I found that there were people who believed that Noah's Ark still existed. I wanted to know more. I studied everything I could find concerning "the Great Deluge" and everything written about it from every culture. My interest in biblical

Explorer Bob Stuplich on the Abich I glacier overlooking the Parrot Glacier
Courtesy of Bob Stuplich 1982

archaeology grew. The implications of substantiating biblical history became paramount for me. I eventually met Dr. John Warwick Montgomery at Biola University in California. He lectured on the Ark history and sightings on Mt. Ararat. I was hooked.

In 1972 I went to Switzerland to study with Dr. Frances Schaeffer at L'Abri in the Alps. While I was at L'Abri a student from the University of Strasbourg stopped in for a visit and we began a discussion. I learned that Dr. Montgomery was teaching at the University of Strasbourg and was planning

on an expedition to Ararat for the summer of 1973. I immediately proceeded to hitchhike up to Strasbourg to inform Dr. Montgomery how badly he needed my climbing expertise for his expedition on the mountain.

Dr. Montgomery carefully explained to me that he had all the members he needed for his expedition, that they had been preparing for months and that all their information for permission to climb had been submitted to the Turkish government long ago. I stayed in Strasbourg and sat in on Dr. Montgomery's classes—he is a great historian and one of the best teachers I have ever

Kurdish woman carrying water in Ahora Village
Bob Stuplich's favorite photo of Ararat 1982
Courtesy of Bob Stuplich

had. I would often meet with Dr. Montgomery after class because he just wasn't understanding how desperately he needed me on his expedition. Finally his patience wore out. He asked me not to mention Ararat or the expedition ever again.

I gave him my phone number and address at L'Abri in Switzerland in case he changed his mind. He graciously took it and put it in his pocket. I left Strasbourg and went to visit some friends in Germany for a week. On my way back to Switzerland from that visit, I had to go right past Strasbourg. I thought that it wouldn't hurt to try Dr. Montgomery one more time. I knocked on his apartment door ready for him to open it long enough to see me and close it right in my face. He opened the door as if he were glad to see me. He invited me into his study and asked me for my passport and some other information. When I asked why he wanted the information he asked me "Didn't you get my message?" I said, "What message?" He said, "I sent a message to you in Switzerland." I apologized and explained that I had not yet returned to Switzerland. He looked me in the eye, pointed his finger at my face, and intensely inquired, "You mean, you had the audacity to come here to ask me one more time to join our expedition after I asked you not to." I

Very old Kurdish woman in Ahora Village
Courtesy of Bob Stuplich 1982

politely affirmed his suspicion. He then explained to me that my persistence, patience and determination were why he chose me to replace one of his members who had to drop out at the last minute. He explained that I would need all three attributes in Turkey. Little did I realize at the time how true his statement would be.

1973 Getting to Know the People

I spent over two months in Turkey without permission to climb. I waited in Erzurum, Dogubayazit, and Igdir getting to know the Turks and Kurds in the area while Dr. Montgomery was trying to get permission to climb from Ankara. I went climbing and fishing with the Turks and visited the Kurds in their villages and worked with them harvesting wheat in their fields. When we explained to the Kurds that we were about to leave the area without Turkish permission to climb Mt. Ararat—my new Kurdish friends explained to me that we needed their permission also. They claimed that if the Kurds did not want us to climb—we wouldn't be able to go up.

At that time, the Kurds claimed they were in control of the mountain since they lived on the mountain. They then invited me to return anytime and we would climb where we wished. I asked if I could bring my American friends (Dr. Montgomery and group) and they said yes. When I explained this to Dr. Montgomery—he decided to send me back a month or so early in 1974 to work, climb, and go fishing for trout (God's fish) southeast of Erzurum with the Kurds for a while before the group would go over. However, this is not the proper legal way to approach climbing the mountain today.

1974 Work, Work, Work

I flew back to Turkey on June 3rd and was finally able to work through the entanglements and difficulties of "arranging" for a climb up Ararat to the Parrot glacier beyond Lake Kop. It took 45 arduous days to work out the details with the competitive and unorganized guides. Much time was spent simply waiting at one spot or another for people to show up. It is difficult to describe how frustrating making these "arrangements" were unless you read my complete report. And Dr. Montgomery and the rest of the expedition kept waiting in the wings for word that it was OK to come to Turkey from Switzerland and the United States.

Huge grinding stones at Korhan 1983
Courtesy of Bob Stuplich

I had many old friends from last year in Erzurum. One of them took me out to see the Citroen that was stored at a brick factory. It was covered in Turkish dirt. We also went to the garage where the trailer was stored and the garage demanded 10,000 Turkish Lira ($700.00) before we could get it out. We had never intended to leave the trailer in that garage but the Turkish friend who said he would take it out and store it in another friend's yard "forgot" to do so. We eventually had to pay about $300.00 to get it out. It was good to be back in Erzurum with old friends and that night I met another Turkish guide who spoke English very well. It was a pleasure talking with him.

The next day was an interesting day. That morning I went to pick up the jeep. It ran quite well after a few minor adjustments. We took it to a stream to wash off the incredible quantity of Turkish dirt that had accumulated in it as well as on the outside of it. I had a hard time starting the jeep and had to make some adjustments on the carburetor. Anytime I opened the hood of the jeep there was always ten or fifteen Turks standing around to "help." I had the hood off and one Turk decided to "help" by pulling the gas line off the carburetor. The fuel pump was working quite well and pumped gas all over the engine. The whole thing immediately went up in flames. I had never seen so many panic-stricken Turks! They all moved so fast that they were running into each other. In retrospect, the incident really seems funny, but at the time I was pretty scared. We finally put the fire out with blankets but the fire had burned out most of the electrical system as well as the rubber gas line. I spent the rest of the day finding parts to do a patch-up job on the jeep.

After a difficult month and a half of "arranging" the permission, guides, horses, and equipment, we were finally able to get on the mountain. Our expedition encountered a July snowstorm on our first night at base camp at Lake Kop. We proceeded up to the Parrot glacier and looked "everywhere" for "Navarra/SEARCH wood"—we found absolutely nothing. We did, however, see a large black object in the ice above the Parrot glacier that got us all excited. Was that "it"? We grouped together to make a plan. While we were planning we realized that Brian Bastian was very sick. He began to lose consciousness. We all got worried. Dr. Montgomery was fearful for Brian's life. Brian couldn't walk. We had to carry him. We began to realize that he had hypothermia. We needed to get him down immediately. When we got Brian down and warmed up, we realized that most of the group had other commitments and they needed to get back to the States or Switzerland.

**Huge and ferocious "wolf" or "sheep" dogs on Mount Ararat
Courtesy of Bob Stuplich 1974**

I determined that I wasn't going anywhere until I went back up to "it." The whole group left Turkey and I stayed. I went right back up the mountain with three Turks and a Kurd. Going up we saw dogs. You cannot get from the bottom of Ararat to the snowcap without the Kurdish dogs finding you at some point. You can watch for the Kurdish tent villages and go around them, but the dogs will sense you and find you and bark, growl, and carry on until their master comes to find out what all the commotion is all about.

We had a plan to approach the "black spot" which was on the north side of the mountain from the south over the summit so we did not have to climb the north side up the Parrot glacier. It would be faster up the south side. We took one day to get to our base camp at about 14,000 feet.

At 4:00 AM the next morning Gaze, Ertugrul and I set out for the top of Ararat. Negmi decided not to press on because the storm the previous day had taken too much out of him. It was very cold and he didn't have the proper equipment. When we reached just above 4,000 meters, Ertugrul said that he couldn't continue the climb but Gazi and I were still eager to try to reach the top, so the two of us continued alone. By the time I got to 4,800 meters I didn't think I was going to make it either. Everything hurt. I could only take 10 or 15 steps before I would have to stop and rest. We could see the clouds below us and it was extremely windy, but we had to climb to the top of the mountain before we could start down the other side towards the "spot." Reaching the summit of the Agri Dagh was the hardest thing I had ever done physically!

Kurdish settlement two miles from Korhan greets their surprise visitor Bob with a lamb which was killed and cooked for dinner 1982
Courtesy of Bob Stuplich

When we finally reached the summit the clouds had met us there. The absence of the sun combined with a strong wind at that altitude made it bitterly cold. We could only bear to stand on the summit for about two minutes before we headed down the north side towards the "black spot." But along with the clouds had come a blinding snow. It was almost impossible to see a step in front of us. We were climbing the huge ice cap glacier, which covers the north side of Ararat from 4,200 meters to the summit at 5,165 meters. The new snow together with the wind had caused huge drifts to cover the crevasses. Gazi and I could descend for only 20-30 meters before I would fall through the snow into a crevasse, as I was going down first. Gazi would pull me out with the rope, which tied us together while we were on the glacier. We would continue but the same thing kept happening. With the cold, wind, and snow it finally became ridiculous to continue our attempts to pass over or around crevasses we couldn't even see. I understood then why no one had ever climbed Ararat from the north face. Finally we were forced to stop because we were in a total whiteout. Gazi finally convinced me that we should return to the base camp. Once again our attempt to reach that "spot" had been frustrated.

We circled around to the west and back to the south toward our base camp. We arrived back at our base camp after 14 hours of climbing, arriving late in the evening. We broke camp and descended the mountain through the night. We arrived at the road between the Iran border and Dogubayazit at about 5:00 AM. I was exhausted. Because of the storm we decided to pack up

Train that Stuplich and Montgomery would occasionally take across Turkey
Courtesy of Bob Stuplich 1973-1975

our gear and start down. When we got to the bottom of the mountain we still had eight miles to walk in the dark with a full pack of climbing gear. We got back to our hotel at 7:00 AM the next morning. Without a doubt that had been the longest and hardest day of my life!

I was also late for a very important date. I was to meet my fiancée in Switzerland and only had a few days to get there. I wasn't flying either. I had to drive our expedition jeep back to Switzerland. We drove the jeep back to Istanbul and then continued driving the remaining 3,800 kilometers back to France. I picked up my fiancée, we got married a week earlier than we planned and got back in the jeep and drove right back to Ararat for our honeymoon. I know you are asking, "How could he do that?" Easy. You are reading this book, aren't you? You have at least a touch of "Ark Fever." I had it pretty bad. Hey, "it" was visible in 1974—we were on our way back across Europe and Turkey to Ararat.

When Dr. Montgomery asked me about going back to Ararat for our honeymoon, many thoughts flooded my mind. I had just left Turkey and I could still remember how good it felt to leave. I was tired and it was a long way back. Who would I climb with? Could I take the time? How could I be sure my Turkish friends would be able to climb? When would we climb? Would it take another month or so of frustration to organize another climb?

I had planned on taking my new wife up with us to our base camp Lake Kop but "winter" had set in on the mountain. I left her in a hotel with friends in Erzurum and took off to see if we (a climbing friend Scott Little from Switzerland and I) could get to "it". Scott and I were both experienced with ice so we decided to just go right up the Parrot glacier.

Explorer Scott Little hiking the Parrot Glacier
Courtesy of Bob Stuplich 1974

We took a van to the place where two men and two horses were waiting for us. It was so cold and windy that one of the Kurds decided not to go up with us. I had warned them the night before that it was going to be "cok cok soguk" (very, very cold). I made sure to explain that when our group went up in July that it was extremely cold and that the Kurds who went with us almost froze to death because they didn't bring suitable clothing to protect themselves. Mehmet, the man with the horses, said that he would be fine. Mehmet, Scott and I started up the mountain at 6:30 AM.

Mehmet was not a guide and had never been to Lake Kop, but I felt quite sure I could find the Lake Kop area and I couldn't justify paying extra money for an extra guide. I had been careful to make sure that I could find my way back when we had gone up to Lake Kop in July. When we got about halfway to the Lake, Mehmet felt sure we were lost. It was very cold and snowing and the dense clouds made it impossible for us to see more than 20 yards ahead. I must admit there were times I wasn't really sure myself that I could find the area again. The only thing that kept Mehmet going was that I had not yet paid him.

At four o'clock that afternoon I finally saw the Lake Kop area. It was a beautiful sight after a long cold climb through the clouds.

We unpacked our gear from the horses and ate. Mehmet started to get cold and scared and he wanted to go back down. He tried telling me that the agreement was to pay $50.00 for him to go up and $50.00 when we got to the site. I knew that he had understood that the agreement was for him to stay overnight so that we could evaluate whether or not it would be profitable to go on to the Navarra site above Lake Kop. There was snow at our base camp and it looked like more was coming. Mehmet started crying when he realized that he would have to stay the night on the mountain. I didn't really know what to do. I could see that if he did stay the night it would certainly be a dangerous situation for him. He had no tent and only a blanket to sleep with.

He unbridled the horses and prepared to spend the night. When I saw that he was going to stay if I did not pay him and that he would almost certainly freeze to death if he did stay, I had to reconsider. I told him that if he promised to come back in 3 days to pick us up that I would pay him, and he could go down. He readily agreed to this and was on his way down the mountain in a matter of seconds.

**Bob Stuplich and Scott Little two-man tent home for 5 days
after snowstorm on Parrot Glacier 1974
Courtesy of Bob Stuplich**

So Scott and I were alone on the mountain. We put up my two-man tent and went to sleep. That night we were hit by an incredible storm! It snowed all-night and dumped more that a foot of new snow on us. It stopped snowing at about eleven o'clock the next morning so we packed our gear and moved up to the Navarra site. It was quite difficult getting to the Navarra site because of all the new snow, especially where the snow covered the huge rockslides and we couldn't find sure footing.

Bob Stuplich climbing out of a crevasse
Courtesy of Bob Stuplich

When we got to the glacier, Scott and I had to remain roped together constantly because the crevasses were completely covered by snowdrifts. When we reached the crevasse where Navarra had taken out wood, we found it frozen completely shut, which made it impossible to do any diving. Dr. Montgomery and I had planned on me diving into the melt water pond and searching for wood since there was so much water there in 1973. The wet suit I had carried up the mountain was of no use. We pitched our tent right on the glacier along side the crevasse and went to sleep in hopes that Thursday would be a better day.

When we woke up the next morning our tent was again covered with new snow and more snow was coming down. It snowed most of that day but Scott and I took every effort to look around. I could see that much of the old snow had melted since July but now the new snow had covered everything, making it impossible to see anything on the surface. I spent quite a bit of time inside crevasses but found nothing but ice and new snow. Later in the day the weather cleared enough for us to see the glacier above us, however, it was also covered with new snow so we were unable to see the "black spot." We climbed about halfway up the glacier but it would have been futile for us to climb any higher because we could not see the exact location of the "spot." After five days in that weather and conditions, we were fortunate to be able to get off the mountain with only minor snow slides and no avalanches. Obviously we never saw "it" again that year.

1975

If I could spend a part of my honeymoon on Ararat, I might as well try for my first anniversary there too. I had already developed a love/hate thing with that mountain. When I went back in 1975 the Turkish/Kurdish problem was so bad that my Kurdish friends had a hard time contemplating risking any contact with the Turkish military which was very present at and around Dogubayazit. My Kurdish friends told me that the Turkish military was watching us.

At the suggestion of our Kurdish friends, Jim Bauch, John Gustafson, and I waited until dark one night, jumped out of the back window of our hotel room, threw our gear in the back of our jeep and headed for the pass between Dogubayazit and Igdir. We had John drop us off at the pass in the dark. John drove down to Igdir and then straight back to Erzurum. Our Kurdish friends told Jim and I that we had perhaps the night and the next day before any search would be sent out for us. We climbed half way up to the Parrot glacier before we realized that we needed to turn back if we were going to get off the glacier before dark. We were off the glacier by dark and proceeded down the mountain to the saddle between Dogubayazit and Igdir at night. Our Kurdish friends were waiting on the saddle to pick us up. We were all nervous. Too

Eryl Cummings and Jim Irwin 1983
Courtesy of Bob Stuplich

little time under too dangerous political conditions. We went back to Erzurum, packed up the Jeep and drove it back to France. The jeep was three years old and completely worn out. I thought I would never see Eastern Turkey again for a long, long time.

1982

By the time Jim Irwin got involved in the search for the ark the stress between the Kurds and the Turks had calmed down a bit. I was honored that Jim asked me to lead the climb for his expedition. We began training immediately in Jim's "back yard"—Pikes Peak. This expedition covered the entire north side of Mt. Ararat. We first camped at Lake Kop with different groups going out in different directions. My group consisted of the two best climbers in the group, Dan Bass from Texas, and Orhan Basher (a Turkish commando—strong, powerful, determined, and confident—a joy to have as a climbing partner).

I was given a $1,000.00 wad of money to go from our base camp at Lake Kop around the base of Ararat to Ahora village to see if I could find anyone who could give us information as to where the ark was. I was sent with Orhan Basher, the Turkish commando who spoke good English. In fact, it is interesting that the Kurds on one side of the mountain can be very different in physical appearance and customs from those on another side. Halis also went with us because he was Kurdish and knew where to go from village to village and could ask the questions. Some of the old time villagers on the north side, however, would only speak Russian. So, for me to ask a question, I would ask Orhan in English, Orhan would ask Halis in Turkish, Halis would ask an interpreter in Kurdish, the interpreter would ask the old timer in Russian, the old timer would answer in Russian, the interpreter would answer in Kurdish to Halis, Halis would tell Orhan in Turkish, and about a half an hour later (if they still remembered the original question) Orhan would give me some kind of an idea of what they had been talking about.

Bob Stuplich went house to house through Ahora and other villages asking for information about Noah's Ark to no avail. Much time was spent in translating between different languages such as the situation with this Russian old-timer and his Kurdish wife talking with the Kurdish guide to the Turkish commando and the English-speaking explorer 1982
Courtesy of Bob Stuplich

We found out the next year that Halis had given me some kind of drug on that little side trip—by the time we got back to our base camp I was so sick that I thought I was going to die. I thought it was because I had just eaten everything I was offered on the little side trip, everything from Kurdish yogurt, cheese, meat, sheep organs of many imaginable kinds, etc.—once I recovered the next day I was fine. Eventually, all expeditions learned how to get up the mountain without the services of Halis.

We had dinner with Kasim Gülek, an elder statesman for the Turkish government, who was educated in the United States at Columbia University by the order of Ataturk himself. Dr. Gülek was one of Ataturk's consultants during the westernizing of Turkey. Dr. Gülek and his wife were extremely helpful in gaining permits during the 1980's as his wife was especially

Kasim Gülek statesman and consultant of Ataturk
Courtesy of Elfred Lee 1985

interested in the search for Noah's Ark. They had beautiful homes in Ankara and eastern Anatolia that contained many archaeological artifacts as well as one of the largest personal libraries in all of Turkey. Dr. Gülek stated the following to Elfred Lee in 1985.

So many civilizations have come and gone here—the Hittites, Ancient Greeks, Romans, Persians, Arabs, Turks—all have left archaeological monuments here. As a matter of fact, the Turkish nation itself is a melting pot... But the real work in Turkey is to dig into the ancient world. Unfortunately many have plundered and took it away. There are whole museums full of archaeological remains that they took away from Turkey! The Purgamum Museum in Berlin; it's a monument of shame! The British Museum is full of archaeological works that they have taken away from present-day Turkey... From that point of view I think you're doing very well in taking up archaeology in Turkey.

When Jim Irwin was introduced to the Turkish military and government personnel he was always introduced as one of the astronauts that went to the moon. They were impressed. Once we got up on the mountain, we still

Jim Irwin giving photo of himself on the moon and a replica of a moon rock 1982
Courtesy of Bob Stuplich

introduced Jim as a moonwalker but we got a totally different response from the mountain Kurds. They would look at Jim, look down at the photo of Jim standing on the moon, look up in the sky with a puzzled look, and then look back at Jim with a silly little grin on their face as if to say, "Sure, I 'believe' that one—got any other good jokes?"

We decided to go straight up the middle of the Parrot glacier to check out the spot we had seen in 1974. We had already checked out both sides of the glacier for wood in the areas of the Navarra and SEARCH expedition sites. We found nothing. The Turkish Climbing Federation had no record of anyone ever climbing the Parrot glacier, so the three of us decided to go straight up the middle of it. It was great ice and we made good time. We bivouacked for the night without a tent high above the Parrot glacier. The next morning we searched the Abich I ice cap to see if we could find any part that might be stationary. I for one do not believe that there could possibly be a boat of any kind in that massive slow moving glacier. That is one huge piece of ice! We searched the area where I tried so many times in the early 70's to reach. There was nothing there but a huge mass of ice slowly moving and grinding anything that may be encased in it. It would be a great place for a ski area but not for a boat. We descended back to base camp.

We then took three groups to set up a high camp above and to the east of the Parrot glacier near the Cehennem Dere above the North Canyon area (great high camp area!). We launched our three different teams in different directions. We had one group make a summit attempt—the first one failed—the second one allowed three to reach the summit. Jim Irwin was in both groups but had to return both times. He was frustrated.

I had been spending most of my time at the western edge of the Ahora gorge rappelling in and climbing out in order to view the whole thing. At our high camp after Jim Irwin's second attempt at the summit I found out that Jim wanted to go down to base camp to get them ready to move to the other side of the gorge for a continued search. We were having perfect weather and felt that we had covered the entire north side of the mountain. I told Jim that he needed to wait for the summit group to return so that they could all go together to base camp. Jim was frustrated and in a hurry. It was a beautiful day and he said he had plenty of time. I explained to him that the mountain

Explorer Bob Stuplich rappelling into the Ahora Gorge 1982
Courtesy of Bob Stuplich

was dangerous and could be fatal if we didn't stay together in our groups.

After I left our high camp for another search - Jim left for base camp alone. We radioed down to base camp at our 7:00 PM usual communication time. Jim was not there. I sent out a search group from base camp and took one from high camp toward base camp. We searched until dark. We could see the flashlights and headlamps of the searchers below but it was too steep to attempt the terrain in between. We didn't sleep much that night. The search group found Jim at 8:00 AM the next morning at the bottom of one of the North Canyon chutes. He had four gashes in his head, knocked out four teeth and his hands were cut and swollen twice normal size. Our three groups from high camp were spread out over the North Canyon area. John Christianson pulled a "Jim Irwin" on us and went a little too fast down the same chute to his father-in-law and ended up in the same rocks with cuts and an injured knee.

When I finally got to John and knew that he was stable, I could hear group two above me calling for help. Group two had a man "paralyzed" or "frozen" on a rock ledge. He had just watched John slide down the chute and now he "couldn't move." I climbed back up and talked him off the ledge. We all got down to Jim just as one of the Turkish commando/medics had him stabilized and we began moving him down the mountain. Our expedition was over. We got Jim to the hospital in Erzurum to have him put back together. All he could talk about was finishing the search on the east side of the Ahora gorge. So, after about a month of recuperation in the good old U.S.A. we went back to Ararat at the end of September. There was too much snow to go up the mountain very far. We went up the middle of the gorge until we felt that it was not safe and returned to Ahora. We set up telescopes at Ahora to view the east side of the mountain. We decided that next year we would cover the east side.

Guide Halis, horseman Memete, and Ahmed Turan
Courtesy of Bob Stuplich

1983

We had 22 people on a combined search of the east side of Ararat in 1983. There was a herd of people at base camp. It was incredible that the Turkish government allowed that and trucked us all over. In my opinion, that was not my favorite way to search the mountain. The weather was not as good as 1982 but the mornings were quite good. We covered a lot of territory. No boats. My climbing group consisted of Jim Kunes and Bill Spear—both climbing friends from Colorado. We covered everything on the eastern side up high. High on the eastern edge of the gorge, and high on the East glacier including the old Anderson sites along the East glacier. The east side of the mountain was the only side I had not been to. I had been up the south to the summit, along the western slopes low and high—twice, all along the northwestern side 4 times, last year we had covered the north and north east sides—even dropping into the Ahora gorge, and now we had covered the east side. My concentration was 15,000 feet and lower. I had ruled out anything being in the 12 square miles of glacier on the mountain unless I could find a glacial lake or area that was not moving. 1983 was a good year though. We were able to take a fixed wing plane around the mountain circling it 4 times. I shot 35mm slides of all sides of the mountain. We had work to do when we got back with our magnifying glasses an "big screens." We found no boats. I didn't go back the next year.

Base camp tents near Lake Kop with the Parrot Glacier above the rock formation
Courtesy of Bob Stuplich 1983

1984

During 1984 I had become a good friend with Jim Irwin and his best friend Bill Dodder. Jim called me one day and asked if he could come to my house for a visit. I assured him that I would be glad to see him at any time. Jim came over and explained to me that he had been angry with me for some time and needed to be relieved of it. He explained that all his anger came from the time he made his second summit attempt in 1982 and returned to our high camp alone. When I saw Jim approaching our high camp alone—I approached him quite frustrated. He had a "habit" of independence on that mountain that concerned me greatly because Jim had placed me in the position of responsibility for all the climbers on the mountain and he was one of them. I flat out told him he had to stay with his group. Jim explained that he may have been able to take it at the time if John McIntosh hadn't been there listening to the whole confrontation. At any rate, Jim said he was mad and when I left to go back to my search group, as I explained above, he proceeded to go down to base camp and fell on the way. Jim asked me to forgive him. I asked Jim to forgive me. It was one of those "you had to be there" moments that I will never forget. I met the real Jim Irwin and he was a beautiful, godly man of peace and reconciliation.

1985

I went back with Jim in 1985. Turkish/Kurdish relationships were again becoming strained. Kurdish terrorists attacked the Probe group and the Turkish government was concerned about Jim going up the mountain. They

finally allowed us to go but not without about 40 commandos with machine guns. Read Dick Bright's account of that climb. We climbed the south side to the summit but the Turks radioed us at the last minute to return without going over to the north side. (By the way Dick, you did get pulmonary edema on that climb—you were just too stubborn to stay up there and die on us.)

Burnt remains of the Probe Expedition
Courtesy of Bob Stuplich 1985

1986

I went back with Jim again because of the possibility of flying again. I didn't go on the first flight, which turned out to be our last. We were arrested for international espionage. I don't recommend it but it was kind of fun (only because we had an astronaut who had been on the moon with us and the international news network knew about it).

1987

I went back with Jim for the last time. By 1987 the political situation in eastern Turkey was again severely frustrating for Ararat search groups. I was able to fly the West Side of Ararat to take 35mm slides with the door off the helicopter but there was too

Bob Stuplich searches Ararat via helicopter
Courtesy of Bob Stuplich 1987

Bob Stuplich on the Abich I glacier looking into the horizon
Courtesy of Bob Stuplich 1982

much snow to be of any benefit. Despite the poor conditions on the mountain, it sure was easier than my previous climbs!

Conclusion

I can't seem to find that boat. That doesn't mean that it is not there. Ararat is a big mountain! I certainly haven't proven that it is *not* there. Bill Crouse seems to think that "it" may be on another mountain. Perhaps. There are a lot of mountains between Iran and Iraq.

One thing is for sure—I have met some great people who have spent quite a lot of time researching and looking for the Ark of Noah—and for good reason. I have also met some very peculiar (a kind word) people over there looking for a boat. Ark search is a passion for some, and a business for others. Some Ark searchers will share everything with you; some are scared to death that someone else will find it before they do. Some have had visions and dreams that God has chosen them to be the "great finder" of Noah's Ark and ordained them to be the next John the Baptist in calling the world to repent one last time. Some are just grateful that God has allowed them to live another day.

Looking for Noah's Ark is an adventure. It provides an opportunity to value and appreciate different cultures. It certainly requires patience and persistence. I enjoy it.

Don has been a veteran Ark researcher since 1984. He was instrumental in the first and only "Ark-a-thon" in June 1986, and author of the book, The Painful Mountain, featuring the alleged Ed Davis. He also discovered the claimed Satellite Remote Sensing expert George Stephen III.

4

DR. DON SHOCKEY

Editor's Note: Dr. Don Shockey, an optomologist who received his doctorate from Pacific University, also received a degree in Anthropology at the University of New Mexico. He participated in a number of archaeological excavations including the 1955 Lucy Site excavation of Sandia Man, "pit-house" dwellings in northern New Mexico, the Stone Age Mexican Tarahumara Indians, a Roman amphitheater in Albania, Qumran in Israel, the temple mount in Jerusalem and a mastodon site. Shockey was also the founder of the Governor Bent Museum in Taos, New Mexico.

Don Shockey's Experiences

One news article caught my eye as I was reading the Albuquerque Journal in the fall of 1983. An explorer would be speaking at a local church the next Sunday evening concerning his four pervious attempts to locate Noah's Ark in Turkey. Being a degreed anthropologist from the University of New Mexico, my latent interest in biblical archaeology immediately surfaced. The time of the lecture would conflict with my position as music director of a local church.

I was following the previous attempts to verify the existence of the Ark on Mt. Ararat beginning with the first American expedition of SEARCH Inc, then Dr. Crawford, Eryl Cummings, and more recently, astronaut James Irwin. I fortunately found a substitute to fill my duties at my church, and at 7:00 PM my wife and I were seated in the audience. The speaker, Dr. Howard Davis of Artesia, New Mexico, was introduced.

Following the lecture, the Davises and the Shockeys drove to a local restaurant for a cup of coffee. Howard told me that one of his team members would be unable to participate in the next expedition scheduled for the summer of 1984. He suggested, assuming the approval of the other team members, that I consider becoming a part of the expedition. I glanced at my wife, she smiled, and without hesitation my reply was "Yes, yes, yes!" The rest is history. I began the most awesome adventure of my life.

During the years following 1984 I've logged nine trips to Turkey and made three climbs on Mt. Ararat. All have been memorable and all different. Preparation was the key. One should expect the worst and if the worst didn't happen, consider yourself very lucky.

Voracious reading and research were only part of the equation for success. I learned that temperatures could drop to -40 F, high winds, rain and snowstorms and lightning were to be expected as a common occurrence and threat. Then there were the ever-present rebels who could kidnap or kill without greater provocation than the fact you were on their mountain. Camera film could be confiscated and equipment destroyed. Should one become ill or injured, medical care would be in the hands of the explorer, as the nearest hospital is hundreds of miles away. The high, upbeat excitement of the expedition would be somewhat tempered by the reality of unexpected delays and dangers encountered each day. Asking God for guidance, protection and discernment was number one priority in all our prayers.

Dr. Don Shockey
Courtesy of Don Shockey

The 1984 expedition did not sight any object on the mountain that we could identify as the Ark or as broken pieces of the Ark. There is absolutely no doubt in my mind that God, according to His divine timetable, orchestrated a number of things related to my Ark-search efforts. Uppermost in these events was meeting Ed Davis and sharing his unique story in my book *The Painful Mountain* so that fellow Ark hunters might benefit from the new information gained from Ed. It was my great pleasure to introduce Ed at the first and only "Ark-a-thon" in Farmington, New Mexico in the summer of 1986 where Ark researchers and explorers from throughout the United States gathered together for the purpose of sharing vital information.

I introduced Ed to archaeological illustrator Elfred Lee. After listening to Ed's eyewitness account of being taken up Mt. Ararat to view the Ark in 1943, Lee began sketching a depiction of what Ed was describing. Ed was the first person to share information that the Ark was in two major pieces. Prior to this time, and using information from the George Hagopian *encounter,* it was assumed that the Ark was still in one major piece. Apparently at some time in the interim between the Hagopian viewing and the Ed Davis viewing, volcanic, earthquake, or other forces had caused the vessel to break into at least two pieces.

Ark-a-thon with Eryl Cummings, Don Shockey, Ed Davis, and Elfred Lee 1986
Courtesy of John McIntosh via Don Shockey

As Ed was describing to me the large structure he viewed on the mountain, he told of huge timbers that extended from both parts of the Ark. He said that if you could bring the two broken sections back together they would fit like an interlocking puzzle. Ed stated that it appeared to be some type of laminated construction. This information was tucked into "file 32" in my mind, and all but forgotten until I was in Dallas Texas for a seminar. On the second day a doctor approached me. He had been told that I had been searching for Noah's Ark, and had some questions to ask. After talking with him and answering his questions for some forty minutes, I asked Dr. Weinstein if he was Jewish. His reply was affirmative. As it turned out, he was born in Israel and was a student of the Hebrew Scriptures. Now it was my turn to ask some questions.

I began, "Dr. Weinstein, when God directed Noah to build the Ark of gopher wood, what is your understanding of what this wood is? The Hebrew word for gopher seems to be rather non-specific."

Without hesitation, he replied, "In the old days there was a particular tree growing in the mideast that when the bark was cut, a gummy secretion would ooze from the cut. This resin was collected and used to apply to the wood to be spliced together. These pieces of wood were coated with the resin and clamped together. After 24 hours the bond was so good and complete that you could not break the splice. It becomes harder and stronger than the wood on either side of the splice. This is 'gopher wood.'"

Ed's account and what Dr. Weinstein was telling me suddenly came

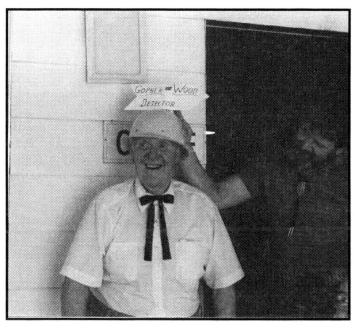

**Al Jenny Holds a Special Ark-a-thon Gift of a Gopher Wood Detector
for Veteran Explorer Eryl Cummings 1986**
Courtesy of Don Shockey

together in my mind as I heard the proverbial bell ring. We have plywood, but not a "ply" tree. Could Gopher wood be a *process* rather than a species? It is apparently a "gophering" process whereby many types of trees could be used in the construction of the Ark. This would have significant advantages in engineering applications for design and for structural strength.

With regard to Ed Davis, it is with personal sadness that I announce the death of Ed Davis in Albuquerque, New Mexico November 17th, 1998. (To those readers who do not recognize the name, Ed was very likely the first American to be taken by an Iranian family to view the Ark of Noah. This occurred in 1943.) Ed was alert until the time of his death, and I enjoyed a visit with him in the Ladera Nursing Home just one week before his passing.

Davis' entire life had been one of unusual adventures. His mother was half Cherokee and his grandmother was a full-blooded Oklahoma Cherokee, hence the name "Chief" used by his close friends was not just a nickname, but one which held much pride and respect. Davis related to me the entire saga of the "Trail of Tears" where his relatives were force-marched from Florida to

Oklahoma and incarcerated in a reservation. Ed's grandfather was an Anglo-Irish wagon master who led pioneers from St. Louis to Oregon, and later became a U.S. Marshall in Indian territory in Oklahoma. He was very proud to be a descendant of his great-grandfather, Jefferson Davis, who was president of the Southern Confederacy during the Civil War.

Chief was born on a train somewhere between Texas and Oklahoma on July 11, 1908. He met his wife Polly in Albuquerque in 1939, and they were married in 1940. There were no children born from this marriage. Ed's involvement with the Ark of Noah began while he was serving in the armed forces during World War II. Soon after his enlistment he was sent to Hamadan, Iran where he worked with the Army Corps of Engineers. Chief's company guarded Roosevelt, Churchill and Stalin when they met in Tehran.

His next orders were to build a supply road from Iran into Russia to support in their effort to defeat Germany. Native Lourds (Lurs) were hired as drivers to assist the army engineers in this endeavor. It was at Hamadan that Davis met Abas-Abas, a Lourd in his eighties. Abas and his family revered the Ark as a holy site.

Ed performed a service of great importance to Abas' village, and in an act of gratitude, Abas-Abas and seven of the patriarch's sons took Ed to Mt. Ararat to climb to the site of the holy artifact. According to Ed this experience changed his life forever. When Mr. Davis saw the Ark it had been broken into two large pieces separated by a narrow ravine. The trek up to the Ark took three days. His entire story is recounted in the book, *Agri-Dagh The Painful Mountain* by this author.

After another stretch of army duty in France, Davis was discharged. Excited to share his experience on the mountain, he soon discovered that most people, including many theologians, dismissed his account of the experience as less than truthful or perhaps total fabrication because he had no photographs to substantiate the story. Ed told me that the doubters placed the veracity of his seeing the Ark on Mt. Ararat in the same category as stories of UFOs and Sasquatch. Disappointed with this reaction, he was silent about the experience during all the following years until 1985 when this author learned about Davis and his incredible experience. Chief agreed to a three and one-half hour polygraph test administered by P.G.P. Polygraph in Albuquerque, New Mexico on May 1, 1988. The following is taken directly from the test results and analysis by the examiner: Target: Whether or not this subject is truthful when he states that he observed Noah's Ark while in the area of Mt. Ararat. On the above date (5/1/88) this subject was tested utilizing the standard Backster Tri-Zone Comparison Specific Examination. Upon final analysis of all of this subject's polygrams it is the opinion of the examiner that he answered TRUTHFULLY to the target issue.

Subject was asked to recall in detail what his recollection of the incident was. His answer was as follows: While this subject was in the U.S. Army and assigned to engineering duties between Iran, Turkey and USSR he met a male later identified as Abas-Abas. Subject stated that Abas' son was working for the government at the time of this meeting. As the subject related the story, Mr. Davis did a great favor for Abas and his tribe.

As a result of this favor Abas was asked by Davis to tell him (Davis) about the Ark or structure that was located somewhere around Mt. Ararat. Davis was told that if the weather was right he (Abas) would take him to see this structure. Some time later Abas and seven (7) of his sons escorted Davis to the site of the structure.

In trying to solicit the information from Mr. Davis the following questions were asked:

1. Are you lying when you state that you were taken to Mt. Ararat by Abas and his seven sons?

2. Are you lying when you state that you climbed Mt. Ararat on horseback and on foot?

3. Are you lying when you state that the object you saw was broken in half?

4. Are you lying when you state that the structure was exposed between 100 and 200 feet?

5. Are you lying when you state that you saw a large wooden structure high on Mt. Ararat?

6. Are you lying when you state that no one ever told you about the Ark other than Abas and the Bible?

Mr. Davis answered all of the above questions with NO. After careful analysis of all of this subject's Polygrams it is the opinion of the examiner that he answered without showing any stress to questions 1-5. Regarding question 6, the subject did show stress and answered that he has talked to a number of people about the Ark. He also stated that not one of the people that he has spoken to have ever seen or known the exact location of where the Ark is.

The following is an account of how the Ed Davis polygraph became a reality.

On Sunday afternoon May 1, 1988 I drove to Ed's home and picked him up before driving to the Albuquerque airport. Eryl Cummings, father of American Ark hunters, and Max Lare had flown in from Farmington. Max was responsible for the name "Ark-a-thon" previously mentioned. We visited in the Continental Airline terminal while awaiting the arrival of Bob Cornuke who at the time was Jim Irwin's chief assistant and vice president of "High Flight" located in Colorado Springs. Larry Williams, explorer and commodities expert from San Diego, California had arranged for the polygraph test. Larry was responsible for financing the Irwin-Cornuke expedition into Egypt to discover the path of the Exodus of the Israelites and the location of the Red Sea crossing. At a later time it was Williams and

Cornuke who located what may possibly be the real Mt. Sinai in Saudi Arabia.

The Ed Davis polygraph test was administered by P.G. Pierangel, who is considered the authority on test procedures and analysis. All law enforcement units abide by his conclusions. Everyone present including the examiner agreed that Ed Davis' account was a truthful one. One huge, major problem remained. Exactly where was the Ark's location on the mountain? Even today nobody knows for sure. Many possibilities and possible locations have been suggested. One area on the northeast side of Ararat has been given the tag of "Davis Canyon", but photos of the mountain in this area have failed to show any suggestive objects. This author has never felt that Davis Canyon was the actual location of Ed's sighting.

Tigris River headwaters at the foot of Mount Ararat 1990
Courtesy of Don Shockey

Early spring of 1988 brought some astounding new information concerning the physical remains of a manmade structure on the northeast section of Mt. Ararat. It began very unexpectedly as I was eating enchiladas at a restaurant in Truth or Consequences, New Mexico where I was introduced to George Stephen III and his wife Kathy.

During the course of our meal together, George asked a simple question: "What are your hobbies, Shockey?" It was an easy question and my answer was immediate. "My number one goal is to verify the existence of Noah's Ark." I continued by giving George a summary of the historic searches and the problems in obtaining any help from our government regarding U-2 and/or satellite photos. George's reply shocked me. "Don", he said, "I have access to special technology, and can within two weeks have information on any square foot of land anywhere on the globe!"

I challenged his statement, and he backed up his claim with information about his military background and the newer technology which he had helped develop for our government in the area of infra-red analysis from satellites located 240 miles in space. He then asked me for some coordinates pertaining to my area of search. He said he would get back to me within two weeks.

George kept his word. It was two weeks to the day when he called from California. Using the technology, he had analyzed the area on Mt. Ararat and found two man-made objects in the Abich II glacier. He determined these objects to be definitely man-made.

"Are you sure, George?" was my next question, and one I should not have asked. He reminded me that this is his area of expertise, then went on to explain why he was so sure. The two pieces are rectangular, and approximately one thousand feet in separation. He said that natural formations are not so specific in shape, and he emphasized his certainty that the shapes were not background rock. He then gave me the approximate elevation and also the depth which the objects were covered with ice and snow.

Aware that he was "sticking his neck out" to help me, I asked him if I flew out to his base location, bringing a map of Mt. Ararat could he, without compromising any secret information, mark the two locations with an "X." He agreed that this was acceptable and would not compromise any classified material.

I met with George a few days later, and the mission was accomplished. George Adams, Robin Simmons, and Chuck Aaron were invited to join me at this meeting where Stephen gave his information. The date was June 30, 1989.

Now for the first time we had hard scientific evidence of something large and foreign on the mountain. Was it the Ark?

There was no way of verifying it without an expedition to reach the area and examine the two objects. If they were found to be anything other than the biblical description in Genesis, they could not be remains of the Ark. The Ark's dimensions would be the first criteria of identification.

The ideal time to explore the mountain is the last two weeks of July through the first two weeks of August when optimum melt down of the snow and ice normally will have occurred. Even this "window" has no guarantee of success.

Armed with Stephen's information, hasty preparations were made for a climb to the location. The necessary equipment was collected. Ahmet Arslan was contracted to be the primary guide for a considerable amount of money, and it was arranged that he would join us in Ankara, Turkey. George Adams stayed in California and would be in charge of financing the expedition.

Despite limited funding for the expedition, Robin Simmons was able to go to Ararat at the last moment. Many problems were faced in getting necessary permission from the Turkish agencies so that we might gain access to Ararat.

While we were granted permission to climb the mountain, Robin's permit was delayed. Timetables were very critical. The climb was begun from Dogubeyasit on the south end of Ararat. Ahmet Arslan had secured the help of a second guide who was from Erzurum, and accompanied by these two men I started the ascent.

My standard trek permit did not allow me to explore the northeast side of the mountain. The only way to verify the objects at the location indicated by satellite was to have the Turkish guides check out the site and photograph any object that might be exposed there. Before we left the hotel, Robin and I gave Arslan a copy of the map showing the specific location. Ahmet said he felt that he could reach the area and take the photographs for us but wanted more money before he would go.

Dr. Don Shockey with Tent at Mihtepe 1989
Courtesy of Don Shockey

At the high camp, I was forced to remain as the two guides left in the darkness of early morning to attempt to carry out our instructions. It was very difficult for me to let them go on without me, but I did not feel it would be right to deliberately violate Turkish laws and regulations.

The wait alone on the mountain seemed to go on forever. Late in the afternoon the two guides returned. Ahmet Arslan was limping, having had a minor accident while jumping a crevice, but he was shouting *excitedly,* "It's there! The Ark is there! It's exactly in the location you showed me, and I took some photographs as instructed! My wife will be so happy because she never believed the Ark was on Ararat. Now I have proof to show her." The three of us were jubilant. Arslan was not able to get on top of the object because of the dangerous terrain and ice.

Ahmet estimated that he was approximately one-fourth mile from the main object. He described it as a "coop, like a chicken coop," meaning that the structure had a slightly pointed roof as he looked into what appeared to be the broken end. Most of the object extended back into the snow and ice—only one end was visible. After arranging with Arslan to send our photos and negatives to us, Robin and I returned to the U.S. After a lengthy wait and two strong legal letters from Adam's attorney, the photos finally arrived. George Adams, Robin and I began a long series of analyses. I contacted Dr. Jim Eberts, a nationally recognized forensic anthropologist who did a great enhancement and analysis of the photos in his lab. "I can't tell you the object in the photo is Noah's Ark," he said, "but it certainly looks like a man-made object."

A short time after returning from Turkey I received a call from Carl Baugh of Creation Evidences Museum in Glen Rose, Texas. He and famed artist Robert Summers would like to fly into Albuquerque to meet me, and would also like to meet Ed Davis for an in-depth interview. Since this first meeting with Carl and Bob, we have become close friends.

A 1990 expedition was planned which would include eight explorers. I would coordinate the logistics and Carl would be responsible for raising the funds. Carl and Bob met with Ross Perot in Dallas, Texas. Mr. Perot at that time indicated that he would finance a helicopter. Carl, Bob and I made a preliminary trip to Istanbul and Ankara to secure permission for the expedition. Having accomplished this, the entire team gathered. Joining me as principal members of the team were Carl Baugh, Dr. Walter Brown, Robert Summers, Dr. Ron Charles, B.J. Corbin, Robin Simmons, and noted photographer George Adams.

We made arrangements to lease a Russian 24-passenger MI-8 helicopter, and signed the papers obligating us to this lease.

Returning to the hotel, we found a message from Mr. Perot, informing us that he had reconsidered, and would not finance the helicopter. With a lot of prayer and phone calls, and the generosity of some wonderful people, and a lot of work by our wives, we were able to raise the funds to cover the obligation for the helicopter. Another obstacle had been overcome.

Having leased the helicopter for one week of service, our group flew from Istanbul to Dogubeyasit in extreme eastern Turkey. It would require another chapter to include all the delays and problems in logistics that were encountered.

We flew the entire mountain twice daily for five days, carefully photographing not only our principal sites, but those of other researchers, some of whom had made claims that the Ark had been located. One particular location thought by some to be the Ark was on the north side of the mountain in an area called the Parrot's Beak. The "object" was unfortunately found to be a natural formation which only from a distance looked promising.

From the helicopter our number one object was clearly seen with very little change in appearance from the 1989 photo. Our original plan was that following our aerial survey we would divide our team and climb from two positions to our primary area of interest. However, when our permit to fly, to land on the mountain, and to climb was translated from Turkish into English, we learned that the words "land" and "climb" had been omitted from our permit. This revelation came as a total shock to all members of our team.

The peaks and saddle of Ararat surrounded by clouds 1990
Courtesy of Don Shockey

After many negotiations the Turkish authorities finally agreed to allow no more than three of the American team to climb. Deciding who should climb and who should return to the U.S. was very difficult. It was finally decided that the two who would accompany me on the climb would be Carl Baugh and George Adams. The entire team flew back to Istanbul and to the International Airport. Following the departure of our other team members, George, Carl and I returned to Dogubeyasit and began our climb.

The Kurdish rebels and the Turkish military were fighting on Mt. Ararat and the authorities were very concerned for our safety. After we had climbed to the high camp from the south side of the mountain we were ordered to get off the mountain.

Disappointment reigned now that we knew where to explore but we were thwarted from physically reaching our objects. This 1990 expedition continues to be the last American expedition on Mt. Ararat although others have since tried to gain permission to climb and have been denied.

I am aware of two non-American explorers who, solo, have been on the mountain and both met with very serious consequences. One gentleman is from New Zealand and the other from Canada. This year (1999), I am aware of at least two American and one Canadian team who plan to attempt an expedition to Ararat. This author also still awaits another return to the Mountain of Noah whenever a "green light" is given. This must be for God's glory and not to bolster an individual or a group's ego. God can and does use people to accomplish His will and purpose.

I extend my thanks to all Ark hunters who have sacrificed time, talent and money and have contributed to the major effort to identify and verify the 100% truthfulness of the biblical account of the flood, the Ark, and its symbolism of Jesus Christ. Thanks should also go out to the many who have contributed in financial and prayer support to all of these various teams. The quest continues and the last chapter remains to be written.

*Charles "Doc" Willis is known for his
intellect and methodical approach to
researching for Noah's Ark. He does his
homework and is always very prepared
when it comes time for an expedition.*

5

DR. CHARLES WILLIS

Dr. Charles Willis, a neuropsychiatrist who holds a degree in religion and a long-term interest in archaeology, became interested in the search for Noah's Ark when he read Eryl and Violet Cummings' book in the early 1970's. He then arranged for his oldest son, John Willis, an Eagle Scout, only

Dr. Willis Snow Tiger Team
Courtesy of B.J. Corbin

sixteen years old, to go with Mr. Cummings on the 1973 expedition to Mt. Ararat. John noted that while climbing up one area, he placed his hand on one rock which suddenly gave way along with 2-3 tons of adjacent rock that went catapulting down the mountain hundreds of feet. Fortunately, he had not placed his weight in that area yet. Such are the dangers of climbing Mount Ararat.

John Willis, Dr. Lawrence Hewitt, Eryl Cummings, Geoff McMahon and Jack Darnell climbed up the Cehennem Dere area. This was the expedition when Geoff McMahon took his 70-pound pack of gear (tent, cooking utensils, cameras, sleeping bag, etc.) up to the high camp area around 14,000 feet on a reconnoitering climb. Unfortunately for Geoff, when they arrived, Jack Darnell (who Dr. Hewitt had placed in charge of the climb) commandeered McMahon's equipment. Disappointed, Geoff had to return down the mountain to base camp without any equipment. He arrived in the dark at midnight. Then the porters wanted Geoff to go straight back up the mountain to show them where the high camp was located. Geoff was worn out and sick but he got up at six to lead the porters back up the mountain. Since the wages for the porters were pre-paid, some of them simply left the baggage along the trail. Because McMahon was sick, the porters with the luggage beat him to the high camp. Finally, Eryl Cummings came chugging along and told Geoff to get himself some soup and minerals which cured him.

The 1973 expedition was able to get a great photograph of the rock at the 12,000-foot elevation which appears to be man-made structure from a distance. This large boulder may have been responsible for several false sightings, possibly including the George Greene, Ed Davis, Ed Behling and George Hagopian accounts. Dr. Willis interviewed alleged eyewitness Mr. Officer personally and believes he was a geriatric liar.

The 1973 team explored the upper reaches of the Ahora Gorge on the north side of the mountain with negative results. Subsequent reading and study led Dr. Willis to the conclusion in the early 1980's that the Ark might have survived under the ice cap. Nicholas Van Arkel, Ph.D., the glaciologist who performed the ice survey of the mountain in 1986, was of the opinion that there might be a stationary ice bowl under the eastern plateau, since this was not a glacier formation. It was theorized that the Ark might lie hidden there.

In 1983, Dr. Willis led an initial probe to the eastern plateau, at which

Dr. Charles Willis at Mihtepe Base Camp 1984
Courtesy of Dr. Charles Willis

time a trenching excavation was attempted with negative results. While valuable insights were developed during this initial attempt, it was later realized that the trench was too shallow. (Members of the 1983 Snow Tiger Team were William Ball, Martin Black, Larry Mast, Gary Meosky, Rod Youngquist, James Willis, and Dr. Charles Willis.)

Dr. Willis and his team have been most appreciative of the providence of God in this search at Mt. Ararat. In 1985, he had obtained a research permit from the Turkish government, but it had a small restriction in it, which precluded effective research. He was advised by his friend, the son of the former president of Turkey, to use it anyway, but after careful consideration he canceled the expedition for that year. In a month or so God's providence became clear as word came of a terrorist assault on climbing groups at Ararat with seizure and burning of equipment at the point of an AK-47. Dr. Willis and his team had stayed home and not lost one penny.

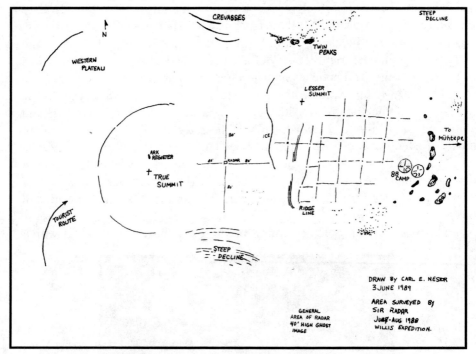

Carl Nestor drawing of Eastern Plateau area surveyed by radar 1988
Courtesy of Carl Nestor via B.J. Corbin

In 1986, the second expedition to the plateau was attempted, this time with a larger team. A metal detector was used and a 16-foot-deep trench was cut in the ice at the base of the western ridge on the eastern plateau at 16,800 feet.[1]

---

[1] The ice cutting operation was performed with a special McCulloch Chain Saw, donated by the McCulloch Corporation, which operated well at high altitude.

The 1986 effort was marked by more efficiency than that of 1983. The local formalities were handled with much more speed. After receiving our local Jendarma Permit in one hour the day after our arrival in Dogubayazit, we were on our way up the mountain in a truck to the 6,500-foot-high village of Eli Koy where the old Chieftain Haji Baba Coktin greeted us with glasses of hot chai (tea). We slept in his walled compound that night, protected from hungry sheep dogs eager to bite into a tender American.

The next morning we started up the mountain with our mountain porters and horses. The first night saw us almost missing our campsite and porters in the twilight, but the emergency whistle around Dr. Willis' neck led to the connection and our camping together by a flowing stream where everyone filled their canteens. A flowing stream on Ararat must never be passed by, since in the morning it will be dry. With hard climbing, some through hail and rain, we finally reached the base camp at Mihtepe (13,565 feet). Here we used some old campsites that had been cleared by the Turkish Army during World War II.

Ice cutting chain saw 1986
Courtesy of Doris Bowers

A comfortable camp was made and then the Snow Tiger Team made a final hard climb with all gear some 3,300 feet higher to the Eastern Plateau (16,800 feet), where a high camp was placed.

Climbing the southeast couloir of Ararat is dangerous because of the many falling rocks, some the size of a Volkswagen, called "widowmakers." However, the Team's courage rose to meet the challenge and this mission impossible was accomplished.

Some eight days were spent on the plateau in accomplishing the tasks needed. Cutting a trench in ice at high altitude is difficult, but it was done. The temperature on the plateau drops sharply once the sun goes down, as Dr. Willis discovered one evening, making him run for his tent and sleeping bag. Several extra trips were made to haul up more supplies and gear to the high camp and this ongoing process was successfully completed.

That same year, Mr. Guy Leduc, a Canadian engineering geologist, in view of the implications of Genesis 4:22, and theorizing that the Ark was probably constructed with some large bronze or iron pieces, completed a careful metal detector survey of the entire Eastern Plateau with a Gemini II instrument donated by the Fisher Corporation. Results were negative. The team then considered that the Ark might have been doweled and pegged to

Willis Snow Tiger Team at Mihtepe 1988
Courtesy of B.J. Corbin

hold it together and that a final answer on the eastern plateau must await an under-ice radar and drilling operation.

On the last day the team climbed to the top of Ararat, and surveyed the Ahora Gorge. They then broke camp and, heavily laden with their packs, inched their way down the slippery rock skree.

At the top of the 3,000-foot couloir, they began to slide down, clutching their ice axes with some degree of desperation. The slide took some thirty minutes, a high-speed trip that beats any roller coaster ride. At the bottom one team member remarked that he had been terrified at the thought of sliding down the couloir, but that it actually was only "mildly terrifying!"

Members of the 1986 Snow Tiger Team were Steve Connelly, Guy Leduc, Pat Frost, Bob Garbe, S/Sgt. Carl Nestor, Richard Froiland, Deborah Redmer, James Willis, and Dr. Willis.

In 1988, the Snow Tiger Team returned with under-ice radar and a glacial ice drill. After securing the proper research permit the team left for Turkey. They spent one night in Ankara, then flew to Erzurum, then traveled overland to Dogubayazit south of the mountain. The next morning they loaded the trucks of the Chieftain, Haji Baba, with the sixteen team members, some 35 duffel bags, the radar and ice drill and drove up the mountain to the little ranch village of Eli Koy where they camped overnight. The next morning 52 horses were packed with the gear and the team started their two-day hike to the base camp at 13,500 feet. The weather was quite good in the early phase of this expedition.

On the way up a Jendarma patrol passed us and a Turkish commando squad heading for the western slope of Ararat came over to check our permit papers which were all in order. They were on a terrorist-hunting patrol and

The 3,000-foot Slide on Southeast Ararat 1988
Courtesy of B.J. Corbin

seemed surprised to see us. Our mountain horsemen were apprehensive about the terrorists, but we assured them that we were under the protection of the Almighty God and that the terrorists would not come near us—which they didn't, although we heard that they did get into a firefight with the commando squad later.

We moved up slowly over a two-day period, across snow fields and many rocky ridges, passing shepherds with their flocks of sheep and the great silver peak of Agri Dagh, the "painful mountain" looming over us. Team morale was high and enhanced by our habit of praying together in a circle, in which our friend and translator joined. He reported that the mountain pack men appreciate how believers treated them in contrast to ordinary tourist climbers who are sometimes rude. The mountain packmen especially exerted themselves for our team via a new route to get their horses and our gear all the way to base camp, a difficult task.

At Mihtepe Base Camp we enjoyed a superb view of the Arax River valley. The next morning our wonderful cook Debbie created a great breakfast. We then acclimated over the next few days and prepared to move camping and scientific gear up the southeast couloir—some 3,300 feet.

The third of August saw teams of determined climbers begin moving up, one climber carrying the 75-pound radar unit. The team did some of this work under stress of a hailstorm. By permission of the Turkish government we were allowed to use a CB radio system which effected easy communication between base and the high camp at 16,800 feet on the eastern plateau. The high camp team was hit by a storm, but made an igloo and waited it out, then slid down the couloir (beats any roller-coaster ride) and climbed again with more gear until the high camp provisions were secure.

The team, under the supervision of Mr. Roningen, completed the radar survey which showed that the plateau was an 80-foot-deep bowl with no sign of an Ark. The team then ran the radar survey over the ridge westward to the

Willis Polar Ice Drilling Team on Eastern Summit 1988
Courtesy of B.J. Corbin

peak of Ararat, revealing that the ice cap thickens to about 95 feet, but again there was no sign of the Ark of Noah. To finally establish the truth of this matter, the team then drilled three test holes with the PICO ice drill in a triangle formation on the plateau to a depth of 40 feet, all with negative results. With the scientific mission having been completed over several days' time, high camp was quickly dismantled. The team then started moving gear down to base camp. Sliding the southeast couloir was, as usual, mildly terrifying! Base camp now became a scene for packing for descent. At night the Araxes River valley with its sparkling diamond lights had an ethereal quality. One gets a sense of how God sees us from a different perspective than we see ourselves. The team burned the garbage—an important point as they saw to it that the camp was left as clean as it was found.

The long, hard descent took two days and finally ended at Eli Koy Village where the team stayed overnight, sang songs with the mountain people and supplied the children with candy. The next day, our mountain friends took the team on a steep upward climb, and suddenly there was before them an ancient lost city! The team walked with wonder through this city. Walls, houses, cisterns, paved streets, and great stone blocks with some features of possible Urartian design. The people of the past had walked these streets and lived in these houses in what could have been the most ancient kingdom of Genesis 8. No archaeological investigation of this city has ever been made.

Dr. Willis, a member of the Archeological Institute of America, checked several sources on Urartu and could find no mention of this city. He prepared a report which may be published soon in an archaeological journal. Though this forty-acre city is after Noah's time it will probably yield some valuable insights into the ancient kingdom.

While no evidence of the Ark of Noah was found, the discovery of this city on Ararat assuaged somewhat the sense of disappointment the team felt.

Of course in an enterprise such as this one must remember the words of President Theodore Roosevelt: "It is better to dare great deeds and fail than to do nothing at all." The discovery of the truth about the eastern plateau, even though negative, was in itself a positive find of truth which is always important.

B.J. Corbin, Dr. Charles Willis, Guy Leduc at Eli
Courtesy of B.J. Corbin 1986

The culminating 1988 expedition was composed of a team of highly-motivated, elite mountaineering Christians who ascended Mt. Ararat accepting the risks of snow, hail, snakes, altitude, falling rocks and terrorists, in view of the potential benefit to the Christian faith and biblical authority. They successfully completed a very difficult "Mission Impossible."

Members of the 1988 Snow Tiger Team were: Robert Baker; Robert "B.J." Corbin; Donald Davis, Jr.; Guy Leduc; Scott Little; Larry Mast; Ross Mehan; Willis Newton, Jr.; Willis Newton, III; Deborah Redmer; Robert, Margaret and Christopher Roningen; James Willis and Dr. Charles Willis.

Guy Leduc conducted a survey with a Gemini II Metal Detector
Courtesy of Dr. Charles Willis

In retrospect, it is obvious that no one has discovered any conclusive proof that Noah's Ark is on Mt. Ararat. Alleged findings of ancient wood have not passed the test of scientific examination, and the alleged sightings have been of little or no value. Mr. F. M. Gurley admitted in writing in 1989 that he had fabricated the alleged World War I Russian Expedition, and that at least his article was a total lie.

In all these efforts Dr. Willis wishes to extend appreciation to Mr. Yavuz Konca, Assistant Professor of English at the University of Erzurum, an experienced mountaineer and a true friend. His help was invaluable in all these rigorous endeavors.

Dr. Willis plans no more trips to Mt. Ararat since he has concluded that the more probable site of Noah's landing was Mt. Cudi, some two hundred miles south of Ararat. He has recruited additional team members and organized new technological instrumentation to investigate Mt. Cudi in the foreseeable future.

Dr. Willis has concluded that the Ark of Noah did not survive into modern times but was broken up for houses and barns since there is nothing that has been found to date to prove its current existence. He hopes to find some evidences of Noah of a different sort. To facilitate this goal he has formed Ancient World Foundation.[2]

In September 1995, after evaluating his own intelligence sources, he launched himself into southeast Turkey for a three-week reconnaissance trip, successfully contacting the proper Turkish officials and ecclesiastical authorities visiting Cizre and Silopi. He finally became the guest of a Kurdish Chieftain at Sirnak on the north side of Mount Cudi (Cudi Dagh). Some brand-new, incredible information was providentially developed as a result of this trip, which Dr. Willis believes, may result in a major biblical discovery.

The final enterprise to discover evidence of Father Noah is about to commence. An expedition is planned to investigate the true mountain of Noah, Mt. Cudi in southeastern Turkey. Funds are needed or it won't happen. You can be part of the greatest biblical archeological discovery of all time. We plan to investigate Noah's original village,

Cudi Dagh 1996
Courtesy of Dr. Charles Willis

[2] Ancient World Foundation, PO Box 3118, Pinedale, California 93650. Phone (559) 439-4905 Fax (559) 447-8418.

Heston; his altar site; the now known Ark landing site; and his now found and photographed tomb. Please send your tax-deductible donation to:

Ancient World Foundation
PO Box 3118
Pinedale, California 93650

Robin Simmons and his wife Heidi are screenwriters. Robin has been a producer on documentaries like the Unsolved Mysteries Ark episode. He played a key role in the photographing of the Stephen Site. A shorter version of this article was originally published in Fortean Times.[1]

6

ROBIN SIMMONS

The story of a cataclysmic flood and a lone family that survives in a hand-made boat is one of the oldest stories of our global culture. Hundreds of similar but apparently independent versions exist all over the planet. Is it possible that this epic myth is based on fact? Even more fantastic, could the great Ark of Noah be preserved, right now, in the icy reaches of Mount Ararat?

There's a well-known account of ten year old Georgie Hagopian, who

Robin Simmons with Helicopter Pilot Yuri Poskrebysheb 1990
Courtesy of Robin Simmons. Photo by George Adams

---

[1] The United States version of *Fortean Times* was published in April, 1999.

saw Noah's Ark while climbing Ararat with his uncle in 1904. The date isn't precise but this was around the time my grandfather was in the region and heard convincing stories of the Ark, preserved in ice and snow, still occasionally visible.

My grandfather died in 1980, aged 106. As a boy, I listened to his adventures as a doctor in eastern Turkey and Russia between 1904 and 1910. He worked in the very shadow of Greater Ararat—the legendary biblical landing place of Noah's ship. My grandfather said some of the Kurds and Armenians he treated confided that the great Ark was preserved on Ararat. They said, it's "high on the northern side, a little below the saddle" of the twin-peaked dormant volcano. He showed me the spot on an old photograph of Ararat. He said the oldest place names of that area preserve antique meanings that translate as "Noah's Village," "First Vineyard," "House of Shem" (Noah's son), "First Market Town" and "Place of First Descent" and so on. Most of these names, he thought, are no longer in general use but are very specific in old-style Armenian.

My grandfather's story so impressed me that over the years I noted any material pertaining to this enduring enigma. It seems as if, every couple of years, someone claims a new Noah's Ark discovery in a book, documentary or TV special. Some are laughably amateurish; others are clumsy hoaxes.

Even supermarket tabloids regularly exploit this mystery. Before long, I had a veritable flood of questionable and unverifiable data. There were Arks everywhere - all over Ararat as well as boat-shaped earthen impressions in nearby lower elevations and many more in the pass between Greater and Lesser Ararat.

The Koran speaks of the Ark landing on Al Cudi; there's a mountain by that name 200 miles south of Ararat. (Some researchers suggest that the Arabic root for Cudi mean "the highest" and refers to the upper part of Greater Ararat.) Kuh e Alvand, yet another 'Ararat' is in Iran. It has a long tradition among locals as the Ark's landing place. More contentious sites exist in other countries and continents. I spoke to several living eyewitnesses—like Georgie—who claimed to have seen the Ark of Noah, or big parts of it, on Ararat.

And there's the tale of a months-long expedition by Czar Nicholas' soldiers, during which the Ark was supposedly entered and photographed. It's location was allegedly mapped somewhere in the rugged, canyon-riddled upper regions on the "Armenian side." This expedition was just prior to the Bolshevik Revolution during which, it is said, many of the Czar's soldiers were hunted down and slaughtered and the Ark photos, maps and artifacts disappeared. Relatives of the few soldiers who survived have family records that seem to confirm the authenticity of the expedition.

A recent story hints that some of Czar Nicholas' personal items may have been transferred from their secret vaults in Moscow and Leningrad to the

Stanford Research Institute (SRI) in California. The SRI is a federally funded 'institute' that serves the intelligence community. Could the cache of alleged transferred items include documents pertaining to the Czar's Ararat expedition?

Then I met the late Ed Davis, an octogenarian and breeder of prized Nubian goats in the American southwest. His story of seeing the Ark has been circulated widely among Ark hunters and dismissed by many as the pipe dream of an old man with a big imagination and a faulty memory. I spent a day talking with this smart and kindly gentleman. This is a condensed version of what he said:

> Something happened to me in '43 that's haunted me all my life... I'm in the 363rd Army Corps of Engineers working out of a base in Hamadan (ancient Ekbatan), Iran. We're building a Way Station into Russia from Turkey. A supply route. My driver's a young man named Badi Abas. One day while we're at a quarry site loading rock, he points to a distant peak that's sometimes visible and says, "Agri Dagh, my home."

Ed Davis
Photo by Robin Simmons

> We can see it clearly on the horizon with its year-round snowcap. "Mt. Ararat, that's where the Ark landed?" I say. He nods.
>
> "My grandfather knows where it is and has gone up there," he says matter-of-factly. I thought, Boy would I like to see that...
>
> One day in July, his grandfather, Abas-Abas, visits our base and tells Badi the ice on Ararat is melting to where you can see part of the Ark. Badi tells me if I want to see it they will take me there. I had done a favor for their village that put me in good stead with the Abas family. In fact, they now have water, where before they had to walk two miles to get it...

So I go to my commanding officer and ask for a leave. He says, "It's dangerous, you'll get killed." I tell him how much I want to go. He says, "I can give you R&R in Tehran and you could take the long

A view of upper Ahora Gorge, the summit, saddle, Abich I and Abich II as well as the relative positions of three possible Ark-like objects.
Photo by Robin Simmons 1990

way." I stock up on extra gasoline, oil and tires.

A few days later, we get up early and Badi Abas and I drive down along the border as far as Casbeen until we get to his little village. This was the settlement I had helped them get water. We spend the night there...

At dawn the next day, we reach the foothills of Ararat and arrive at another primitive village. Abas tells me the name of the village means "Where Noah Planted The Vine." I see grapevines so big at their trunk you can't reach around them. Very, very old.

Abas says they have a cave filled with artifacts that came from the Ark. They find them strewn in a canyon below the Ark, collect them to keep from outsiders who, they think, would profane them. It's all sacred to them. That night, they show me the artifacts. Oil lamps, clay vats, old style tools, things like that. I see a cage-like door, maybe thirty by forty inches, made of woven branches. It's hard as stone, looks petrified. It has a hand-carved lock or latch on it. I could even see the wood grain.

We sleep. At first light, we put on mountain clothes and they bring up a string of horses. I leave with seven male members of the Abas family and we ride—seems like an awful long time.

Finally we come to a hidden cave deep in the canyons of Greater Ararat. They say it's where T. E. Lawrence (of Arabia) hid when he was doing reconnaissance. There's a huge pot of hot food waiting for us. There's fungus there that glows in the dark. And they say Lawrence put it on his face to convince the Kurds he was a god and get them to join him in his war against the Turks.

We eat and then climb back on our horses and continue riding higher on the narrow trail. They tell me we're going through the "Back Door." It's a secret route used by smugglers or bandits.

Along the way, they point out a pair of human legs sticking out of the ice and tell me he shouldn't have been up there. I believe them.

I don't know how the horses are able to follow the route. In some places you can tell we were riding along a high cliff but most of the time it's hard to see because of the rain and fog. A freezing wind is blowing and it feels like it's going right through me. Soon, Abas tells me to be quiet because we're at a place where Russian sentries, stationed below, might hear us.

We ride in silence for the rest of the day. Sometimes they'd communicate in their own private code by short whistles.

Eventually we run out of trail. Someone from the Abas family is waiting for us, takes our horses and we are roped together and climb on foot much higher to another cave. I can't tell where we are. The rain never lets up...

After three days of climbing we come to the last cave. Inside, there's strange writing, it looked beautiful and old, on the rock walls and a kind of natural rock bed or outcropping near the back of the cavern. Another pot of food is waiting for us. Everything's prepared for my visit by the Abas family. It rains hard all night.

The next morning we get up and wait. The rain lets up and we walk along a narrow trail behind a dangerous outcropping called "Doomsday Rock." I guess it's called that because it's a place you could easily die and many have. Some not of their own doing. We doubled back around behind the imposing rock formation and come to a ledge. We are enveloped by fog.

Suddenly the fog lifts and the sun breaks through a hole in the clouds. It's a very mystical sight as the light shimmers on the wet canyon. My Moslem friends pray to Allah. They speak quietly and are very subdued...

After they finish praying, Badi Abas points down into a kind of horseshoe[2] crevasse and says, "That's Noah's Ark." But I can't see anything. Everything's the same color and texture. Then I see it—a huge, rectangular, man-made structure partly covered by a talus of ice and rock, lying on its side. At least a hundred feet are clearly visible. I can even see inside it, into the end where it's been broken off, timbers are sticking out, kind of twisted and gnarled, water's cascading out from under it.

Abas points down the canyon and I can make out another portion of it. I can see how the two pieces were once joined — the torn timbers kind of match.

They told me the Ark is broken into three or four big pieces. Inside the broken end of the biggest piece, I can see at least three floors and Abas says there's a living space near the top with forty-eight rooms. He says there are cages inside as small as my hand, others big enough to hold a family of elephants.

I can see what

An illustration based solely on description of one of the Ark-like objects Ed Davis saw. Compare it to the third object photos.
Illustration by Elfred Lee

[2] It is interesting to note that on the Tom Pickett Corona Satellite picture in the Introduction, there is a horseshoe-shaped valley in the Abich II glacier below the saddle of the peaks

looks like remains of partitions and walkways inside the bigger piece. I really want to touch it—it's hard to explain the feeling. Abas says we can go down on ropes in the morning. It begins to rain and we go back to the cave...

Next morning when we get up, it's snowing. It had snowed all night and it's at least belt deep on me. I can't see anything down in the canyon. The Ark is no longer visible. Abas says, "We have to leave, it's too dangerous."

It takes five days to get off the mountain and back to my base. I smell so bad when I get back, they burn my clothes. And no one seems interested in what I saw, so I quit talking about it. But I dream about it every night for twenty years.

There's something up there...

As part of my ongoing film project called *RIDDLE OF ARARAT*, we (producer George Adams, cameraman Paul Zenk and myself) recorded Davis' amazing tale. Although Ed Davis' story struck me as unusually detailed and unpretentious, it was almost too good to be true. When it was privately printed and distributed by one of his friends, Davis says he received bizarre phone threats warning that he had betrayed an ancient family secret and as a result "the Black Hand of Allah was upon him."

Intuitively, I believe Davis but have many questions about his details. For instance, how is it possible to see Mount Ararat from Hamadan, over 400 miles away? Davis supposes peculiar atmospheric conditions that create mirages. Again, Kuh e Alvand, the Iranian 'Ararat' is close by Hamadan—did Ed go there?

Using archival photos and old maps, I see a likely and possible route for Davis from Hamadan to Tarlabas ("Village of Abas"?) near the new village of Ahora (some say the old name translates as "Where Noah Planted The Vine") into the Ahora Gorge and to a place beneath the massive ice finger that curls off the Abich II glacier (but it's difficult to clearly discern an obvious route to the higher elevation just below the saddle).

About this time Adams and I got a promise of full funding for *RIDDLE OF ARARAT* from entrepreneur Ed Shaida, a man referred to me by Eryl Cummings. An initial deposit of a $1.5 million to cover initial filming and expedition set-up expenses was to be made on a specific date.

I had accumulated a great amount of data pertaining to Ararat and the possibility of the Ark, or parts of it, being preserved. In fact, a specific target area that stretched from below the twin peaks into the upper Ahora Gorge seemed a very likely and unexplored zone to explore. We needed a helicopter and pilot and permits. We also wanted to frame our movie around a colorful Ark hunter and we decided on Don Shockey, an optometrist-treasure hunter with pronounced cowboy tendencies. Shockey agreed to let us pay his expenses for multiple trips to Ararat in exchange for all filming rights.

Out of the blue, Richard Bright called and suggested that I contact Chuck Aaron, a fellow pilot who had a Turkish military approved permit to fly a chopper around and on Greater Ararat. I invited him to join our team. Assuring him that in the event we found something, that information would be made available to all. That our film project was to record the steps that led to any initial discovery so people could decide for themselves without bias or preaching. I liked Aaron a lot and we hit it off immediately. Adams and I invited Aaron to check out a remote sensing expert that we planned to visit with Shockey. It seemed to me that the pieces of the puzzle, to not only locate the possibly preserved Ark but to document it, were falling into place almost too easily. Chuck Aaron and I were especially in agreement that this was not just another treasure hunt and that personal agendas, or profit, were not to be motivating factors.

George Stephen III examining Infra Red satellite image (not Ararat but Alaska) taken by space shuttle astronaut with a 35mm hand-held camera
Photo by Kathy Stephen

George Stephen III is a military-trained, 30-year veteran of remote-sensing, high-resolution, infrared and other satellite type photo interpretation - a specialist who says he had access to "every square foot" of planet earth. When Stephen was asked to look at upper Ararat for any man-made anomalies, he agreed. When we met some time later, Stephen said:

> I looked at the mountain from the 10,000-foot altitude to the top.
> I'm a hundred percent sure there's two man-made objects up there

on the north side of the mountain above the 13,000-foot elevation. What amazes me is a structure at this altitude. The terrain is just treacherous! And the amount of ice on it...

It's definitely not a military object or device because it couldn't be used since it's under ice almost all the time.

The process I use is a Photo Analysis Material Spectra (PAMS). We pull up a photo from a satellite, I can't tell you which one, but it's available. The photograph is put into one of our own processes which is a laser process that takes a spectra reading. We work with 64 different shades of *every* color. Each one of those shades means something that is going on with that anomaly or target. Then we use "perforation" in which we take "plugs" out of that area. In other

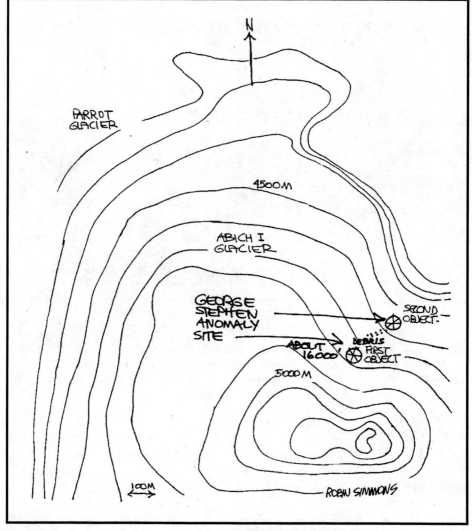

George Stephen III Site Anomaly Map 1989
Courtesy of Robin Simmons

words, instead of looking for the needle in the haystack, we remove the haystack. We perforate the area and pull those plugs until we come up with an "image" of whatever is in the target area.

On that mountain (Ararat) is the rectangular shape of two man-made organic objects. One above the other. Looks like maybe 1,200-foot difference. Both objects look like they were joined at one time because there's a spectral trail going down from one to the other. They're sitting in a fault on a ledge. The upper one is hanging. They are both in a glacier. Last time I looked there was about 70 foot of ice over the upper object. The lower one I can't tell because it's at too steep of an angle.

I can't tell you what it's made of, but it's not metal and it's not rock. It would have to be organic, perhaps wood. It's ancient but I'm not saying it's the Ark because I haven't "seen" it. All I can say is that I'm a hundred percent sure it's a man-made object. But for

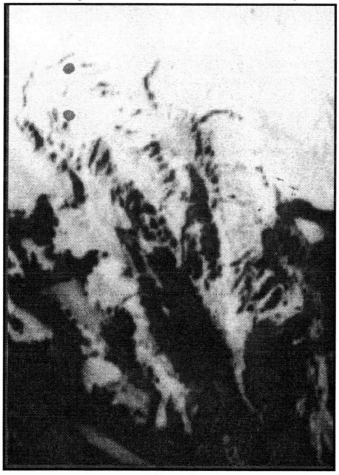

George Stephen marked sites on Corona sat. photo
Courtesy of Robin Simmons 1999

somebody to take something up there, to haul it up there, to build a thing of this size would be an amazing feet.

The most peculiar thing about this anomaly is that there are no trails to it that indicate it was constructed on this site. I don't know if this is the original location of this object. Maybe it's been raised up from a lower elevation. Or maybe it was higher and slid down throughout the centuries. It's almost like it crashed or landed there...

Perhaps this glacier melts back and this object being hollow, up there on this ledge like it is, with thousands of tons of ice in it and around it, breaks off and takes part of it on down the canyon.

Personally, I don't believe in Noah's Ark. And frankly, I've no idea what it is.

When Stephen marked his two part, broken anomaly site on the topo and satellite graphics we gave him, Shockey, Aaron, Adams and I leaned in unison like novelty dipping birds. We couldn't get close enough! I immediately saw that the Stephen site was in the same area my grandfather indicated to me many years before—a little below the saddle. Actually it was the upper Abich II Glacier.

However, this area did not mesh with Davis' story—he never mentioned crossing ice fields on being anywhere near the summit. Is it possible to reconcile the apparent discrepancy? Was the Abich II cleared of ice in 1943 and did Davis get there without going over the ice cap? Or is the Ark broken into at least two more pieces in a lower location?

Immediately after our meeting with Stephen at his former lab near Ridge Crest, I noticed a somber change in Chuck Aaron. Much later I learned that Shockey talked privately with Aaron and made certain private contractual demands. Shortly thereafter, Aaron disappeared and went to Turkey and Ararat to fly on his own. I was puzzled by this turn of events and even more disappointed at Shockey when I found out why Aaron exited our team. A real loss. What else was in store for us? To some, it seemed like certain dark forces were conspiring to prevent us from accessing and documenting this potentially significant anomaly. What else could go wrong?

Our promised funding was delayed, but Shaida said to go ahead and secure confirmation of security permits, research, photo and trekking permits from Turkish Embassy in Washington, DC, and we would be reimbursed. Adams and I flew to DC and got clearances in writing from the Turkish Embassy—a building with no name or street address marker—for filming in all areas except Korhan, which they said "did not exist." A further curious restriction: we were allowed only 35mm still and 8mm cameras on Ararat. We also were required to use an approved guide for Ararat.

While in Maryland, Adams and I met with Turkish citizen Ahmet Arslan, a former Azerbaijani broadcaster/translator for *Voice of America*, who agreed to be our guide and to film on Ararat—off the trekking route if necessary—for a fee in the thousands in addition to, of course, round trip air fare and hotel, meals, etc., as well as his hiring a climbing assistant of his choice and his fee, also in the thousands!

I was determined to visit the area in a recent August when the thaw

**Shooting of *Riddle of Ararat* with Director Robin Simmons, Don Shockey,
Pilot Yuri Poskrebysheb, Producer George Adams
Background Russian Navigator, Turkish Co-pilot 1990
Courtesy of Robin Simmons**

should be at its maximum. George Adams, my film-making partner and I made arrangements to get funding to document this anomaly, the security clearance and research and climbing permits for Greater Ararat.

I kept in touch with Stephen as he updated the amount of ice covering the upper object. I calculated that at the apparently extraordinary rate of evaporation and melting, that by mid August something would be visible.

Even though Shaida's promised funding inexplicably evaporated like the ice over the anomaly, I was determined to get a camera aimed at the target! On our own, George Adams and I arranged payment and airfare for Shockey, around whom we still planned a documentary. In addition, we officially hired Ahmet Arslan—an Azerbaijani-Turk who grew up in the Ararat foothills—to hike to the target zone and take some pictures for us.

Shockey and I took off for Turkey. We met Arslan in Ankara. He seemed surprised, and strangely upset, to see me. Somehow Arslan got the impression that he was working solely for Shockey. I went to the various government agencies to get confirmation of my permits and security

Photo of first, or uppermost object as pinpointed by satellite interpreter George Stephen III. The object looks like the end of a boxcar embedded in the ice. Photo similar to 1973 Hewitt slide 1989
Photo by Ahmet Ali Arslan was taken about 1,200 (?) feet distance

Writing on photo by Robin Simmons of first, or uppermost object as pinpointed by satellite interpreter George Stephen III. The object looks like the end of a boxcar embedded in the ice 1989
Photo by Ahmet Ali Arslan was taken about 1,200 (?) feet distance

clearances. All were in place. Arslan said he would pick them up and arrange

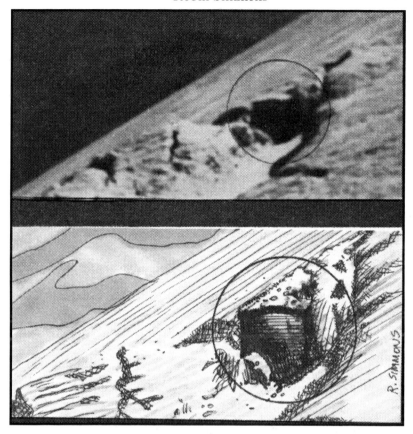

**Drawing of first or uppermost object based on eyewitness description
of Ahmet Ali Arslan and an Armenian businessman in Istanbul 1989**
Courtesy of Robin Simmons

to have them wired to the Ararat region where the military would hold them.

Arslan talked about his previous fifty some climbs to Ararat's peak as well as stories he heard from childhood regarding the legends of the Ark being preserved. Arslan received a doctorate (University of Edinburgh?) collecting mostly Kurdish folktales from the Ararat region. Unfortunately, these stories did not pertain to the Flood or the Ark. Strangely, Arslan also spoke of a 40 day mission, guiding and accompanying the late Bud Crawford onto Ararat's ice-cap when an electronic cache of listening devices were planted in the ice for the CIA. Bud Crawford died alone at 1:45 AM on 16 October 1970 in what some say was a bizarre and suspicious auto accident on an otherwise empty Colorado road.

We went to Ararat and prepared for our trek. We showed Arslan the Stephen's site on the topo map and told him what we wanted him to do. I showed Arslan how to operate the personal video cam and where and what angle to shoot footage as well as still photos. Suddenly, Arslan demanded that an additional $5,000 plus be wired into his wife's Maryland bank. Since the anomaly was off the approved trekking route, and since my climbing permits had "disappeared" during the transfer to the Ararat region, according to Arslan, Adams and I felt we had no choice and arranged to have the money wired as demanded with the understanding that Arslan was being hired to photograph the anomaly site and it, the photographs, were our property.

At the last minute, Arslan refused to take the video camera and battery belts. He only wanted to use a own still camera. Shockey accompanied Arslan and his climbing assistant part way up the sanctioned tourist trek route on the easier southern slope. Early the next morning, I waited in the foothills by my short-wave radio as Arslan set off by himself, leaving the sanctioned climbing route to a place overlooking the Stephen site on the upper Abich II.

Arslan left Shockey on the trekking route and continued to our target area. Eventually, I got an excited coded call that he had reached an area overlooking the target, that something was visible and he was going to photograph it from a safe distance then come and get me as agreed.

The next day he arrived back at the base camp shaken and apparently frightened. His behavior was odd, punctuated with unexpected outbursts. He refused to take me back up the mountain as originally agreed. He would hardly talk but, gradually, I pieced together his account: "I grow up with mountain behind my village." He said, "I climb to peak over 50 times. As a boy, I hear all the Ark stories but I never see anything before this time when ice is melt back more than I ever know... I see a dark area in ice... Like a coop (barn) but still most inside the glacier. You can see the object—backside

About a year after Ahmet took the photo of the first object area it then looked like this. There was about 24 feet of ice covering it according to George Stephen III. This photo was taken from a distance of about 1,500 feet 1990
Photo by Robin Simmons from Helicopter

stuck in the ice—front exposed. Looks like a roof with snow on it. Shaped rectangular. I see timbers and brown gray color. Not rock or natural. Very dangerous there. Ice crust—but under it is empty! Deep crevasses. Can hear water rushing beneath. Gorge breaks off down below. Steep. I couldn't push in closer..."

Arslan claims he got about a quarter mile from the object, from where he took a few photographs. Later, when George Stephen saw the pictures, he

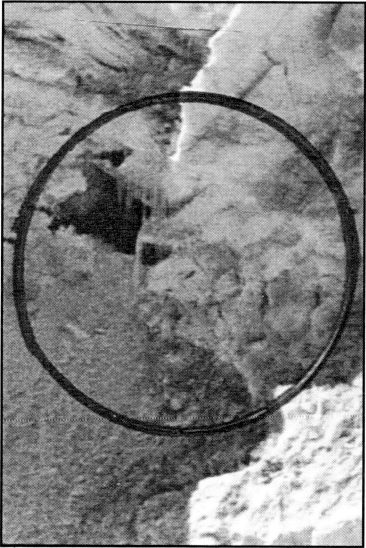

This shadowy shape similar to the first and third objects, seems to protrude from a place about 1000' below the first object. It is approximately the position of a broken part of object one as "seen" by George Stephen III. Are these parts of the same object? Are they Ark parts? 1990
Photo by Robin Simmons

said it was indeed the uppermost of the two objects he 'saw' using his specialized satellite software.

Dr James Eberts, a highly regarded forensic archaeologist, examined Arslan's photos under a high-resolution process and said: "This does not appear to be a natural part of the landscape. Looks strikingly man-made to me. With a peaked roof and rectangular sides or walls. The only way to be sure is get on it."

Strangely, Ed Davis did not recognize the high altitude photos as resembling what he saw. Months later, I am flying over Ararat in a sturdy Russian built MI-8 chopper with my filmmaking partner George Adams. The Turkish military refused to let us land on the mountain so we photograph and videotape Ararat and the Ahora Gorge from the air. Despite the estimated 23 feet of additional ice over the object area, we quickly identified the spot. It looks like a frozen wave-like formation of ice hanging over something embedded in the glacier.

As we circle the mountain, I look for evidence of the lower, broken part of object that Stephen says is perhaps 1,200 feet below in a steeper part of the glacier. I take some long-range shots of what appears to be a similar-shaped broken-ended, roofed structure barely visible in an ice wall. Is this the second, broken object Stephen described?

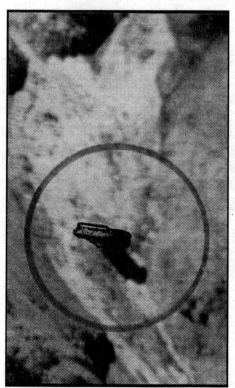

Hand drawn outline of third object. From extreme enlargement (1000x Plus) taken from below in Ahora Gorge. Notice shadow of protruding rectangular object embedded in scree.
Photo by John McIntosh

As we make another pass over the awesome Ahora Gorge, I look down to the spot, about 2,500 feet distant, where I theoretically located Ed Davis' object. In a debris-ridden canyon of ice and rock, there appears yet another similar-shaped anomaly jutting out from a steep skree. Water courses under it. The end appears broken and there's a peaked roof-shape with parallel sides. It looks battered. Is it a rock formation? Or something man-made?

This object closely matches Ed Davis' description. If it is that Ark-object, then there's another big part buried in the rubble above it.

There are those who call it a rock (McIntosh, Van Dyke, Kneisler) and those who see something provocative and worth investigating

Upper Ahora Gorge and Abich II Glacier 1990
Photo by Robin Simmons

Upper Ahora Gorge and Abich II Glacier and objects of interest 1990
Photomap by Robin Simmons

(Setterfield, Thomson). No one has been on it, to my knowledge. McIntosh, Thomson and myself have looked at it from a distance and widely different perspectives including from above and below.

All three anomalous shapes are extremely similar and could in fact be broken parts, all fallen from the same singular source still lodged in the fault line high in the icecap. Unfortunately, there's no accurate scale cues for any of these objects. The biblical original is described as at least 450 feet long—longer than that length if the cubit is a "royal cubit." So is it possible that the Ark could have broken into at least four large pieces? The answer is just out of reach—but maybe not for long.

Now the story gets even stranger. According to a source, who would talk only if guaranteed anonymity, in 1974 a US "special operations" team was engaged on a secret mission to photograph a Soviet radar device that was tracking SR-71 flights out of Turkey into Soviet air space. Returning over Ararat to avoid detection, the team was caught in an ice storm and sought shelter in a crevasse. They literally fell into a huge structure they at first thought to be an ancient Byzantine shrine. As one, the team suddenly realized the elevation was far too high for such a structure and they all concluded it must be the Ark of Noah. Code named "Black Spear," their report apparently went to the White House for the President to read. A friend of a Presidential advisor told me that he (the advisor) saw the still classified report in the Oval Office and it included a specific reference to what the special ops team believed to be a preserved, ice-encased portion of the true Ark of Noah.

From an illusive source, another story has recently come to light, full of details which seem to partially check out. Between December 1959 and April 1960, a pilot made between 40-50 flights from a secret base in Turkey into the Soviet Union as a 'decoy' for Francis Gary Powers' U-2 flights under an ID of 'DET TWO TEN TEN'. Many of these flights included documentation

An Armenian explorer made this drawing around 1973. It is an object he saw protruding from the ice of upper Ararat. Compare it to the photo of the first object. Notice the "ice wave."
Courtesy of Robin Simmons

of the construction of the Chernobyl nuclear power plant. They would return to Turkey over the Russian/Iranian border zone and head up towards Ararat. Out of his left window, the pilot said he saw, many times, an oblong, rectangular Ark-like object protruding from the ice at an altitude maybe between 14,500' and 15,000'. The pilot says the photos are stored, today, seven floors below the Pentagon. A request has been made to obtain these high-resolution close-up images of the anomaly in Ararat's ice cap.

In 1968, a teenager named Dave Duckworth was a volunteer worker in the Smithsonian Institution in Washington, DC. Duckworth told me that for several days that Autumn large shipping crates marked 'Smithsonian Institution/National Geographic Ararat Expedition' were deposited on pallets at the loading dock. A visiting specialist named Robert Geist was in charge of the material, which all went to the vertebrate paleontology wing (where Duckworth worked under the supervision of an Albert Myrick). Duckworth says he saw infrared aerial photos, taken from an anchored balloon that showed a boat-shaped object under the ice. He was told they had found Noah's Ark. He saw old style tools, pottery and an alabaster sarcophagus that contained a body. He heard Geist say there were more bodies. Dave was told to keep quiet. Several years pass, sometimes Dave spoke openly about his strange Smithsonian experiences.

In 1974—the same year as operation "Black Spear"—and long after Duckworth's story became known, two "FBI agents" visited Duckworth (at a different place of employment) and warned again: "You were in a place you shouldn't have been and saw something that doesn't concern you."

In talking to people about this persistent enigma, there's one thing I hear over and over; the notion that the Ark has been preserved for a purpose as a witness in our time. But a witness to what?

At the University of Erzurum, [an Islamic scholar told me]: "The Ark is a bomb in the world." There is a widespread belief in the region that the revelation of Noah's ship will be a sign that Mohammed is returning to purge the earth of heretics in a holy war. All true believers will then go to heaven in a restored golden Ark. One of Ed Davis' guides told him: "When the Master returns, a light will shine on the Ark and restore it."

An Old Testament professor at a respected liberal arts university once reminded me of the Gospel's warning—"As it was in the days of Noah so shall it be at the coming of the Son of Man." The text's true meaning, he said, a reminder that when the 'sons of God' (the fallen angels in Genesis 6) again breed with the 'daughters of man', the great deception of the Antichrist that precedes the Second Coming is imminent. This puts so-called alien abductions in a whole new light.

The same scholar asked me: "What would happen if the Ark were conclusively proved to be preserved in the ice of Ararat and then it became apparent that it had been looted by the West? And further, that it was a long-known secret kept by the powers that be? That this sacred mountain and its treasure had been profaned by the 'great Satan' (America)?" He went on: "And what if the Ark were revealed to be on Ararat and not on Al Cudi, as some translations of the Koran say? Would that further aggravate the situation by making it appear that Mohammed was a liar?"

The idea of the great Ark of Noah actually existing—to say nothing of being preserved into our day—goes against consensus academic and scientific opinion. However, as every researcher knows, geologic anomalies abound that challenge standard models of slow, uniform changes over millennia.

Colonel James Irwin, the late moon-walking Apollo astronaut, apparently had access to information not generally available. He made several high altitude explorations of Ararat. He told me he thought the preponderance of evidence indicated there was something ancient and meaningful hidden on the heights of Ararat. Something that would affect the way all mankind relates to each other—and the Creator. Irwin said, "It's not about walking on the moon, it's *who* walked on earth."

Perhaps the real riddle is why the solution to this mystery remains just out of reach. Are there forces that actively protect it? As of this writing, Greater Ararat is off limits to trekking and exploration. The Ahora Gorge is a forbidden zone to climbing and to photography of any kind. The trails have been mined and military encampments ensure enforcement.

If this ancient riddle can't be satisfactorily explained, then a new

Robin Simmons Photographing Mount Ararat from Helicopter. Next to Robin is George Adams who is roped into the open door while filming Mount Ararat from thousands of feet above the mountain 1990
Courtesy of Robin Simmons

paradigm is needed to explain the observed out-of-place artifacts. Perhaps they are evidence of an antedeluvian world that included human beings like us who were suddenly drowned in a global cataclysm. On the other hand, perhaps it's too late and too dangerous for the true identity of the Ararat anomaly to be revealed?

Robin Simmons can be contacted at FindTheArk@aol.com.

Bill Crouse has contributed much to Ark research with his critical analysis and series of newsletters called Ararat Reports. Anyone truly interested in the search for the Ark should obtain a bound full set of Ararat Reports.

7

BILL CROUSE

Bill Crouse

Bill Crouse is the founder and president of Christian Information Ministries, International, a Texas-based ministry concerned with defining and defending the Christian World View. Bill traveled to Mt. Ararat on two expeditions in 1984 and 1985 to investigate the claims that remains of Noah's Ark might still be there. He was also the editor of *The Ararat Report* a Noah's Ark newsletter from 1986 to 1993. In 1989 Bill went to Armenia, a small country in the shadow of Ararat. While there he visited the monastery at Echmiadzin where he was only the second person this century allowed to examine what is purported to be a piece of Noah's Ark.

Bill's interest in the search for Noah's Ark is primarily as a journalist. He is deeply concerned about the many false and misleading claims that have been perpetrated by many well-meaning individuals since the early sixties. While he once held to the possibility that the Ark could be found on Ararat, he now believes it is virtually impossible for reasons given in his article. The modern evidence does not stand up to close scrutiny as scintillating as it is. Rather, the ancient evidence, he believes, gives a strong case for the region south of Lake Van.

Christian Information Ministries, under Bill's guidance, operates a page on the World Wide Web geared to issues of the day as they relate to the Christian faith. The address is http://www.fni.com/cim/index.html

A Critical Evaluation of the Ancient Sources

Since the early 1950's the search for Noah's Ark has been the subject of many books and movies.[1] What gave rise to this interest was the distinct

---

[1] For the beginner who wants to survey the literature we recommend the following three books: John Warwick Montgomery, The Quest for Noah's Ark (Minneapolis, MN: Bethany

possibility that actual remains of Noah's Ark might be found. The spark, which set off this burning interest among Christians, was the claim in 1948 of an eyewitness who said he stumbled onto the Ark high on the snowcap of Mt. Ararat.[2] Since that time others have made similar claims. Based on these alleged eyewitness accounts many expeditions have been launched, countless hours have been spent in research, and large sums of money have been spent to verify what many critics said was an impossible quest.

More recently in the decade of the eighties, Col. James Irwin, the late moon-walking astronaut, and his associates combed most of the mountain on foot. Still not satisfied, they surveyed and photographed the mountain from various aircraft. While the efforts of Irwin and others have received much attention from the media, there is still no tangible evidence of an Ark on Ararat. Indeed, many who have been involved in the search, are now becoming convinced that the Ark may have merged with the elements, or that God may not want it revealed at this time.[3]

Bill Crouse 1998
Courtesy of Bill Crouse

In this chapter I would like to propose a third reason why the search for Noah's Ark has been unsuccessful, namely, that it may have landed on another mountain and the remains may no longer be extant. From the perspective of history, there seem to be compelling ancient sources which argue for another site as the final berth of Noah's Ark. Before we look at this evidence, it might be helpful to the reader if we give some of the reasons why the search has been concentrated on Mt. Ararat in eastern Turkey.

First, and foremost, are the alleged eyewitness accounts. If it were not for these, it is doubtful that a search would ever have taken place on the mountain the Turks call Agri Dagh and the Armenians call Masis (Mount Ararat).

Fellowship, Inc., 1972), Tim LaHaye and John Morris, The Ark on Ararat (Nashville, TN: Thomas Nelson, Inc., 1976), and Violet Cummings, Noah's Ark: Fable or Fact? (San Diego, CA: Creation-Science Research Center, 1972).

[2] For a complete account of this report see: LaHaye and Morris, *The Ark on Ararat*, pp. 115-116.

[3] Many Ark enthusiasts link the discovery of the Ark with end-time prophecy, an idea which could be true, but as far as we know is without any biblical support.

A second reason given for searching for remains of Noah's Ark on Mt. Ararat is its altitude. At nearly 17,000 feet, it has a permanent ice cap, which would lend itself to the Ark's preservation.[4] Indeed, an Ark perpetually frozen in ice would never decay. It could lie undisturbed for thousands of years.[5]

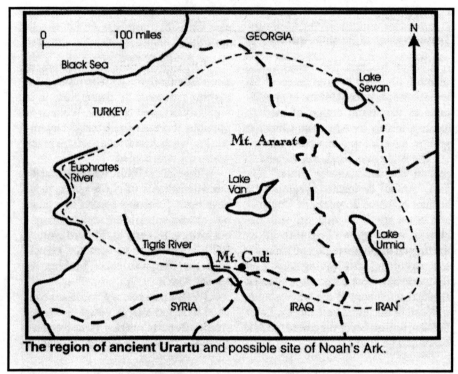

The region of ancient Urartu and possible site of Noah's Ark.

Ancient Urartu, the "mountains of Ararat"
Courtesy of _Bible Science Newsletter_

The third reason given has to do with the level of the floodwaters. Since Mt. Ararat is the highest mountain in the region it is assumed by some that the Ark must have landed on the highest mountain, since Noah could not see the tops of any other mountains for some time after the Ark grounded.

After the many expeditions of the last several years, some questions should now be raised as to the validity of the above reasons for looking for the Ark on Ararat. The eyewitness accounts have not been helpful in locating the lost artifact. The accounts are often contradictory, and under close scrutiny most are suspect. Some of the sightings have been made by pilots who appear to be of reputable character. However, these sightings, in our opinion, are explainable by the fact that the mountain has an abundance of

---

[4] This icecap is approximately 17-20 square miles in size. In some places it is 200-300 feet thick.

[5] As readers may be aware, wooly mammoths have been found in the far north which science dates at over 10,000 years. The flesh was still edible!

large blocks of basalt, and when seen under the right conditions, they can easily resemble a huge barge.[6]

Some question the age of the mountain itself. Is it not of recent origin? That is, was it not formed after the Great Flood? There seems to be almost a total lack of evidence this mountain was ever under water.[7] If the Ark landed on Ararat, why is there not some evidence of flooding, such as sedimentation, fossils, etc.? Geologically, we can conceive of a scenario where the mountain may have risen during the flood, but we still need evidence of the floodwaters.

Ancient ruins near Ishak Pasa
Courtesy of Elfred Lee

Others have been attracted to the mountain because of its altitude and its ability to hide and preserve the ship in its ice cap. Certainly this could be a valid reason, and it is one that this author once maintained. However, we again have geological problems in that the permanent ice cap is not stationary.[8] It flows down the mountain in several glacial fingers. Any structure would be gradually destroyed because of the uneven rate at which a glacier flows. Like water in a river, a glacier flows faster on the surface than near the bottom.

---

[6] The author has in his possession a collection of photos of these "phantom Arks." Some of these are heart-stoppers. Given the right combination of light and shadows Arks can be seen all over the mountain!

[7] Clifford Burdick, a scientist and early Ark searcher, claimed to have found pillow lava on the mountain as well as sedimentation. Neither claim can be substantiated. The sedimentation he found was shown to have been laid down by volcanic action and not by water.

[8] There are some areas of the icecap which some thought might be stationary. These areas have recently been bored into and examined with sub-surface radar with negative results.

In conclusion, it is difficult to be optimistic that remains of the Ark of Noah might someday be found on Mt. Ararat. Not only has it been thoroughly searched in recent years, an intact Ark five hundred feet in length would be difficult to hide. Besides the geological reasons, and the dubious eyewitness accounts, there are compelling historical reasons for believing that Noah's Ark will never be found on Mt. Ararat. We now turn to these arguments.

If Noah's Ark did indeed land on the 17,000-foot peak of Mt. Ararat one should reasonably expect reports of this event to have support from antiquity. When the search for Noah's Ark became a hot topic in the early seventies, this was assumed to be the case. Evangelical scholar Dr. John Warwick Montgomery argued this case in his well-documented book *The Quest for Noah's Ark*. It is our contention that Montgomery erred in his interpretation of these sources. As some readers may know, the Bible gives only a general reference as to the landing place of the Ark. Many enthusiasts of the Ark search, however, mistakenly believe the Bible names Mt. Ararat as the Ark's specific resting-place. This is not the case. The Bible says only that the Ark came to rest on "the *mountains* (plural) of Ararat" (Gen. 8:4). (Author's emphasis.) At the time Moses wrote Genesis "Ararat" was a very remote region north of Assyria centered around present-day Lake Van. Modern archaeological studies have pretty well delineated the boundaries of this ancient kingdom.[9]

A careful study of historical sources indicates that the earliest undeniable (a key word) reference for Ararat as the landing site of Noah's Ark is the middle of the thirteenth century A.D.[10]

The "Ship of the Prophet Noah" on Cudi Dagh
Courtesy of explorer Gertrude Bell 1911

By the end of the fourteenth century it seems to have become a fairly well established tradition. Prior to this time the ancient writers argued that the remains of the Ark of Noah could be found on a mountain known as "Cudi Dagh." Let us look now at what we believe to be the compelling evidence of those ancient sources.

[9] For more information on the land of Ararat, or Urartu as it is known in non-biblical literature, we recommend: Edwin M. Yamauchi, *Foes from the Northern Frontier* (Grand Rapids, MI: Baker Book House, 1982), and Charles Burney and David Marshall Lang, *People of the Hills* (New York: Praeger Publishers, 1971).

[10] We do not regard this as a settled issue; we are still searching for any references prior to this.

Cudi Dagh is located approximately 200 miles south of Mt. Ararat in southeastern Turkey, almost within sight of the Syrian and Iraqi borders.[11] The Tigris River flows at its base. The exact coordinates Latitude and Longitude are 37 degrees, 22 minutes North, and 42 degrees, 26 minutes East. In literature it has also been called "Mt Judi, Mt. Cardu, Mt. Quardu, the Gordyene mountains, Gordian mountains, the Karduchian mountains, the mountains of the Kurds," and by the Assyrians, "Mt. Nipur." It is also important to note that at times this mountain has even been called "Mt. Ararat." At an altitude of about 7,000 feet (2114 meters), it is not a terribly high mountain, though it is snow-capped most of the year. The current edition of the Encyclopedia of Islam lists it as "over 13,000 feet and largely unexplored." The Euro Map and Microsoft's Encarta Visual Globe 99 appear to substantiate the 7,000 foot altitude, and it seems strange that it would not be noted on our modern aerial navigation maps if it were 13,000 feet high.

Most modern maps do not show the location of Cudi Dagh (the Euro Map for Eastern Turkey is one of the first to do so). Those that do show it to be about 25 miles from the Tigris River (see map), just east of the present Turkish city of Gizre and still within the bounds of the biblical region of Ararat (Urartu).[12]

Cudi Dagh overlooks the all-important Mesopotamian plain and is

Bridge Ruins on Tigris River in vicinity of Cudi Dagh 1911
Courtesy of explorer Gertrude Bell

---

[11] This area was in the news early in 1992, as it was the area to which the Kurds fled from Hussein's murderous troops.

[12] Readers should be aware that there is another Cudi Dagh in Turkey (a mountain of about 2100-foot height) located near the city of Urfa not far from the biblical city of Haran.

notable for its many archaeological ruins on and around the mountain.[13] There are also many references to it in ancient history.[14] The Assyrian king Sennacherib carved rock reliefs of himself on the side of the mountain.[15] The Nestorians (a Christian sect) built several monasteries around the mountain, including one on the summit called "The Cloister of the Ark." It was destroyed by lightning in 766 A.D.[16] The Muslims later built a mosque on the site. In 1910, Gertrude Bell explored the area and found a stone structure still at the summit with the shape of a ship called by the locals "Sefinet Nebi Nuh—The Ship of Noah." Bell also reports that annually on September 14, Christians, Jews, Muslims, Sabians and Yezidis gather on the mountain to commemorate Noah's sacrifice.[17] As late as 1949 two Turkish journalists claimed to have seen the Ark on this mountain—a ship 500 feet in length.[18]

The evidence for this site as the landing place of Noah's Ark is not so strong that it demands a verdict, yet it is indeed compelling. If we only had the ancient references, the evidence for this site would easily outweigh the evidence for Mt. Ararat (excluding modern sightings, of course). These ancient witnesses are as follows:

Berossus

A Chaldean priest and historian (third century B.C.). His writings in Greek were published about 275 B.C. but his work survived only as far as it

Bill Crouse in 9th century B.C. Urartian cave next to Ishak Pasa Castle 1984
Courtesy of Bill Crouse

was quoted by others, notably, Polyhistor (first century B.C.), and Josephus (first century A.D.). He is also quoted by a few others as late as the fifth century A.D. Berossus' account is basically a version of the Babylonian Flood account. He notes that the Ark "...grounded in Armenia. Some part still remains in the mountains of the Gordyaeans in Armenia, and some get pitch from the ship by

---

[13] The Euro Map shows that a cave, the ruins of Kale, and the archaeological excavation of Heribi Marabasi are located near Cudi Dagi on the Hezil Suyu river.

[14] One of the most descriptive of the area is by Xenophon in *Anabasis* (fifth cent. B.C.).

[15] See L.W. King, "Sennacherib and the Ionians." Journal of Hellenic Studies 30 (1910), 327-35. See his footnote on p. 328.

[16] Gertrude Bell, *Amurath to Amurath* (London: MacMillan, 1924), p. 292.

[17] Ibid., p. 292.

[18] Andre Parrot, *The Flood and Noah's Ark* (London: SCM Press LTD, 1953), p. 65. We cannot vouchsafe for the accuracy of this report. We do know that Kurds in the area say that wood has been found there as late as 30 years ago.

scraping off, and use it for amulets." Some believe that Berossus was acquainted with both the Hebrew version, which puts the Ark in Armenia (Urartu) and the Babylonian, which puts the Ark in the Gordyaean mountains. They conclude the reason he mentions both territories is that he is trying to reconcile the two accounts. This may be true, but it is an argument from silence. The fact is, this location, Cudi Dagh, is both in the Gordyaean mountains and within the borders of ancient Armenia (Urartu). It may be that Berossus is just trying to be precise.

The Samaritan Pentateuch

This manuscript contains only the first five books of the Old Testament. It puts the landing place of Noah's Ark in the Kurdish mountains north of Assyria. The Samaritan Pentateuch was the Bible used by the Samaritans, a Jewish sect who separated from the Jews about the fifth century B.C. They were Israelites of mixed blood dating from the time the Assyrians deported many from the Northern Kingdom. The area was then colonized with citizens from Assyria. Intermarriage that occurred when some of these Assyrian colonists married Jews who were not deported resulted in a people who became known as the Samaritans. Their version of the Pentateuch shows a definite propensity to update geographical place names and harmonize difficult passages. There is much evidence that the Samaritan Pentateuch arose during the fifth century B.C., though the earliest manuscript extant today dates from about the tenth century A.D.

The Targums

The Targums are paraphrases in Aramaic which were made for the Jews after they returned from the captivity in Babylon (See Nehemiah 8:8). During their long captivity, many of the Jews forgot their native Hebrew, and only understood the language of their former captors—Aramaic.

Chalked Ahora Gorge petroglyph 1983
Courtesy of Doris Bowers

These paraphrases were originally oral. They were rather loose paraphrases, and in some instances were more like running commentaries. These Targums later were written down and preserved. They give Bible scholars a valuable tool for textual criticism and interpretation. Three of these Targums (Onkelos, Neofiti, and pseudo-Jonathan) put the landing place of the Ark in the Qardu mountains. It should be remembered that this mountain was not far from where some of these Jews spent their captivity. They probably did not know of the kingdom of Ararat since this kingdom had ceased to exist around the seventh century B.C.

Josephus

Living and writing during the first century A.D., Josephus was a man of Jewish birth who was loyal to the Roman Empire. He was a man of great intellect and a contemporary of the Apostle Paul. As the official historian of the Jews for the Roman Empire he had access to all the archives and libraries of the day. He mentions the remains of Noah's Ark three times. All are found in the Antiquities of the Jews. The first is found in Vol. IV on p. 43 of the Loeb edition.[19]

> Then the Ark settled on a mountain-top in Armenia. . . Noah, thus learning that the earth was delivered from the flood, waited yet seven days, and then let the animals out of the Ark, went forth himself with his family, sacrificed to God and feasted with his household. The Armenians call that spot the Landing-place, for it was there that the Ark came safe to land, and they show the relics of it to this day.

Bill Crouse far right with German climbers crouching next to rocks to get away from 50 m.p.h. wind 1984
Courtesy of Bill Crouse

---

[19] The most popular translation of Josephus is by William Whiston in 1737. However, the most accurate translation is the Loeb edition from the Classical Library. We also used this

First, note that Josephus says the remains of the Ark existed in his day though he himself was not an eyewitness. Second, the mention of the Armenians assigning a name to the landing site is intriguing, even that he calls them "Armenians." They were first called "Armenians" by the Greek historian Hecataeus, who wrote of the "Armenoi" in the sixth century B.C. Josephus, who also undoubtedly used the Septuagint (the Greek version of the OT), knew that it substituted "Armenia" for "Ararat" (in the Hebrew original) where it occurs in Isaiah 37:38. At the time Josephus wrote (near the end of the first century), the Armenians were still a pagan nation. However, there is a tradition that some Armenians were being converted at this time through the missionary efforts of Bartholomew and Thaddeus. The big question is: Was Josephus quoting Christian Armenians at this early date, or, did pagan Armenians know of the flood? Regardless, it might be significant if the Armenians had this tradition at this early date. We continue to search for the evidence. Third, concerning the Armenian name for the landing place, William Whiston, in his translation of Josephus, has the following footnote:

This *apo bah tay reon* or "Place of Descent," is the proper rendering of the Armenian name of this very city. It is called in Ptolemy, Naxuana, and Moses Chorenensis, the Armenian historian, Idsheuan; but at the place itself Nachidsheuan, which signifies "The first place of descent," and is a lasting monument of the preservation of Noah in the Ark, upon the top of the mountain, at whose foot it was built, as the first city or town after the flood. See Antiq. B. XX. ch. ii. sect. 3; and Moses Chorenensis, who also says elsewhere, that another town was related by tradition to have been called Seron, or "The Place of Dispersion," on account of the dispersion of Xisuthrus's or Noah's sons, from thence first made. Whether any remains of

Kurdish children with eight crosses on rock at Eli village 1983
Courtesy of Doris Bowers

edition to enable us to consult the original text. In Whiston's translation this quotation is in Book one, Chapter 3.

this Ark be still preserved as the people of the country suppose, I cannot certainly tell. Mons. Tournefort had, not very long since, a mind to see the place himself, but met with too great dangers and difficulties to venture through them.

Whiston wants to identify "the place of descent" (*apo bah tay reon* in Greek) with the modern city of Nakhichevan situated southeast of Ararat about 65 miles inside the former USSR. Ark researchers in the past have used this footnote as an apparent early evidence for Mt. Ararat's being the site of the Ark's landing.[20] However, we must ask if this is the intent of Josephus, or the eighteenth-century interpretation of Whiston (from his footnote). There seems to be linguistic and other evidence that such is not the case.

First, to identify the current Mt. Ararat as the landing place of the Ark, as per the footnote of Whiston, is contrary to Josephus clearly identifying it as a mountain in Gordyene. Second, the early Armenian historians identified the Gordyene ("Gortuk") mountains as the landing place of Noah's Ark at least up to the eleventh and twelfth centuries.[21] Third, According to the Armenian language scholar Heinrich Hubschmann, the city of Nakhichavan, which does mean "Place of First Descent" in Armenian, was not known by that name in antiquity. Rather, he says the present-day name evolved to "Nakhichavan" from "Naxcavan." The prefix "Naxc" was a name and "avan" is Armenian for "town."[22]

The second, and perhaps most important reference is found on page 45 of the Loeb edition and is a quote from the above-mentioned Chaldean priest, Berossus.[23] We quote here the entire paragraph.

This flood and the Ark are mentioned by all who have written histories of the barbarians. Among these is Berossus the Chaldaean, who in his description of the events of the flood writes somewhere as follows: "It is said, moreover, that a portion of the vessel still survives in Armenia on the mountain of the Cordyaeans, and that persons carry off pieces of the bitumen[24], which they use as talismans." These matters are also mentioned by Hieronymus the

---

[20] Montgomery apparently makes this assumption. See his book, *The Quest for Noah's Ark*, p.60ff.

[21] See Lloyd R. Bailey. *Where is Noah's Ark?* (Nashville, TN: Abingdon Press, 1978), p. 102ff. See also V. Kurkjian, *A History of Armenia* (New York: Armenian General Benevolent Union, 1959), p. 1-2.

[22] See the work of Heinrich Hubschmann in "Armeniaca." Strassburger Festschrift zur XLVI Versammlung Deutscher Philologen und Schulmanner (Strassburg: Verlag von Karl Tauberner, 1901), Section V. cited in Lloyd R. Bailey, *Noah* (Columbia, SC: University of South Carolina Press, 1989) p. 190ff.

[23] Found in Whiston, Book 1, Chapter 3.

[24] Bitumen is various mixtures occurring naturally or obtained by distillation from coal or petroleum, found in asphalt and tar, and used in surfacing roads and waterproofing.

Egyptian, author of the ancient history of Phoenicia, by Mnaseas and by many others. Nicolas of Damascus in his ninety-sixth book relates the story as follows: "There is above the country of Minyas in Armenia a great mountain called Baris, where, as the story goes, many refugees found safety at the time of the flood, and one man, transported upon an Ark, grounded upon the summit; and relics of the timber were for long preserved; this might well be the same man of whom Moses, the Jewish legislator, wrote."

Again, note that Josephus is not an eyewitness. Rather he is quoting all the ancient authorities he had access to. Most of these are no longer in existence, and indeed, are known only from his quotations of them. It is impressive to this researcher that Josephus seems to indicate there is a consensus among the historians of his day, not only about the remains of the Ark still existing, but also concerning their location.

Josephus also quotes the work of Nicholas of Damascus, the friend and biographer of Herod the Great. Nicholas claimed that he put great labor into his historical studies and apparently had access to many resources. It is possible he was one of Josephus' main sources. His story of the flood, however, deviates from the biblical account in that he has some surviving the flood outside the Ark. His location for the final resting-place of the Ark seems to be in harmony with the Gordyene site. He claims the Ark landed above Minyas on a great mountain in Armenia. According to ancient geographers, Minyas was a country slightly to the southeast of Armenia, below present-day Lake Urmia in Iran. The name he gives this mountain, "Baris, is a mystery. According to Bailey, the Greek word baris means "height," or "tower" and can also mean "boat!"[25] The third reference to the remains of the Ark is found in Volume XX, p. 403 of the Loeb edition.[26]

> Monobazus, being now old and seeing that he had not long to live, desired to lay eyes on his son before he died. He therefore sent for him, gave him the warmest of welcomes and presented him with a district called Carron. The land there has excellent soil for the production of amomum in the greatest of abundance; it also possesses the remains of the Ark in which report has it that Noah was saved from the flood—remains which to this day are shown to those who are curious to see them.

The context of this citation of the Ark's remains has to do with a certain royal family (King and Queen of Adiabene) who converted to Judaism. In the immediate context of the above citation, Monobazus, the man who converted,

---

[25] Lloyd R. Bailey, *Noah* (Columbia, SC: University of South Carolina Press, 1989) p. 216, see footnote #19.

[26] In Whiston it is found on Book 20, Chapter 2.

gives his son Izates the land of Carron. The clues given as to the location of
the Ark's remains in this passage are not unequivocal. The remains are said to
be somewhere in a country called Carron which must be found in the greater
country of Adiabene. Why? Because the king could not have given what was
not his, therefore, Carron must be found within Adiabene.

It is fairly certain that Adiabene is bounded by the Tigris on the West
and the Upper (north) and Lower (south) Zab Rivers. Today this would be
northeastern Iraq. The land of Carron presents some difficulties. It is
mentioned only by Josephus. There does seem to be some doubt about the
text here since the Loeb edition amends the text to read "Gordyene" where
the same "Carron" is mentioned elsewhere in Antiquities.[27] If this is the case

The Probe Expedition with Bill Crouse and Jim Irwin 1985
Courtesy of Bob Stuplich

then Josephus is not giving us a second location for the remains of Noah's
Ark. He may have associated Adiabene with Gordyene since they were next
to each other. There is precedent for this. Pliny, a Roman author and
contemporary of Josephus, places the city of Nisibis in Adiabene when it is
actually located to the west of Gordyene (*Natural History*, 6.16). It is
interesting to note also that Hippolytus (second century) agrees. He says,

---

[27] The Greek is *carrown*. The Loeb edition suggests in a footnote that the original reading
may have been *cardu*. This is certainly within the realm of plausibility. This, then would just be
another variant spelling of Gordyene, the country of the Kurds. Interestingly enough, there is a
land called "Kirruri" located southwest of Lake Urmia. See L.D. Levine, "Geographical Studies
in the Neo Assyrian Zagros." *Iran 11* (1973) p. 105. This land is a small district adjacent to,
and north of Adiabene, just across the Little Zab River.

"The relics of the Ark are . . . shown to this day in the mountains called Ararat, which are situated in the direction of the country of Adiabene. This would be correct since he wrote from Rome." (*Refutation of All Heresies*, 10, Chapter 26).

From the above there seem to be grounds for arguing that Josephus pinpoints the Gordyene site (Cudi Dagh) as the landing place of Noah's Ark. While we cannot say this with absolute certainty, we feel we can conclude that nowhere does Josephus say anything definitive that might lead us to assume that present-day Mt. Ararat is in view. We also disagree with Bailey who believes that Josephus gives three different locations for the Ark's final resting-place.[28]

Eusebius

In the third century A.D., this early church father noted that a small part of the Ark still remained in the Gordian mountains.

The Pershitta

The Pershitta is a version of the entire Bible made for the Syrian Christians. Scholars are not sure when it was translated but it shows up for the first time around 400 A.D. In Genesis 8:4, it reads "mountains of Quardu" for the resting-place of Noah's Ark. This version shows a definite influence from the Targums mentioned above.

Faustus of Byzantium

Faustus was a historian of the 4th Century A.D. Very little is known about him except that he was one of the early historians of Armenia, though he was of Greek origin. His original work is lost but his writings have survived in translations.

It is from Faustus that we first hear the story of St Jacob of Nisibis, the godly monk who asks God to see the Ark.[29] After he repeatedly failed to climb the mountain an angel rewarded him with a piece of wood from the Ark. It is this story that is often quoted in succeeding centuries, and the location given for the event in these later sources is Mt. Ararat. However, please note: Faustus, the one who presumably originated the story, puts this event, not on Mt. Ararat, but in the canton of Gordukh. The St. Jacob of the story is the Bishop of Nisibis (modern Nusaybin) a city which is only about 70 miles (not quite within sight) from Cudi Dagh.[30]

---

[28] Lloyd R. Bailey, *Noah* (Columbia, SC: University of South Carolina Press, 1989), p. 66.

[29] Montgomery's translation of this story from the French can be found in *The Quest for Noah's Ark*, p. 66-69. It is important to note that Faustus wrote from the same century as St. Jacob.

[30] St. Jacob of Nisibis was one of the prominent figures at the Council of Nicea (325 A.D.). He was known for his ability to perform miracles and was known as the Moses of Mesopotamia. He may also have figured in the evangelization Armenia.

To the bishop Mt. Ararat would have been near the end of the known world. If Faustus had meant this mountain he undoubtedly would have called it by its Armenian name of Masis, as he does elsewhere in his work. Armenian historians are in agreement that early Armenian traditions indicated the southern location as the landing place of the Ark. Up to the tenth century all Armenian sources support the southern location as the landing place of the Ark.[31]

Would it not be strange for the Syrian bishop to ignore what his own Syrian Bible (the Pershitta) told him was the landing place of Noah's Ark? Also, St. Jacob's own student, St. Ephraem, refers to the site of the landing as "the mountains of Qardu." It is hard to believe that one of his intimates could be that confused! The natives of the area today tell the story of St. Jacob, the Bishop, and similar traditions associated with Mt. Ararat, i.e. the city built by Noah, and his grave, etc.[32]

Epiphianus

The Bishop of Salamis (Epiphianus) was a fierce opponent of heresy in the fourth century A.D. On two occasions he mentions that the Ark landed in the mountains of the Gordians. In fact, he says the remains are still shown and that if one looks diligently he can still find the altar of Noah.

Isidore of Seville

Isidore wrote during the sixth or seventh century A.D. He is quoted in the sixteenth century as saying the Ark landed in the Gordyaean mountains.

Eutychius

Eutychius was the Bishop of Alexandria in the ninth century. He says, "The Ark rested on the mountains of Ararat, that is Jabal Judi near Mosul." Mosul is a city near ancient Ninevah about 80 miles south of Cudi Dagh.

The Quran

Written in the seventh century, the Quran says: "The Ark came to rest upon Al-Judi..." (Houd 11:44). The Modern Muslim Encyclopedia is familiar with the early traditions that the Ark came to rest on Cudi Dagh. However, the writer of the article under "Jebel Judi" believes Mohammed was referring to the Judi mountains in Saudi Arabia. This is not certain. Mohammed was very familiar with Christian and Jewish traditions, not to mention the fact that he probably traveled to this area during his days as a merchant. In the English translation of the Quran made by George Sale in 1734, a footnote concerning

---

[31] See endnote # 20. Also see the tenth century Armenian historian, Thomas Artsruni: Robert W. Thompson, *History of the House of the Artsrunik* (Detroit, MI: Wayne State University, 1985), p. 81.

[32] Bell, *Amurath to Amurath*, p.294.

the landing place of the Ark states that the Quran is following an ancient tradition.[33] At least the following Muslim sources seem to agree.

Al Masudi
Masudi, writing in the tenth century says "The Ark came to rest on Jabal Judi...8 P(F)arasangs from the Tigris. The place can still be seen." Eight P(F)arasangs is approximately 25-30 miles—the distance Cudi Dagh is from the Tigris.

Ibn Haukal
Also writing in the tenth century, Ibn Haukal places Al-Judi near the town of Nesbin (modern Nusaybin) and mentions that Noah built a village at the foot of the mountain.

Benjamin of Tudela
Benjamin of Tudela wrote in the twelfth century he traveled "two days to Jezireh Ben Omar, an island in the Tigris on the foot of Mt. Ararat...on which the Ark of Noah rested. Omar Ben al-Khatab removed the Ark from the summit of the two mountains and made a mosque of it." Several things to note here: the ruins of this city, Jezireh Ben Omar, are located at the foot of Cudi Dagh; here is evidence that this mountain was also called "Mt. Ararat"; it does have two peaks and remains were still there at this date.

Ibn Al-Mid
This thirteenth century Muslim historian informs us that an emperor (Heraclius) wished to climb Jabal-Judi to see the site in the seventh century.

Zakariya ben Muhammad al Kazwine
Muslim geographer Zakariya of the thirteenth century also reports that wood from the Ark was used to construct a monastery. He does not, however, give a location.

Conclusion
The above evidence to us seems impressive. As stated it is not conclusive, but certainly is compelling when compared to the evidence for Mt. Ararat in Turkey. This of course does not include the eyewitness accounts for Mt. Ararat, which taken at face value, are spectacular.

Only one verified eyewitness would invalidate all of the above. However, since we have no absolutely verifiable eyewitness, we wonder if any of the eyewitnesses in the lists given in various books about the search for Noah's Ark could have possibly been at this southern location. We feel

---

[33] This footnote is found in the Appendix on p. 496. The footnotes were the responsibility of Frederic Mynon Cooper.

that some of them can, and at least one, seems to us to be certain. Here are two examples:

Bill Crouse Studying the Echmiadzin Monastery "Ark Wood" Cross 1989
Courtesy of Bill Crouse

First, we are not entirely convinced, but it is possible that the discovery of the Ark by Prince Nouri might have been at this southern site, and perhaps what he saw was the stone reconstruction somewhat covered with snow.[34] We find it interesting that he was traveling from India to take over the leadership of the Nestorian church, which just happened to have its center a little to the east of this mountain. Certainly he would have been acquainted with the Nestorian tradition which puts the Ark on Cudi Dagh. The Nestorians once had a famous monastery called "The Cloister of the Ark" upon the summit of this mountain. It was destroyed by lightning in 766 A.D. as mentioned earlier. Question: Why did he say he was on Mt. Ararat? Because to most Christians, if the Ark is there, it had to be Mt. Ararat.

We believe a second and more certain possibility is the chance discovery of the five Turkish soldiers who were returning home after World War I who were leaving from Baghdad to return to their homes in Adana when by chance they came upon Noah's Ark.[35] Why would they deliberately go several hundred miles out of their way toward Ararat to climb a 17,000-foot mountain which was still under the control of their enemies (the Russians) when their home was in the opposite direction? These questions need answers. If you look at a map, they most likely followed the Tigris River right to their country's border. This would have put them right on target to Cudi Dagh. They could not have gone a more direct route through Syria because of the British Army. This explanation makes sense.

The above arguments and historical references may not constitute a conclusive argument for the Ark's final berth, but they are compelling, and to us, overwhelming. More digging is necessary, perhaps even in the literal sense, on Cudi Dagh.

---

[34] For an account of this story see Violet M. Cummings, *Noah's Ark: Fable or Fact?*, p. 188ff.

[35] Violet Cummings, *Has Anybody Really Seen Noah's Ark?* (San Diego, CA: Creation-Life Publishers, 1982), p. 103ff.

References:

For Ark researchers who wish to do further critical study of the above-mentioned ancient texts we recommend the scholarly work of Jack P. Lewis, *A Study of the Interpretation of Noah and the Flood in Jewish and Christian Literature* (Netherlands, Leiden: E.J. Brill, 1968), and Lloyd R. Bailey, *Noah: The Person and the Story in History and Tradition* (Columbia, SC: University of South Carolina Press, 1989).

This is a slightly edited version of the article that originally appeared in the journal: *Archaeology and Biblical Research*, Vol. 5, No. 3. Summer, 1992. Copyright 1992.

Robert "Bob" Garbe enjoyed a variety of Ararat experiences in the mid-1980's with Dr. Charles Willis and later forming his own team with Chuck Aaron and myself. Bob (with help from others) also built a portable subsurface radar unit for our 1989 expedition to the Western Summit of Mount Ararat.

8

ROBERT GARBE

I do not presume to know God's will concerning the resting-place of the Ark of Noah in our time in history. However, my participation in the search has given me some opinions on the matter. Bible scholars indicate that finding the Ark has no significance in New Testament revelation other than the many references to the flood and the faith of Noah. This simple observation may actually be the key to the part the Ark plays at this time in history. I will attempt to explain this concept as I describe my part in the search for the Ark.

Polls indicate over ninety percent of the general population believe there is a God. There are many religious "experts" with opinions about who God is. However, do we know the truth about God? Each of us creates a comfort zone about the subject that we can live with. Opinions about God range from the belief in an impersonal entity that started the universe and plays no part in our lives to belief in a God who is in control of all things. In the middle is an all-loving God who is in all of us. My participation in the search for the Ark has helped move me from a belief in the first description to a confidence that God is indeed in charge of all things and nudges our lives as he sees fit. My search for the Ark has developed in me a great appreciation for God's ability to create and sustain his universe.

Investigating the feasibility of the flood account has convinced me the Bible is our comprehensive instruction manual about who God is, how we should conduct ourselves, and what specifically must be done to honor him. In dealing with God it must be emphasized that we want to be careful not to make a mistake about what He wants us to do. The account of the flood and the story of Noah's Ark are among the first Bible stories we learn. We often learn about the flood from some kind of cartoon depiction. This is unfortunate because under close scrutiny the geological record supports the flood story. Understanding the flood can be a first step in understanding other miraculous events recorded in the Bible.

My background included a belief in theistic evolution. Although very little evidence was supplied about evolution I assumed it to be more grounded in fact than God's creation as depicted in Genesis. I brushed aside all the conflicts by assuming God just used the most current scientific rendition of the beginning. The biblical flood story never bothered me, primarily because I had only a surface knowledge of geology and did not fully understand the flood story.

Bob and Gerry Garbe at Durupinar Site
Courtesy of B.J. Corbin

My first contact with creation science was through the *Bible Science Newsletter* published through the efforts of Walter Lang, William Overn, and Paul Bartz. In it, Charles Willis reported on his 1983 expedition to find the Ark. He had an interesting theory that the Ark should be high on Mt. Ararat in order to fit its grounding within the time frame of the receding waters. According to Willis the Ark would likely be in a depression like the mouth of an extinct volcano such as is found on the eastern plateau. This would reduce the destructive effects of grinding glacial ice. The ice would need to cover the Ark except for a few periods of great melt-back as occurred at the times when sightings were reported. It would have to be in a position for Noah to see an adjacent mountain peak like Little Ararat.

This theory was compelling because it fit the biblical account precisely. One problem with the theory is that it is difficult to fit it into any eyewitness accounts. At the conclusion of his article explaining his theory and the progress he had made, he asked for those interested in becoming team members to contact him. I sent a resume expressing interest in joining his team.

On Thanksgiving eve that same year (1983) he called and we began a friendship that has extended through two expeditions. It was at this point that I began learning why a search for the "mythical" boat called Noah's Ark was reasonable. I believe God's purpose for my participation is found in this exercise. I encourage others to do the same thing. A wonderful world of the compatibility of science and the Bible will be opened to the person who pursues this truth. The first book to read is *The Genesis Flood* by Whitcomb and Morris. It lays out an explanation of the biblical account of the flood and construction of the Ark in layman's terms. It also gives much geological evidence supporting the flood story as recorded in the Bible. The authors give convincing arguments that this is no mythological story. There is good reason to believe the events actually happened and that this account is more than a symbolic story to illustrate God's judgment and Christ's salvation as is theorized by some. In fact, Christ uses the flood story as an illustration in his teaching many times, stating it as fact, not allegory.

In 1984 (Willis' second trip) we were victims of the usual problems presented by the local government officials in Turkey. In spite of the fact that permission to search was granted by the Turkish embassy and senior government officials in Ankara we were delayed by the local governors and military commander. Willis stated that the reason for the failure was due to the fact Ankara had issued a sport climbing permit not a research permit. In Turkey, there are also other issues to consider: (1) Make sure to bring gifts to the officials. While this is a custom in Turkey we don't usually use this tactic in the United States. (2) There is an inability among bureaucrats to make decisions. (3) The military commander, charged with providing security, was unsure of the level of security on the mountain and did not want to risk our safe passage. The mountain has many hiding places for Kurdish rebels who have a hatred for the Turks. News reports are received almost daily of the deaths of Kurdish rebels and Turkish soldiers in conflict.

The risk we feared in 1984 was demonstrated to be real in 1985 when the team Bill Crouse helped organize was driven off the mountain in the middle of the night after having all of their equipment burned by a gang of rebels wanting to emphasize their authority in the area.

We sat around in our hotel for over five days waiting for the permits to be put in order. We also visited as many sites as possible without going too far and losing time should the research permits suddenly be granted.

Finally the time frame for meaningful research was lost. We needed at least seven days to excavate just one spot on the plateau. The delay was taking these days from us. Five of us decided to climb the mountain for sport during the last few days. There is a climbing route on the south side that was open for a three-day climb. With very little time for planning we shifted gear around and prepared to climb. This climb would significantly add to our familiarity with the mountain in preparation for future trips.

Our guide, Yavuz Konca, was indispensable in helping to get through the permit formalities. An English teacher at a university, he became our primary communicator as none of us spoke Turkish.

We moved up the mountain from the south, climbing to a base camp area at about 13,000 feet. The next night after a day's rest we would make the summit attempt. There was little time to rest and discuss plans or problems as we started at 1:30 A.M. up this strange mountain, following guides on trails rarely marked with even a path. If you lost sight of the person ahead of you and got lost your problems would just be starting (or ending permanently). The wind was blowing very hard at thirty to fifty miles per hour at all times.

The guide went first then Bill Crouse, Ken Alexander, myself and Jim Willis. We used two flashlights and moved at what seemed to me a reasonable pace. Actually it was as fast as I could possibly go. As dawn came we were near 15,000 feet. By about nine A.M. we were a few hundred yards from the edge of the ice cap. The winds were so strong we stopped and waited, hoping they would abate.

After an hour the wind was still as fierce as ever. Now other climbers were catching up to us and we were all waiting together behind boulders trying to keep out of the cold wind. There were as many as six rope teams preparing to move to the summit. The time had come to make our move or risk running out of daylight on the descent back to base camp.

Someone in another group developed hypothermia and Bill Crouse loaned him his sleeping bag. Bill had been elected to bring the only bag we had in case of emergency. I did not realize the importance of this fact until later in the day. Our water supply was very low, a fact that should have concerned us, but no one noticed. I drank a quart of water before we started at 12:30 A.M. and about a half quart during the next 18 hours, yet on a climb like this we should have been drinking four quarts a day to prevent dehydration. Dehydration causes many physical and mental problems at higher altitudes. Hypothermia and disorientation can quickly lead to catastrophes. Pulmonary edema and blood clots can be fatal in a matter of hours or days. We shared our water with each other, but did not think to ask other groups to share their water with us. We had been so accustomed to being polite to one another that we shared water on the climb as we had bought soft drinks for one another at the hotel. It is critical on any mountain climb to discipline oneself and use water wisely and we had not. It is especially critical on Ararat because free-flowing water is not easy to find at night. This caused one of our team members to run out of water on his way up the mountain.

When we reached the edge of the ice cap we put on our crampons and the five of us connected to the same 150-foot rope. About twenty yards onto the ice Bill's crampons fell off. The guide helped him put them back on, but they fell off again within minutes, so Bill left them off. We were walking on slick ice ninety percent of the time and Bill was having a lot of trouble staying on his feet.

I have to admit Bill Crouse has more guts than a lot of people I know. For a person to continue to climb that mountain for the first time and crawl across an ice cap for a mile and a half on his knees, so blind (caused by severe dehydration) he could only see shadows, the man has to have courage. Bill even apologized for holding up the rest of us.

Abich II and beginning of Abich I Glacier 1986
Courtesy of Bob Garbe

We reached the summit about 1:00PM and sat down for about fifteen minutes to take pictures and record our names in the summit register. The summit was a beautiful elevation overlooking wavy ice stretching for miles in all directions. Beyond the ice was a vast emptiness to the plains 10,000 feet below. The winds were still blowing at over forty miles per hour and stirred up the snow, obscuring the view to the east in the area we wanted to search. We were only 200 yards from the place we were convinced the Ark rested. Visibility to the west was good and I remember seeing a pair of abandoned skis poking out of the snow north of us, about two hundred yards away. The ice could have been hundreds of feet thick and the Ark could be hidden anywhere under it. How could we hope to find it? I'm sure each of us hoped to get a glimpse of the Ark while on this climb just as several eyewitnesses claimed to have done in the past.

We had to descend from 17,000 feet down to our base camp at 13,000 feet before night. When we got off the ice we unroped and sat down to remove our crampons. I coiled the rope and Ken carried it down. Ken and

Yavuz went first and when they got 70 to 100 yards ahead of me I lost sight of them. I tried to keep up while still keeping Bill and Jim in sight to my rear.

Descending from a mountain can be more dangerous than climbing it. Exhaustion brings on a tendency to use poor judgment. If we unknowingly climbed down to a cliff edge and then had to climb back up to seek a better way down, a lot of time and energy would be wasted when there was none to spare.

Bill and Jim seemed to be looking at rocks on the way and were in no hurry (because Bill could not see where he was going). Then I saw Yavuz (our guide) sitting on a rock waiting for us. I stopped and sat with him for about a half-hour but Jim and Bill did not show up. Yavuz was exhausted and not feeling well from a lingering infection that had started several days before.

We decided Jim and Bill would have to come down this way because there were snowfields and ridges on both sides almost forcing their descent between them. I thought they would be safe if they did have to stay out overnight because Bill had the sleeping bag. It was at this point I found that Bill had given the bag to the hypothermic mountaineer earlier in the day.

Now I became very worried. If the winds returned the chill factor would produce very cold conditions that could be fatal. I emphasized to the guide my concern and we agreed he should move on down since he was sick and we could get help from those at base camp for Bill and Jim. I would hang back and continue to try to spot the stragglers and direct rescuers to their approximate location. I worked my way to an elevated area to get a better view.

I saw Chuck Willis coming up about 800 feet below me. I yelled down that Jim and Bill had not kept up with us and that something was definitely wrong. I worked my way down to Willis to tell him the problem. Fortunately, he was fresh, as he had not made the summit climb. We looked up to try to find Jim and Bill. We could see two people on the western ridge of the slope. We could barely make them out because they were silhouetted in the setting sun 500 feet above and 200 yards away. I spotted Jim's jacket but could not see Bill's blue parka. They hesitated and were not moving down in our direction. They seemed to be avoiding us. They didn't answer our calls to them. We wondered if they might be two bandits who had attacked Jim and Bill. Dr. Willis moved up rapidly to intercept them. He lost sight of them from time to time because of the terrain, so I spotted for him and kept my flashlight on so he could keep his bearings. Nightfall was fast approaching and it became very difficult to stay oriented.

Two men came up with a sleeping bag and supplies and I pointed out where they should go to help Willis. They seemed fresh and full of energy. I was relieved to see them. They would be able to help Willis if a rescue became necessary.

It was dark now and there was no moonlight. I felt like I was in a rock jungle with boulders taller than I. I was 300 feet above and a quarter mile from camp. I was able to yell to camp to shine a light so I could know in which direction to go. They heard me and I was able to feel my way down to them.

I was very thirsty and drank over a quart of water (what a drink!) before I got into my sleeping bag and I still remember shivering cold in the bag. I had dozed off, exhausted, when Bill came into the tent and told the story of his descent and rescue. Thank you again God for keeping us safe!

We learned a great deal in 1984—everything from Turkish politics to mountaineering preparedness. These lessons went a long way toward making the next trip more profitable. A common problem with Ark searchers is that we usually meet in transit on the expedition and never have time to practice working together except on the phone or in letters. It has been my experience

Garbe Object (Left Middle of Photo) This photo was mistakenly credited to Jim Irwin and a Dutch TV Crew as an airplane photo in Balsiger/Sellier book and videos. The reality is that Bob Garbe took this photo looking down from the Northeast edge of the ice cap 1986
Courtesy of Bob Garbe

that those of us with a common belief still experience stress-related problems interacting with each other. Our faith does not immunize us from our human personality traits.

So far God's purpose in the Ark search seems to be to remind the world of his judgment. Every three or four years someone claims to have found the Ark and it hits the headlines throughout the world. When this happens many are reminded of the stories they heard as children. Many scoff at the claim.

Some say, "Hasn't the Ark been found years ago?" I was a Bible-believing Christian who started out as a theistic evolutionist and now am a young earth creationist with a high degree of confidence that science confirms my faith. The adventure continues every time I come across new and old scientific evidence corroborating my beliefs in biblical events and concepts.

My second visit to Turkey was also on Dr. Willis' team. There are success stories with each expedition. Often we feel we have failed if we return and have to admit we were not successful in finding the Ark. In reality each expedition adds a segment to the pool of information about the Ark and each builds on the other. A major reason this book is being published is to document the progress that has been made for future searchers. Since 1982 when Col. Jim Irwin was instrumental in renewing the modern search for the Ark, more than a dozen sites have been ruled out, thus narrowing the search. Dr. Willis ruled out the eastern summit plateau.

An interesting sidelight of this second trip was a photograph I took while on the edge of twin peaks on the northeast side of the mountain at 16,800 feet. I was unroped and curious to see what was beneath the edge of the twin peaks. I worked my way as close as possible to the edge, then leaned out to photograph over the edge, panning the full width.

After I returned home, I began to examine the photos with my son's microscope. I was amazed to see an object that at first looked like the Ark. The characteristics of the object were amazingly like those described in eyewitness accounts. A row of windows the length of the top, proportionally correct, and a square outline of a door in the side were very convincing. The area in the photograph was the spot Ahmet Arslan had reported having seen timbers coming from the glacier. This "was" the Ark for about two weeks.

After conferring with Bill Crouse and John Morris, I learned Carl Nestor had also photographed the same area and had adjacent shots that convincingly rule out this object as nothing more than a rock formation. The photo's angle and focus led Bill Crouse to suspect the object may have been a rock close to the camera and not large enough to be the Ark. We are now convinced the object is nothing more than a rock with a remarkable resemblance to the Ark. This is an illustration of how a strong bias influences what we see on these trips and is something of

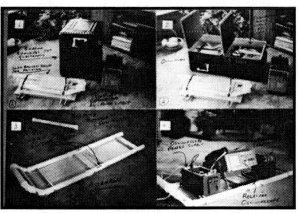

Portable Ground Penetrating Radar built by Bob Garbe 1988
Courtesy of Bob Garbe

which we all need to be cautious.

In 1986 when the Willis team excavated fifteen feet into the eastern ice cap at 16,800 feet, it became clear we needed to profile the ice to a greater depth using less time-consuming methods. The department of polar studies had experience with ice-penetrating radar that had potential for this purpose. Lambert Dolphin from Stanford and Lonnie Thompson from Ohio State University had used this technology on the Great Pyramid and on glaciers in Peru with some success. I contacted these two scientists for advice on its application in Ark exploration. It seemed feasible for a relatively small investment. To rent a profiling radar would cost $20,000, which at the time seemed beyond our budget. I pursued the idea and by late 1988 had developed a working model that we could put on a backpack. In the meantime geophysicist Bob Roningen was able to fund and operate a profiling radar for the Willis expedition in the summer of 1988. This commercial radar was very useful in spite of its weight to profile the eastern plateau. Despite the weight, the team was able to extend their search through the ice westward from the eastern plateau all the way to the peak. They found ice of 90 feet in depth but no sign of any Ark ruins.

In 1989, the Chuck Aaron lead team determined that the depth of the ice on the 15,000-foot western plateau was sufficient to qualify it as a possible site. Areas on the ice cap have potential in spite of the ice flow as demonstrated by the discovery of "Ice Man" in the glaciers of the Alps.[1] The Ark could also be buried under rock, gravel and silt. There may be ground penetrating radar in satellites capable of revealing the Ark structure.

Chuck Aaron heard about my radar and we linked up to use his helicopter expertise to deliver the radar to the mountaintop. The team Chuck led consisted of B.J. Corbin, Chuck, a photographer Paul, and myself. We met at Seneca Rock, West Virginia, to go over plans and practice climbing together. Seneca is an ideal climbing area in the eastern United States, having been used by the U.S. military for technical rock climbing training.

**B.J. Corbin, Chuck Aaron, Bob Garbe at
Seneca, West Virginia 1989**
Courtesy of B.J. Corbin

B.J. came to the meeting with a broken collarbone and was unable to climb. We did some light climbing and spent most of the weekend planning. Chuck

[1] See: "The Iceman's Secrets," *Time*, Oct. 26, 1992, p.62.

flew a helicopter to Seneca and we could tell he was highly competent as a pilot by the way he handled the helicopter landing. Dave Montgomery and John Wanvig joined us that weekend and had some interesting information on areas of the mountain from which there had been eyewitness accounts. One sketch was a map to what later turned out to be the "eye of the bird," now shown beyond a doubt to be a rock formation.

When we got to Turkey we had the usual political problems, but the delays were minimal because Chuck had done very good preparatory work with the permits and our Turkish pilot knew the best ways to get by the stumbling blocks. In Dogubayazit we stayed outside of town in order to minimize our contact with distracting influences. We needed to stay focused on the flight to the 15,000-foot plateau. The weather was perfect.

We made a reconnaissance flight around and over the mountain so Chuck could get a feel for wind patterns and we could photograph everything possible. We were at maximum weight for the helicopter and over service ceiling for a vertical landing on the 15,000-foot plateau, so Chuck did a glide-in landing, taking full advantage of the rotor lift. We unloaded within minutes and the Turkish pilot flew off for a second load, B.J., and the photographer Paul.

We began erecting tents and securing them in case the winds increased dangerously during the next several days. Within an hour, two men dressed in civilian clothes, carrying AK-47's, approached from the south summit plateau. They barged into our camp, grabbing cameras and pulling out the film. We spoke little Turkish and they spoke no English. We all felt these men were Kurd rebels and might decide to kill us after robbing us. I had two principle thoughts running through my mind: first would the bullets hurt and second was every one going to heaven.

I knew we had to find a way of communicating so they would know we meant no harm to them. I pointed to the radio in hopes we could get the gunmen to talk to our Turkish pilot down at the hotel. Chuck was able to reach him after walking over to the edge of the plateau. He explained our predicament to the pilot and the pilot proceeded to talk to our captors. We learned that the gunmen were actually Turkish military patrolling the mountain. They dressed in civilian clothing to foil snipers who frequently shot Turks in retribution for attacks on them. This solved the problem. The soldiers embraced us as friends and even handed us their loaded rifles as a good-will gesture. They didn't want us to keep any photographs of them because they could be used by Kurdish rebels to identify them as targets for ambush.

They left our camp and we continued to set up our equipment. The photographer, who was not a Christian, then asked to be flown off the mountain. He had not bargained for this kind of danger. Chuck was able to get the pilot to bring up Dave Montgomery in place of the photographer. We set up the radar and started to mark a grid pattern on the plateau with survey flags. Under our camp the ice was 250 feet deep. It appeared we were over a trough that may have been the head of the southwestern glacier.

Six hours after the landing, we all became very nauseated, with severe headaches and weakness from the sudden change in altitude. We learned firsthand the lesson that acclimatization is unavoidable, requiring over a week at altitude. We had to rest for an hour and then try again to get back to work.

B.J. Corbin and Bob Garbe after 1989 Descent
Courtesy of B.J. Corbin

On one excursion B.J. and I looked for an exit route should the weather prevent the helicopter from picking us up. The northwest area of the ice cap looked promising. While scouting in this area we noticed that the ground broke through the ice at the edge of the plateau. This was an additional clue to the profile of the ground under this portion of the ice cap. From the northwest edge of the ice cap to 150 yards south, the ice thickness increased to 250 feet!

At our next radio contact we were informed the military had demanded we exit the mountain within 24 hours and told us the helicopter could not pick us up. This meant we could not remove all of our gear. This was quite a dilemma because we needed at least another week to finish the survey. They wanted us to move off to the south. A southern exit would be less exposed to Kurdish rebel interference, but much more dangerous to a sick crew attempting to avoid the cliffs and dead-end ravines.

About that time an individual (Ibrahim) ambled into our camp wearing, believe it or not, a tweed suit and tattered boots. We conveyed our plight to him as best we could and he indicated he was willing to lead us down to a high camp he maintained on the southern sporting route. I was convinced we had met an angel sent as a result of our prayers. We gave him a new pair of wool socks and my favorite hat. He carried two packs to our one as we followed him in the direction of his camp about four miles away. On the way we had to cross a glacier and some crevasses.

Nightfall forced a stop in our descent. The danger of a fall at night was too great. We stopped and crawled into our sleeping bags among the boulders and slept as best we could. At dawn we continued down to this man's camp and had tea, bread, cheese, and honey for breakfast. Chuck had us help clear a landing site near the camp. He was able to contact the Turkish pilot but could not convince him to land on our hastily made landing zone. He did agree, however, to pick us up a few hundred feet below.

That same summer the melt-back on the mountain progressed beyond what any of us had seen before. Eyewitness accounts coincide with periods of low precipitation and hot summers, according to reports in "The Ararat Report" published by Bill Crouse. The mile-long snowfield leading up to the eastern plateau was completely melted off during our August trip. The summer heat persisted into late September and Chuck Aaron felt it would be prudent to return that same summer to do aerial reconnaissance. If the Ark were exposed we would have a good chance to photograph it. Chuck was able to penetrate the permit maze very quickly and we returned to Turkey.

In Dogubayazit we were disappointed by high winds every day. It was impossible to approach the mountain safely. On Friday, Chuck and I climbed up the mountainous terrain behind the now abandoned Simer Hotel (the same place B.J. found fossils). We videotaped the excursion and documented marine fossils of sand dollars and shells. Obviously this area at a 10,000-foot elevation had been under a sea in the past. We were ten miles south of Ararat and 300 miles from the Persian Gulf, site of the closest marine life at present.

Fossil sand dollars and clams embedded behind Dogubayazit Hotel 1984
Courtesy of Doris Bowers

At about 2:00 P.M. the wind died down dramatically and the clouds covering Mt. Ararat thinned out. We ran down the mountain and suited up for a flight before dark. Turkey has one time zone, making darkness fall around 6:30 P.M. in the east. Our first choice for photography was on the northwest slope, where B.J. Corbin had seen an interesting object in our recent photographs.

On the approach to the mountain we passed the "Eye of the Bird" or Ice Cave. Both Chuck and I did a double take when we saw it. It bore a striking resemblance to eyewitness descriptions of the Ark. It had what looked like two decks, which corresponded proportionally to those reported by eyewitnesses, and what seemed like planking. Half of the object seemed buried at an angle in the ice cap. Chuck made at least two flights around the mountain before nightfall and we returned to the motel. That evening we reviewed the video and became convinced from the video that we had discovered the Ark. The video even seems to show partitioning like rooms in the Ark.

The next morning we made another flight and flew around and over the mountain, photographing everything. We got some excellent photos of Little Ararat and the north face of Mt. Ararat. These photos have since revealed several interesting structures that should be investigated in the future. Shapes like an arched cave opening and projections that could be parts of a broken Ark. We have learned photos are often deceiving so we will reserve judgment for now.

Significance of the "Eye of the Bird" or Ice Cave Object

A friend and scientist has made an analysis of the helicopter sighting we made in September of 1988. It is noteworthy that he wishes to remain anonymous because his credibility would be challenged in his field of research if he acknowledged an association with Ark searchers. This is true of many scientists who fear persecution if they imply any belief in the harmony of scripture and science. It is all right to believe in God, but any reference to this harmony can lead to ostracism by others in the scientific community, including loss of jobs, tenure and ability to get papers and books published. This paradox has become the lie of our century and is partially responsible for the moral decay in our society. I recommend reading *Evolution, The Lie* by Ken Ham to anyone interested in becoming better informed on this subject.

The analysis of "the eye of the bird" is significant because it rules out as many as eleven eyewitness accounts of Ark sightings. Thus the search is narrowed to help us avoid constantly repeating past error. The quoted analysis follows.

General Description of the "Eye of the Bird" or Ice Cave Object

This object is at least intermittently visible as a dark mark in the Ararat ice cap from at least as far as Dogubayazit. It lies at an altitude of about 14,500 feet and 500 feet below the main plateau that exists northwest of the highest peak. A straight line from Little Ararat through the highest peak of

Ararat proper and projected just beyond the main plateau will pass very close to the object's location. The Aaron-Garbe photos taken from the air show the peaks of Ararat in the upper right-hand side of the picture.

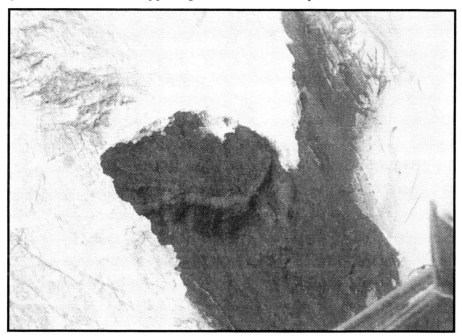

Ice Cave or "Eye of the Bird" 1989
Courtesy of Bob Garbe

The object itself is poking out of an ice-pack and is tilted slightly downwards. It lies in an approximately north/south direction on a rock bench or shelf above a steep cliff. At suitable times each year, there is a frozen lake or pond at the base of the cliff. Furthermore, extending down the hill from the cliff is a debris-covered snowfield. There appears to be a buildup of debris at this point under the snow cover, and rubble is continually being added by the cascade of ice from above the object. The object itself appears to have a covering of rubble or debris on top that is at least a yard deep, and may be significantly more. For this reason, the object looks more "natural" when viewed from above.

Earlier Observations' Points of Agreement

There are a series of observations of an object claimed to be Noah's Ark on Mt. Ararat that are in accord with the above description. (Page numbers refer to *The Ark on Ararat* by Tim LaHaye and John Morris.)

1. The monk Jehan Haithon wrote in 1254 A.D.: "Upon the snows of Ararat a black speck is visible at all times: this is Noah's Ark." (p. 22) It

certainly exists as such in a number of photos of the mountain (p. 106). Apparently, it also is very prominent in the Spot Satellite photos, even after extensive snowfall. It was suggested as a consequence that it may be a volcanic hotspot. Anything with a different thermal capacity, such as pitch-covered wood, may behave the same way.

2. Sir John Chardin visited Ararat in the 17th century. In an engraving of the mountain he etched out the position of the Ark as on the western end of the main plateau (pp. 21, 24). This description agrees closely with that of the above object.

3. In 1940, Sister Bertha Davis showed pictures to her Bible class of the Ark protruding above a debris-covered snow field (p.113). Similarly, in 1969, film footage taken from a helicopter was shown in Philadelphia. In it the Ark was shown protruding from a similarly rubble-covered snow field (p. 107). These photos appear very similar to the above object.

4. George Greene in 1953 located the Ark on a rock bench on the side of a cliff, protruding from a glacier/snow field. It was covered with rock debris and was lying in a generally north/south direction. The latter point is important in assessing any object as to whether it is the one which Greene saw. The altitude was given as about 14,000 feet (p. 135). Both of these facts are basically in agreement with photos of the object.

5. The Russian airborne photos taken during 1938-48 were taken at an altitude of approximately 14,500 feet, and showed the Ark tilted slightly downwards and poking out of the ice. One key point is diagnostic in determining where these aerial photos were taken of the object purported to be the Ark. The photos all had the peaks of the mountain in the upper right side of the picture (p. 111). If the 14,500-foot contour is traced around the relevant portion of Ararat, there are only two places where those conditions apply. One is where the above object is located. The other extends from about the Abich II glacier eastwards. If the Russian photos were indeed of Noah's Ark and not some other formation, then these are the only two possible sites for the Ark's location.

6. Finally, the record of Turkish soldiers in 1916 is important. They located the Ark as resting on a rock on the west side of the mountain and lying in a north/south direction (p. 91). This agrees with several elements of the object's descriptions, but, how would one know that this really was the Ark and not some other object?

First, the soldiers did not view it from the air or from some distance. They were on the ground. Second, they got close enough to make another diagnostic comment. George Hagopian and Ed Davis, who have both given extensive personal testimony of their sighting of the Ark, claim that wooden pegs or dowels were used to hold the planks together (p. 71). These Turkish soldiers also claimed that wooden pegs held the Ark together (p. 91). This would indicate that the object on the west side of Ararat may be at least part of the Ark.

Final Comments

1. A discrepancy is noted between conclusive sightings such as those of George Hagopian and Ed Davis compared with some recounted by persons who were airborne. The Ark or portions of it which they saw or thought they saw, was in a region whose description fits with near certainty the upper portions of the Ahora Gorge. All told, Ed Davis saw a total of 300 feet of the Ark as two fragments of about 150 and 100 feet long. The object described above is about 200 feet long. It would therefore seem that at least two and possibly three major portions of the Ark exist on Ararat. It seems logical to me that the Ark exists on Ararat and that it landed high up on the mountain. It then became petrified as many reports insist, and broke up due to either earthquake or ice movement. The separate portions were then carried to different parts of the northern sector of Ararat by ice flow and other natural forces. Sundry smaller pieces and timbers would then be accounted for in other locations.

2. It is also probable that some sightings claimed to be of the Ark are merely rock formations. Several such formations have been misleading in the past (p. 177, 198, etc.). It seems that an aerial survey may be more prone to this error than ground-based observations. It is thus important that all likely objects from air surveys be checked on the ground.

3. This latter point is particularly essential for the above object investigated by Aaron and Garbe. It has eight features in common with at least six other reported sightings of the Ark and so cannot be dismissed lightly. If a ground-based expedition and/or radar prove it to be a natural formation, then one conclusion is inevitable. Namely, that this is the object that has been mistaken for the Ark on several significant occasions.

4. Finally, one important characteristic needs close examination. On all the photos and the videos of this object, there are what might best be described as "icicles" hanging from the "roof." On close examination they can be seen to be spaced at regular intervals. Furthermore, there is a similar set of "icicles" coming up from the bottom of the object directly below the top set. In addition, the shots taken looking along the object from its end show that both top and bottom sets of icicles follow a slight curve. They do not hang

vertically. These facts lead to the conclusion that the photo taken by John McIntosh at a distance of about five hundred feet from the object in 1984 shows the icicles in essentially the same positions then as now.

It is therefore not beyond the realm of possibility that they mark some man-made feature such as internal compartments or ribbings—if indeed it is the Ark. If it is not, then it will be interesting to discover what they really are. The explanation that this object is simply a volcanic vent or an ice cave is insufficient. Someone needs to brave the ice cascade and look inside the "cave" with a strong light and see if there are any signs of wooden dowels, pegs or other evidence of human ingenuity at work. At the very worst, one more object will have been eliminated as being the Ark—one which has almost certainly given rise to a number of reported sightings. At the best—a portion of the Ark may have been discovered and its location fixed.

This report by my anonymous friend is dated February 26, 1990.

Conclusion

Has it been worth spending thousands of dollars to search for an Old Testament artifact? Could not hundreds of Bibles or meals be purchased with the money to nourish the poor in spirit and health? Why expose oneself to the dangers in eastern Turkey? Who cares if the Ark is found or not? We live by the New Testament, don't we? There is no biblical indication the Ark has any significance in end times!

I have had to ponder these questions over the past ten years and the answer has come unmistakably that the search for the Ark is very important. Christ used the illustration of Noah and the flood many times to illustrate Noah's faithfulness and God's judgment. Was Christ using a myth to make illustrations?

Anyone seriously in doubt of the Bible's authenticity needs to do a scientific study of the feasibility of Noah's adventure and the geological features all over the earth confirming the water deposition of the earth's surface features. This maligned story in the Bible will lead you to many other wonderful illustrations of compatibility with science, the "god" of our time.

Genesis contains fundamental principles of our faith. We cannot allow these events and principles to be trampled one by one by those who hate God. It is all true. As far as purchasing Bibles and feeding the poor goes, God has given us the capacity to do it all if we really wanted to do so.

Chuck Aaron is one courageous guy. He has made more helicopter flights around Mount Ararat than any other American civilian I know.

9

CHUCK AARON

Disappointed? Yes. Discouraged? Sometimes. Defeated? Never! I am forty-seven years old and have owned and operated my own helicopter business for the last twenty years. I have logged more than sixteen thousand hours as a pilot and am rated in both helicopters and airplanes. I am also a certified airframe and power plant mechanic. I consider myself a very stable and objective individual who tries to examine all sides of an issue before I make decisions. I am very active in reading, studying and researching the Bible, especially the Old Testament. This is because I am interested in eschatology or the study of end times, which I see as the bud of the tree. In order to understand the bud of the tree you must first learn the root of the tree and what makes it grow. I believe that root is the book of Genesis.

I became interested in the search for Noah's Ark before the first time I read the Bible. My son Shawn, who had always wanted to be an archaeologist, came to me one night in 1984, right after he had seen the movie *Raiders of the Lost Ark*. He asked me if there was anything else out there that would be neat to look for. As if a light bulb had just come on, I thought of Noah's Ark. Why don't you look for Noah's Ark? I don't know that anyone else has tried. His immediate response was, No! That triggered in me an impulse to take down the Bible that my mother had given to me several years before. It was just sitting on my bookshelf collecting a lot of dust. As a matter of fact, I had never opened it since she had given it to me. My mother loved God very much and had been trying for years to get me to read the Bible. I always thought it would be too difficult to understand and I just was not motivated spiritually enough to even try. I decided I could see what the Bible had to say about Noah's Ark, and I knew that it was in the front of the Bible somewhere. Sure enough, I found it in Genesis and I read what it had to say so I could tell Shawn when he came home that night.

After reading chapters six, seven and eight, I thought since it was so close to the front of the Bible I should read from the beginning just so I would not miss anything else about the Ark that might have been mentioned. I flipped back to the beginning, and what did I see but a note from my mother that she had written in 1981. I did not even known it was there. It said, "To my very dear son, Charles Patrick Aaron. About 3/4 of the way through this book begins the New Testament. Read it slowly so you learn more about him whom you seek. I love you, Jesus loves you, Mom, Christmas, 1981."

I was in shock! My mother by this time was in a nursing home in St. Cloud, Florida. She was the victim of poor judgment, which had left her with little or no mental faculties. I hated the place she was in, but she needed 24-hour-a-day care for almost all her needs, as she was completely bedridden. She finally passed away a couple of days before Easter in 1987.

What happened next was really neat. God obviously had his own agenda that was different from mine. By the time I got through chapter eight that night, I found myself really enjoying the picture that was forming in my mind about God and man. I decided to read on a little more. By the time I went to sleep that night I had read through Genesis. I was able to follow the Bible and was beginning to have a new understanding of God.

When I woke up the next day I decided that since it was Saturday I would read Exodus until I got bored. By the end of the day I had finished Exodus, and while I was reading it, I had cried, laughed, and cried and laughed, all at the same time. I was hooked. It was by far the best book I had ever read and I could not put it down. I finished the whole Bible within six months. The most important thing I can tell you is that my whole life changed from just reading this one book. I had a totally different outlook on life on this planet earth. Now I could understand the meaning of life itself. I could spend eternity telling how this book changed my life.

I remembered that in the New Testament Christians are called to use their God-given talents for the glory of God. I was a well-seasoned helicopter pilot and God knows I'm the type of guy who carries through a project once I have it in mind. I've always been an extrovert and involved in all kinds of sports and activities. My friends have always told me that grass never grew between my toes.

Now that I had accepted the Bible, I asked myself what I could do with my talents to serve God? I remembered my conversation with my son, and decided to look into the possibility of locating Noah's Ark myself. I also decided that as long as the doors opened up for me I would continue, but if they closed, then they were closed. I began by getting two 36" X 36" NASA photos of Mt. Ararat taken by satellite. I started jogging every day to get into shape, because I knew that someday I would go to Mt. Ararat. I didn't know when or how, but I knew I would go, I could just feel it.

Six months later, by which time I was jogging up to twelve miles a day, I got a phone call from an individual in Istanbul, Turkey, who wanted to buy one of my helicopters. He said that he wanted to give me a deposit on my JetRanger, but preferred to meet me before transferring $300,000 into my account. He suggested that I fly to Turkey to meet with him for a week. He

Chuck Aaron Flying Helicopter Over Mount Ararat
Courtesy of Chuck Aaron via B.J. Corbin

said he would pick up the tab and show me Istanbul. Of course, I said that would be fine! That was on a Thursday. Two days later, Federal Express showed up at my house with round trip airline tickets. The plane left the next day, and on Monday afternoon I found myself in Istanbul.

The Turkish gentleman picked me up at the airport and we drove over to one of his offices right on the airport. We had been sitting there, chatting for about twenty minutes when the phone rang. For the next several moments I became very nervous as he spoke in Turkish to the caller, but kept glancing over at me. "Am I going to be taken hostage?" I thought.

I was not feeling good about this at all. Finally he hung up the phone and said, "Chuck, that call was from a friend of mine in Ankara. He needs one of my helicopters in eastern Turkey. It seems there is a man there named Jim Irwin, an American astronaut, who is looking for Noah's Ark. My pilots are afraid of that area and don't really want to go there, but I could convince them to go if they knew that someone with your experience was with them. What do you think?" He stared at me in disbelief when I began to cry. I could not believe what I was hearing. I had difficulty keeping my emotions under control. I was in shock. After I got hold of myself I told him the whole story about my personal quest to look for the Ark. Now he was in shock.

The next morning at 7:00 A.M., one of his pilots, one of his mechanics, and I lifted off the ground in his JetRanger helicopter and began the twelve hundred mile trip across Turkey. We arrived at the foot of Mt. Ararat around 9:00 P.M. and the first person to meet us was Jim Irwin himself. I told him the story of my getting there and he became visibly shaken. At that point, Jim and I became the best of friends.

Because of legal issues with Russia and the border agreement between Turkey and Russia, we were not allowed to fly the helicopter on the north side of Mt. Ararat, which is where we wanted to search. In spite of this, the trip was not at all a loss for me. On the contrary, I met many great people who were with Jim: Bill Dodder, Bob Stuplich, Bob Cornuke, Dr. John Morris and John McIntosh. All these men were soldiers for God who were willing and able to risk their lives in the service of God.

Now that you know a little bit about me and how I got involved in the search for Noah's Ark, let's press on to the facts that I have found after eight expeditions to Mt. Ararat. There are two basic questions each person must answer. First, is there a God? Does God exist only in our minds? For me, the answer is easy. Of course there is God, and only one God! That became very evident to me after I read the Bible. Second, is the Bible inspired by God through the Holy Spirit and is every word factual? Again I overwhelmingly say yes. If these two essentials are agreed upon, we can proceed to see what God has to say about where Noah's Ark landed.

In the New American Standard Bible, Genesis 8:4 states, "And in the seventh month, on the seventeenth day of the month, the Ark rested upon the mountains of Ararat." We know from Genesis 7:20 that "the waters prevailed fifteen cubits higher, and the mountains were covered." For the definition of a cubit, we turn to 2 Chronicles 32:30 where it says, "It was Hezekiah who stopped the upper outlet of the waters of Gihon and directed them to the West side of the city (of David)."

An inscription found in 1880 near the mouth of the Siloam tunnel describes this remarkable engineering feat by which water was brought from the spring of Gihon to a place inside the City of David. Diggers worked from both ends, meeting almost exactly in the middle of this self-described twelve hundred-cubit-long tunnel. Since we know from excavations that by today's measurement it extends 1,777 feet, we know that the cubit was about 18 inches in length.

According to the Bible, the Ark landed on Mt. Ararat and the waters were twenty-two and a half feet higher than any mountain in the world. We know the elevation of the highest mountain in the world today, Mount Everest at 29,029 feet. If one assumes that Everest were the same height at the time of the flood, that would put the depth of the floodwaters at about 29,051 feet. I have researched this subject thoroughly, and while there are some who question what happened to allow the waters to abate after being at that depth, I will not go into the answer to that question now. The answer however can be deduced fairly easily using scientific data available today.

In Genesis 8:5 we read, "and the water decreased steadily until the tenth month, in the tenth month, on the first day of the month, the tops of the

Bob Garbe, Chuck Aaron, and Alparslan Demirural 1989
Courtesy of B.J. Corbin

mountains became visible." Noah landed on the mountains of Ararat in the seventh month and the seventeenth day, and no mountain could be seen at that time. This is a very important point to remember. It was not until the tenth month on the first day of the month (or 74 days later) when Noah first saw another mountaintop. It is certain that the only mountains he could have seen would have been the top of little Mt. Ararat to the east, or if for some reason the summit of Ararat blocked his view, the next mountain tops would be 33 miles to the west at an elevation of 11,014 feet.

I have flown a helicopter around that mountain many times. I have landed a helicopter on the 15,200-foot western plateau, and have even camped and walked around there for three days with the author of this book, B.J. Corbin, and another Ark researcher, Bob Garbe.

Greater Mount Ararat is about 17,000 feet at its summit, and Little Mount Ararat is beside it five miles to the east-southeast at 13,500 feet. I conclude that when Scripture refers to the "mountains" (plural) of Ararat, it is referencing these two mountains. Since no other mountain could be seen for 74 more days, that leads me to the conclusion that Noah landed on the taller of these two mountains.

The next step is to find out where Noah landed this 450-foot-long, 75-foot-wide and 45-foot-high barge on Mt. Ararat (see Genesis 6:15 for the dimensions). But first we have to ask the all-important question, did God plan to save the Ark to allow it to be seen again at some future date or not? To answer this I refer you to Genesis 6:14 which says, "Make yourself an Ark of gopher wood; you shall make the Ark with rooms, and you shall cover it inside and out with pitch."

Pitch? What is pitch? Pitch is the sap of the tree. It was used between logs as a sealer that kept water out.

The thing that has always puzzled me is why God told Noah to put this sticky pitch or sap on the inside of the Ark. Putting pitch on the outside of the Ark was understandable, but why the inside? To me that only makes sense if you want to preserve the Ark. By putting pitch inside and out and placing it on Mt. Ararat, which has a perennial ice cap, it makes sense to believe God intended its preservation. If the Ark is on Mt. Ararat and in the ice cap, and if it was originally manufactured of wood covered with pitch both inside and out, then it could easily be preserved indefinitely.

In Matthew 24:36-38 Jesus is talking about the second coming (or as some call it, the end of time):

> But of that day and hour no one knows, not even the Angels of heaven, nor the Son (Jesus), but the Father alone. For the coming of the Son of Man (Jesus) will be just like the days of Noah. For in those days which were before the flood they were eating and drinking, they were marrying and giving in marriage, until the day that Noah entered the Ark.

Jesus was hinting that we would know when the time of his second coming is near because we will be reminded of how far people had turned from God in the days of Noah. This leads to the whether God is planning to show the Ark again at some future time. If not, why did he seal it up so well and put it on a mountain, so that it would be preserved for as long as God wanted. Furthermore, why would God preserve such minute detail as to the size of the Ark and the number of days of the receding of the water? These seemingly meaningless facts can actually be clues that lead to a possible location.

My understanding of God according to the Bible is that God often uses man to fulfill his prophecies, and he uses things in the past to reference the present and future for warnings and heavenly reasons. It doesn't take a rocket scientist to figure this one out. I believe that if God holds true to his long-standing dealings with man, He not only will disclose the location of the Ark, but also other items like the Ark of the Covenant. Why? To show the glory of God and act as a silencing agent to man. A sort of divine "I told you so." Furthermore, these things could be strengthening agents to the Christians on earth during the tribulation period, because they will need a lot of encouragement in that time. I know that these things will not "save" anyone. When I first began my search for the Ark I believed that proof of the existence of these items might help convince people of the truth of the Gospel, but I found after reading and studying the Bible, that only God himself can do that. Because Eve and Adam ate the fruit, gaining the knowledge of Satan and sin, that knowledge passed to their offspring, causing the corruption of mankind. We are therefore incapable of saving ourselves.

I believe the Ark to be on Mt. Ararat in the ice cap somewhere between 13,500 and 17,000 feet. That is the altitude range of the perennial ice cap. As to where on Mt. Ararat, that is another question?

I can tell you for certain, as can many of my close friends who have been with me on these eight different expeditions, that it cannot be seen with the naked eye. We have been all over that mountain by helicopter many times at very slow speeds and right up next to the mountain also. We have seen every square inch of it, photographing it as we went. But don't lose hope, we haven't finished yet.

So where could it be? There are only a few places on this mountain that a 450-foot-long barge could hide. There are three peaks: the center peak, the western peak and the eastern peak. Approximately one-half of the ice cap covers the east and south sides right up to the eastern peak. It is thin on this side because it receives the sun's direct rays. I have photos and videos of this area taken from a helicopter in September 1989 showing little or no ice on it at all.

The center peak is the highest at about 17,000 feet, and between this and the western peak is a possible caldera (a large crater formed by the collapse of a volcanic cone, very common to volcanic mountains) located at 16,500 feet. This is one place the Ark might be. The presumed caldera is about 700 feet in diameter. There is also another huge caldera on the northwest side of the summit at 15,200 feet. This area is called the western plateau.

I believe this caldera has a lot of potential for being the resting-place of the Ark. Imagine God looking down on the earth at the end of the flood. He sees Noah floating around in this huge boat, knowing that it has all the life on earth inside it. God not only wants them to be saved from the flood, but after the flood as well. God certainly would not let the Ark land on the mountain at its summit where the steep angle of the ground makes it difficult to disembark.

He would plan for it to be as flat as possible and have a route down the mountain for all the animals and Noah's family to be able to get down safely. Also, you can imagine how rough the waters might have been during the flooding because of the incredible altering of the earth's plates and bodies of waters. The scene certainly was not an idyllic setting like "On Golden Pond."

We know by comparing Genesis 7:11 and Genesis 8:14 that Noah was in the Ark for a total of 370 days from the time he and his family entered the Ark and God locked the door behind them.

Basing our calculations on the 30-day month that ancient calendars generally used, we find that Noah landed on Mt. Ararat exactly five months later, and had therefore spent 150 days floating before the Ark actually touched hard ground. But why did Noah stay in the Ark for another 220 days after landing? Anyone, who has seen Mt. Ararat from a helicopter's perspective, knows why.

The mountain is very steep on all sides, and continues to be steep from the summit down 12,000 feet before the piedmont, or level ground, is reached. We know that Noah had problems: rough seas and a tall, steep mountain, virtually pointed on the top with very little flat terrain to support the Ark in rough water. How did they get down once they landed? The western plateau. Actually, this western plateau was a small lake roughly 2,000 feet in diameter.

Immanuel Expeditions Team David Montgomery, Kathy Montgomery, Paul Schiemer, Chuck Aaron, Jr., Chuck Aaron, B.J. Corbin, Bob Garbe, John Wanvig, Debbie Redmer 1989
Courtesy of B.J. Corbin

Noah had been floating around in very rough seas, and as the water subsided the summit of Big Ararat appeared, and the dove that Noah let out came back with an olive branch in its beak (Genesis 8:12). Note that this dove was gone for one day at the most (Genesis 8:10-11). At this point there was no land in sight, so the dove came back in the evening. The nearest mountain to Mt. Ararat that is as high or higher is found in the Caucasus mountain range in southern Russia, 248 miles to the northwest. The name of that mountain is Mt. Shkhara. Its elevation is 17,064 feet, only a few feet higher than 17,000-foot Mt. Ararat. The next highest mountain is in the same range but is located an additional 37 miles beyond Mt. Shkhara. This mountain is 1,461 feet higher than Ararat, having a summit of 18,481 feet. These two peaks of Ararat would be the only two peaks visible above the water at this point from which the dove could have retrieved an olive branch, unless it went to China.

Based on these facts, I take the position that this dove got the olive branch from Mt. Ararat itself. If this theory is correct, then the summit of Ararat was higher than sea level before the Ark had landed. This would leave only one other place for the Ark to land on relatively level ground. I think that God put the Ark on the western plateau-lake. It would be easy for God to get the Ark inside the rim of the caldera just as the flood was subsiding, and there it would float naturally and calmly, safe from winds and weather, while the porous volcanic mountain allowed the waters to subside slowly in the caldera. This is one explanation as to why Noah waited an additional 220 days in the Ark. Furthermore, it would be an easy walk for Noah and all the animals if they had walked down the northwest face. That is the path the locals usually use when they climb the mountain, and I have excellent photos showing how easy it could have been.

In 1989 I had the opportunity to lead three more expeditions to Mt. Ararat. The first one, in July, was made up of fourteen people. On this trip B.J. Corbin and Bob Garbe assisted me in a company we formed called "Immanuel Expeditions." On this expedition we were able to prove that the western plateau was indeed a caldera, using the subsurface radar unit that Bob Garbe had brought with him.

I had the opportunity to camp on top of that western plateau at 15,200 feet. B.J. Corbin, Bob Garbe and myself were able to use a special radar unit that Bob had brought. This instrument was for the purpose of looking into the ice on that plateau and seeing how deep the caldera was, perhaps even finding the Ark itself. That was the plan, anyway. What actually happened was that two men with AK-47s who had a different agenda from ours. A Turkish Major told me later that there were a group of four PKK who were caught by the Gendarma and were executed. Just before that incident, however, we were able to conclusively prove that we were reading depths of the ice right underneath our tents of 256 feet. In other

South side of Mount Ararat 1988
Courtesy of Chuck Aaron

words, that caldera we were on was now a frozen pond or lake all the way to rock bottom. That is the reason this area is so flat on top. I believe this caldera's frozen lake may be the hiding place of Noah's Ark.

My next trip was in September of 1989. On this expedition there were just Bob Garbe and myself. You have possibly heard about this trip. It was on this trip that the claim was made that we had "found" Noah's Ark. That statement hit the papers and TV all around the world.

We were sure. Anyone with us would have been sure too! The object that we saw fit most all the clues that some "eyewitnesses" had stated about the Ark over the years. It was on the side of a steep wall, encased in ice, protruding out at an angle, etc. What we saw at 14,500 feet on the west side of Ararat, fit that description exactly, and we had never seen it before, even though we had been all over that mountain many times in the past. The only reason we saw it this time was because of the tremendous amount of melt-back that had occurred that summer.

Many of the past sightings had been by pilots flying past Mt. Ararat. Astronaut Jim Irwin made the comment, right after he saw our videos of it, saying, "It looks like it could be Noah's Ark, and it probably is what other pilots have claimed to be Noah's Ark. But what is it, really?" There is no question that it looks like Noah's Ark to a pilot in an aircraft, but confirmation by a ground team was still necessary.

A Mr. Gunner Smars called me from Sweden. He had seen our videos of what we thought was Noah's Ark on TV in Sweden and he called me in Orlando, Florida, asking me to send him a copy of the tape so he could analyze it. I sent him a copy immediately and after reviewing it, he also thought it was the Ark. He arranged an immediate expedition and went to Ararat and climbed up to it. He was able to get to it by traversing the mountain, and even then was only able to get above it. He wrote a letter to Jim Irwin (which I have) in which he told Jim that he did not think it was the Ark. He said the place where he stood was solid rock and that he could not see any wood. Therefore he surmised that it could not be the Ark.

Thanks mainly to a brother of ours in the faith, Mr. Robert Van Kampen, a third expedition was made possible that year in October 1989. By then I was completely out of spare funds and Bob was gracious enough to fund the entire trip. On this expedition we took Grant Richards and John Morris, both experts in archaeology and geology, as well as experienced mountain climbers.

The thing I personally appreciated most about them was that they loved the Bible. We got a helicopter in Istanbul, flew it out to Ararat, and on this trip were able to fly within 100 feet of the object that appeared to be the Ark. After close inspection we all agreed that it was not the Ark after all. We also agreed that from a distance of five hundred feet or more, most people would swear that it was.

A man who wants to remain anonymous once contacted me after reading an article about me in an Orlando newspaper. He told me a story which, after having talked with him on many occasions, I sincerely believe to be true. He is about 70 years old now and has no reason in the world to track me down just to tell me a lie. I will call him Caleb.

Caleb told me that about 1945 he was loadmaster on a U. S. Air Force C-47 (DC-3) cargo airplane. While based in England he made many trips into Turkey to re-supply military bases. On one of his trips he had to go to eastern Turkey to drop some supplies. After they dropped off the supplies, the pilot said to the crew (four people in all), "Let's fly over Mt. Ararat and see if we can see Noah's Ark." Sure enough, Caleb told me details of the mountain that he would not know if he had not been there. He told me that they saw Noah's Ark complete, not broken up, and he described it as a long, dark, wooden barge made of logs.

He said it was lying in a north to south position, and it looked like it was half-sunken in the ice. It was on the west and north side of the mountain at around 15,000 feet. He said that the pilot indicated they were at 16,000 feet, and they made two passes by it. The passes they made were flown north and south, and when they were flying south on the final pass the summit of Ararat was on their left (east) side, and was above them. The sight mesmerized everyone on the aircraft. They couldn't believe what they were seeing.

He said over and over again how positive they all were that it was Noah's Ark. The sky was clear, and the view of the Ark was perfect, leaving no doubt in any of their minds that it was the Ark. Because of the secret military mission they were on, when they returned and told their commander of what they saw, he ordered them to forget about it and to never mention it again.

When Caleb and I first met, before he told me this story, he wanted me to check with the military to see if he would get into any trouble for telling me. He was afraid that I might repeat it to the general public and mention his name. I assured him of the constitutional rights of a writer, and told him not to worry about my revealing his true identity. I can say with God as my witness, this is a true account of the story that this man told me.

Astronaut Jim Irwin personally told me that he was told by an active duty Air Force General that there was a secret file on Noah's Ark. It was so "top secret" that not even Jim Irwin could see it, but the general assured him that the file does exist.

So where do we go from here? If anyone knows any way to get permission from our military or CIA to use the so-called "top secret" radar satellite that looks underground (the one used in the Gulf War to find underground bunkers), or if anyone has access to the archives of the satellite data recorded on tape, please contact me and I will give you the exact coordinates of the place where I believe the Ark is located. The best time of the year to look would be during the coldest part of the winter, because when the ice is frozen solid, radar, set at the right frequency, will penetrate ice as if it was not even there. I believe that with the right equipment, at the right place, at the right time, Noah's Ark could be easily found by one of these satellites.

Others have different ideas about where Noah's Ark is located. Many of them are friends of mine. May God bless them. All I have said here are my thoughts and ideas about where I believe it is located and why. The fact remains that none of us has actually found it. However, a photograph of the summit of Mt. Ararat hangs in the hallway of my house and that keeps me pressing on. I took the picture on one of my expeditions and at the bottom of the photo I have a note that reads:

Disappointed? Yes.
Discouraged? Sometimes.
Defeated? Never!

I just keep reminding myself that this is God's plan. This is a test. This is only a test. I believe that God, not Chuck Aaron or any other person, will decide if and when he wants to show the Ark. Whether the Ark is substantiated or not, I am content with my search for the Ark and to continue living my life based on the Bible.

*John Morris has been a leader in the search
for Noah's Ark since the early 1970's.
Though his responsibilities as President of
the Institute for Creation Research (ICR)
keep him busy, he remains very interested
in the search for the Ark today.*

10

DR. JOHN MORRIS

About John Morris

John Morris earned his B.S. in Civil Engineering from Virginia Tech in 1969. He received a M.S. in Geological Engineering from the University of Oklahoma in 1977. Morris gained his Ph.D. in Geological Engineering from University of Oklahoma in 1980. He is the president of the Institute for Creation Research (ICR) near San Diego and the son of well-known creationist Henry Morris.

From John Morris

It has been a privilege and a blessing to have participated and been a leader in the search for Noah's Ark for over 25 years, during which time I participated in thirteen trips to Mt. Ararat. By God's grace I was able to write several books on the subject. When asked by my friend and Ark research colleague, B.J. Corbin, to excerpt segments from those books and articles detailing some of my Ararat expedition experiences for this collaborative effort called *The Explorers of Ararat*, I gladly agreed.

[Excerpts taken from *The Ark On Ararat*, by Tim LaHaye & John Morris; 1975]

1972

In the early 1970's, I became actively involved in the Noah's Ark search as field director of the Institute for Creation Research (ICR) expeditions. In October of 1971, I went to Turkey to gain a working knowledge of the mountain, and in 1972, led a small group of mountain climbers representing ICR, consisting of John (J.B.) Bultema, Bill Ellison, Roger Losier, and John (Skip) Seiter. We ventured far into the Ahora Gorge, searching the vital western face from below. We then spent five days in the area above the

Ahora Gorge, Cehennem Dere and on the Parrot Glacier, where we were able to take many excellent photographs of the upper reaches of Mt. Ararat.

It was felt that if the Ark remains on Mt. Ararat it must be in an area where the glacier is stationary, because a moving glacier moves with such tremendous force a wooden structure such as the Ark could not survive in its path. A glacier moves unevenly due to friction forces applied at areas of contact with the rock below, generating shear forces, which would grind to powder anything with which it came in contact. For the Ark to have been preserved since Noah's time, it would have to have been frozen almost constantly in a quiet and stable area protected from these destructive forces. The ICR team studied and photographed several such stationary ice packs.

The hardships faced by climbers of Mt. Ararat are well known, but let me tell you an incredible story that happened to our team on our first expedition.

Dr. John Morris
Courtesy of John Morris

Struck by Lightning

As we neared the top of the finger glacier, the wind and snow increasingly worsened. At one point J.B. sat down beneath a large rock to rest and gain some relief from the blinding snow. I had seen lightning strike this rock several times and returned to warn him, but as all three of us stood or sat on this huge rock, lightning struck it again, sending unbelievable jolts of electricity through all of us.

J.B.'s back was frozen to the rock with his arms, legs, and head extended out into the air. He felt no pain at that time even though he sensed the current surging through his body. From that vantage point, however, he could see Roger and me thrown off the rock. The force of the lightning seemed to suspend us in the air and then drop us far down the slope. Simultaneously, J.B. succeeded in forcing one of his legs to the ground, completing the electrical circuit. The current somersaulted him down the mountain following Roger and me.

I had been standing on the rock (now known as "Zap Rock") thanking God for protecting us once again, feeling that we would not be harmed. I no sooner finished praying when the bolt struck. My whole body went numb. I couldn't see or move, but I never lost consciousness. I fell over backwards, still wearing my heavy pack. Expecting an impact that never came, it seemed as though I was floating very slowly for several seconds, and was gently placed on the snow by unseen hands after which began sliding down the steep slope. I knew I must stop, but for an instant my eyes and arms would not function. When they did, I responded and grabbed a boulder in the snow, halting my slide.

Ahora Gorge, Cehennem Dere, and North Canyon, and upper Parrot Glacier near where lighting struck Dr. John Morris, J.B. Bultema and Roger Losier
Courtesy of Dr. John Morris

For a few seconds I lay there, not moving, aware only of intense pain. I foolishly reasoned that since the pain was so great I must have received the full force of the bolt, and that the other two were unaffected. I tried to roll over and sit up, but to my horror found that both legs were paralyzed! There was no sensation of touch or life in them, just burning, searing pain!

I called to my friends for help, thinking they were unharmed, but the only answer was a call for help. Looking back uphill, I saw J.B. sitting in the snow, about 20 feet away, obviously also in great pain, with one leg twisted underneath him. He too was paralyzed and thought one leg was broken.

We remained there for several minutes, crying out to God for relief from the pain and deliverance from the horrible death that surely was to be ours. Suddenly I realized Roger was missing, and frantically began calling and looking for him. J.B. spotted him first, much farther down the mountain. His face was in the snow and one side of his head was covered with blood. We were unable to go to him, but prayed for him and called to him from above. Finally he stood up, looked around, and walked up the mountain toward us. His face was at least as white as the snow, and his eyes were filled with confusion and fear. When he was a short distance from me he stopped and began to bombard us with questions. "Where are we? What are we doing here? Why don't we go sit under that big rock and get out of this snow"? J.B. patiently tried to explain to him that we were on Mt. Ararat looking for Noah's Ark, and that we had just been struck by lightning under that big rock.

Roger was in shock and was experiencing total amnesia. He didn't know anything. He didn't know who he was or who we were. Furthermore, he didn't even like us. He wondered who these two nuts were sitting in the snow, freezing to death, when they could gain some shelter from the storm up among the rocks. J.B. finally convinced him to go get our ice axes, but that was the only thing he would do to help us.

So J.B. and I, unable to help ourselves, had to rely totally upon God. We reasoned that Roger would soon slip into deep shock and would need medical attention. J.B. thought his leg was broken and both of us were paralyzed, unable to move. We discussed a painful descent of the mountain, but ruled it out as impossible.

Our situation was, in short, critical. Unless we were able to get to some shelter, we would freeze to death in the storm within a few hours. And so, being unable to alter the situation, I prepared to die.

That's a weird feeling, rationally knowing that you are about to die. I never once doubted my salvation and did not fear death. In fact, I felt real peace, feeling that soon I would be in heaven. I had always envisioned meeting Jesus face to face as a rather exciting experience, but I now felt no excitement, just comfort. In fact, I wanted to get on with it—to die quickly, rather than slowly over a period of hours.

As I sat there contemplating horrible death, the Holy Spirit seemed to interject some of his thoughts into my mind. First, I was reminded of the hundreds of Christians who had suffered and died while following God's leading, and how they considered it a privilege to suffer for Him. Then I was reminded of the marvelous way in which our group had been led in the past months and particularly the past weeks in Turkey. I thought of the miraculous acquisition of our V.W. minibus, of the Christian friends who had helped us, of the granting of the impossible permits, of all the many dead-end streets down which we had wandered, only to find an open door at the end. I was reminded of the Christians back home who were praying for our safety and success, and of the job we had been called to do, and of its implications, importance, and urgency.

And then the conclusion. No, I wasn't going to die! God still had a purpose for us to accomplish. He wasn't going to let us die up in that frozen wasteland. Somehow, He was going to remedy the situation, heal and strengthen our bodies, and allow us to continue the search for the Ark.

Miracle on Ararat

During those moments I was reminded of many passages of Scripture, including James 5:15, which states that "the prayer of faith shall save him that is sick," and I John 5:14, 15, stating that "this is the confidence which we have in Him, that if we ask anything according to his will He listens to us. And since we know that He listens to us in whatever we ask, we also know that we have the request made of Him."

These thoughts were all whirling around in my head at dizzying speeds. I knew that I wasn't going to die. I knew that God was going to heal us, and knew that this was according to his will. Since I knew these things, suddenly the realization came that I also had faith to believe that these things would come to pass. And if I had that faith, then I could pray the prayer of faith. And so, with my heart pounding wildly I prayed that prayer of faith, knowing that God heard me and that He would answer my request and heal my body.

Before the Holy Spirit had directed my thinking, I had prayed for relief from the pain and for healing. But it was a prayer of desperation, not of faith. This time I expected a miracle. I tried to move my legs—no response. Or did that toe move? Frantically I began massaging my legs and could gradually feel the firmness return. There was no sensation of touch in them, just a burning numbness. Before, when I had felt them, they resembled a balloon filled with water, shapeless and pliable. But now they were hard. I continued to massage, covering them with snow to ease the burning sensation. Their strength gradually returned, but still no feeling. Within thirty minutes my knees would bend! Within an hour, I could stand!

Using an ice axe as a cane, I hobbled over to J.B. and massaged his legs. He had been unable to reach his ankle and still thought it was broken. We determined that it was not broken, but both legs felt like jelly. Amazingly, he was quite calm and relaxed and felt that Roger needed attention more than he.

Explorers on steep vertical slope of Ararat
Courtesy of Dr. John Morris

Roger was sitting on a nearby rock, obviously cold and shivering in shock. He didn't even have the sense to put on heavier clothing. So I retrieved his pack and re-dressed him—nylon pants, down parka, wind parka, and poncho. As I was tying his poncho up around his chin, a look of recognition crossed his face, and his memory began to return. When he asked why I was dressing him, I knew he was going to be all right. He did not fully recover for several hours, but in the meantime he was able to heat some water for a hot drink. But in doing so we lost nearly all of the coffee, cocoa, tea, and soup. All hot drink material slid down the hill, along with some valuable equipment.

J.B. had been massaging and flexing his legs during this time. His right leg had recuperated somewhat so that he could at least move it. Roger and I helped him over to a rock where he was able to don warmer clothing and find shelter from the storm.

Finally, I began to dress myself, but my legs were very weak and shaky. I had walked up and down the slope gathering gear until totally exhausted. Then we huddled together under the rock to gain shelter from the storm, drank a hot drink to ward off hypothermia, and prayed to gain victory over

Snow-capped peaks of Big and Little Ararat
Courtesy of Dr. John Morris

the situation.

Earlier, I believed that it was in God's will for us to be healed and to survive the ordeal. Now we were partially healed and growing stronger each minute, but we still faced a cruel blizzard with few options open to us. Lightning was still flashing everywhere, snow was still coming down in buckets, and gale winds were blowing. We knew we were going to survive, but that it wouldn't be easy.

The only possible area of safety was on top of the ridge away from the big rocks. We needed to find a flat place to pitch our tent and gain shelter from the storm, so as soon as the lightning intensity lessened, Roger and I began searching for a way to the top. The wind was blowing the snow with such intensity we could not see more than ten feet ahead of us, but eventually we located a path between several huge rocks. It was nearly vertical and the footing was treacherous at best. Once we reached the top, however, we found the weather was even worse. We were right on the edge of the Abich I Glacier, and the wind velocity had doubled; in spite of it we found a flat place to camp and returned to J.B.

In our absence J.B. had been massaging and exercising his legs. His right leg had regained its strength, but there was no response from his left. He was still unable to move, so Roger and I climbed the slope again with our packs and made plans to anchor to a rock and assist J.B. in his ascent. I was nearly

Dr. John Morris with packing gear
Courtesy of John Morris

exhausted after this second climb. My legs were shaking like rubber, so I rested in the snow for several minutes. We descended once again to J.B., and much to our surprise found him standing up waiting for us. His legs still had no feeling, but their strength had returned enough to allow him to stand, so Roger carried his pack, and with little assistance from me, J.B. climbed that vertical slope on two numb weak legs!

Within minutes of the time we reached the top, the storm broke. I guess God figured that we had had enough. The snow and wind stopped, and the clouds disappeared as suddenly as they had formed. In complete comfort and peace we were able to pitch our tent and eat a hot supper. In fact, that evening before the sun went down, it was rather warm and pleasant.

(Back) Durnal, Losier, Bradley, Davies (Front) Morris, Ikenberry, Dewberry
Courtesy of Dr. John Morris 1973

Throughout the day, I had felt that this would be the day we would find the Ark. This feeling was strengthened by the fact that Satan was so determined to stop us. It's not hard to imagine what I was doing and thinking as we pitched the tent and set up camp. As soon as time permitted, I wandered off to the edge of the Ahora Gorge, positive that the Ark was in full view. I didn't approach any dangerous cliffs, but with binoculars searched in all directions from a safe vantage point. Much to my disappointment, I did not see the Ark; but the view of the Gorge from above was magnificent. The freshly fallen snow covered everything above 9,000 feet elevation including, I suspected, the Ark. So we had to settle for a comfortable place to sleep, hot food, and our lives that night. We were satisfied and gave thanks to God. Very few people have ever camped that high on Ararat, and I'm sure no one else has ever had such a wonderful time of prayer and singing hymns as we had that evening.

1973

Cooperating Turkish officials had assured the ICR team that permits for another expedition would again be issued in the summer of 1973, so plans were made to return. Preparations were made to take a larger, better-financed, better-equipped group to Mt. Ararat, capable not only of relocating the Ark itself, but also of thoroughly documenting it. Professional photographers, a

Western side of the Ahora Gorge 1983
Courtesy of Dr. John Morris

medical doctor, and various Christian explorers and mountaineers were chosen for the job, in hopes of producing a 16-mm documentary film of the relocation of the Ark, as well as other ancient sites in eastern Turkey. Team members included John Bradley, Jim Davies, Jim Dewberry, Luke Durnal, Jim Leeper, Roger Losier, Larry Ikenberry and myself.

Meanwhile, Turkey was undergoing a period of political unrest. Several months of bitter parliamentary fighting had divided the country's leadership until April 26, when an overwhelming vote of confidence was given to the new coalition government formed by President Koruturk and Prime Minister Talu. Plans were made to gradually lift the martial law, which controlled the country.

By the time our ICR advance team reached Turkey in July, only a few areas were still under martial law, and even those were quite peaceful. However, two potential problems loomed ahead. In October, almost every elected official in Turkey was up for re-election, and on October 29, Turkey planned to celebrate its 50th anniversary. All things considered, it was not a good year for a group of foreigners with sophisticated gear to explore one of Turkey's most sensitive zones. Mount Ararat overlooks both the Russian and Iranian borders.

Although a number of sympathetic officials in the Turkish government actively attempted to acquire permission for the ICR team, they were unable to do so. When the decision was finally reached forbidding the issuing of permits, these officials promised more effective support of the ICR efforts in the future. So the team left Turkey with not only a deep love and burden for its people and a sincere respect for its government, but also a sense of accomplishment, even elation over the prospects of future work.

However, the weeks the advance team was in Turkey were not spent entirely in the capital city of Ankara. Some members of the team twice journeyed to Ararat, again exploring and photographing ancient ruins, as well as thoroughly photographing the critical areas of the mountain with high-powered telescopic equipment. While these photographs did not reveal the Ark, they would be strategically helpful in planning future endeavors.

Dr. John Morris searches by binoculars above Parrot Glacier crevasses 1973
Courtesy of Dr. John Morris

On subsequent trips to Turkey and the base of the mountain, a pattern of not granting permits to research Mt. Ararat unfortunately became the norm for the next several years; however, we continued to establish and maintain contact with Turkish authorities. Efforts to search for the Ark were additionally hampered by several other groups climbing Mt. Ararat without the required permission. This only caused the Turkish government to mistrust the Ark research effort even more. There can never be justification for a Christian to directly disregard the law of the land.

Though I remained active in the search for Noah's Ark, I did not return to Mt. Ararat to lead another expedition until 1983. In fact, access to the mountain was extremely limited until former astronaut Col. Jim Irwin expressed an interest in exploring it. His visibility made him a celebrity in Turkey with officials granting him a rare permit in 1982. Asked to participate, I was unable to do more than help Col. Irwin assemble a capable climbing team. But once again expeditions were possible.

1983 Excerpts from November 1983 Impact article No. 125—*The Search for Noah's Ark*: 1983

We returned to the mountain on August 19, with a scaled-down crew of four Americans and one Turkish resident of America. The permits, which had been requested beginning in early July, were delayed until a very detailed screening was conducted and the Turkish government completed the evaluation process. Unfortunately, two members of the proposed team, Dr. Howard Carlson, a Sumerian archaeologist, and Dave Elliot, a professional

Ahmet Arslan, Brian Bartlet, and Dr. John Morris south of Parrot Glacier
Courtesy of John Morris

cinematographer, were unable to accompany the group at such a late date. Three of the team were mountaineering experts, two of whom were also trained in mountain rescue and medicine. One of these mountaineers, Donald Barber of San Diego, re-activated a previous injury at the 9500 foot level and was unable to continue the climb. The other mountaineers, ex-medic Brian Bartlett of Samuels, Idaho, and Dr. Ahmet Arslan of Washington, D.C. area, an expert on Turkish folklore, native of Mt. Ararat, as well as professional climber, did make the climb. They were joined by Ed Crawford of Edmonton, Alberta. We were accompanied on the mountain by Ahmet Shaheen, vice-president of the Turkish Alpine Federation, and two Kurdish residents of Mt. Ararat. A return date of September 7 was necessary because of prior commitments, the group having planned to begin the work earlier in the summer.

In contrast to nearly all past expeditions, ICR applied for and was granted full scientific research permits by the Turkish government. The group proposed to study archaeological remains in the Ararat area, make linguistic and cultural comparisons with remains at sites known to be of great antiquity and to test the ICR position that all civilizations had originally sprung from a common source, the survivors of the flood who lived on Mt. Ararat. Specific plans had originally included careful documentation and evaluation of known inscriptions, relief drawings, underground chambers, and structures previously discovered in the vicinity of Mt. Ararat, while also searching the area for other ancient relics, including the remains of the Ark. All members of the ICR team were specialists—capable of accomplishing these goals.

Although the permits were finally granted and research visas issued by the Turkish Embassy in Washington, D.C., finalization of the necessary

Ishak Pasa 1973
Courtesy of Dr. John Morris

paperwork kept the ICR group off the mountain for still another week and a half of precious time. While waiting they re-visited an unexcavated cave in the foothills of Mt. Ararat which had been dug into an upturned layer of sandy limestone near the ruins of Ishak Pasa. Many more aspects of this site were discovered, including a series of prepared ledges and a facade which had been smoothed off near the cave opening in preparation for additional inscriptions or openings. Unfortunately, much deterioration of the area had taken place since 1973 and an interior room (tomb area?) as well as an arched tunnel had collapsed. The excavation of this promising site remains of paramount importance in the understanding of the early civilizations which sprang up after the flood.

The other important archaeological site which ICR had hoped to document is known as Korhan, studied first in 1972. Unfortunately, it was declared a restricted zone and access was impossible. Objects discovered on past expeditions include a large semicircular altar, a cave with eight Sumerian crosses on its entry, inscriptions in a pre-cuneiform script, and many other objects of obvious antiquity. Much fruitful work could be done at this site.

Instead of beginning their climb on the northern side, which lies within the sensitive zone adjacent to the Armenian border, as they had hoped, the ICR team was forced to climb from the village of Ortulu on the south side and then to traverse around to the west and north. Implications of this ruling included losing four days of the limited remaining time in ascent and descent, inability to establish a base camp with proper documentary and climbing gear, and many miles of dangerous climbing on loose glacial skree.

Once at the Ahora Gorge, however, the team did check out what were thought to be the most promising sites, from vantage points above as well as below. No wood of any sort was discovered. Two new inscriptions were discovered on loose rocks in the bottom of the gorge made of a granite stone commonly found on the west face of the gorge. Another hand-carved cave which is easily seen on the vertical west wall of the gorge is reported to contain objects of religious significance by Kurdish villagers, none of whom have ventured there for superstitious reasons. Indeed, it would be nearly impossible to do so without technical rock climbing skills and equipment. Due to the reduced quantity and type of technical equipment brought on the long climb from the starting point on the south side of the mountain, the ICR team was disappointed in its efforts to enter the cave. Vertical climbing from below halted about 10 meters below the cave in rock too weak for pitons.

.   Those knowledgeable on the Ararat project know that late August is considered the optimum time to search. The weather becomes much more unpredictable and potentially violent in September and climbing may become quite dangerous. Reports of a record winter snowfall had dampened expectations for the summer's work, as did news reports of bad weather in mid-August. However, the ICR team found the mountain rather hospitable for a change, although cloud cover hampered photography and two midday snowstorms forced temporary bivouacs. Each day more snow melted and very little remained below 14,000 feet elevation, while glaciers had receded farther than in anyone's memory. The conditions seemed optimum for a discovery.

Other aspects of danger were also avoided. Relationships with the local Kurds on the mountain were enhanced by participation of the two Turkish guides and the assistance of the two well-respected Kurdish villagers. Thankfully, only a few minor skirmishes occurred with the usually vicious Kurdish wolfhounds. Furthermore, even though the team spent many hours and traveled many miles over loose "crumbly rock," only rare avalanches caused concern, with no injuries. We did encounter a bear in an ice cave on a hot afternoon in the Ahora Gorge, but thankfully he was not interested in us.

Despite the favorable conditions, no remains of the Ark were discovered. Those sites thought to be the most likely resting places for the Ark were thoroughly investigated and photographed. Other sites of less interest could have been checked out, but time was short. (As it was, I had to miss the first three weeks of teaching duties for the fall semester and could not stay longer.) The team returned to the States on September 8 and 10, satisfied that they had done everything possible under the circumstances. They and their financial and prayer supporters were predictably disappointed that the Ark was not discovered, but rested in the fact that God would allow the discovery in his time, and not before.

Turkey had recently changed its long-standing position against research and travel in the Ararat area. Whereas for the previous 10 years or so, i.e. 1973-1981, access had been quite limited, many groups from countries around the world were allowed to climb to the summit this year. (1983) Several expeditions were not restricted to the standard summit route and were allowed to look elsewhere in search of Noah's Ark.

One such expedition consisted of Pat Frost, Howard Davis, Dr. James Davies, and others who linked up with a Turkish group doing medical research on the mountain. They achieved good coverage of the North Canyon area, and the area west of the Ahora Gorge. Another, headed up by Dr. Charles Willis, excavated a portion of an interesting ice pack east of the summit at 16,000 feet elevation with a modified chain saw adapted to ice. Still another group, John McIntosh and friends, spent some time searching the area east of the Gorge and toward the saddle between the two peaks. They then joined still another group headed by Col. James Irwin and including Eryl Cummings, Marvin Steffins, Ray Anderson, and climber Bob Stuplich. This latter expedition was even allowed to make plane trips around the mountain. The plane made four circuits at 11,000, 12,000, 13,000 and 14,000 feet elevation, with several hand-held cameras on board. Unfortunately, their photos showed no objects of interest. Neither did their ground search, which explored the east side of the Ahora Gorge and toward the saddle.

The obvious thought has now crossed each explorer's mind—perhaps the remains of the Ark are not really on the mountain at all. Yet the eyewitness evidence remains. Something must be up there. But where? Seemingly, every possible location has been checked. On the other hand, it may be that our methods are no longer productive. Since none of these difficult and expensive foreign expeditions has been fruitful, in part due to their inability to spend large amounts of time on the mountain, perhaps it

John Morris, Brian Bartlet, Ed Crawford 1983
Courtesy of Dr. John Morris

is time to turn the search over to the actual inhabitants who have ready access to the mountain.

Just such a solution has been proposed and is being carefully considered. An ICR supporter has recently pledged a substantial sum of money to be offered through ICR as a reward to any Turkish discoverer of the Ark during 1983 or 1984. The money would be placed in a Turkish bank and would be released once an ICR observer has documented the discovery. Until the Ark is found, no money would be spent and no lives endangered. If approved, the offer will be extended to the proper Turkish groups within the next few months.

Those who might question such a plan should bear in mind that the combined 1983 expedition expenditures of the various groups totaled well over a quarter of a million dollars. A reward may well be a better use of

Colonel Jim Irwin Walking on the Moon with Apollo 15 Lunar Lander 1971
Courtesy of John McIntosh

limited finances, and seems now to offer a greater chance for success.

1984 Excerpts from Acts and Facts, Vol. 13 No. 10 October, 1984 by John Morris

On August 25, 1984, the news spread around the globe. Noah's Ark had been found! A group of American and Turkish explorers, including ICR's Dr. John Morris, had discovered the remains of a huge boat on the slopes of Mt. Ararat in eastern Turkey, so the papers claimed. But discriminating readers soon began to question the continuing news releases. Something seemed wrong.

Indeed things were wrong, so wrong in fact, that what promised to be the most productive Ararat expedition ever turned into a nightmare of worldwide proportions, at best, producing questionable results; at worst, the end of all searches.

Several expeditions were approved for research on Mt. Ararat that summer, the most prominent one being a combination of three subgroups: International Expeditions headed by Marvin Steffins; High Flight Foundation, with former astronaut Jim Irwin; and Institute for Creation Research, with Dr. John Morris. These three had received broad approval for search and research, including the use of a high-altitude, military helicopter beginning August 20.

The ICR group, consisting of mountaineer Don Barber, Halil Husrevoglu of Turkey and Dr. John Morris, arrived in Ankara on August 5, to accomplish the preliminary work for the entire team, including filing of a detailed flight plan for the helicopter and clarification of certain aspects of the permits. Numerous crippling problems had surfaced for all of the other expeditions by this time. Thus forewarned, Morris and the others were able to eliminate many problems before they occurred, but quite a few remained, which were faced as they arose. In all, about ten days were spent in government offices in six cities throughout Turkey.

. Photo analysis by Ray Anderson of the United States had identified an Ark-shaped formation half-buried by snow and rock at the 12,500-foot elevation on the western side of the mountain near the Parrot Glacier, which the ICR group desired to investigate before the enormous cost of the helicopter was incurred. As soon as final paperwork was done, they climbed to the site but the Ark was not visible. They were back down in four days to meet the Steffins party on August 19, consisting of Steffins, his wife and daughter, Turkish physicist Dr. Bulent Atalay, and helicopter expert "Watcha" McCollum.

Within a day it was made known to the team that the high-altitude helicopter promised was in need of repairs and would not be available. The substitute which was offered could only reach elevations of 10,000 feet, much too low for research purposes. It was refused, and the groups turned to secondary objectives and methods.

The Irwin subgroup arrived on August 20, consisting of Jim Irwin, John Christianson, Dick Bright and Ron Wyatt. Wyatt had, on several occasions, visited the Ararat region with particular interest in a strikingly ship-shaped formation in the foothills some 20 miles southeast of Mt. Ararat. The site had first come to light in aerial photos in 1959 and had been studied by expeditions in 1960 and 1973. Both groups had concluded that the object was merely an unusual geologic formation. Wyatt convinced Irwin to visit the site, and although Irwin was intrigued, he was not convinced the formation was Noah's Ark, and left the site to climb Mt. Ararat.

After consultation with Steffins, the ICR group traveled to Kars to obtain permission for both groups to study archaeological sites on the mountain's north face. But, while the ICR group was gone, Steffins and Wyatt returned to the formation, this time with a metal detector which identified several discrete, metallic anomalies on either side of a central rock outcrop. Fragments were collected which bore superficial resemblance to petrified wood. Needing to wrap up certain details with the government regarding the helicopter, Steffins then left the mountain area and returned to Ankara without having conferred with Irwin or Morris.

Once in Ankara, rumors were flying among members of the press that Steffins had found the Ark. In order to squelch the rumors, Steffins called a press conference to explain that he had indeed found a boat-shaped, Ark-sized object on the mountains of Ararat, which given more research and documentation might prove to be the Ark of Noah. But the press exaggerated and so twisted the story that it appeared Steffins was announcing a discovery. Furthermore, over the next week the incident became a national scandal. All expedition members were accused of being treasure hunters and smugglers, "proved" by the fact that Wyatt had announced from New York City that he had removed portions of the boat. Pictures of him with a sack of samples appeared in newspapers throughout Turkey. Wyatt had rushed to New York to announce the site while Morris, Doris Bowers and others were just beginning to critically examine the site. Productive work on the search was over at that point, with the Irwin, Morris and Steffins groups harassed, threatened and forced into hiding. Fortunately, everyone was eventually able to leave the country and return home.

On the day of Steffins' infamous press conference in Ankara, Morris and his group had been visiting the boat-shaped formation. Careful study indicated to them that the studies in 1960 and 1973 were correct, and that the formation was merely a geologic formation, although an unusual one. It is approximately 510' x 160' with walls 30' high in places. It was evidently formed as a brecciated mud flow descended a hillside and flowed around a prominent rock outcrop, producing a "boat-shaped" formation, as does river water when it flows around a rock. The mud consists of various rock types, from coarse

The Durupinar Formation 1984
Courtesy of John McIntosh

sandstone to basalt, in a matrix of clay and fault breccia. Underlying the area is a layer of organic, rich, black limestone which looks somewhat like partially petrified wood. The formation is rather unusual but appears to be of natural causes. Its coincidental location in the foothills of Ararat, coupled

with its boat shape and huge dimensions, is puzzling. The presence of magnetic anomalies demands that more careful research be done, and final judgments must wait.

Although the overall effect of the summer's work is uncertain, one important discovery was made by an unrelated group, that of the ruins of a major city near the village of Eli, which appears to be of great antiquity. Located and photographed were many ancient inscriptions and structures which may hold the key to understanding the origins of ancient civilizations.

Metin Karadag Crossing Life Threatening Crevasse 1984
Courtesy of John McIntosh

1985

To test my proposition that Turkish nationals could search with less opposition, ICR sponsored an expedition by Mr. Halil Husrevoglu and three of his Turkish friends. Halil who lives in the states, had been with me on several previous expeditions, so he knew the area, the officials and the research.

Unfortunately, while Turks have better access, they have less protection. After an effective but unfruitful week studying crevasses in the Parrot Glacier, Halil was attacked by a well-known expedition horseman by the name of Halis. Left for dead, Halil was rescued by the local tribesmen. When the incident was reported to the police, they were not interested.

1987 Excerpts from Impact No. 175—A Report On The ICR Ararat Exploration, 1987 by John Morris

It has been obvious for some time that ground-based expeditions to Mt. Ararat in search of Noah's Ark have very little chance of succeeding. All who have seen pictures of the mountain and heard of the difficulties and dangers fully understand the necessity of using other methods.

In August of 1987, the Institute for Creation Research (ICR) participated in an international expedition composed of representatives of four organizations in cooperation with two Turkish companies. This consortium was granted permission by the very cooperative central government in Ankara: 1) to survey and photograph all areas of interest on the mountain from a fixed-wing airplane, 2) to investigate with a high-altitude helicopter any promising sites discovered from the aircraft or aerial photos, and, 3) to document any discovery by a ground-based climbing party. As a requirement of this permit, we were asked to do an equivalent study of the boat-shaped formation some 15 miles away from Ararat, which others have suspected might be the decayed remains of Noah's Ark. (I have studied this formation and am convinced it is merely an unusual geologic formation.)

Although all involved organizations participated in planning at all stages, primary responsibility for the acquisition and interpretation of aerial photographs rested with ICR and International Exploration, Inc. (Interex, Mr. Rod Keller, president), a Canadian-based aerial exploration company. A Cessna 206 aircraft was leased from a Turkish aircraft dealer in Ankara, capable of flying to 20,000 feet elevation and equipped with a high-resolution camera. The request to use a sensitive infrared video camera was withdrawn during permit negotiations.

High Flight Foundation of Colorado Springs (Jim Irwin, director and former astronaut), accepted primary responsibility for the use of the helicopter—a Jet Ranger II with pre-engine, also leased from a Turkish company, as well as direction of potential ground exploration and documentation. Plans to use the helicopter to build a mountaineering shelter, at the request of the Turkish Mountaineering Federation, were canceled since the final permissions were not granted until mid-August—much too late for transportation of materials and construction. The structure had been required by the Turks in the early permit negotiations in return for permission to explore. A "log cabin" design was chosen with pre-cut timbers to be flown up by helicopter and assembled on site.

Evangelische Omroep (EO), a branch of official government television in the Netherlands, (Jon Van Den Boesch, director) under separate permits to film in Turkey (including an interview with President Kenan Evren to discuss Turkish involvement in the European Common Market) was joined to the Ararat expedition to document all activities and discoveries. EO has had a long and fruitful involvement in creationist activities, including the original filming of the movies now known as the award-winning series, "Origins: How the World Came to Be."

As is always the case, difficulties and opposition surfaced at every turn. Our permit received approval on August 14, but getting the specific aspects nailed down and paperwork completed turned out to be a trying process. By August 25, however, we had explicit documents allowing all phases of our work, including the basing of both helicopter and airplane in Dogubayazit, the town at the base of the mountain. Precise flight plans had been approved by the Turkish Civil Aviation Agency, and although cautious, our hopes were high.

Earlier in the spring, however, a directive had been issued from the Prime Minister (not normally involved in the permit process), mandating that no exploration of any sort would be allowed on Mt. Ararat, evidently in response to requests for exclusivity from certain American groups including Ron Wyatt who were interested in promoting the boat-shaped formation as the Ark. Even though the evidence favoring this site is quite meager and speculative, there is a government effort to capitalize on the attention given it, including the building of a "visitors' center" on the site and improvement of the road to it. I had been told of this directive, but assumed our permission constituted an exception to it.

Unfortunately, therefore, provincial and local officials with responsibility to implement our permits had two conflicting documents, and clarification and coordination turned out to be impossible. At 10:00 P.M. on the night before we were to begin flying, we were told by the local officials that the more restrictive of the two was to be honored, and the flights were canceled.

A second major problem dealt with the nearness of both Russian and Iranian borders. By agreement with these countries, Turkey maintains a 20 km buffer zone along these borders, within which activities such as our proposed exploration and photography are kept to a minimum. However, our permits specifically allowed us to land in Dogubayazit (about 10 km from Iran), and specifically approved the areas of research on the mountain (slightly over 20 km from Russia, but only about 15 km from Iran). Again, local officials had two conflicting orders, and chose the more restrictive.

A third problem was the weather. The winter of 1987 had seen extensive snowfall in eastern Turkey, and since snow cover might obscure anything on the ground, this was thought to be detrimental to the search. Conversely, the summer had produced record heat waves. All Ararat veterans felt the snow melt-back was at least better than average. More importantly, the night on which our permits were canceled, a major snowstorm hit the mountain, leaving at least 18 inches of new snow, covering everything above 11,000 feet elevation. This had melted within a week, but by then our permits had been totally revoked.

After extensive negotiation, we were finally allowed to make one flight, of course restricted to air space outside the 20 km buffer zones. This meant we could photograph the west side of the mountain and see the promising north side only obliquely, from high altitude. Unfortunately, low-lying clouds covered the mountain below 13,000 feet, and the recent snowfall obscured much of what remained. Fortunately, these same clouds hid our plane from view as we ventured as close as possible to the Ahora Gorge and the Davis Canyon. The photographs taken, however, are of excellent quality, and do provide insight into a few areas of interest. They were taken in such a way as to provide stereoscopic coverage of the areas photographed, allowing three-dimensional viewing. The photos have now been carefully studied, and sadly no hints of the Ark have been seen, but all areas were shrouded in snow.

Even though we didn't do all we had hoped to do, in the final analysis, we were able to secure governmental permission for an aerial survey—an answer to a 16-year prayer of mine. We now know much more of the implementation process and of Turkish law bearing on this issue, and know ways to minimize the specific problems which stymied us. Now is hardly the time to quit! The mechanism is in place and relationships established which might yield a proper survey in the future.

Meanwhile, efforts are continuing to evaluate recent high-resolution satellite imagery of Mt. Ararat. Computer enhancement techniques, developed for the data from the French "SPOT" satellite, make it possible to "see" objects as little as three meters in diameter. ICR is committed to this study, and is involved in two such efforts.

The evidence continues to mount that God has protected the Ark over the years since the flood. In spite of volcanic eruptions, earthquakes, the erosion by the glacier, and the effects of time, the data [through eyewitness accounts] strongly assert that the remains of the Ark lie somewhere on Mt. Ararat, buried by volcanic debris and ice, awaiting discovery at the proper time. God answers prayer, and we can be thankful for the progress made in the summer of 1987. In his time and to his glory, the obstacles will be overcome and the Ark will be found. Even with the disappointments and frustrations, I am convinced the discovery is near.

1988 Excerpts from Acts & Facts Vol. 17, No. 11, November, 1988

The summer of 1988 saw a number of investigators journey to Mount Ararat in search of the remains of Noah's Ark. Considered together these efforts compose the most complete study of Mount Ararat ever made in one year.

In July a joint Turkish-American effort studied the boat-shaped formation some 10 miles south of Greater Ararat, which some have maintained is the Ark. Cores of the formation were taken down to some depth, but they yielded nothing of direct archaeological interest. Unfortunately, a group promoting this site soon plans to release a feature-length film claiming discovery of the Ark here.

Late in July a helicopter was used to search a hidden area known as the Davis Canyon. I was involved in the initial planning and ICR helped to a limited degree in the funding. Only moderate snow cover hampered the search, but no discovery was made. An effort to return at a better time to do a more complete survey was delayed until September 13. Even though late in the season, recent snow had melted, and good photographic coverage of many areas of high interest was obtained at that time. Again, there was no discovery.

Dr. Willis' group received Turkish permission to use a radar device to investigate beneath the ice cap on the eastern plateau summit region. No anomalous shapes were discovered under the ice in this area. There were a few other ground-based expeditions, also unsuccessful.

The many eyewitness accounts [included in an appendix], however, old and new, which have always been the main reason to search for the Ark on Mount Ararat, still remain unexplained, indicating something significant may indeed be up there, awaiting the right timing and conditions for discovery.

1989 Excerpts from Acts & Facts, December, 1989

As reported in Acts & Facts as well as in numerous news reports around the country, American explorers by the name of Chuck Aaron and Bob Garbe, claimed in late September 1989, to have discovered the remains of the Ark of Noah, high on the slopes of Mt. Ararat.

The object of interest can be seen as a dark spot in the southwest glacier. Turkish climbers call it "The Eye of the Bird," after the bird-shaped look of the finger glaciers. It has come to be known as the "Ark Cave" or "Ice Cave." I had participated in the planning and fund-raising for this helicopter-based search. I did not accompany the explorers on the September trip, but did return as part of a team of six in late October, in an attempt to verify and document the discovery. The ICR contingent consisted of Bob Van Kampen, geologist Grant Richards, my brother Henry Morris, III and myself. We joined Chuck Aaron and Bill Dodder, representing Jim Irwin.

Enjoying cooperation from the Turkish government, the group quickly acquired permits which allowed not only helicopter flights, but ground-based study and sampling. Unfortunately, complete implementation of the permits was delayed for several weeks. Finally, however, the team was able to study the object of interest from the helicopter once again, with even less snow cover than in September, but was prohibited from getting the much-needed samples.

From the air, the object looks long and rectangular, an estimated 70' x 100' x 300' protruding from the glacier. It seemed to consist of a basaltic ledge overlying an unconsolidated ash layer, which has partially eroded, revealing the interior. Since petrified wood can sometimes look superficially like basalt, samples are needed to settle the matter. Microscopic investigation of the samples would clearly show remnant cellular structure of the wood, or interlocking crystals of the rock.

Ice Cave or "Eye of the Bird" rock formation 1984
Courtesy of John Morris

The object appears visually much the same as eyewitnesses have frequently described their encounters with the Ark, and as such, will remain of interest until samples can be obtained and studied. However, each of the team members was convinced at the time of viewing from the helicopter that the object was most likely of natural origin.

1999 Conclusion

Several of the eyewitnesses have mentioned that the Ark is covered by rock or rock rubble, perhaps mixed with ice and snow, but not actually in the glacier. My current thinking is that the structure has likely been engulfed by volcanic ash, ejected in one of the mountains by many post-flood eruptions. Once buried in ash, the Ark could be preserved by petrifaction, injection with or replacement by silica, common in igneous rock. This could explain why several eyewitnesses have insisted that the Ark is "as hard as rock." Numerous layers of ash and volcanic flow rock are exposed in the Ahora Gorge and elsewhere, forming a "stair-stepped" terrain. Such topography is mentioned time and again by eyewitnesses, with the Ark resting on a ledge, protruding from the mountain and near a cliff.

While I remain interested in exploration of the glacier, I feel the bulk of the eyewitness evidence favors a lower site, in rugged, rocky terrain, but still accessible to non-technical climbers with knowledge of the proper route. Indeed, without these eyewitness reports, there is absolutely no reason to search at all.

Thus, I maintain a primary interest in the Ahora Gorge, and other similar features, from approximately 12,500 to 14,500 feet in elevation. I suspect only 50 feet or so might be protruding from an ash deposit, but even that would be covered by snow or rock debris on most years, forcing a continued revisitation of the many potential hiding places.

For nearly two decades, the search for the Ark was paramount in my thinking. Even at night I would dream of climbing the mountain several times a week. The Ark search gets into your blood. It's like having gum on your shoe. You can kick and kick, but can't get it off. I'll always be hooked. My study of the Turkish language, of Muslim writings, of Anatolian history, and of Turkish customs has been fascinating, and on my thirteen trips to the mountain, the many dear Turkish friends and experiences have been enriching.

I have memories which will last for a lifetime. But in recent years my passion has turned to other projects, as responsibilities have grown at home and at ICR. I no longer seek to return to the mountain, although I maintain a deep interest in the search and contact with active search groups. But if the right opportunity arose...

Ray Anderson is a seasoned veteran of Ararat exploration. He can recall the days of Dr. Lawrence Hewitt and Eryl Cummings, when permission to climb in and around the Ahora Gorge was commonplace.

11

RAY ANDERSON

An innocent trip to a bookstore in Los Angeles one Saturday in 1972 changed my life forever. After selecting several books from the shelves, I took them to the cashier and while waiting for her to finish with the customer ahead of me, I thumbed through a book from a stack beside the cash register. It was *Noah's Ark: Fable or Fact* by Eryl and Violet Cummings. What I saw in the couple of minutes of browsing caused me to add a copy to my other purchases. When I got home and read it through without stopping, I was hooked! I was an instant "Arkeologist!"

Ray Anderson studying Mount Ararat through a telescope 1982
Courtesy of Bob Stuplich

In 1972, I called Eryl at his home in Farmington, New Mexico, and asked how I might join one of his expeditions to Mt. Ararat. He was not very encouraging. During our conversation he mentioned one of his expedition partners, Dr. Lawrence Hewitt, a medical doctor in Huntsville, Alabama.

He suggested I contact Dr. Hewitt as he was putting together an expedition for the next summer (1973). Dr. Hewitt was an experienced Ararat explorer, having been on the mountain four or five times searching for the Ark. I did call Dr. Hewitt, and found in the course of our conversation that we had a mutual friend in Huntsville. His medical partner was my wife's cousin. The next day he called and told me I could join their next expedition.

In the next few years I was on two Ararat searches with Dr. Hewitt and a friend of his, Jerry Williams. During these early years we usually confined our efforts to the northeast, north, and northwest sides of the mountain. We also concentrated on areas below 14,500 feet elevation, as all early evidence, such as it was, seemed to indicate that was where the Ark would be found.

During these periods, Dr. Hewitt had very little difficulty securing permits to search anywhere we cared to on Ararat. We would leave Ahora village and go onto the mountain with only one Kurdish guide and a Turkish soldier. Dr. Hewitt always brought a good supply of basic medical supplies and medicines, and when we stopped on the mountain at the Kurdish shepherd camps, the natives would appear from out of the hills bringing their families for his medical attention.

Ray Anderson Northeast Side of Ararat 1993
Courtesy of Ray Anderson

From the beginning, some of the early search groups scorned anything coming from Adventist efforts, feeling that God would surely not reward them with credible information. To this day, I think some are still uncomfortable with my findings because it came through my association with Adventists. I had a close relationship with Hewitt, Williams, their families and friends.

Around 1984, I received a telephone call from my old climbing companion, Jerry Williams, the Adventist minister. In a conversation with a high official of his church, the subject of his involvement in the Ark search arose. This official told him that he was working with a new member of their lay-missionaries who was a former U-2 pilot but was now out of the service. He had shared some of his experiences as a pilot during the 1960's with this official. Some was still classified but he felt he could tell him about seeing what he believed was a section of Noah's Ark. He had been flying a very low-level photographic mission along the border of Turkey near Mt. Ararat. Another highflying U-2 was flying a very high flight to decoy radar away from him. Before heading back to his base in Turkey, he made a low sweep up the north side of Ararat, just to the right of the Ahora Gorge. As he swept across the mouth of the gorge at a very low level, he looked out of the left side of his cockpit and saw at the top of the ridge, a bowl shaped formation which he also described as an inverted fish hook. Inside this, against the wall, he saw protruding from the glacier, about 20-25 ft. of what he believed to be a man made structure. It was rectangular in shape and had some damage. He made a quick turn and flew over it again, getting his left wing tip within 200-300 ft. of it. He was convinced it was man made and being a religious man, concluded it had to be Noah's Ark. Through church connections, my friend Williams was able to contact the man who confirmed the story.

Sometime later I contacted Williams again and he refused to talk about it, saying that I must have misunderstood him. He claimed no recollection of the conversation. I tried to locate the pilot through the Adventist church offices but found no one who knew anything about him.

I traced the pilot to his hometown in Louisiana and located his father who confirmed that his son had been a U-2 pilot but had given him orders to not reveal his name or location. The father thought it was something about security and classified information. I believe the pilots story because several years later, Ed Davis told me the object (long piece) the Kurds showed him was resting against a wall of a bowl or horseshoe shaped formation just above the mouth of the Ahora Gorge at the top of a ridge. Just as the pilot described it and as my picture shows it. The Kurds told Ed that a few feet of the north end is exposed almost every late summer regardless of the winter temperatures and ice cover, because very hot winds sweep up the north slope of the mountain coming from Armenia and the hot summer plains. This will melt the ice off a few feet of the end of the Ark.

Dr. Hewitt's tea felt no need to search above about 14,000 feet, so needless to say we found no evidence of the Ark. Shortly after returning from our second journey Dr. Hewitt died, and from 1976 through 1993 I went on five more expeditions with various groups, including one with simply my son John and myself. On one trip I was fortunate enough to be included in three flights around the mountain in a Turkish Air Force aircraft secured by Apollo astronaut Jim Irwin. The granddad of all Ark searchers, Eryl Cummings, was with us and I believe it was his last trip to the mountain. Both Eryl and his wife Violet have since passed away.

None of these expeditions, including the aircraft search, revealed any clues concerning the location of the Ark. But we were still looking below the 14,500-foot level. Around 1990 I began having serious doubts that the Ark

This is a color copy enlargement of a slide taken across the top of the Ahora Gorge. The Ray Anderson object long piece is circled at the top of the photo. The Ray Anderson short piece is circled at the center of the photo which is the disruption in the Abich II glacier. At the upper end of the disruption is a box-like structure. This is the area specified by Satellite Remote Sensing Analyst George Stephen III and given by Don Shockey and Robin Simmons to Ahmet Ali Arslan in 1989. Arslan photographed the same area and it appears that this Hewitt/Anderson slide and the Arslan photo may be showing the same object. This slide, taken in 1973 (probably August) by explorer Dr. Lawrence Hewitt, appears to show fresh snow on the ground. Note that Ed Behling claimed to see a similar structure in late May/early June of 1973 and the Navy's Al Shappell sighting was in 1974.
Courtesy of Dr. Lawrence Hewitt via Ray Anderson

was hidden below that altitude. By the time of our 1986-87 expedition every square foot of the mountain below that altitude had been thoroughly explored.

During my association with Dr. Hewitt, we had exchanged many photos and slides, including some he had taken on searches before I met him. I have a low-power binocular microscope which can be used to study 35mm slides. It reveals small details not seen even when the slide is projected onto a screen or viewed through the usual viewer.

I decided to take another look at my collection of Ararat slides through the scope and examine the areas above 14,000 feet. About halfway through the slides, I came to one taken by Dr. Hewitt in 1973. As I examined the upper right-hand corner at about the 15,500-foot level, BINGO! I saw what appeared to be a small section of the end of the Ark protruding from the glacier.

I took this slide to a photo technician in Nashville who specializes in enlarging and optimizing 35mm slides. She became very interested in the Ark and spent many hours bringing out as much detail as possible in the object and the surrounding area. Unfortunately this slide was taken quite some

Slide scan of upper Ahora Gorge and Abich II depression 1973
Courtesy of Dr. Lawrence Hewitt via Ray Anderson

distance from the object and the camera was pointed across the Ahora Gorge at another area about 2,000 feet lower.

The technician was able to enlarge the object and its immediate surroundings onto both 35mm and 4 x 5 transparencies. I have studied both of these under my scope for many hours and am convinced it is a small section of the north end of the long section of the Ark.

I mention the long section specifically because of another event that occurred shortly after my find on the slide. I decided to try and contact Ed Davis and get firsthand details of what he had really seen on his trip to Ararat in 1943.

I got acquainted with Ed over the phone, eventually becoming a very good friend with him, and we talk with each other every few weeks. Ed had convinced me that the Ark is in two pieces. He described in detail where the

Photo showing the area of the Ray Anderson long piece object 1989
Courtesy of Ray Anderson

short piece is located in relation to the long piece. That convinced me I should take another look at the original Hewitt slide showing the north end of the long piece. Ed had told me that the short piece is about 110-125 feet of the south end of the Ark which has slid down the glacier about 500 feet below the long piece. It is captured in a large crevasse with one end butted against a rock wall under the ice.

I looked down the glacier to about the 15,000-foot level and there was the crevasse with an object in it that appeared to be a small section of the Ark roof and superstructure. My photo technician enhanced this photo as she had the slide of the north end of the long piece and produced transparencies showing detail that has convinced me that it is the short piece that had broken off the south end of the Ark.

I have seen a number of photos and slides taken of this area during other years, and while the outline of the crevasse is clearly visible, my 1973 slide is the only one with enough ice melted off to show the object. I have seen photos and slides taken in other years that do show the outline of the north end of the long piece, so evidently the ice melts off it quite often.

I am convinced the long piece of the Ark is resting on a rock shelf, inside a bowl or horseshoe-shaped valley, sometimes described as a fishhook. It is at about the 15,500-foot elevation. The short piece is down the slope of the glacier at about the 15,000-foot elevation, and this is usually covered with ice.

I realize that other explorers feel the Ark is at other locations, and I respect their views. I feel that we must all continue our efforts to reach the sites with equipment and witnesses who will be credible to the world. I expect that while the tensions continue to exist around the mountain, none of us will get permission to make ground approaches to the sites.

Our best hope to find the truth seems to be helicopter flights up to the glacier. This, unfortunately, makes any expedition quite expensive and complicated. I believe, however, that God will in his timing overcome all of these problems and allow the Ark to be exposed to the world in order to help people build their faith.

I hope Richard "Dick" Bright will not mind me considering him to be the "bulldog" of Ark researchers. His persistence in the search for the remains of Noah's Ark is nearly unmatched. (I say "nearly" where John McIntosh may be his equal in this regard) This is a much-needed quality to overcome the many frustrations associated with searching for the remains of Noah's Ark.

12

RICHARD BRIGHT

Richard Carl Bright is a professional airline pilot. His education includes a Bachelor of Science degree from Bemidji State University in with major areas of study in geography, geology, and earth science. In some of the courses he took to obtain that degree, he was taught that the doctrine of uniformitarianism and the theories of evolution were, in essence, the basic background of the earth's and our human history. It was in an anthropology class that he began to have some trouble, which he will discuss later.

In recent years I have studied areas of Theology, which I find to be very important in my life, and have led to both a fully accredited Masters and a Ph.D. through external studies. I don't pretend to make any special claims, and I don't do this kind of work for a living. I consider myself still a student, and I love the subject matter. I'm an airline captain. That's what I do for a living.

My involvement in the search for Noah's Ark was in great part due to the impression upon me by Violet Cummings' book *Has Anybody Really Seen Noah's Ark?* There was also the meeting I had with Violet and her husband Eryl, who are now both deceased. Eryl Cummings, a very knowledgeable investigator, was considered by many, as the "dean" of modern Ark research. Then came the meeting with one man who, I believe, had an incredible impact on my adult life.

From the pages of my book *The Ark, A Reality?*, I give you my impressions, as recorded at that time:

I wrote to Mr. and Mrs. Eryl Cummings. Mr. Cummings called me one evening. We set a date and I flew to Farmington, New Mexico, to meet them both. Mr. Cummings, who had been to Ararat fifteen times by then, is now in his eighties, and Violet Cummings is the author of the book that first got my attention. I found Mr. and Mrs. Cummings to be two of the most gracious people I have ever met. I am very thankful for the hospitality and courtesy extended to me. I asked them how I could become a part of the next Ark expedition. How I would go about it? Whom should I contact? One of the names given to me was that of the former astronaut I had read about in the newspaper clipping, Colonel James B. Irwin, a man who had walked on the moon. I wondered to myself how I would ever be able to talk to such a man. I wrote Col. Irwin and he was kind enough to answer. I then called him on the phone, but I was at a loss for what to say. I mainly stuttered; I don't think that impressed him much. I went to his office unannounced to meet him, and I was to find him to be one of the most down-to-earth people I had ever met. He also was most gracious in taking time from his schedule to let me stumble across my words as I attempted to express myself. I stood in awe of the man; I was nervous. Nothing was decided.

Two days later I went to work. It just happened that I had to fly to Colorado Springs for a twenty-minute stop to pick up passengers en route to Denver. This stop just happened to be on my schedule that month. Colonel Jim Irwin was due to fly to New York on business and just happened to pick Frontier Airlines out of Colorado Springs that day. One of the flight attendants, on reserve status, just happened to pick up that trip. She just happened to graduate from the same high school that Jim Irwin had attended years earlier, and recognized him from a picture. She came to the cockpit and to tell us who was on board, and I almost jumped out of my seat to go back to the passenger cabin and reintroduce myself to the man sitting in

Professional Airline Pilot Dick Bright
Courtesy of Dick Bright

the first seat in the first row, Colonel Jim Irwin.

After his flight to Denver, Colonel Jim Irwin and I talked for a few minutes. Then he was on his way to New York on business, and I was on my way to begin one of the greatest adventures of my life.

I had prayed, and had received my answer. It was not to be in 1983. My year to join the team was 1984. Sixteen months would pass from the time I had applied for acceptance as a member of the expedition team until I would at last be on my way. In the meantime, I involved myself in considerable research and physical training.

In preparation for the expedition, I searched eight libraries for information pertaining to anything helpful in finding the location of Noah's vessel. I spent a lot of time looking for a photograph, which reportedly existed, to no avail. I read books by various authors and spent many late nights poring over the pages. I prepared myself physically by losing 28 pounds.

I took instruction in ice and rock climbing and technical procedures, and did quite a lot of climbing by myself, and with others. Long's Peak was the last big climb, and was with Jim Irwin and John Christensen, another member of the expedition.

**Eryl Cummings with Elfred Lee
Painting in Background
Courtesy of Elfred Lee**

I jogged almost daily, with my personal best reaching twelve miles at an average elevation of 9,500 feet. I camped and climbed in rain, and spent a lot of time at the Nautilus.

I wrote to Jim Irwin in June of 1984 and briefed him on my preparations, giving a synopsis of my reading research. I hoped to convey to him my enthusiasm and sincere desire to join his expedition.

At 7:00 A.M. on August 15, 1984, I began what was the first of eight expeditions to the date of this writing. I expect there will yet be another in the not-too-distant future.

I must take a minute here and thank B. J. Corbin for asking me to contribute to this work compiling reports by the explorers of Ararat. In order for me to best do this, I can only relate to the reader my personal experiences. The reader should know that every expedition has proven to be costly, challenging, and disappointing. Each year the names on a team change. Yet, as in quest of a great goal, in body and spirit, we go on. I'm very blessed to be among a group of people dedicated to the search, to the solving of the questions surrounding his mystery.

In my mind, the questions which surround this particular mystery should not cause us to doubt the existence of the Ark, but rather should encourage us to find just exactly where the ship rests, and when God will choose to reveal it. Then, of course there is the question, "Am I to be a part of this tremendous event?"

I include a few highlights from previous expeditions to give the reader an idea of what we went through in our searches. These excerpts are taken from my own book and give the impressions and details of that time. The information presented here is accurate to the best of my recollection.

My First Expedition—1984

It was a peaceful year, and the expedition of 1984 went well as far as the travel and the climb of Mount Ararat was concerned. Jim Irwin, John Christianson, Ridvan Karpuz (our guide), and I were the principals in this attempt. We began near the borders of Iran and the USSR, in Dogubayazit, Turkey, on Thursday, August 23, 1984. Following are excerpts from the record:

We left the hotel at 6:37 A.M., and now we are on our way to Eli village near the base of the mountain. By 8:20 A.M. the horses are being saddled with our packs. The friendly Kurdish folk at the village are filling us full of juice, and the members of the press and the photographers who have accompanied us are in fine form. They are doing what they are paid to do. At the village during the photo session, the lady of the main household of Eli Village was asked to pose with Jim. She originally declined but decided that since Jim believed, she would allow her picture to be taken with him. John and I handed out gum and candy to the children. There were many of them who came back several times holding out both hands for our offerings. That was fun. I noticed that John was particularly good with the kids, and they seemed to love him. I believe it is his gentle, kind nature that attracts the kids to him. In my case, I expect it's the gum. Leaving the village at 9:15 A.M., our four-man operation, plus reporters, photographers, and followers, totaled 16 people and three horses. By 9:30 A.M. we were at low camp, about 10,500 feet (3,200 meters) or so. I'm told that it is time for a light lunch and rest.

The plan now is to sit around all day and get acclimated. I'm very impatient, but Jim is wiser than I and agrees with the guide that we're to sit tight. I must keep in mind that its God's timing that will take us to the Ark, not mine; but I hope it's soon. It is now 7:25 A.M. on Thursday. We went to a river and filled our water bottles. The water was cold and dirty. We had to purify the drinking water with iodine tablets, a must from now on. It's interesting that all of a sudden, water is of such importance. Clean water is one of those things you seem to take for granted back in the States, or in any area of plenty. Friday, the 24th of August, at 6:30 in the morning: We're up and breakfast is underway—a quick one to be sure. We're leaving a duffel bag full of stuff behind, and still we seem to be taking too much with us. The Turks and Kurds kept us awake well into the night; there must have been a party of sorts. It's 9:00 A.M. and we're finally underway. It's a slow start. The reporters are left behind; still one photographer sticks with us. It's noon now and we are at 4,200 meters, which is as far as the horses can go. That's somewhere around 13,800 feet. We made good time this morning, now we will carry our own packs. Our high camp will be at 4,900 meters, which is approximately 16,000 feet. There are a lot of loose rocks and it's a difficult climb. Water is at a premium. It amazes me how these Kurds can smoke so much and still climb like they do. We have a break now, then the toughest climb to come.

By Saturday night, August 25th we had reached our high camp. This is an overview of the day and plans for tomorrow. We made it to camp by noon. We rested until about 1:10 P.M., then we hiked to the west glacier and looked it over from above. We then climbed a finger glacier to search for the wood sighting of which Jim was made aware last year. We found it...a pair of skis

and poles at 16,000 feet on Inonu Peak. We reached that summit with crampons and ice axes. We don't know why the skis are here. I can't imagine anyone actually trying to use them on this mountain. A photograph of the skis at a distance would cause them to appear like pieces of wood, or hand-hewn timber, sticking out of the ice. Were they

**Dick Bright, John Christensen and Jim Irwin
with skis on Ararat's summit 1984
Courtesy of Dick Bright via John McIntosh**

planted to bring Jim back? I wonder why they are here. It's just past midnight early Sunday morning, August 26th. I find it hard to sleep at night; twelve hours is too much. Anticipation of tomorrow is great, and I'm slept out. The temperature is 22 degrees, a mild evening, and the sky is incredible. Stars are everywhere like I have never seen before. Like the lines in a Robert Service poem, "Night's holy tent, huge and glittering with wonderment."

With an early start at 8:00 A.M., we explored the west side on the ice, the north side above the Cehennem Dere (a "U" shaped cut-out or canyon in front of the Abich I glacier on the north-northeast side), above the Ahora Gorge, and across the Abich I and II glaciers to the saddle between Ataturk peak and Cakmak peak. I was looking forward to exploring the northeast area of the mountain.

It is now Monday the 27th at 8:55 A.M. I'm not sure where or how to begin. A lot has happened since my last entry. I'll try to begin where I left off. We were on the saddle between Ataturk and Cakmak peaks. At times we disagreed on some points and I began to wonder if we were under the influence of the principalities and powers the Bible talks about.

Discussion took place on how to reach the northeast side. We had to descend at least 2,000 feet to be near the edge of the ice where I'm sure the Ark must rest. When Ridvan and I unroped and took a walk to look down the ice and snowfields that were to be negotiated, he was not in favor of descending the steep slope. I felt that I could have made it. To me, it appeared as though the trip down would have been easy enough, hopefully not too fast. Climbing back up again, however, might well have been another matter. There was an area of jagged rocks, or peaks that I wanted to get down to, but Ridvan the guide, said "No." At the time, I was beginning to become confused. The northeast area was an area to which I felt we had to go. It was a must, but now, all of a sudden, we couldn't get there.

John and I agreed that the area needed to be searched. Jim wanted us to search the area. But Jim knew we could not get down and back up before dark and our camp was on the other side of the mountain. A plan was devised to approach the area from the bottom. We would need to descend the mountain, circle it, and climb up from that side. A move such as this might have caused legal problems in that the northeast side of the mountain was closed to all climbers.

Although Jim had been given complete search privileges of the mountain we might need additional police approval from Dogubayazit, the town and area whose jurisdiction we were apparently under. Also, Ridvan mentioned that it would take more time than we had, to negotiate a hike to that side, search and return. There was confusion and some disagreement. In retrospect, we probably should have moved the camp and stayed another day. However, we descended.

The trip down was exhilarating. We spent four hours and forty minutes on the descent to base camp.. The ascent had taken two days. We dropped our packs and ourselves for a few minutes rest. Then, in preparation for the rest of our day's journey, we changed boots and clothes while drinking several bottles of pop that a few enterprising young kids had packed and offered to us for a price. We then descended from base camp to arrive in Eli village at 10:10 that night. From there it was a pickup and van ride to Dogubayazit.

On Monday, August 27th, we received news that a British climber had been shot somewhere on the north side of the mountain while climbing alone. Reports of who shot him, or why, varied from the military, because of improper papers, to bandits, to villagers, for any number of reasons.

Jim and John had planned to stay for only two more days because of schedules and other commitments. There were no teams left on the mountain, and those that had been there had not been allowed to search—just to climb on the south and west sides. If I alone had stayed to continue the search, my guide would probably have been replaced, as he had a schedule, too. Chances are the replacement would not be able to speak English. Even had I been able to get a permit to continue the search alone, it probably would have been a sport permit and not one for research. I decided to leave with Jim and John. At that time, I did not have definite plans to return to Ararat. Because of time constraints and decisions made, 1984 was a disappointing year. But that was only the beginning of the Ararat experience.

Second Expedition—1985

My second trip began August 12, 1985. I said an emotional good-bye to my wife and daughter and was on my way to Ararat once again.

We had heard that Bill Crouse and his Probe Ministries group were chased off the mountain by an armed band of Kurdish terrorists. All of the group's equipment was burned or stolen. John McIntosh, one of the Crouse group, was reportedly waiting for us in Dogubayazit, near the base of Ararat. Whether he wanted to join us, or just to brief us on the activities at this point, I did not know.

Mount Ararat rises above the streets of Dogubayazit 1985
Courtesy of Bill Crouse

On this trip we had a big group of climbers. There were twenty-four climbers in all. Six were on a research permit which would supposedly allow us access to all areas of the mountain in our search for the Ark. Eighteen climbers signed on with a sport permit which would only allow them to climb the mountain on a guided tourist climb, using only one path to climb the south side of the mountain to the summit and back down again.

There was a report that there was a lot of melt-back this year. That would possibly make the Ark easier to find. That is assuming, of course, that it was there for someone to find. It is our belief that it is. Now all we had to do was wait for the mountain to open. The military had shut down legal access to it, while they attempted to solve the terrorist problem.

Upon our arrival in Turkey, Jim had scheduled meetings with the local police about additional permission needed for our climb. He was also to meet with the Agri Army Corps Commander, but it turned out the commander was out of town. Permission from the Army was necessary because of the current military operation. Even though we had received our government-issued permits, Jim and Ridvan spent four hours with the local authorities while the rest of us enjoyed sightseeing, bread by the homemade loaf, meysu juice, and watermelon (karpoos). Finally, we were again underway to Dogubayazit.

The road was dusty, and the ride was rough. Passing traffic as we hang on the side of the pavement or on the shoulder, which normally drops off rather quickly into a ditch or a canyon. This while going as fast as possible, with the driver continuously honking the horn. Little villages situated near the roadway occupy what seems to be a semi-fertile, tawny-colored landscape with scattered flocks of sheep, while the low-lying "mountains of Ararat" flank us on both sides. We view piles of hay and teams of horses and wagons, an occasional tractor, and the local farmer cutting his crop by hand sickle. Finally, late in the afternoon, Mount Ararat was in sight.

Mount Ararat towers above the landscape in all its glory, the undisputed ruling citadel, magnificent and beautiful in the western sun and clear skies. It is purple in the distance, crowned with the splendor of its white ice cap. The sight of the mountain, strong and majestic, sends chills across my spine. This is an incredible mountain; I had almost forgotten the power in its awesome appearance. We met John McIntosh who reported that the situation was not exactly positive. Jim needed to see the Army Corps Commander in Dogubayazit. The situation on the mountain sounded serious, and it was now doubtful the military would solve it anytime soon. Still, I was not overly concerned. We have more than two weeks to accomplish our task.

The terrorists seemed to be in control of the mountain. Apparently, they were Kurdish Communists seeking to have their own republic, and had chosen Mount Ararat as their own territory. To a certain extent, I can understand the Kurdish situation. Terrorist activities, however, are not welcome in the Republic of Turkey.

Margaret Kahn, in The Children of Jinn, explains it in the following way.

Kurdistan is a real place with its boundaries in the mountains of Turkey, Iran, Iraq, Syria, and the USSR. It has its own cities and language, even a national anthem. The Kurdish population outnumbers the combined populations of Denmark, Norway, and

Sweden, but Kurdistan has a way of appearing and disappearing. The last few decades of modernization have seen the Kurdish people fighting for their lives, and control of their land. The Kurdish people are fighting for recognition in a self-determined struggle, and the Communists are there to help.

Fortunately, only a very few have accepted their help, and are intent on establishing their new government on Mount Ararat. I'm sure these people have grounds for a legitimate complaint, and maybe should even raise a fuss, but this, no doubt, is the wrong way to go about it, and I was not too excited about their timing. The Turkish military was apparently having a difficult time finding the terrorists. I guess that's understandable, as the mountain is big, and places to hide are many.

Our group was ready to climb. However, the Turkish government wouldn't approve our climb because they wouldn't take the responsibility for our safety. The publicity would not be in the best interest of the Turkish government if they could not control their own territory. Neither would it be good publicity if we were to come into harm's way. If this terrorist group intercepted our large group, led by Jim Irwin, and we were to be detained, all the news services would soon be aware of the situation. The cause of these Kurdish terrorists would receive worldwide publicity, especially with ABC coming to town and CBS already here. A meeting was arranged between Jim and General Varol, the Army Corps commander. I was at the meeting. The general initially promised his support. However, subsequent "required" meetings with local police and local Jendarma officials cast a shadow of doubt on the seriousness of that support.

There were several phone calls back and forth about the size of our group and our exact intentions. We intended to climb the north side of Ararat with military protection. Since the Ark is reported to be near the edge of the ice on the northeast side, several people on the sports team would actually be involved in the search—those that would make it to high camp. We felt that since there were fifty or more commandos and only eight terrorists who had actually been seen at any one time that the protection should have been adequate.

While waiting between phone calls, we listened to stories about who the terrorists were, and that one of them had killed seven people. When the decision was finally made, the mountain was to be off limits until August 22. (We were there on the 16th.) We were told there was a military operation on the mountain, which was the reason for the closing.

Most of the team was scheduled to return to the United States in about eight days. Consequently, they would not be able to climb. It was a time of anger, disappointment, and disgust at the situation and the powers that be in the offices of the Turkish authorities. Perhaps we should have been happy that the authorities wanted to keep us out of harm's way, but that was not the case. We wanted to climb no matter what the Kurdish separatist threat was claimed to be.

Finally, on August 23rd, with only the six members of the original research team remaining and available to climb, we received permission to climb—with an armed escort. The team members were Jim Irwin, John McIntosh, Elfred Lee, Dr. Ole Honningdalsnes, Bob Stuplich and me. A guide was also with us. His name is Ahmet Turan. There were also a number of Turkish soldiers.

By Saturday, August 24, we were at Eli village at Ararat's base. There were no children begging for candy this year and the presence of the heavily armed Jendarma reminded us that photographs were forbidden. A French and an Austrian team joined us. A *20/20* news team that was in Turkey to monitor our progress wanted to get us on film, and was trying to negotiate with the military to at least take our pictures as we were walking out of camp. None were allowed. Jim observed this exchange, but regardless of what he may have thought about it, he wisely thanked a military officer for providing our security, and we began our climb. We were allowed to climb the south side of Ararat—not the north side as we had desired, but at least it was on the mountain. We intended to work on the rest of it later.

Finally, at 5:36 P.M. (long after our scheduled departure time of 9:00 A.M.), our group, totaling in the neighborhood of sixty-one people, plus ten horses was at last under way.

Before continuing, let me assure the reader, and especially the Turkish people, that the climbing experience depicted in this chapter, is written from my personal and timely point of view only. It was written during, and shortly after, the heartfelt emotions of a difficult and troublesome time. My impressions of the events were without a doubt influenced by the struggles of the delays and the climb; nonetheless, they were my impressions, and I give them to you.

There is no intent whatsoever to insinuate that the government or the military of Turkey was less than cooperative with our efforts. If that had been the case, we would not even have been allowed into the country, let alone be protected as we were. We owe them a debt of thanks for their efforts.

At our first camp we were allowed no fires and no flashlights but I wondered why. The terrorist attacks had all been in the area of 4,000 feet higher than we were. I wondered if the Jendarma would be with us the next night when we really might need them. We found that our "escort" would take us only to approximately 3,200 meters, or about 10,500 feet. Here, they would wait for food to be brought to them, and we were to go no further.

After a series of delays, it turned out that the military unit along to protect us was not prepared to go on. This was in part because they hadn't brought along any cold weather gear. Eventually the military stayed behind at

3,200 meters, but allowed us to climb further, taking the guides and horsemen whom came with us.

We arrived at 4,200 meters and found the remains of many burned tents, packs, and other camping and climbing gear strewn all over the place. Piles of dried camping food littered the site of one of the burned tents. This camp had been hit by terrorists just two weeks prior to our being here. The Probe Ministries expedition group was the fortunate folks to survive it, and our own John McIntosh was there. If the terrorists would return now, they would meet

Explorers Roped Together Hiking up from Mihtepe 1983
Courtesy of John McIntosh

no resistance. Our military "protection" was camped at least one thousand meters (over three hours) below us. We had shown Ahmet Turan, our guide, photographs of the northeast side, and the area in which we intended to search. Turan seemed to understand completely, and agreed. To this point at least, everything seemed to be okay, and we had been approved by all the necessary authorities for our area of search. The only restriction was that we couldn't take pictures. Turan had been talking about leaving all cameras behind when we left on the next leg of the climb. If this happened, we still had Elfred Lee, our artist and illustrator, and he had brought his pencil and paper.

We moved on early the next morning. Jim, Ole, Bob, and I started out first, along with Ahmet. John and Elfred were to follow behind us after packing the campsite and would later join us on the ice. Ahmet was in contact with the Turkish military by walkie-talkie, and about three hours into our climb, he received instructions that would cost us nearly half a day. We were not to be separated and were to wait for John and Elfred.

We realized that we were wasting time while sitting still. Knowing that this may cost us a half-day because of the new instructions, Jim made a decision that was of great sacrifice to himself, John and Elfred, but was designed to be a great time saver for the purpose of the expedition. He decided to go down and meet John and Elfred, and tell them they had to go down with him to the soldiers' camp, thereby freeing Bob, Ole and me, with Ahmet, to continue our climb. This was the only way Ahmet would agree to climb and save the time we so desperately needed for our search. We had prayer, then Jim began his descent. Bob, Ole, I, and our guide (who, as far as I was concerned, was playing his walkie-talkie entirely too much)—we were now on our way up.

My notes and memories of the next part of the climb are sketchy at best. The incline was very steep, and with 60-pound packs on our backs, it seems our energy level was somewhat taxed. We were climbing on rocks that roll with every other step. Sometimes one step up takes a climber two or three steps back. There were the occasional small rockslides to contend with, and along with the increase in altitude, comes the decrease in oxygen; the heavy physical workload proved to be a real challenge. Ole is quite the climber, but he was hard to keep awake. He scrambled fast for a few yards, and then sat down to rest, then began to fall asleep because of the altitude. We would holler at him, he would get up, scramble a little further, sit down, and go to sleep. This happened over and over again; I've never seen anyone climb like he does. Bob is steady and strong, and led the three of us. Ahmet had a light pack and climbed, or scrambled, way ahead of us. He would then sit and wait for us, who were more heavily laden, to catch him. Ahmet was in pretty fair shape, and had climbed this mountain many times over the last 20 years. For me, it was a difficult climb. My notes read like this: "Tough climb for me. We're near 16,000 feet now, on the ice—next, the ice cliffs—cold wind—slow going—slight mountain sickness—must overcome—3:22 P.M."

We finally got on the ice, and with my crampons on, the climb became a little easier for me, even though the slope was quite steep, but Bob and Ole were concerned about my chest congestion, which was beginning to get worse. From my notes: "I've got a headache—I'm not feeling very well. We're above 16,000 feet, just below the summit." (The goal here was not to get to the summit, but rather to go around it and down to the northeast side, to set up camp before dark) also, "We won't be able to do much searching today—a little slower than planned—I am the reason for that."

As Bob, Ole and I decided on our strategy for accomplishing this, Ahmet got on his walkie-talkie again. He came back with this short and shattering statement: "Northeast is forbidden!" The military establishment at Dogubayazit had decided the northeast side of the mountain, the area of our search, our reason to be there, was now off limits and forbidden.

At first, I didn't think there was a problem, as Bob and Ole were the first to understand what Ahmet was saying. Ahmet, at our most earnest request tried again and again on that radio of his to convince those on the other end to come up with another decision, but it was like talking to the wind; the answer was always the same. Bob got on the walkie-talkie and tried to reason with the military on the other end, asking that we just be allowed to camp on the other side of the summit, and get out of the wind. Ahmet tried again, then I took a shot at it. I mentioned that Jim Irwin had permission from the higher echelons of command at Ankara, Erzurum, and even Dogubayazit. Still, the answer came back "forbidden."

We had not come all the way to Turkey, waited at the base of the mountain, and delayed our climb for nearly two weeks, all at a great expense financially and emotionally, then risked our lives at the possibility of a terrorist attack, and endured the hardships of the climb, just to get a few hundred yards away from the northeast, our prime goal, to have some person in a stuffy office tell us our goal was "forbidden!"

Bob decided we should go to the summit and take a look. I wasn't at all interested in going to the summit. I could not have cared less, but it would give us time to think, which was what Bob had in mind. We dropped our packs and climbed the 500 feet or so to the top of the big mountain, and signed the book, which was encased in ice. We also wrote a word or two about being disappointed that we could not continue our quest.

From the top, we could see where Ridvan and I had stood the previous year, on the other side of second peak. We were five minutes from that spot, and maybe twenty to thirty minutes from the jagged peaks I had seen the previous year. We could see the place we wanted so desperately to set up our camp and begin our search operations. The word for the day now seemed to be "forbidden." Bob said he had agreed with God in prayer that if the Turkish government wouldn't allow us to go to a certain area, then he wasn't going to go. Bob has a cool head. I don't know exactly what Ole said. I just remember he was not exactly happy with what was going on.

We stood on the 17,000-foot summit of Mount Ararat, had a lengthy discussion with the people on the other end of that walkie-talkie, then, we did as we were told. Had we not done so, the situation might have gotten worse. Still, I am not convinced all the decisions we made were the right ones though making wrong decisions could impact research years down the road.

We descended to a protected area in the rocks around the 15,300-foot level, set up camp, and slept on it. We hoped that by tomorrow the problem would just go away, and we could continue on. This move took us further away from our goal, back in the direction from which we had just come. As I look back on it, this did us little good psychologically. We were concentrating then on just finding a place to camp in the protection of the rocks, but it was a retreat.

It took us about an hour or more to descend to the rocks where we had decided to set up camp. The wind was very strong. I think out of the southwest, and we were on the south side of the mountain. Setting up a two-man tent became a four-man job. We were cold. My head ached like the devil, and I was congested to the point of concern. Bob and Ole were concerned; I wasn't yet fully aware of the potential problem. We didn't eat anything. No one was hungry. Bob said he was cold; he had chills, and was going to bed. This seemed like a smart idea. Ole bundled up in every piece of warm clothing he had, then crawled into his sleeping bag. We all settled down for a long, long night.

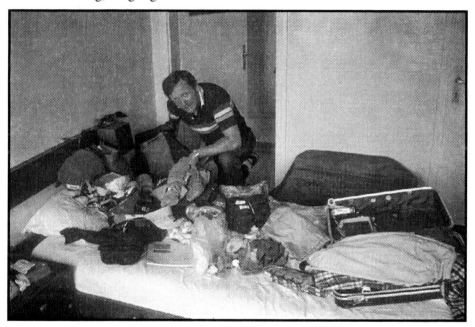

Dick Bright packing for his climb up Ararat
Courtesy of Bob Stupliich

Bob suffered alternate bouts of chills and sweating, and probably fever, with no sleep at all throughout the night. I began to cough, a cough that seemed to start from somewhere close to my toes. I had been diagnosed as having a touch of pulmonary edema by Bob, the experienced mountaineer, and as also having a virus, by Ole, the doctor. Ole had given me pills to combat pneumonia. I understand pulmonary edema has to do with a leakage of blood plasma into the lungs, and its early symptoms are similar to those of pneumonia. All I knew was that I had an aggravating cough that I hadn't had a few hours earlier, and also one heck of a headache. It seemed as though an invisible someone was continuously hitting me on the head with a club. I was aware that this miserable headache, on which painkillers seemed to have little effect, was a definite sign of mountain sickness. Ole gave me a sleeping pill that put me out for about 3 hours, and that helped. It helped Ole too, as we were in the same tent. Bob and I had a long night, and Ole slept. I have to admit that I wasn't really concerned about Ahmet. The wind howled and the temperature dropped. I couldn't seem to get warm.

The morning found us not only thankful the night had ended, but also somewhat depressed. The weather on this morning however, was very good. Other than that, my body hurt from a cough that seemed to mean business, and my head still felt as though someone were beating on me. My lips were chapped and bleeding, and the Blistex was frozen.

At 8:00 A.M. Ahmet came back with his radio report that said that it was still forbidden for us to go to the northeast side. I don't know if we really cared. By this time we just wanted to get off that mountain. But we would certainly have gone back up and over to the northeast, had permission been granted. I'm sure Bob and Ole still had the reserve to get there, and I would have stumbled along too, but the word was "forbidden" and we, for some reason, were playing by the rules. We descended the mountain and were probably in the area of 12,000 feet when we were suddenly given permission to return to the summit and continue our search. We didn't have the strength.

We looked at each other and then at Ahmet. I could do nothing but shake my head in utter disappointment. We knew there was no way we could go back up there, we just didn't have the strength. I felt as though we had been taken. It was as though we were the victims of a cruel joke, and the prankster had no intention of allowing us access to our area of interest. But he was able to save face by now making it legal for us to do so. Our inability to accomplish this was, from this point on, no longer prevented by limitations put on us by the Turkish military. They said we could go, but we were too weak, too sick, and out of time. There must be another explanation for this behavior of the authorities. The rest of the day passed with very few words. Blisters, sore toes, dehydration and fatigue accompanied us the rest of the way down the mountain.

We were later told that terrorists were again on the mountain and that had been the reason for withholding permission for us to go further. Whether this is true or not, I don't know. Disappointed, we went home. Elfred Lee later stated that he was on a flight with the American Ambassador to Turkey Robert Strausz-Hupé. When Lee asked the Ambassador about the team being asked to go back down the mountain he stated, "The Soviets were engaged in military maneuvers near the border and Turkey has an agreement to be outside a 20 kilometer zone from the border when that occurs whereas we were 14 kilometers away. Also, there was a serious terrorist threat and because of his high profile, they were looking for Jim Irwin and coming up the other side of the mountain."

Third Expedition—1986

In 1986, I was a member of two expedition teams. The first one we called the "Summit Expedition Team." There were three of us on this climb. The first was Ron Lane, a retired lieutenant colonel in the U. S. Army Rangers. Ron lived in New York and was employed as a civil engineer. There was Ahmet Arslan, guide and translator, who holds a Ph.D. in International Comparative Folklore. Ahmet lived in Washington, D.C., where he was a voice on "Voice of America" to Azerbaijan. I was third. We were also expecting Dr. Ole Honningdalsnes, but he had not arrived by the time we were scheduled to leave.

On August 9 we began our long ascent on Ararat. Everything seemed to have gone quite smoothly, except that I was concerned about Ole. He was at least a day or two behind us, and we didn't have time to wait. We didn't want the mountain to close before we were able to climb. We left a letter of explanation at the hotel for Ole, and a guide will meet him right away as soon as he arrives, to assist him with the paperwork and the climb to join us.

Fortunately, we didn't have the restrictions placed on us by the military that we had last year. But we were told not to take pictures of the local inhabitants. The reason for this seems to stem from a picture of the Kurdish villagers which is said to have been published in a French magazine depicting how the people of Turkey live. It was embarrassing, and not necessarily an all-encompassing, accurate portrayal.

Our research permit allowed us the opportunity to check our state of health as we climb. Each hour or so, we recorded our pulse, altitude, time of day, and state of health. Medical doctor, Ole Honningdalsnes was to be in charge of this, but since he wasn't there, we improvised.

Ron is having trouble catching his breath. He had had heart trouble in the past, and this was beginning to become a concern for the three of us. By Ron's own choice, he elected to stop at the 3200-meter camp (10,500 feet). He reasoned that Ahmet and I could climb faster without him, and the plan was to move as quickly as possible. A group of Kurdish horsemen stayed with him. I know he was disappointed, but it was better for him to rest than to be in a bad way higher up the mountain. I know.

B.J. Corbin Handing Candy to Eli Villagers with Deborah Redmer Looking On 1988
Courtesy of B.J. Corbin

I remember the bad shape I was in just a year ago. Perhaps Ron's condition would improve after some rest. He seemed to require a lot of water, and may be dehydrated.

The Summit Expedition now consisted of just Ahmet Arslan and me. A Moslem and a Christian climbing and living together for a week, facing together the moods of Mount Ararat, in search of Noah's Ark.

Ahmet and I, along with one Kurdish horseman and two rock-scrambling donkeys carrying our packs, reach the 4200-meter camp (approximately 13,800 feet). We had made excellent progress, and the Kurdish horseman stuck right with us. I'll never understand how those mountain Kurds can climb as they do and still smoke so much. I seldom see a Kurdish guide without a cigarette in his mouth.

It is good that Ahmet and I hadn't stopped at the 3200-meter camp, as it could have affected our morale. We had climbed 1000 meters higher on this first day than I had in either of the two previous years. This had been a good day for Ahmet and me, though not quite as profitable for Ron. Ahmet said we must stay here and acclimate for a day and two nights. For me, the impatient one, this would be a long rest.

While we spent a day resting at the 4200-meter camp, Ron had climbed up to join us. In his weakened, exhausted condition he had climbed and struggled alone for eight hours to reach us. He climbed for two reasons: first, to satisfy himself that he had met the mountain with his best effort; second, to let Ahmet and me know we didn't have to return at a previously decided date of August 16. Since he was the only one with a timetable requiring an early departure from Turkey, he would make his own arrangements, first to get down the mountain with the aid of another guide, then on his own go to the nearest airport, which is in Erzurum. I was proud of him. On August 11, Ron saw Ahmet and me off, before beginning his own descent.

Ahmet and I reached the summit and took the usual tourist pictures. Then we headed toward the place, which was to be our high camp near Cakmak Peak. It is the area just below this peak, the area of jagged peaks, that I thought so intensely interesting just two years ago. We arrived at Cakmak with only one minor slip. Ahmet fell to his knees in a crevasse, but got out easily. By 4:20 P.M. our camp was set and we were resting. I was now utterly exhausted. The night was one of very little sleep, ferocious winds, and temperatures cold enough to freeze solid the water bottles we had inside our tent.

The next day, loaded with climbing gear and cameras, we roped up and proceeded toward the head of the Ahora Gorge, the top of the pie-shaped area, and the small jagged peaks we wanted so much to search. I walked down the steep ice slope to the jagged peaks (with Ahmet belaying me), the rocks of which top a vertical drop into the gorge. At the edge of the rocks I looked straight down about two miles, and into some of the adjacent canyons.

Then, moving the anchor to several other vantage points, we searched with binoculars. For an hour and a half we searched. Our cameras photographed everything in sight—east, west, and down, trying to catch hidden areas on film. It is my belief that any areas we might have missed were too small to have hidden a ship.

We noticed one object on the east side of the gorge, and quite a bit lower

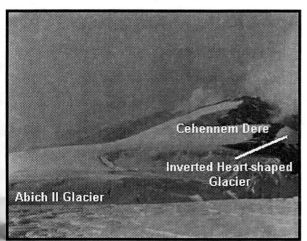

Photo From East Summit Overlooking Upper Ahora Gorge 1988
Courtesy of B.J. Corbin

down than our position. There appeared to be something resting on a ledge. I was more than willing to attempt a closer look at this object, but Ahmet succeeded in talking sense to me. He said the soldiers would see us, and if we were caught, we would, at the very least, be arrested. After an attempt to warn us three times, they could shoot at us. I wasn't concerned about that, but when he said that the shepherds would surely see us, and that they would shoot at us just for sport, trying to hit our legs. I decided that I probably should think it over just a little while longer. (In retrospect, I now doubt that would have happened. Ahmet simply didn't want to go down there). A solo descent and climb back out wouldn't have been wise on that steep ice. It takes two people and a rope. Ahmet wasn't about to go. The object on the ledge might be something to get a closer look at as soon as government restrictions are lifted, and we're legally cleared to search that area.

I was looking in the direction of what could well be a very special area of the mountain—the east side of the Ahora Gorge on the northeast side of Ararat, which is closed to climbers, and where the Ark may well be permanently parked. What sense did it make for me to be there if I couldn't go down there and take a closer look? Ahmet insisted that we not go down. It was illegal. So again, for some reason, I obeyed the rules.

If God had brought me here, then I believe I was here for a purpose. If this is only my idea, then I guess I'm just here. I did feel close to God, closer than in any recent time. I thought then that this must be his will. I prayed that this trip to the top of this mountain of rock and ice was not just my idea, but that He had a part in it. Did He? I don't know. I prayed very simply: "God,

You are all wise. If You'll show me Your big wooden boat, then maybe through this book, it will have an impact on a few lives, even mine. But, if this is not to be, if this wasn't your idea, then you know that I'm just here, and I guess, on my own. I have tried to do what I thought I was meant to do, and I've done my best. Whether it is your idea or mine, thank you for bringing me here."

On the next day, August 13, we left the first plateau and descended to the Parrot Plateau for our look into the west side. We traversed the ice and crevasses in sort of a zigzag pattern, trying not to slip. We could hear the water running under the ice, and knew that if we slipped and fell, we could start some of this loose stuff moving, and possibly start an avalanche. We were roped together for safety, and thanks to the crampons we had strapped to the bottoms of our boots we did not slip.

Upon reaching the plateau and an area of rocks on the west side, we removed our crampons and walked the rocks, managing to get a good look across the gorge to the east, and up across the Abich Glaciers to the pie-shaped area at the head of the gorge. My notes state the following.

We crossed above the heart-shaped glacier, moving in a westerly direction. We were between the Cehennem Dere and the heart-shaped glacier, when I asked Ahmet to stop. I wanted to drop down to the very edge and look straight down in an attempt to see what was below. This area of the mountain holds a high interest, not only to me, but also to most of us who search for the whereabouts of the large vessel. Ahmet says this is a dangerous area. I remind him that's the reason we have the rope. We found a "bomb-proof" anchor in two boulders leaning against each other. Three long pieces of webbing tied together and threaded through the space below, where the boulders come together, and wrapped around one of them, eliminate the possibility of the webbing skipping over the top. Two carabiners, a third just for a little something extra, a figure eight connected to my harness with the rope in between, and I was on my way to the edge of the ledge. Ahmet fed me the rope as before, and asked if I were planning to rappel down. I said I'd take a look first. Ahmet told me to be careful. We joked. "Ahmet," I said, "You've got my life in your hands. It'll be a piece of cake." "Yeah," he said, "New York cheesy style."

I walked about 50 feet down to the front edge of the heart-shaped glacier to what appeared to be a conglomerate rock outcropping that stuck out about 25 feet beyond the ledge. A conglomerate is usually made up of many small rocks cemented together, normally by some type of water action. Ahmet says these rock outcroppings are known as "shaky-teeth" that is, they have a tendency to fall out.

I told Ahmet to put some more tension on our three-millimeter rope. (A 3mm. rope is a little small but it will hold a thousand pounds, and is lighter to carry than a larger rope.) That he did, to the point I had to pull just a little slack. I walked out on the conglomerate outcropping, and looking straight down and beyond the ledge of the plateau, I could see another ledge. I looked left and right, and saw only rock. I moved out toward the end of the formation, and because the wind was strong, I lowered myself to crawl on my hands and knees. I was thinking that Ahmet is very capable with the rope, and I'm glad he's there, but just in case my educated Moslem friend needs a little help, I said quietly, over and over, "Jesus, Jesus, Jesus, Jesus." It was a prayer. I looked below, left and right, anticipating to see what I was after, but the canyons in my view held only what appeared to be rocks, and the glaciers to my right were heavy with snow and ice. I saw shapes that were interesting, but as far as I could tell, all I saw was rocks and ice.

Except for descending the east ridge, or dropping down from the Parrot Plateau and into the canyons below, we had done all we could do from here. To drop into the canyons would be against Ahmet's promise to the military, and put us closer to the Kurdish mountain people who, no doubt, would not revel in our being there. We would have to get the necessary permission from the Turkish authorities to legally enter the area.

It took us two days to descend from the domain of ice and bitter winds to the blistering heat of the plain, on which is built the village of Dogubayazit. Ahmet made the statement that in his 21 years of climbing this one was the toughest. We had covered a lot of area in the time we had spent on the ice. We had given a determined and concentrated effort to the search. I was pleased we had worked together as well as we did. We made a good team. My only problem was in agreeing to obey the rules.

Fourth Expedition—1986

At 3:30 P.M. on the 20th of August, a Lufthansa flight from the United States and Germany arrived in Ankara. On the plane were Jim Irwin, Mary Irwin, Bob Stuplich, Bill Dodder and Bob Cornuke, who had arrived to start the second phase of our 1986 expedition to Ararat. I met them at the airport. This phase of our expedition was to attempt to fly around Ararat, locate the Ark, then climb the north side of the mountain to locate the structure.

Upon arriving at the Hotel Apaydin in downtown Ankara, we were greeted by Eryl Cummings, who had come to Turkey for the purpose of negotiating to arrange the flight around Ararat. With Eryl were two gentlemen, Mr. Eran Cakir from the office of the Department of Interior and Mr. Mahittium Baskam from Shell Oil Company. The Department of Interior is above all the police, Jendarma, all the offices of tourism, and of foreign relations in Turkey. Eryl, Jim, and Mary had been informed, in confidence, that permission had been given for us to climb the north side, but we must wait until August 25. There was to be a change in command at Kars, the controlling Jendarma facility for the north side of Ararat, and our climb

Chris Roningen Watching Guy Leduc Toss a Snowball
Past B.J. Corbin at Mihtepe 1984
Courtesy of B.J. Corbin

would be discussed with them at that time. Meanwhile, there was a moratorium on the mountain for all climbers.

We discussed using a Cessna 206 or a Cessna 421 from the Em-Air Flying Service in Ankara to fly around the mountain to see and photograph as much of the mountain as we could in the meantime. This could be done either in conjunction with our climb, or before it. The flying service said we could have the C-206 on the 27th of August for three days, at the minimum pay rate for three hours flight time per day. In addition, we would pay for the flight from Ankara to Mount Ararat and back, plus for a truck required to carry barrels of fuel into the area.

It's 7:30 A.M., August 21. Jim and Mary asked for our company (all of us) in their room for a conference. Direction is given to each of us for the day's activities, with each of us having something to do. Items of high priority concern the possibility of flying the C-206. We have decided to use the C-206 mainly because of cost savings over the C-421, and because of its better visibility due to its high wing, versus the low wing of the C-421.

In a nutshell, here's the plan. The plane, a Cessna 206, is loaded with two 50-gallon drums and one 25-gallon drum of fuel, with the seats folded and carried as baggage. The pilot alone will take it to Erzurum early on the morning of Saturday the 23rd. Bob Stuplich, Eryl Cummings, Ahmet Arslan and I will drive a rented van all night to arrive in Erzurum sometime around 8:00 A.M. We will then refuel the aircraft from the barrels of fuel which were its cargo on the flight over. We would fly from Erzurum to Ararat, an hour and a half away, spend up to three hours flying around the mountain, and return to Erzurum, arriving with at least one hour's fuel remaining. That would total six hours of flying in an aircraft that holds seven hours of fuel. Hopefully, in that time with the weather cooperating, we would be able to find and photograph the remains of Noah's Ark. The plane would then return to Ankara. Price? $1,575 minimum. Permission for this project was denied by the Turkish Civil Aviation Authority.

There were many problems with obtaining the required permission over the next few days. There were problems too with scheduling aircraft availability. It would take pages to list it all. Six days later, on August 27, Eryl and I met Jim, Mary, and Ahmet, Willem Van Schaayh, a Dutch cameraman, and Jan Van Den-Bosch, an official of the Dutch Christian Television Network at the Erzurum airport.

The Cessna 206 that we had rented arrived and I got a special clearance from the airport authorities to go out on the ramp and meet the pilot, Engin Akaltan, and the mechanic, Alisan Soylu. Also, for my own peace of mind, it was a chance to look over the airplane over. Engin Akaltan from Ankara, was the well-qualified pilot. A former fighter pilot, he had 500 flight hours in Cessna aircraft, 300 of them as an employee of Em Air. He also seemed to understand English pretty well. I was pleased with that. I, unfortunately, do not understand the Turkish language and have to rely on English-speaking Turks in order to communicate. The mechanic, Alisan Soylu was the head of the maintenance department of Em Air, and had a few other jobs in the operation of the company. He had an excellent command English and could act as interpreter when needed.

Alisan told me that we had the necessary Civil Aviation Authority's

Kurdish children doing back breaking work
Courtesy of Bob Stuplich

approval for the flight over Ararat. That was wonderful news! After talking with Engin, I mentioned that I would ride as his copilot, and probably encourage him to fly where I wanted to go. Engin and Alisan agreed that would be just fine. I looked the airplane over, and I must say that I was pleasantly surprised. It appeared to be very well maintained.

The following day, August 28, after what seemed like interminable delays for no discernible reason, we received the authorization to fly. We were told we could take off at 3:00 P.M. However, there was another problem. The airport closed at 5:30 P.M., and we wouldn't get back until after 7:00 P.M. According to the rules, we wouldn't be able to land. It was an interesting turn of events. We had permission to take off, but now we needed permission to land. The Army Chief of Staff and the Governor of Agri say it is okay to fly at 10:30 tomorrow morning, if we can't take off this afternoon. We contacted the Governor of Erzurum asking him to keep the airport open, and allow us to land a little late. We must fly today. They might change their minds tomorrow.

We lifted off shortly past 3:00 P.M. that same afternoon. The Cessna 206 didn't perform as I had hoped it would. The opening in the aircraft's fuselage, and the spoiler, which is a six-inch wide strip of aluminum, 90 degrees to the air flow (to help direct the air out around the photographers) caused extra drag, and worsened the aircraft's performance. We circled the field once, climbing at 300 feet per minute. I suddenly realized that of all the flight time I've logged over the past 19 years, this might well be the flight of my life! By 4:30 P.M. we had reached 14,000 feet, and Ararat was in sight.

At 5:00 P.M. we crossed over the west glacier of Ararat. As we flew over the ice rim of the Cehennem Dere, and by the Abich Glaciers, I looked up to the 16,000-foot peak, the top of the pie-shaped area atop the Ahora Gorge, and saw from a different perspective the area on which I had stood just 16 days earlier. We were doing what some people had wanted to do for many years. We were searching for Noah's Ark by air, and we had two still and one motion picture camera to document everything we could hope to see, everything, including the remains of a big wooden ship.

We crossed the gorge at 15,500 feet, and made a 180-degree turn just past the east ridge. There were clouds over and beyond this point. I wished the clouds had not been there, but we took what pictures we could and were thankful for them. We flew back to the west with the sun in our eyes. We made the next pass at 15,300 feet, directly over the edge of the ice, looking at the rocks below. Each pass we made was two or three hundred feet lower than the previous one. We were getting a closer look at the terrain, and testing the air for stability and effects of the winds. We wanted to make sure that if we caught a downdraft, or ran into severe turbulence, we would be somewhat prepared for it.

With each pass, the cameras recorded what we could see. Up to this time, Engin and I had taken turns flying. Now, Engin was doing the flying, and also doing his job exactly as I was telling him to do. Turn here, turn there, slow down, fly at 80 knots, stay here, drop 200 feet, let's go try it again, do this, do that. Whatever I asked of him, Engin did, and did very well.

We crossed the heart-shaped glacier and Cehennem Dere—it seemed just a few feet above the ice—in order to get a better look into the canyon areas below. The canyons weren't as open to view as I thought they would be, and the long shadows of the afternoon didn't help. We were looking for a dark object in the dark rocks covered in the shadows of the early evening.

We had flown the mountain for 50 minutes, and no Ark had been seen. We were due at the airport by 6:30 P.M. We knew we'd be late. I didn't much care; I guess I was disappointed. We didn't see the Ark, but, of course, that didn't mean we didn't have it on film. Only a slide-by-slide and frame-by-frame inspection of what was photographed would determine this.

At what we guessed to be approximately 20 minutes before landing, Engin called the airfield and we found we had "special permission" to land. That was nice, but I don't know what else they could expect us to do. We sure couldn't stay up here all night waiting until the airport opened in the morning. Nor could we go anywhere else. We had one hour's fuel in our tanks, and the next closest airport was over an hour away, and was military. I can't imagine the permission we'd have needed for that landing! We touched down in Erzurum at 7 minutes past 7:00 P.M. It was sundown.

Friday, August 29, 1986, we were at the airport by 9:00 A.M. when it opened, prepared to make a second flight. Em Air had ferried enough fuel from Ankara to allow us two flights to the mountain. If we could get permission to buy fuel from the military, we were prepared to make two flights on this day, so everyone on our team would have an opportunity to fly, and photograph. The military said, "No!" Also, our permit had been put on hold. The governor of Erzurum said we did not have the proper authorization to fly on this day. He didn't have any written authorization from the Army Chief of Staff, so he would not allow us to take off.

We were then told that we hadn't had the proper permission yesterday. We had only had verbal permission, and not written permission. Apparently, the chief of staff hadn't signed the proper piece of paper. It had only been reported that he had. Everyone was supposedly in trouble. Apparently, there was so much red tape to go through to authorize this flight, that someone got tangled up in it, and sent out the wrong information. We had not been given the permission we actually received.

The following morning, August 30th, we were arrested by the police and our film confiscated. Our rooms were searched and the team of police entering Ahmet's room took not only the film he shot over the mountain, but also rolls of film he had shot of his family on vacation. This was

Turkish tanks south of Ararat guarding the border area
Courtesy of Bob Stuplich

understandable, as they had no idea which rolls of film Ahmet had shot over the mountain, and which he had not, but it made Ahmet angry. They didn't trust or believe him, and he's a Turk.

The police even took Willem and Jan's unexposed film. It irritated Willem when they delayed in giving him a receipt for what they took. Bill Dodder is the only tourist among us who didn't bring a camera—hence, no film. Bob Stuplich and Bob Cornuke also lost their unexposed rolls of film. Jim and Mary's room was searched. There was no film there for anyone to take. Some tempers were beginning to flare a little by this time, but not Jim's. He was as cool as he always is.

I had left five rolls of film on the plane in a little blue pouch. One of the Turkish policemen who had searched the plane tossed my blue pouch, with the film still inside, on the bed in Ahmet's room during the search. I casually walked over, picked it up, and put it in my back pocket. Then, I stepped out into the hall and stood there. In about five minute's time, there was a frantic search for my blue pouch by at least four men. Ahmet translated their concern, and asked if I had seen it. I said, "Yep!" They all gathered around me and asked, "Where is it?" I said, "Right here." I pulled it out of my pocket and handed it to them. This thwarted an emergency of some sort, I'm sure. Then, I went to my room, and a police commissioner searched through my climbing gear.

We were later to get the film back—at least most of it. What we did receive back had been developed by a Turkish photo lab and viewed by the authorities. We were actually held under house arrest and were not permitted to leave the hotel. The events of the next couple of days fill a complete chapter in *The Ark, A Reality?*, but rather than drag the story on here, I will

Eastern Face and Ahora Gorge 1988
Courtesy of John McIntosh

simply say that we were released from house arrest in due time and had a party to celebrate. It was a combined celebration—that of our release, and a birthday party for Jan Van Den-Bosch.

As an apology two bouquets of flowers were presented to Jan by members of the Turkish press. The gesture was accepted and appreciated by him. The press represented a fine people in a country plagued by a very complicated bureaucracy. Ahmet summed it up when he said, "Our people are embarrassed by the police action, and I must say what has happened doesn't reflect the sense of the nation." I don't know if this was a kind exaggeration, or not, but I do know that the feeling at our table was one of "All's well."

Bill Dodder led the group of us in a very special grace. We stood with clasped hands around the table and sang a victory song: "Stand up, stand up for Jesus, you soldiers of the cross." Ahmet, the friend on my left, sang right along with us.

Fifth Expedition—1987

In 1987, I went to Turkey again. John McIntosh and I met in Dogubayazit. Ole Honningdalsnes was there as well. It turned out to be a time of interviewing (through an interpreter) a few of the local citizens to determine what they knew, or were willing to tell us, about the location of the Ark. The results are recorded in my book. The bottom line for that year, is that after eleven days in Turkey I left for the United States. Why? Because permission for us to climb was denied.

Sixth Expedition—1988

On September 3rd, 1988, I once again arrived in Dogubayazit, Turkey. In my pocket I had a copy of a letter from the Turkish Embassy in Washington, D.C., that read: "I wish to inform you that you/your team have been granted permission to climb Mount Buyuk Agri (for expedition purposes) on the basis of the application forms you submitted to this Embassy." The mountain referred to is Ararat.

The letter had been written to John McIntosh, and I was to be a member of an eight-man team he was to organize and lead. That particular expedition had been canceled, but not the permission to climb, which was valid through the month of September. My name was included in the letter as a team member, so to this point at least, I had permission to do what I intended to do. I had been through this before. The second paragraph of the embassy letter requested that the Directorate of Security of the Turkish Province be contacted in order to obtain an additional permit.

The expedition McIntosh had intended to lead was canceled, in part because of a snow cover on Ararat that was heavier this year than in recent years, making discovery of the Ark less likely. After the expedition was canceled, John, who then expected to enjoy a complete summer in sunny California, was asked to join a very small group whose plan was to fly completely around the mountain in a helicopter. Having accepted this great opportunity, John was also in Dogubayazit, Turkey. He was now on a permit to fly, and for him it had become another expedition entirely.

John flew, and the snow was heavy; nothing was seen. In fact, the day after I had arrived in Dogubayazit, it had snowed. No doubt that anything I was looking for on that mountain was now hidden under its new white blanket. The highlight of the year for me was in a jeep ride up the mountain to a shepherds' camp and back again.

Early in the morning of September 5th, I left Dogubayazit in the company of two new acquaintances in an old, beat-up, four-wheel drive vehicle. To honor their request, I will not mention their names, nor will I elaborate on the details of the venture. I will only say that I was looking for an "open door."

We stopped in the village of Igdir and purchased a fair volume of fruits and vegetables. I wasn't planning a feast; they were to help extend my hand in friendship. We then drove toward the city of Arilik. The Soviet Union, its border area, and the city of Yerevan were on our left, and the northern side of a white, snow-covered Mount Ararat was on our right. Weaving to dodge potholes, at least some of them, we passed cars, trucks, tractors, hay wagons, horses, oxen, cattle, sheep, pedestrians, bicycles, buggies of various types, wagons, and even pushcarts. It was a normal drive on an average highway in the far reaches of eastern Turkey.

We left the main highway and proceeded on small dirt roads and trails toward the big white mountain that seemed to appear larger than I had ever seen it before. We drove through villages constructed of stone and mud and surrounded by haystacks and pyramids of animal dung, the fuel chips used to heat the home and cook the evening meal. There were green bushes and a tawny landscape in the sunlight of the morning. We drove alongside and in riverbeds, several of them, then across fields and rocks; four-wheeling will never be the same. I wondered how the skeletal frame of the human body could handle it.

After passing a few shepherds' camps, sheep and sheepdogs, we arrived at a certain camp a short distance up the lower slopes of the mountain. I was welcomed after an uplifting introduction by my new friends. The hosts accepted our gifts, and I was invited to their tent. I took my shoes off before I entered, in accordance with the local custom, and then I was extended the comfort of a rather large pillow to sit on. We ate. Naney lewas and penir, a bread and cheese combination, along with chi (tea), stabilized my stomach after the thrilling ride I had just experienced. Then we had an interesting conversation.

I was told there were many, many soldiers on the mountain. This was because of the activities of the Kurdish terrorists, or freedom fighters, depending on whose point of view you were speaking from. Since my new friends were not able to interpret for me to the extent that I was able to understand, I do not know the shepherds' point of view. I had no intention of taking a political stand of any sort on that situation, so I didn't question them about it.

I don't have a well-informed point of view to express on the matter of terrorists or freedom fighters. However, my experience with the Kurdish people I have met has been one that I have thoroughly enjoyed. They have always treated me very well, and I admire their family unity and the contentment with their simple, slow-paced lifestyle. To visit a shepherd's camp is to step into the pages of the distant past. The "giving" hospitality and courtesy extended to me, a guest in their land, is far superior to much of what I've seen in the fast-paced, selfish, sophisticated, complicated, cosmopolitan world to which I am accustomed.

I asked the shepherds if they knew where the Ark was. The response was very encouraging. It was, "Maybe." I asked, "Will you take me there?" The elder person of the group said, "We have never seen it; we hear that it is there. We have not allowed anyone to go there." I responded, "But, will you take me there?" He replied, "This is the Kurdish freedom fighters' war area against the Turkish soldiers. There is killing. Many people have died and it is very dangerous to go there." I wasn't sure if the elder had said terrorist or freedom fighter, but the one who was doing his best to interpret said "freedom fighter." That could have been his own opinion. He did appear to be one with a tendency toward rebellion. It is quite probable that if he hadn't had this tendency, then he wouldn't have taken me to meet these people. The fact that there is killing would certainly be a valid reason for the Turkish military to want to keep people out of the area. No doubt, they wouldn't appreciate it if I had gotten in the way. I might have had a problem with that myself.

The shepherd told me, "There are so many soldiers on the mountain that a bird can't fly by without being seen. You cannot go any higher on the mountain without being seen or stopped."

I answered, "You mentioned that you have never seen the Ark. Do you know anyone who has?" "No," he said. I asked, "Then how do you know that it's there?" He said, "We hear that it is there."

I asked, "Where is it?"

"It is in a place where it is very steep and one must be very brave to

John McIntosh and Dick Bright 1988
Courtesy of John McIntosh

climb to it. It is above steep walls where there is a flat area that changes every year, or it could be in another place that never changes, and looks like ice."

It became apparent through conversation that they did not know where it was. They had mentioned two places. The description of both places made sense to me. I was not convinced that they knew where the Ark was, but I was convinced that they all believed that it was on the mountain.

We had more discussion as to where they thought the Ark may rest, but having failed to bring a picture of the mountain with me, and the mountain being now shrouded in clouds, it was difficult to determine what they were saying to me. I drew what I hoped would be an illustration of the mountain, and had one of the shepherds mark the spot, but he marked two spots with big circles. That didn't help much, but it was a lot more than I had before I made the trip. (At a later time I would conclude that the two circles could have been drawn to represent two pieces of one broken ship.) I was reinforced with the shepherds' belief that the Ark was indeed on the mountain. It's an encouragement to continue on. The "open door" I had been looking for led me to those nice people, beyond that, the door was closed. I had an inner peace about it.

In the late afternoon, as we made our way back down the slopes toward Arilik, seemingly from nowhere an army vehicle appeared and out of it piled about fifteen armed soldiers. They spread across the road and ditches and it looked as though an encounter was inevitable. My three Kurdish companions were in the front seats while I was in the back with two climbing packs. We pulled to a stop and as the soldiers approached us, I could sense a little tension coming from the front seat, but not so much as to draw attention. I was sure the focus was going to be on me, and what I was doing there. Then, of course, there was the matter of the climbing packs. We pulled to a stop and the soldiers approached us.

As I am an American and not Kurdish, I was not supposed to be on the mountain. If I were found out, it would no doubt have caused me great difficulty. However, By God's grace, I was somewhat prepared for this potential meeting. To explain: Many of the Kurdish men wear a sport coat or a suit coat and pants that reasonably match, even when they are in a shepherd's camp. It's common attire, and not to be dressed this way would almost always tend to draw attention. As it happened, because of my desire to partially assimilate with the Kurds for communication purposes, I was dressed that way. I wore a wrinkled and dirty brown suit coat and a pair of pants that almost matched. I had a faded shirt on under the open jacket, my hair was a mess and my face was dusty and dirty from the day's activities. One of the Kurds said I looked like a "yellow-colored Turk." The Army looked us over, never said a word, and let us "shepherds" pass.

Seventh Expedition—1989

In 1989, I was in Turkey again. I spent some time near Ararat but was not allowed to climb. I didn't return to Turkey again until 1993. There were other expeditions during the intervening years in which I did not participate. Chuck Aaron and Don Shockey each had a team. Jim Irwin was there again. It was to be his last trip. You see, there was one event that hurt me deeply. My friend, and mentor, Colonel James B. Irwin had a heart attack and left this world in August of 1991. I had just spoken to Jim a few days before it happened. I was leaving the country to fly a trip to Europe when I called him. Jim was peddling a stationary bike and talking to me on a speaker phone. Jim's heart stopped beating twenty years and one day after his return from the moon, August 1991. I miss Jim Irwin and think about him often.

Eight Expedition—1993

Ararat and the search had been on my mind every year since '89. Still, I probably wouldn't have gone in '93, except that I had been encouraged by a few people to lead a team on another search. I must have been ready because a considerable amount of planning went into the expedition. I really jumped in with both feet this time. Our team originally consisted of twelve people and was called "The Search for Truth."

Truth is, it began to unravel the day before we left the States. We had intended to use a subsurface radar unit to look into Ararat's ice and locate the Ark if the melt-back of the summer hadn't left it at least partially exposed. However, a freak accident during a systems test left the radar unit inoperable. Consequently, two members of the team who were to operate the radar, remained in the states. Ten of us crossed the ocean. One man from our group, Al Jenny, a manufacturer and businessman from Cocoa, Florida, went to Moscow. He intended to do research on the reported Russian sightings of years past. In Moscow, Al managed an interview with a science/religion magazine and asked its readers for information pertaining to reports of previous Ark sightings by Russians. He succeeded in obtaining two reports from relatives of soldiers who had taken part in the 1917 expedition to the Ark, which had been ordered by the Czar Nicholas II.

The reports also mentioned a Russian flyer that had seen the ship. This information gives credence to the much-debated Roskovitsky story first published in the New Eden magazine about 1940. In this story, a Russian flyer saw the ship and reported it to his commanders. Upon verification of his sighting, word got back to the Czar, who then sent a 150-man expedition team to climb Mount Ararat and locate the structure. It was found, photographed, measured, and documented, but the information was lost as the Bolsheviks took over in 1918. With this new information, it does indeed seem that there is some truth in the Roskovitsky story and that it was not totally fabricated as some modern researchers now contend.

The rest of the team ran into considerable difficulty. The next few paragraphs are from the 1993 "Search for the Truth" report.

We departed our homes to join up on August 16th in Newark, New Jersey, where eight of the twelve-team members met. Present were Gary and Barnett Duce, Ray Anderson, Al Jenny, Richard Perkins, Joe Presti, John McIntosh, and myself. Missing was Ross Wutrich who would join us in Antalya, Turkey one day later. Ron Lane was delayed because of a painful back problem.

The eight of us arrived in Antalya, Turkey on August 17th. By the time we had arrived, the Kurdish workers Party, an illegal workers party, otherwise known as the PKK, had increased their offensive action dramatically. Thirteen foreign hostages (tourists) had been taken and, quite possibly, eleven of them were on Mount Ararat. People in eastern Turkey were being killed. These included local residents (mostly Kurdish) and Turkish military, along with Kurdish terrorists. The situation had become volatile and that turn of events was definitely not in our favor.

The terrorists (PKK) have claimed to be fighting for a place of their own. For centuries Kurdistan has been a nation without borders, a people living mainly in the mountainous areas of Syria, Iran, Iraq, parts of the former Soviet Union and Turkey. They have their own language and songs, but no official country of Kurdistan. Naturally, there has been some suppression of this vast group of people by the governments of the lands they live in.

The PKK have taken it upon themselves to violently change this. However, they realize that an independent State of Kurdistan, which would primarily be located in eastern Turkey and northern Iraq, and maybe other places as well, would not receive the financial benefit that Turkey offers them. They now want recognition and to be provided for. I am told by the Turks that as Turkey builds its economy and tries to increase the economy of eastern Turkey, the PKK ruin it. They blow things up and kill even their own kind. They raid Kurdish villages and kill people they claim to be fighting for. The Kurdish have their own story, somewhat different then the Turks, but I won't get deep into politics in this writing.

Because of this ever-present problem, obtaining permission to climb again appeared doubtful, and the backing we had from certain senators and congressmen in the U.S. didn't necessarily have the positive impact we had hoped for. I spent a week in Ankara bouncing between offices of the Turkish ministry trying to obtain the necessary paperwork.

This was actually my second trip to Turkey in '93. The first trip, a month earlier, was in part to ensure the required permissions would be granted. There was no guarantee then, but there never has been, even in years past. I had the assistance of a reputable Turkish citizen, Mehmet Noyan of Attalos Travel, Inc., of Antalya, who was to walk the papers through the proper channels for me. I also met with the U.S. Ambassador to Turkey, Richard Barkley, and Mr. Gursan of Em-Air who owned two helicopters.

On this second trip, I was told the problems with the PKK in eastern Turkey were getting worse. A major concern was for our safety. On the one hand, that we wouldn't get killed, and on the other, that we wouldn't get captured by the PKK. An excerpt from the '93 report read:

The bottom line here is that neither the Turkish government nor the U.S. Embassy will take any responsibility for our safety. The easiest thing for them to do is to deny our requests for research permits and assistance in obtaining them. Turkey will deny us in such a way as to politely encourage us to leave the country. I spoke with Mr. Akin of the Office of Foreign Affairs and I told him we would take that responsibility on ourselves and give it to God. Then they wouldn't have to worry about us. But that didn't do much good. He said they would not allow us to be responsible for ourselves.

Beyond that, Mr. Akin was most kind and hospitable, but offered no encouragement at all. He said that the ministries, five of them, have our applications, and that they will each have to make a decision. I asked which ministries had the applications, and was told that he couldn't tell me. He did say that a rejection from any one of them would be a rejection from all.

Even though he didn't tell me, I found out that, in addition to the Office of Foreign or External Affairs, there are also ministries of the Chief of Staff, Internal Affairs, the Erzurum Governor, Turkish Security (like our CIA), and Education and Culture. We were told that we must wait. I assumed that the process would take time—too much for our stay.

The Turks might have had a dilemma, of sorts—they had letters of support from members of the Congress and Senate in the U.S. and they had the Embassy, whose main interest was to see us out of the country— What to do?—Wait! They would wait us out until we had to leave the country and go back to the U.S.

In addition, authorization was needed from the Civil Aviation Authority before we could fly the helicopter. The helicopter itself was not up to the job I had contracted it for. The "job" was to lift what was now a nine-man team to the ice cap of Ararat, let us do our job, and then to get us out of there again. From the '93 report:

If we do see something that needs investigation, will we be allowed to land on the mountain? Will we even have a helicopter that can do that job? The pilots are firm (so far), in that they can't land any higher than 4,000 meters, which is only 13,200 feet. On Ararat, that's PKK country. We must land on the ice at 4,400 meters minimum (14,500 feet) to be above the danger to the team members and the helicopter. Then, there's the problem of weight. I'm told they can take only three passengers at a time to 4,000 meters. Therefore, a shuttle would have to be set up, which would then subject some members of the team to the PKK possibility as they wait at a lower elevation in order to go in the chopper.

None of this is satisfactory. The MI-8 helicopter under the Em-Air registration operated by Attalos Travel cannot do the job I contracted for. The answer had to come from the Ukraine in the form of the M-17 helicopter. It is bigger, and is powerful enough to do the job. Ersan, the number two man at Attalos Travel was supposed to be working on this while Mehmet and I were in Ankara. If we could not arrange the use of an MI-17, then I would have to find a way to convince the Turkish and Russian MI-8 pilots that the job could be done. I would get the aircraft performance charts myself and work with them to figure it out.

If we were not allowed to land, I believed the MI-8 does have the power to reach 5,000 meters (16,500 feet) and fly around the mountain with all of us on board. The aircraft's service ceiling may indicate less than 5,000 meters, but if we were light enough, I believed it could be done. I believed therefore, that as a last resort, a visual fly-by would be possible with the helicopter we now had. But how would I handle it if we saw something that needed investigation? We would find a way!

On Friday morning, August 27, I was in the office of the chief pilot, Mehmet Sakir. He and I and a Russian captain studied the manuals and talked about what his twin engine MI-8 helicopter could actually do. They seemed to be stuck on this 4,000-meter figure with only three people on board (plus the pilots) for a high landing capability. I did my best to convince them there is a safety factor built into the performance charts and the aircraft would perform better if they pushed it just a bit. We added in a wind factor and found that just 15 knots of wind would allow the MI-8 to make the landing at 4,400 meters with three people in addition to the pilots. They were reluctant, thinking they wouldn't have 15 knots of wind, but I assured them that we would. It's windy on mountaintops!

We were making progress. However, there was no way I would accept a landing at 4,000 meters. That's PKK country, and below the ice at 4,000 meters would put the team and the chopper in jeopardy.

If the MI-8 were used, we would land three of us, then the chopper would shuttle a second three-man team to follow the first three. The second team would be a four-man team if the wind were strong and the chopper performed well above their expectations. Two men would not get on the mountain, but they would be able to see Ararat, as we all would, on the initial fly-by. All nine of us would then be on board. I knew that the fly-by was possibly all we would get. The landing shuttle might not be approved, but we had the plan just in case. Because of the concern for the safety of our team regarding the PKK, the shuttle would have to originate in the security of the Kars Airport, just over 40 miles from Ararat.

Time, as expected, along with the other problems we were experiencing, began to be a factor in the possibility of an expedition. It had been two weeks since we had left the States, and the return trip was scheduled in just a few days. Still, we refused to give up. Also, the more powerful MI-17 helicopter would not be available to us. It would have to be the MI-8. From the report, our expedition attempt:

Monday, August 30th: This morning, I wore a jacket and tie to the Attalos Travel office. I told everyone at breakfast that it was an "attitude change day." Because I was doing my best to hide a deep concern, the positive outlook was probably going to do me more good than anyone. I asked Ron and John to join me and we went to the Attalos Travel office where we met with both Ersan and Mehmet and discussed the flight. Sakir, the Turkish chief pilot, was there, and he fell back to the concern surrounding the landing. I was tired of dealing with this. Ron and I simply laid it on the line. We told him: "We are landing at 4,400 meters. Period! You figure out how you're going to do that, but that's what we will do!"

I then told Mehmet that we expected a green light in the morning. We wanted the flight to take off at 11:00 A.M., fly to Erzurum, and on to Ararat with two fuel stops along the way. (We had already considered our route of flight and were ready to file it with the Civil Aviation Authority.) I said,

"Tomorrow is the last opportunity for the entire group. We have to fly tomorrow. Plan on it!"

That night, I prayed with the team and planned our flight. I shared with them that we would have the word by 11:00 A.M. and we would leave then. It was a faith thing. We still did not have permission.

Tuesday, August 31: I'm in Mehmet Noyan's office by 9:00 A.M., and we're on the phone to Mr. Akin in Ankara. I asked him, "When can I expect the permission?" He replied, "One of the ministries has said 'No.'" He wouldn't tell me which ministry. The phone call ended. Okay, now that we've gotten that answer, how do we get around it? I need a miracle!

Then, Mehmet got mad. He phoned the President of Tourism in Turkey, Mr. Basaram Ulusoy. I'm not sure what was said because I don't have a clue how to understand that language. All I know is that whenever a Turkish man operates a telephone in an agitated state of mind, he gets very loud!

Fog looking down from Mihtepe 1990
Courtesy of B.J. Corbin

I so believed we were going to get this permission that I think I had convinced Mehmet as well. We actually had the pilots standing by at the airport preparing for an 11:30 departure with the flight plan already filed! Mehmet had a van driver standing by to take the team to the airport, and we still didn't have permission. Mehmet ended his phone call seemingly in utter frustration that nothing could be done.

Then, the door opened! Mehmet Sakir, the chief pilot, informed us that the Governor of Erzurum had gone on holiday and a very good friend of his was the army commander of that region. Mehmet said the commander was now in charge of everything that happened there with regard to permissions out of Erzurum.

We knew that we could legally fly as far as Erzurum without any special permission. It was east of there that was the problem. Sakir called his friend and spoke with him for just a short time and the word came back, "Yes!"

It was a verbal approval and in a few short minutes, due to the marvelous invention of the fax machine, we had written approval. The restrictions were that we wouldn't be allowed to fly below 9,000 feet (so we wouldn't get shot down,) and we wouldn't be allowed to take photographs. It would be a visual flight around Ararat only.

We were on the move—two weeks to the day from our arrival in Turkey. The Bible verse from Isaiah 40:31 spoke to me in a big way: They that wait upon the Lord shall renew their strength—they shall mount up with wings as eagles. Finally, at 5:08 P.M. We lifted off!

I noticed something very special. The registration letters of the helicopter were TC-HER. I read it as "Touch Her." Mount Ararat is known by the Armenians as Masis, the "Mother of the World." We wanted very much to touch her. I expected we would.

I got out of my seat and walked up to the cockpit and watched the crew perform their duties. The nomenclature of the flight instruments, switches, and circuit breakers were all in Russian, so, much of what I was looking at I couldn't quite figure out, but I did recognize the vertical speed indicator, the altimeter, and the air speed indicator. The engine instrument needles were all registering in the green arc (or blue, as it was,) and this told me that both engines were performing very well.

We climbed at about 145 km/hr (90 mph) to an indicated 4,450 meters or approximately 14,685 feet above sea level. We were heavy with three pilots up front, three relief pilots in the back, and nine team members, plus a lot of heavy luggage and a full load of fuel. Sakir told me that the helicopter was performing very well at this altitude.

We landed at the Adana Airport at 7:15 P.M., while it was still legally daylight, because the rules specified that we could not fly at night. We spent one night at the Sedef Hotel and were up by 4:15 in the morning. By 5:55 A.M. we were in the air again. In the early dawn we saw the full moon as the sun reached to try and find its way above the horizon in a clear sky. I watched the blades of the blue and white MI-8 spin above me as they lifted this grasshopper-shaped machine upward. Below, the valleys were shrouded in fog that wove its way into a blanket of white sprinkled randomly with specks of green, as the trees tried to claim the early dawn.

This particular helicopter had been the private aircraft of the onetime Soviet President Brezhnev. A thought occurred to me: Wouldn't it be ironic if this machine, once operated by an atheist government were to be the one to carry a Christian team who would sight the structure of Noah's Ark on the mountain called Ararat?

We rode above the top of an overcast and were "on top" till mountain peaks pierced the blanket of white on either side. Then, at 7:25 we saw the terraced green hills below, along with a river. We touched down on Runway 31 at Elazig for a fuel stop that took longer than anticipated, but we used that time to modify our plan.

Originally, we had planned the next leg of the flight to go from Elazig to Erzurum, then have a fuel stop and go on to Kars for a landing. I had wanted to fly around Ararat before landing in Kars. The legs would go as such: Elazig to Erzurum to refuel, then Erzurum to Ararat on a fly-by, and on to Kars for a landing. The pilots had argued that the helicopter didn't have the range. They said what I wanted to do would have them landing at Kars with less than minimum fuel and the Russian pilot who was the aircraft

Bottom - unknown, Don Shockey, Yuri (pilot), Carl Baugh, Robin Simmons, Walt Brown, George Adams Top - unknown, crew, unknown, crew, Ayfer (flight attendant), unknown, unknown, Ron Charles, B.J. Corbin very top Ed Cassidy and Turkish co-pilot 1990
Courtesy of B.J. Corbin

commander said, "No." They wanted to land in Kars first, refuel, then fly the mountain.

The Russian, who was in command of the aircraft, knew the machine. He was supposed to know the range it could fly. He was to have a fuel reserve on board when he reached his destination and he had to plan the flight appropriately.

However, as I studied the map and figured the distances involved, I believed his educated guess on the amount of fuel, which would be remaining after an Erzurum-Ararat-Kars flight, was an especially cautious one. I think he was extremely conservative and wanted a very large reserve of fuel upon landing at Kars. I believe the flight I proposed, which included a quick fly-by of Ararat, then a landing at Kars, could have been made with an adequate reserve of fuel. The captain had said, "No." In retrospect, I think he and I could have discussed this further. Still, even if our discussion had reached an intense level, he was the captain; what he says is law. I certainly understood that.

I knew also that a fuel truck had been dispatched to meet us in Kars and it should be waiting there when we arrived. To the best of my knowledge, the military authorities in Kars were not part of this permission game yet, so we could possibly get in and out of Kars en route to Ararat before they stopped us. There was also the fact that according to our "permission," this was to be a visual fly-by of the mountain; no photos. However, I wasn't about to go along with that. We had our cameras. During an inspection by the military at Erzurum, our cameras, (those not very well hidden) could be confiscated. Bypassing Erzurum may indeed be the right plan. Because the chopper captain had said, "No" to the Erzurum-Ararat-Kars flight, I had proposed, and because of the reasons just given, I decided to bypass Erzurum and go straight to Kars. I believed we would be able to do the job from Kars as long as we moved quickly.

At 9:30 A.M. we lifted off and climbed above the rugged terrain enjoying an eagle's-eye view of eastern Turkey. A few puffy summer clouds accented the hot summer sky. Then flashes and smoke of artillery or tank fire were seen somewhere in front of us. We were about to touch down in bandit country. The PKK and the Turkish military were at war. At 11:46 A.M. we touched down at the Kars Airport. I had known the airport was reported to be secure so we hadn't tossed away safety, but I hoped the security police would leave us alone just long enough for us to refuel and take off.

We looked for the fuel truck, but it was nowhere to be seen. Sakir went to phone the company in Antalya to find out what happened to it. Ersan told Sakir that the fuel had been dispatched out of Erzurum and was supposed to have left there by 8:00 this morning. The condition of the eastern Turkey highways would mean a four-hour drive for the fuel

Doris Bowers in white surrounded by Kurdish villagers amazed by her blonde hair 1983
Courtesy of John McIntosh

truck. According to its timetable it should arrive at any moment. We waited, and waited some more.

Time dragged on and the pilot said it was now too windy to fly. I disagreed. He said he had just talked with a police chopper pilot and the policeman told him that it was too windy. Now we were getting the police involved. This was not a good sign. Sakir said that it was getting too cloudy. Well, the summertime convectional buildups can be expected, but from where we were, we couldn't see Ararat. We didn't know if it were covered or not. I didn't agree with that excuse, either. Then he said that the airport closed at 5:30 and that we could never get back by then. Sakir said that we would have to pay a fine.

I remembered the flight in 1986, when two Turks, a Dutchman, and I flew Ararat in a Cessna 206. We arrived in Erzurum after the airport had shut down and that probably contributed to the authorities' closing down our flight and not allowing us to fly the next day.

I quizzed Sakir on how much the fine would be. He didn't know, but he was tired and the flight was shut down for today. We had been awake since 4:15 in the morning, so he was probably tired. It was 3:00 P.M. and the fuel truck still hadn't arrived. A military officer who could speak some English walked up and asked to see all of our passports. I guess he was Passport Control. Then he asked to see my permission. I showed it to him. He looked at it, said it wasn't enough, then asked to take it. He promised to copy it and bring it back to me. I just smiled, said "Of course, you may copy it." I gave it to him and said nothing else. He smiled and walked away—with our permit.

That evening, when Mehmet Sakir showed up at the Turistik Hotel Temel in Kars, where our team had checked in, I was informed that the fuel truck had arrived and the helicopter was now about ready to go. The seats were being removed to lighten the aircraft and theoretically help our climb. I was then informed that the base of the mountain we wanted to land on top of was under artillery fire from the Turkish military and that aircraft were bombing PKK targets in the same vicinity.

We had been invited to dinner at the Turkish military officers club (at our cost) which we were enjoying when the Military Passport Control officer who had taken our permit walked in with a couple of other officers. Sakir and they sat together near me and had a conference. After about half an hour, the military officer turned to me and said, "I don't think it is a good idea to fly. A military operation is starting and it's very dangerous and we cannot give security." I replied, "We fly." The military officer then handed back the permit and said, "No photos, no landing, visual okay." That meant that we could still fly. I thanked him and smiled. Shortly thereafter, we thought it was best that while we were still ahead, the team should leave and return to the hotel. We thanked everyone and did just that.

It turned out that on this day and the previous day, in addition to the killing of a number of PKK, several Turkish soldiers were also killed. Eighteen were killed in the border town of Aralik in an ambush and twelve more were killed, apparently by a mine, as their truck drove over it while they were on the way to help the eighteen. Thirty-four soldiers were killed in a fight, primarily by a missile, or missiles, fired from the hidden areas of Ararat's base. It seems our timing for this trip was really lousy.

During the night, the local police chief had found out about us and arrived at the hotel demanding to see the pilots. I'd seen it happen before when we were able to get military permission, but some police chief would stop us. It had happened to me in 1985, and 1989, in Dogubayazit on the southern side of Mount Ararat.

Also, during the night, and on a larger scale, Iran attacked Armenia in defense of Azerbaijan. This angered the Turks who were friendly with Azerbaijan. If anyone were to help Azerbaijan, the Turks wanted it to be themselves, not the Iranians. The main reason the Turks hadn't come to the aid of Azerbaijan was that they were waiting for the go-ahead, or for some action, from the United Nations. That action hadn't yet happened.

The border of Iran and Armenia is only a short dozen or so miles from Mount Ararat. Turkish troops were pouring into the area and they were on alert. This was not good for us. What was good for us was that anticipation ran high, and we expected a great day—we were greatly excited about what we believed would happen. Also, Ron woke up without a back pain for the first time since before he left the States to join us. This, too, was an answer to prayer. Everyone felt great!

About 5:00 the next morning upon reaching the helicopter we found it to be surrounded by armed policemen. We were then told that the governor of Kars had ordered the police chief to stop our flight. The stopping of our flight wasn't legal, because we had prior permission, but that was only my point of view. The permission we had was from the army commander in Erzurum. Up to now the military authorities in Kars had also allowed us to continue, but now the town cop had gotten the governor involved. Had the fuel truck been on time, and if there had been no war, we could have flown yesterday.

However, this was today, there was a war, and now we were in Kars. The governor of Kars had not been asked for his approval for our flight, and he didn't like that. We were told to wait until 8:30 or 9:00 A.M. until the governor arrived. Sakir was in an argument with the policeman present, and then on the phone to the police chief, but to no avail. We were not allowed to board the chopper and complete our mission.

Time passed, policemen came and went, and Sakir went with them to speak with the governor. We waited. There was silence and the team rested. More time passed. The local military commander showed up and took an interest in what was going on and decided he would see that we didn't go anywhere any time soon. Also, a telex or a message of some sort had come down from the powers that be in Ankara to order that our flight be stopped. Things were rapidly going from bad to worse.

We were ordered to fly back to where we came from and abandon the mission. They insured that we would do that by putting a policeman on the chopper with us to be our onboard escort. I became convinced then that it was time to pull back as far as Erzurum and regroup. Also, telephone contact out of Kars to Antalya in an attempt to reach Mehmet and Ersan was extremely difficult. Phone connections in the larger city of Erzurum should be better.

We landed in Erzurum and I checked us into the Grand Erzurum Hotel. We stayed there that night and into the next day. We were then told by Attalos, the people who owned the helicopter, to return to Antalya. Permission had been revoked for us to continue our mission. The telex from Ankara stood. Our expedition was over.

No Expedition—1994

In 1994, there were no expeditions to search for Noah's Ark in eastern Turkey. Instead, there was only war. Still, I was in the country. I went to Turkey during July to renew friendships and as a fact-finding trip. Ultimately, I learned (as had been expected) that because of the conflict between the Turkish military and the Kurdish separatists, no permission to climb Ararat would be allowed by Turkish authorities.

No Climbing—1995

I was in Turkey during August of 1995. Again, because of the conflict, the military would not allow me to receive permission to climb Ararat.

No Climbing—1996

Ron Lane, a very good friend of mine, died in 1996. I met Ron in 1985. He and I were members of Jim Irwin's team. Now, like Jim Irwin before him (1991), my friend's body rests in Arlington Cemetery. Both had been military officers—one a lieutenant colonel and the other a colonel. Ron had been on the 1986 and 1993 Ararat expeditions. Ron was there whenever I needed him. He was the publisher of my book. Like Jim, I'll miss Ron a lot.

An expedition was proposed for an American team to both fly a helicopter and climb Ararat. Included in this expedition were up to four Turkish climbers and Turkish Mountain Federation guides. We called it the "Turkish-American Scientific Quest" (TASQ). The American ground team was composed of three climbers, a photo documentation expert, a climber who was also a computer expert and myself. The helicopter team consisted of another photo documentation expert, a science teacher who also knows his way around a camera and an eyewitness of the Ark's location. An archaeologist was waiting "in the wings." Did I say an eyewitness?

A minister, Vincent Will, of Springfield, Missouri tells us that he saw Noah's Ark in the late summer of 1944. At that time, he was a young military man, an avionics technician on a flight from Italy to the city of Yerevan in the former Soviet Union. Yerevan sits near the base of Ararat. The pilot of the C-47 (DC-3) knew of reported sightings by other pilots of what appeared to be the remains of a massive barge-like structure locked high in the ice cap of Mount Ararat. Taking advantage of the opportunity afforded them by the military flight, Vince and the pilot flew close to the mountain, and they identified what appeared to be a very large wooden structure protruding from the ice cap. Vince was able to see inside of the broken front end of the structure. I met Vince in 1995 and his contribution to the rediscovery of the Ark is of tremendous importance.

Even though my team had applications hand-carried to the Turkish Embassy in Washington, D.C., and also to the offices of the ministry in Ankara, Turkey, permission was again denied. While our American team waited patiently in the States, I flew to Turkey to negotiate with the authorities in Dogubeyasit(at the base of Ararat) in Agri in an attempt to gain the legal permission to climb.

During this trip I met up with two mountain climbers from Switzerland—Karim Presti and Guiseppe Rezzonico. They also had intentions of climbing the mountain in search of the Ark. This was a prearranged meeting between the Swiss climbers and myself. We had considered that they would work with TASQ. If permission for TASQ was again denied, the hope was for the three of us to get permission to climb. Guiseppe and I had communicated for several months. Guiseppe had first contacted me in 1994 and sent me an Ararat photo which he had taken in 1993. He had been held on the mountain as a captive of the Kurdish rebels. He was one of at least 13 people who had been caught on or near the mountain that summer and held as captives of the PKK. While being a captive, he was given limited freedom to climb on the ice and take a few pictures. Guiseppe told me that they actually treated decently by the rebels.

The photo he sent to me seemed to indicate a possible structure in the Araxes glacier. I matched his photo with my own file photos and three which matched the object in the Araxes glacier. I had taken two of the photos from an airplane in 1986 and John McIntosh had taken the other one from a high ridge on his first climb in 1978. Until I received the Swiss photo, neither I nor John had noticed the apparent structure in the glacier. Although the evidence on the photographs was not conclusive, I decided this location needed more to be searched more.

During out time in Dogubayazit, Karim and I (Guiseppe was sick) spent some time with the local military authorities. We had a discussion that lasted about an hour, and were politely informed that Ararat was off limits to everyone including Turkish citizens. It was even off limits to the Kurdish shepherds who would normally have their flocks of sheep on the lower grassy slopes of the mountain. I asked about the possibility of a ride in a military helicopter and told that also was impossible. Then on a table which was between us, I put two photos of what I then believed was part of the Ark. The two military officers immediately showed a level of excitement and interest that was new to our conversation. They wanted to know where I got the photos. I told them that I took the pictures ten years ago. One thing led to another and I said, "I know the Ark is on the mountain, and you know the Ark is on the mountain." The reply was, "We don't care! That is your problem. We have another problem." He was referring to the PKK problem but I think they knew more than they were telling us. I was not disappointed. I expected this answer but it was necessary that I ask. That's why we were there. Their parting words before good byes were "It's impossible to go the mountain. It's forbidden, maybe next year, maybe not for five years."

No Climbing—1997

I went to Turkey twice in 1997. On the first trip, which took place from mid-July to the end of August, John McIntosh and I traveled together. We spent nearly five weeks in the country. Much of our time (three weeks) was spent with Dr. Salih Bayruktutan of Ataturk University, located in the city of Erzurum. After phone contact and with our requests again denied by the authorities in Ankara (Salih had been in Ankara to personally request permission just before John and I arrived in Erzurum). We traveled from Erzurum toward Ararat while stopping to speak with every civil and military authority we could contact. Even with the backing of the university, the military would not allow us on or near Mount Ararat. During the two remaining weeks that John and I spent together, we tried everyday to get the legal permission to climb. We also met some interesting Kurdish locals in Dogubeyasit. One of these men claimed to know of the structure in the ice on the mountain. I asked if he would take me there and was told no. He said that it was too risky. I then asked if he would got to the mountain, climb it, and take photos for me. He would use my cameras and I would pay him well for success. It took our Kurdish friend about nine days to first make up his mind, come up with a plan, and make the round trip to the structure and back. I met him upon his return and he was a very tired but happy man. He said I would be very proud of him. I was informed that he did indeed see part of the structure sticking out of the ice and he did photograph it. However, on his return he had to hide the cameras and film in a villager's home because of the military presence in the area, who would have searched him as he left the villages at the base of the mountain. I told him that he had to go back after the cameras. He and another Kurdish friend did just that. A day later the Kurdish friend returned. The military had caught the climber with the cameras. The military had caught him with the cameras, confiscated them, put him in jail and were searching for the American who gave him the cameras. Now, although I had not really broken any law, I guessed that the Turkish military was probably getting a bit irate with me. So I got advice from the Kurds and John and I were in a fast taxi out of town within ten minutes. I later learned that the military arrived at our hotel about 45 minutes after we had left.

I made a second trip in 1997. This was at the end of September. Canadian Ark explorer George Kralik went with me on this trip. We met other local Kurds who attempted to help us by climbing the mountain with our cameras but a heavy snowfall hampered their efforts. After a little more than two weeks, we left the country.

Dick Bright, Dave Larsen, and John McIntosh 1998
Courtesy of Dick Bright

No Climbing—1998

I arrived in Turkey on August 19th and left three weeks later. Most of the time John McIntosh and Dave Larsen (a friend and educator/businessman from Pasadena, CA) were with me. Because of discretion, the full details of this trip cannot be discussed. The full story will be published at a more opportune time. In spite of the problems, I have reason to believe that the Ark is indeed on Ararat and a discovery may be soon. I fully intend to make another trip—my 15th—to Turkey. As in the past, I intend to again be in the company of individuals who are highly dedicated.

The next year there will in fact be several fully financed organized teams entering Turkey. Revealing the Ark may have an impact on some people. On others, they could care less. Regardless, I believe it is our place to try and succeed in finding the truth, to tell others, let them make their own decisions and to God be the glory.

Conclusion

This should give the reader an idea of some of the problems many of us go through in an attempt to search for the Ark. Along the way, we've made mistakes, and hopefully, learned from them. It hasn't been easy, but then if it were, the Ark would have long since been revealed, and perhaps its impact on future events would be lessened.

Many of us are convinced the Ark is on Ararat and, even though we have trouble along the way, there is a level of commitment to make every effort to reach it. Why? I imagine each person who gets involved in this quest has his own personal reasons for his desire to do so. Could it be to do what we believe is the will of God in our lives? Maybe. Is it to do something to show where we stand in our beliefs? Maybe. I've heard it said that people may doubt what you say in your life, but they will believe what you do. Is it to hope God will say, when the time comes, "Well done, thou good and faithful servant?" Is it, that in doing this, we hope to reach the lives of other people? Is it to help get the Word out? Maybe. Is it just the adventure? I think most of us have reasons that are similar, and those reasons are, for the most part, good, and hopefully acceptable to God. In my mind, some of the people mentioned here in this small effort are giants in this undertaking for God. Among them are such people as Jim Irwin, the ex-astronaut, evangelist and team leader, who had a tremendous impact on my life; Eryl Cummings, who researched Ark stories for over 40 years; and Violet Cummings, who wrote two books on the subject. John Morris, Ph.D., a creation geologist, author, and veteran of Ararat was once struck by lightning while on a climb. He survived, is a leader in this effort and he was kind enough to write the foreword to my book. There are others not mentioned here. Their contributions and efforts, according to their own beliefs, I think, will be accepted as gold.

From a personal standpoint, I was taught in college that theories of evolution, particularly the Darwinian Theory, natural selection, and chance, were responsible for my existence and that of every person and type of animal. In essence, life was an accident. I was taught that Uniformitarianism was the guiding geological principle in the history of the earth. There was no room for cataclysm.

I sat in anthropology classes and listened to the way anthropologists, paleontologists, and other scientists of one name or another could take a tooth, a jawbone, or a portion of a skullcap determined to be of great age, and then build a model of some gigantic beast to fit the fragment. They even put fleshy and hairy exteriors on the products of their imaginations and sold it to the students as part of our heritage. I didn't buy it.

I took the classes, passed the tests, giving the appropriate answers, and I graduated. But, down deep, I didn't believe that which I was being taught was, in fact, the complete truth. The subjects are too involved and complicated to be discussed here. It would mean defining evolution and natural selection, and discussing mathematical probabilities of chance and mutation. It would involve discussing creation, the Laws of Thermodynamics, and the fossil record. It would involve defining Uniformitarianism as a geological doctrine versus the extent of cataclysm. I discussed these things to the best of my ability in *The Ark, A Reality?*

I will not attempt to do so here. There are many books by creation scientists who do a far better job than I could. Besides, I don't think those topics necessarily fit in well with the topic of this book.

The bottom line is that I am of the belief that we are not here by random chance, having so evolved from as simple a form as a unicellular organism. Accidents and random chance cannot be the creator. I believe there is purpose to life; there is someone with a "blueprint." We were created by purposeful design. "Chance" is not my God.

Geology has not been uniform throughout history. The geologic column in its entirety does not exist outside of the textbook. The history of the earth has signs of cataclysm all over it—cataclysm by water. All of this is obvious as we open our eyes and do our own study apart from the college classroom. This is my opinion, and I was heading in this direction even before I opened page one of the Bible.

According to the Bible: "For we shall all stand before the judgment seat of Christ...So then every one of us shall give account of himself to God" (Romans 14:10,12). The problem, I think, is first a spiritual problem. At age 35, I bought my first Bible and started reading it voraciously. Then I started to read the scripture. A couple of years or so later, I read Violet Cummings' book, Has Anybody Really Seen Noah's Ark? I then met her and her husband Eryl, and Jim Irwin. You know the story.

During the years since I read that first book concerning the Ark, I have read as much as I could find on the subjects of Noah's Ark and the Genesis Flood. Over the years, I have read many accounts of reported sightings of the Ark. I have even spoken with people who claim to have seen the ship many years ago as it lay in the ice and rocks of Ararat. By the vast numbers of reported sightings alone, (200 or more since antiquity) one would tend to believe there is something to the reports. When one considers the similarities of many of the reports the tendency to believe is further strengthened.

Details vary from one report to another. Some of the reports may have no basis in fact, or there may have been a misidentification of what was seen. However, it takes just one true sighting to put the Ark on Ararat. Let's consider the possibility of truth by a comparison test.

From the pages of my own book:

"There are four reports of the Ark with the door off. There are seven reports of one end broken off, and eighteen of its sticking out of the ice and snow or with snow on the structure. There are nine reports of a meltwater pond, eight reports of a ledge, and ten reports of a ravine, valley, gully, or some such place, which the Ark, sitting on a ledge, could be in. There are three reports of a very difficult or hazardous climb to reach the ship.

There are at least two reports to my knowledge of the Ark's leaning against a rock or ridge, and two reports of its sitting in a north-south direction. There are three reports of the pond's overflowing in a stream down the mountain and two reports of the Ark as having openings around the top. There are many more comparisons that I could include, and with the addition of more reports, the numbers you have just read would increase. However, these should be enough for us to come to a conclusion and to the point of this exercise. We can choose to believe that all of these reports are based upon lies, or, based on the information presented, we can choose to believe that the Ark or a large wooden barge is on Mount Ararat, if just one of the reports is true."

So, what does this all mean to me? It means I believe the Ark is on the mountain. If so, why hasn't it been verified? By what you've read in these pages, you can understand that it is presently difficult to even get to the mountain. Beyond that, I can only guess that the time hasn't been right. There is other evidence not mentioned here that leads me to believe the time for the Ark to be revealed will be soon.

Will there be other expeditions? Absolutely! Why? It's a search for truth. Pilate said to Jesus, as recorded in John 18:37-38, "Art Thou a King, then?" Jesus answered, "Thou sayest that I am a King. To this end was I born, and for this cause came I into the world, that I should bear witness unto the truth. Everyone that is of the truth heareth my voice."

Pilate saith unto him, "What is truth?"

If a huge, partially petrified, frozen wooden structure, resembling a barge or ship with cages built inside, were found in the ice and rocks high on a mountain, what would you think? Jesus said, as recorded in John 8:32, "And ye shall know the truth and the truth shall make you free."

We have all heard so many times that the new millennium, the approaching turn of the century, signals the return of Christ. Is this true? Is the Ark of Noah a biblical type of the Ark of salvation through Jesus Christ? When will Christ return?

From Matthew 24:36-39:

> But of that day and hour knoweth no man, no not the angels of heaven, but my Father only. But as the days of Noah were, so shall also the coming of the Son of man be. For as in the days of Noah were before the flood they were eating and drinking, marrying and giving in marriage, until the day that Noah entered into the Ark.

And knew not until the flood came, and took them all away; so shall also the coming of the Son of man be.

The discovery of the Ark will not be expected by the majority of the people. I would guess that most of the people do not believe in its existence now or probably even in the past. If the Ark is revealed, could that be a warning—maybe a final warning that Jesus Christ is on his way? That also would not be expected by most people. Again, as I hate to say it, most people may believe very little about Jesus, and the fact that he will return as he promised. I believe it will happen. When? "As the days of Noah were, so shall also the coming of the Son of man be." (Matt 24:37) It could be a day like today. It will be "business as usual" and he won't be expected. Will the Ark be discovered first? Whether or not this is to be the case, I believe we have a responsibility, and that responsibility is in part, to give reason for, and to share with the best of our ability, what we believe is the truth—To God be the Glory![1]

[1] *The Ark, A Reality?* by Richard Bright, Ranger Associates, 1989. Reprinting and updating by New Leaf Press, 1995. (Title pending)

The Report of the *Search For Truth Scientific Research Team and Expedition* of 1993, by Richard Bright.

I consider myself to be the "regular guy" of Ark research. I attempt with this book and my web site to bring Ark research and researchers closer together in a spirit of unity and harmony. We can accomplish much more when we share information and resources. I provide a forum and clearinghouse environment on my web site for all Ark researchers.

13

B. J. CORBIN

I hope the preceding chapters have given you an appreciation for the explorers of Ararat. Searching for the remains of Noah's Ark is a very difficult task.

I will attempt to summarize some of the key points expressed by the explorers and offer some thoughts of my own. Of the explorers that still believe the remains of Noah's Ark exist on Ararat, most of them favor the northeast summit and Abich II glacier areas. There is still interest in the Western Plateau, Parrot Glacier and Ahora Gorge areas.

Though the focus of this book is on the exploration of Mt. Ararat, I should mention there was attention given to a boat-shaped object researched by Ron Wyatt, David Fasold and others, approximately 18 miles south of Mt. Ararat. Most of the explorers of Ararat, including myself, have been to this site and find it interesting, but believe it is most likely a natural formation. I have actually seen similar-shaped objects between Big and Little Ararat from a helicopter. I visited the Durupinar or boat-shaped object in 1998 with Dr. Salih Bayraktutan, Professor Robert Michelson, Dr. Bill Shea, David Deal, and fellow Ark Research Team (ART) members. Primarily, Bayraktutan, Michelson and Deal are interested in conducting a more in-depth analysis of the boat-shape and surrounding area before dismissing it as a natural formation. Ron Charles theorizes that Durupinar may be an old Mongol fort possibly used and fortified by Tamerlane's army in the conquest of Armenia.

Albert Groebli has an interesting alternative premise about the Ark landing in Iran. A summary is included in an appendix. The details are listed on the author's website.[1] It should also be noted that Pierre Daniel Huet

---

[1] B.J. Corbin's website is http://noahsarksearch.com

created a conception map in 1722 A.D. entitled "Terrestrial Paradise" which placed the Ark on top of another traditional "Mount Ararat" in Iran, "Kuh e Alvand." The map was placed in Calmet's *Dictionnaire historique del la Bible*. Of course, it should be noted that "Kuh e Alvand" is outside the biblical "mountains of Ararat."

This book also includes two explorers who surmise the Ark may have landed on Mt. Cudi. I have included a summary table of promising locations for Noah's Ark by the various explorers.

Ark Research Field Team 1998
Driver 1, Jerry Kitchens, Driver 2, Mark Jenkins,
Matthew Kneisler, Michael Holt, Robert Michelson
Salih Bayraktutan and B.J. Corbin
Courtesy of B.J. Corbin

For those of us who search for the Ark, it is frustrating to know that the potential discovery and validation of the Ark seems so close, yet still eludes us. Many people believe Noah's Ark has already been discovered, or at least had that impression prior to reading this book. Given all the news stories, books and movies claiming the discovery of Noah's Ark over the years. This book was not meant to confuse or challenge your beliefs. It is intended to take a deeper look at the evidence (or lack of evidence) for the discovery of Noah's Ark. I am currently unaware of any evidence that would validate the discovery of Noah's Ark.

I have not given up on Mt. Ararat as the location for Noah's Ark, though historical text and references seem to point towards Mt. Cudi. I believe some of the eyewitnesses may have been telling the truth about Noah's Ark on Mt. Ararat. The biblical account of the flood in Genesis states that it took over seventy days for the water to recede and the tops of other mountains to appear. This would seem to indicate a summit or near-summit landing of the Ark. Mt. Ararat, as the tallest mountain in the region, would be a likely place for the Ark's landfall. Its height and the difficulty of climbing Mt. Ararat does concern me with respect to the people and animals of the Ark descending the mountain. Mt. Cudi, with an approximate elevation of 7,000 feet, would seem a more reasonable location to unload the Ark's passengers and cargo.

B.J. Corbin next to Tent at Mihtepe 1988
Courtesy of B.J. Corbin

In 1988 the Willis expedition, using subsurface radar, eliminated as a possible landing site a large area of summit snowfields called the Eastern Plateau. If one suspects that the Ark landed near the summit of Mt. Ararat, there are only a few places remaining that could contain Noah's Ark.

Location	Elevation
Northeast Summit Area	16,500 feet
Abich II Glacier	14,000-16,500 feet
Western Plateau	15,000 feet
Upper Parrot Glacier	14,000 feet
Ahora Gorge	12,000-14,000 feet
Northwest	13,000-14,000 feet
Mt. Cudi	7,000 feet

Northeast Summit Area / Abich II Glacier

Much of the evidence for the Ark's existence on Mt. Ararat seems to point to the upper northeast ice cap. One would expect major ice disruption caused by a petrified Ark moving slowly down a glacier. We find such ice disruption in the Abich II area. This would be consistent with the scenario of the Ark landing between the two summit peaks, with all or a portion of the structure moving slowly moving down the ice. There is a large box-like shaded area on the northeast summit that appears to be the right size. Many people underestimate the size of Noah's Ark when observing objects of interest. I am fortunate to have good helicopter photographs that scale a known area 500 feet in length on the Ararat ice cap. In Dick Bright's book *The Ark, A Reality?* displays a composite drawing including many of the alleged sightings of the Ark on Mt. Ararat. Most all of the sightings appear in the northeast area of the ice cap.

Another reason the northeast ice cap may be a likely resting spot for the remains of Noah's Ark, is a lack of access to that part of the mountain. Permission to climb that region of the mountain is rarely given, partly because it faces the border of Armenia. It is one of the most dangerous areas to climb on the ice cap. The general tourist route to climb Mt. Ararat approaches the summit from the south.

There is a rock outcropping located at approximately 14,000 feet on the northwest side of the mountain called "Ark Rock." I have heard that some of the locals were afraid to approach the Ark for fear of spirits guarding it. You can view the entire northeast ice cap and upper Parrot Glacier area from Ark Rock. One could speculate that people would view the Ark or what they thought was the Ark from this vantagepoint.

B.J. Corbin at Mihtepe 1988
Courtesy of Ross Mehan via BJ Corbin

There is also a claim that satellite photos exist indicating two unnatural objects at approximately 15,000 feet in the northeast Abich II Glacier. Like so many other Ararat clues, it is difficult to confirm or validate the evidence from the original source.

It is not my intent here to summarize in detail all the various Ark sightings on Mt. Ararat throughout history. There are many claims of discovering the Ark on Ararat by dozens of people. I tend to trust the testimony of the late George Hagopian. He seemed an honest Armenian Christian who lived in the vicinity of Mt. Ararat as a boy when the mountain was still part of Russian Armenia. I have listened to a taped interview of Hagopian by Elfred Lee many times. I perceive Hagopian as telling the truth about his two experiences with Noah's Ark. Hagopian claimed the Ark rested between the two peaks, what is also called "The Saddle." For those interested in researching alleged sightings in more detail, a recommended reading section can be found at the end of this book.

Western Plateau

Many of the local mountain people who live on or near Mt. Ararat communicated to me that the Ark lies beneath the western part of the ice cap.

There is a military photograph that was recently declassified showing an Ark-like structure on the edge of the Western Plateau at approximately 15,000 feet. It is interesting to note that the ice on the Western Plateau was measured with subsurface radar at a depth over 200 feet thick. As you have read, Chuck Aaron and some others believe that the Western Plateau is a caldera (collapsed volcano cone). This could explain why the ice is so deep in this area of the mountain, which would explain sightings of Noah's Ark high on Mt. Ararat partially submerged in a lake. While hiking and camping on the Western Plateau, I could see and hear water running under my feet. A picture I have by Chuck Aaron and Bob Garbe shows how the Western Plateau could melt enough to appear as a small lake near the summit of Ararat. From airborne photos one can see the Western Plateau as the largest and most stable "landing area" on the entire ice cap.

Parrot Glacier

This area of the mountain became a prime search target after the claimed discovery of wood by Fernand Navarra in the 1950's. A book and movie

transpired from several expeditions and discoveries made at this site. Problems began when conflicting reports emerged regarding the age of the recovered wood. In Navarra's book *Noah's Ark: I Touched It* he reports the wood is approximately 5,000 years old. Other independent reports using Carbon-14 dating revealed the wood to be considerably younger in age. What is more puzzling, as described earlier by Elfred Lee, is that Navarra claims to have discovered wood in other parts of the mountain. Also, consider that Navarra may have observed a large dark structure under the ice while he was climbing the Abich II Glacier, not the Parrot Glacier.

B.J. Corbin at Mihtepe 1988
Courtesy of B.J. Corbin

I recently received some information of a claimed discovery of Noah's Ark by an Italian named Angelo Palego. The photographs appear to place the location of the Ark in the Upper Parrot Glacier region at approximately 4600 meters (14,000 feet). He identifies his discovery as a continuation of Navarra's original discovery. The photographic evidence that is available to me does little to convince me of the claim. Please understand that I have seen dozens of more interesting shapes on Mt. Ararat. The more one researches objects of interest on Mt. Ararat, the more cautious one becomes. Many claims of discovery have been made to newspapers prior to any validation of the actual discovery. We wait for evidence that will prove this claim of discovery and others beyond a reasonable doubt.

I should note that the upper Parrot Plateau continues to be an area of interest for veteran Ararat climber Ahmet Arslan. Ahmet has climbed Mt. Ararat at least fifty-four times. He is originally from Turkey and knows many of the local Ararat people, and the folklore concerning the whereabouts of Noah's Ark on the mountain.

B.J. Corbin at Durupinar Site 1998
Courtesy of B.J. Corbin

Ahora Gorge

The Ahora Gorge area of Mt. Ararat gained popularity in recent years after Dr. Don Shockey and other veteran Ark researchers interviewed a man named Ed Davis. Mr. Davis was in the Army and stationed in Iran during World War II. In 1943 Mr. Davis earned the confidence of a man who claimed to know where Noah's Ark was located. Davis later climbed Mt. Ararat and viewed the Ark from a distance and in cloudy conditions. It is interesting to note that Mr. Davis was stationed in Hamadan, Iran. Not far from Hamadan is a mountain called "Kuh e Alvand" that also has a Noah's Ark tradition. Perhaps more interesting is the fact that it has a history of being called "Mount" Ararat. Mr. Davis, in his initial interviews, referred to the local people as Lurs or Lors from Luristan (a region in the Zagros mountains of western Iran) and not Kurds. Though most Ark researchers believe that Davis was on the Turkish Mt. Ararat, one can only speculate that he may have been taken to the Iranian "Mt. Ararat."

I have some concern regarding Ed Davis' testimony. I understand that he passed a polygraph examination, but I have two separate interviews in which he places the location of the Ark in different places. In his original interviews, veteran Ark researchers surmised that Mr. Davis viewed the Ark in the Ahora Gorge. This site in the Ahora Gorge became known as the "Davis Canyon." In a taped interview with another Ark researcher, he concurred that the Ark was located near the northeast summit (some 2000 feet higher), where he had earlier testified that he was not on the permanent ice cap.

Though Davis' story lacks consistency, his description of mountain landmarks and drawing of the Ark is similar to other accounts on Mt. Ararat. It is possible that Davis unintentionally allowed himself to be led during some of his interviews. It is a natural tendency for Ark researchers to harmonize accounts that favor where we expect to find Noah's Ark.

The Ahora Gorge has been extensively photographed with no definitive Ark discovered. There was some excellent aerial photography of Mt. Ararat orchestrated by Scott Van Dyke. I understand that he discovered several objects of interest in the Ahora Gorge, but awaits a ground expedition to confirm whether they are artifact or rock.

Several climbing expeditions took place in the 1970's by Ark researchers in the Ahora Gorge. There were some close-up helicopter flights of the area in the late 1980's and early 1990's. The close proximity of the Ahora Gorge to the Armenian border and civil unrest make it unlikely that any permission will be granted to search this area in the near future.

Jim Willis, Scott Little, Willis Newton, Jr. at Mihtepe
Courtesy of Dr. Charles Willis 1988

Ark researchers Dick Bright, John McIntosh, Ken Long, and others have "objects of interest" located in the Ahora Gorge area. Ed Crawford is interested in an object between the Abich I Glacier and the upper Parrot Glacier.

Northwest Site

In the 1970's there was a man who supplied Ark researchers with very specific details and maps of Noah's Ark and its location. Knowledge of the mountain was apparent by the landmarks and details he described. He claimed that his father had actually been to the site some two-thirds of the way up the north-northwest side of the mountain and that he had seen the remains of Noah's Ark. To my knowledge, this site has not been fully identified. I have helicopter photographs of what may be the location described by the gentleman. In one of the ice-laden valleys near the location is a large rectangular-shaped shadow under the ice. I believe the best practice is to fully eliminate all possible sites until the remains of the Ark are found.

Mt. Cudi

Of the explorers highlighted in this book, two of them believe that Noah's Ark did not land on Mt. Ararat, but on Mt. Cudi (pronounced Judi), which is located approximately 200 miles to the southwest of Ararat. Both of these men have previously explored Ararat and originally thought Ararat to

B.J. Corbin with Immanuel Expeditions Flag
Courtesy of B.J. Corbin 1989

be the landing area for the Ark. Based on what I have read by Lloyd Bailey and other Bible scholars, they may be correct about their assumptions about Mt. Cudi. Though Mt. Cudi has little in the way of sensational eyewitnesses, ancient historical texts and documents seem to favor Mt. Cudi over Mt. Ararat as the landing site for Noah's Ark. None of the Ararat eyewitness accounts have proven the Ark's existence on Ararat beyond a reasonable doubt.

The various opinions and conclusions expressed in this book demonstrate that good people can disagree. The key for researchers is to respect each other and keep the lines of information and communication open. It seems that many of us who search for Noah's Ark have pieces of the puzzle, but would gain a better understanding if information were more openly shared. Attempts have been made in the past to bring Ark researchers together. I did not attend the last Ark-a-Thon, but understand it was beneficial. Other attempts to bring Ark researchers together have failed. Though the primary reason for the book was to offer some straight talk about Noah's Ark from people who have been to Mount Ararat, another reason for this book was to promote unity among Ark researchers. I also wanted to include some new information and clues for future Ark researchers.

I hope you have enjoyed this attempt to bring together some of the world's leading researchers and explorers of Mt. Ararat as they shared their hopes and frustrations of searching for the elusive remains of Noah's Ark.

What is Really Important?

Searching for what could be one of the greatest archeological discoveries in all of human history is very exciting. But what is really important? Even if the discovery of Noah's Ark could be validated and proven beyond a reasonable doubt, what would it mean?

If you have read this book because of an interest in the search for Noah's Ark and you are not a Christian, please consider the following:

When you look at a watch, you can reason that there must be a watchmaker. Though you may not know the watchmaker personally, you know he exists by his creation. Take a good look at this world and universe we live in, at the uniqueness of mankind, especially in comparison to the other creatures in nature. There is just too much design for creation to be mere chance. I have studied evolution at the college level and would contend that it takes more faith to believe in evolution than in creation. If a person is interested in these subjects, a couple books to study the issues.[2]

The Bible says that God considered Noah a righteous man living in a wicked world. In the Old Testament, God provided a plan of salvation for Noah and his family through the building of the Ark. God convicts our hearts when we sin and have done something wrong. In the New Testament, God now writes his laws (The Ten Commandments) in our hearts. God in his mercy and love provided a permanent "ark of salvation" through the sacrifice of his son, Jesus Christ. If you would like to learn more, the New Testament of a Bible is the place to start. For if we search for the remains of Noah's Ark for any reason other than to build trust in the Bible, we are *missing the boat*!

---

[2] *In The Beginning* by Dr. Walt Brown (http://www.creationscience.com) and *Is There A God?* by Dr. John Oakes (http://greatcommission.com).

B. J. Corbin Fourth Trip to Turkey

Thursday 10/1/1998

I left Salisbury Regional Airport on a commuter to Philadelphia, only to find out that my connecting flight to Washington Dulles had been cancelled. My only option was to fly to Washington National Airport and hope to catch a shuttle bus to Dulles. When I arrived at Washington National and asked the US Airways representative at the gate about getting to Dulles to catch my International flight, he said there is no way to make the flight. A young man overheard my dilemma and suggested the only way possible to make the connection would be to take a cab for around $50 dollars to Dulles, and he offered to split the fare with me.

We race to Dulles, then I dash to the Lufthansa ticket counter out of breath and give the short version of the story to the ticket agent. She completed a fast transaction and quickly directed me to the appropriate security checkpoint (which I cut in line to the front) and then to an airport shuttle to the correct terminal.

I run through the airport with two fairly heavy bags and see Jim Hall, Matthew Kneisler and Mark Jenkins (with wife and two sons to see us off) already in line to pre-board the flight. It takes me several minutes to catch my breath and cool down. I make the flight from Dulles to Frankfurt/Ankara!

Friday 10/2/1998

We arrive in Frankfurt, Germany very early Saturday morning. Michael Holt and Jerry Kitchens are waiting at the gate for us. Michael Holt, an employee of United Airlines, coordinated special accommodations for the team, including a place to rest, eat, and take showers. We are soon joined by Rob Michelson and discuss tentative plans for our trip to Turkey. We all fly to Ankara, then take a 15-20 mile taxi ride to the Tunali Hotel.

Saturday 10/3/1998

We leave Ankara airport to fly further east to Erzurum, Turkey. We stay at the Oral Hotel and get settled in. We have dinner at the hotel and Salih stops by to meet everyone and to pickup Rob.

Later that evening the Ark Research Ministries (ARM) team meets in Jim Hall's room. Jim shares his overall goals and visions for the project, then shares a long and detailed testimony. We have a time of fellowship and prayer, then it seemed only minutes afterwards that Jim goes into the bathroom and sounds sick. Most of us figured that it was something that he had eaten. He returned with us for a brief time, then returned back to the bathroom. The group broke up and decided to give Jim some privacy.

Only minutes later did Michael Holt knock on our door (Matthew Kneisler and B.J. Corbin) and said we need to get Jim a doctor. There was a large amount of blood in Jim's bathroom floor that had been coming out "both ends." I ran downstairs to the front desk and attempted to explain the situation. We soon had an ambulance to take Jim to a hospital in Erzurum. Michael rode in the ambulance with Jim as Salih Bayraktutan and Rob

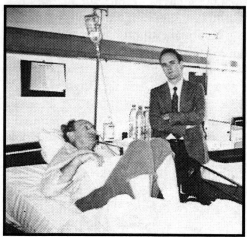

**Jim Hall in Bed at Hospital in
Erzurum with Matthew Kneisler 1998**
Courtesy of Michael Holt via B.J. Corbin

Michelson returned to the hotel from a pre-conference meeting. Salih Bayraktutan and family, along with the management and staff of the Oral Hotel, and the staff at the hospital all need to be commended for the excellent care and concern expressed to Jim in his time of need. They even donated their own blood to help him.

The team was obviously very concerned for Jim's well being, and had felt like we had witnessed a spiritual attack on Jim and the team, though logical explanations were offered.

Sunday 10/4/1998

This was one of the longer days of the trip. We were all concerned about Jim and visited him at the hospital. We were supposed to have a pre-meeting with Salih around 5 P.M. that evening, but later received a call from Rob stating that the meeting would be moved to 7 P.M. Around 9 P.M. the rest of the team is getting both anxious and frustrated. I recall Rob returning to the Oral Hotel around 10 P.M. to a semi-hostile crowd.

Monday 10/5/1998

The workshop began around 10 A.M. with opening statements from Dr. Salih Bayraktutan. He expressed an interest in having an international team of researchers investigate all sites and areas of interest relating to the flood of Noah.

Professor Robert Michelson gave a detailed presentation for the Durupinar (boat-shaped) formation, though careful not be make any claims of discovery. He also echoed the call for collaborative scientific efforts for sites related to the flood of Noah.

David Deal followed Rob with his interpretation of aerial photos and historical references regarding the Durupinar site and to a new claim of discovering "Naxuan" or "Naxuana" in the hills above Durupinar. He boldly proclaimed that Durupinar was indeed the remnants of Noah's Ark, and the upper site was probably Naxuan. I personally found these statements to be total conjecture since Mr. Deal had never even been to either of these sites, and presented little in the way of conclusive evidence.

B.J. Corbin at Kazan west of Ararat with large stone that has a hole in it 1998
Courtesy of B.J. Corbin

After lunch, Matthew Kneisler of ARM presented the team research proposal, in proxy, for Jim Hall who was in the hospital for intestinal bleeding.

B.J. Corbin presented a brief history of research on Mount Ararat and concluded with the most likely areas left to search on Mount Ararat, including the ruins at Eli, Korhan, and the St. Jacob's monastery.

Tuesday 10/6/1998

We left in three rented cars for Dogubayazit, which is just south of Mount Ararat. We stop in Agri for lunch and photos opportunities. We encounter some typical communication problems at the entrance of the governor's office building because of the video camera. The situation was soon resolved and we were escorted out of town by police and registered with Turkish security.

After passing through several military checkpoints, we arrive in Dogubayazit late in the afternoon. Salih needs to meet with local police, security, mayor, and military that we are in town and the nature of our visit.

We checked into the Hotel Grand Derya which was quite nice by eastern Turkey standards, and noticed that we had two Turkish security assigned to us in the lobby. There were also security posted outside of the hotel on our behalf.

Wednesday 10/7/1998

We stop at the military headquarters to see about our escort for the day. Two Turkish soldiers are assigned to protect us as we ventured on the Durupinar site, where a short, but solemn memorial service was held in honor of David Fasold, as David Deal sprinkled some of the ashes of David Fasold on the site.

The group also went up near the Iranian border to search for ruins of an ancient settlement. We did hear some gun shots, and were hoping these were only from target practice, or maybe warning shots from Turkish military, as we were very near the Iranian border. No ruins or artifacts were easily discernable to most of the group once we reached the upper site of interest.

Ark Research Team in Richmond, Virginia 1998
Courtesy of Jim Hall

We concluded the day with a drive to Kazan, a small village west of Mount Ararat, where some claim large stones are actually sea anchors or drogue stones from Noah's Ark. We arrived in the Kazan near dark, and it was decided to wait until morning of the next day to visit the stones.

Thursday 10/8/1998

We went to Kazan to see the large stones. After about an hour or so, we returned to the Durupinar site, where the ARM team conducted an interview at the visitors center, and the others went back up to the upper site. We heard more gunshots, and could only hope for the best.

There was a brief period of tension during the afternoon, where most of the ARM team was left at the visitors center with no car or person that spoke Turkish. At one point, we got a little nervous where someone was crouched in the brushes for over a half an hour. Too long for a mere bathroom break! Not to mention the occasional gun shots in the background.

Salih, Rob and Dave announced the discovery of what they believed to be the top of a tomb at the upper site. I recall them saying that they found corners of a 3' by 5' stone slab. Due to some confusion, I did not go up to see the sites, but Rob later showed me some photos of the sites, which seem to warrant further investigation. Some members of the group claim to have found pieces of pottery and bone.

We eventually left for Erzurum around 4 P.M., stopping again in Agri for dinner, this time without incident.

Friday 10/9/1998

Matthew and I went to Erzurum airport to catch an earlier flight out. We arrived at Ankara and spent several hours changing tickets. We also alerted Lufthansa of Jim Hall's condition and had phone numbers of doctors and wheelchairs waiting. We were able to make a standby flight to Frankfurt and were very pleased. We celebrated by staying at the Sheridan Hotel at the airport, mostly at our own expense.

Saturday 10/10/1998

I catch a train to Augsburg, Germany, to stay with good friends for a few days before returning to the United States. I leave Matthew at the airport to catch a flight back to Dulles and then on to Tulsa.

Only after receiving an email from Matthew, did I learn that the remainder of the ARM team had been traveling behind us and actually met Matthew at the airport gate in Frankfurt. They said Jim was bleeding a little, but was in good spirits and made it home safely. Jim Hall and the ARM team are now making diligent plans for a possible expedition in 1999.

Regarding the larger group that met in Turkey, there are other plans to raise about $2.5M for a 30-day scientific expedition that will consider the Ararat sites, Durupinar, "Naxuan," and any other sites of interest. They plan to use advanced remote sensing technologies under a coordinated research effort called the Search for Early Post Deluvial Anatolian Culture (SEPDAC), between Ataturk University and the Georgia Institute of Technology.

RECOMMENDATIONS FOR FUTURE EXPEDITIONS

By B.J. Corbin

I must admit there is a strong spiritual presence on Mt. Ararat that I cannot fully explain. I can remember having one of my most powerful prayers while camping under the stars of Mt. Ararat (my whole body felt electrified). I have also been fearful of what could happen while on Mt. Ararat.

It sounds like a cliché and oversimplified, but if you are interested in the search for Noah's Ark, you really need to pray constantly for God's will concerning any involvement. As you have read, it is a very dangerous expedition.

If you are planning an expedition to Mt. Ararat, I recommend the following:

1. Try to establish contact with established veteran Ark researchers to avoid common pitfalls and mistakes—have them join your team, or join their team, if possible.

2. Start early establishing government agency contacts to secure permits—even though a permit will not guarantee you will get on the mountain. Do not climb illegally by going up the mountain without a permit.

3. Follow standard mountain climbing protocol—many Ark researchers seem interested in a quick helicopter landing on the ice cap to avoid unfriendly confrontations below. I was part of the 1989 expedition that actually landed on the ice cap by helicopter. We struggled with mountain sickness and were still confronted with machine guns at 15,000 feet! I would only recommend a helicopter landing if the climbers were fully acclimated (say on a nearby mountain) prior to takeoff.

4. Guard against the lack of water on the mountain—most camp fuel stoves do not melt water efficiently at high altitudes.

5. Start ascents to the ice cap early (pre-dawn) before the ice melts and rocks begin to loosen and fall from above.

6. Have a good Turkish/English-speaking guide or translator with you at all times—things can get confusing real fast.

7. Learn the culture of Turkey and show respect for the authorities. Like in any other country in the world—it pays to know the right people.

8. Have strong leadership that will provide team correspondence every week / month or as needed, starting at least a year or two before the actual trip—have the entire team meet prior to the expedition (preferably a practice climb or two with glacier training).

9. Be cautious of what you eat—many a climber has suffered from stomach and intestinal problems on Ararat. I found success in this area by eating the local yogurt. Elfred Lee says that charcoal saved him and Navarra drank lots of "Roke."

10. Maintain proper diet and exercise prior to an expedition—if you drink coffee and/or smoke cigarettes—plan on some extra problems at high altitudes.

11. Explore the latest subsurface radar and satellite technology and consider a high altitude remote sensing airplane with multiple sensors—I believe if the Ark is on Mt. Ararat, it is under the ice cap or buried most of the time.

12. Avoid the common tendency to "harmonize" all claimed sightings of the Ark that are unrelated. Some accounts have to be wrong!

Hopefully, these recommendations and suggestions will benefit future expeditions. I am glad to share my thoughts and experiences with any individual or group who are searching for Noah's Ark with a heart for God's will.

Searching for Artifacts Related to the Flood of Noah

We have the technology...but can we obtain the permission to use it? Since the mid-1990's, the use of the Internet has enabled Ark researchers to better communicate and coordinate research information and options. With advanced communication and high-tech research tools, i.e., high resolution satellite imagery, ground penetrating radar, unmanned aircraft, and many other techniques, we can now safely say that we have the capability to answer the question as to whether actual remains of Noah's Ark are still existent today. The question remains as to whether the government of Turkey will allow extensive research to be conducted in the eastern and southeastern regions? The lack of permission to search in these sensitive areas is understandable, with Mount Ararat located on the Armenian and Iranian borders, the Durupinar (boat shape) located on the Iranian border, and Mount Cudi located on the Iraqi and Syrian borders. When you combine historical and geographical factors along with the Kurdish PKK separatist conflict in the region, one can start to understand the scope of the research problem. Our prime research areas of interest are under military control and restrictions.

In an attempt to "open" the doors to research in this part of the world, Professor Robert Michelson at Georgia Tech in the United States and others (Dick Bright, John McIntosh, etc.) have been working very closely with Professor Salih Bayraktutan of Ataturk University in Erzurum, Turkey. Professor Bayraktutan is the initial contact person in Turkey for permission to search the eastern region, which includes Mount Ararat and the Durupinar (boat shape) formation. Many Ark researchers do not fully understand the complicated and bureaucratic permit process. Even if Professor Bayraktutan submits a research application for approval or further processing, it must move through various government agencies, governors, mayors, and the military before full permission can be granted. Even if all permissions are in-hand, there is still no guarantee of access to the desired research sites.

During the summer and early Fall of 1998, I worked with Professor Michelson who was coordinating a conference with Professor Bayraktutan at the Ataturk University Earthquake Research Center in Erzurum, Turkey. The title for the conference was "The First International Workshop on the Noah Flood and The First Settlement in the Agri Mount Region." Where I was also acting as a consultant to Jim Hall and the Ark Research Ministries (ARM) team, I quickly put Jim in contact with Rob to ensure the ARM team would be represented at the conference.

The planning session was held on October 6th, with fieldwork conducted on October 7th and 8th at the Durupinar (boat shape) formation and what is believed to be remains of an early settlement in the hills above the site. Some in the group are prematurely calling the site "Naxuan" or "Naxuana," which according to Josephus, refers to the place of first decent. The field group also spent an hour or two at Kazan, which is just west of Mount Ararat, to see large stones that some speculate are sea anchors or drogue stones from Noah's Ark.

During the workshop and at other informal meetings, most people expressed a desire for all potential sites related to Noah's Ark and the flood to be researched. In reality, most participants could be divided into two research paradigms, Durupinar and Mount Ararat.

The first group included Salih Bayraktutan, Robert Michelson, David Deal, and Bill Shea, who are interested in the Durupinar (boat shaped) formation and the site above. To be fair, Bill Shea was more of a neutral observer who added a sense of balance and perspective to the two groups. I would also place Jerry Kitchens, the primary fund-raiser into the category of neutral observers.

The second group included Mark Jenkins, Matthew Kneisler, Michael Holt, and B.J. Corbin representing the Ark Research Ministries (ARM) group directed by Jim Hall. Unfortunately, Jim Hall suffered from intestinal bleeding and was forced to stay at the hospital in Erzurum during the workshop and fieldwork. To Jim's credit, he remained in good spirits and was continually encouraging the ARM team to accomplish specific tasks. The ARM group is primarily focused on researching Mount Ararat. We met Ed Crawford at the hotel and nearby restaurant in Dogubayazit, the small town south of Mount Ararat. Mr. Crawford is interested in the Abich I glacier just above the Ahora Gorge on the north side of Mount Ararat. His assumptions for potential discovery of Noah's Ark are based on cave inscriptions found in the Ahora Gorge and from a variety of photos of the glacier. He admittedly stated that he preferred to work independent of other Ararat research groups.

(Crawford's web site http://www.vonbora.com)

A third research group interested in the Mount Cudi or Cudi Dagh site, some 200 miles south of Mount Ararat, was not represented at the workshop or in the field group. Currently, I am only aware of Dr. Charles Willis of Fresno, California, being active in the search of this site, though Lloyd Bailey and Bill Crouse have expressed written support of the site. Dr. Willis, a veteran of several expeditions to Mount Ararat in the 1980's, has made a couple of trips to the Cudi site to prepare the way for a future expedition to search for wood and other fragments that may still remain.

Though the workshop and fieldwork experiences were unorganized, key contacts and relationships were developed and several people had an opportunity to visit the Ararat region for the first time and gain useful experience.

What Sites Remain to be Investigated?

Additional and supplemental information to this book can be obtained at http://www.noahsarksearch.com

The three prime candidates that fall within the ancient "mountains of Urartu" are:

Mount Ararat
Mount Cudi
Durupinar

Mount Ararat

Mount Ararat in eastern Turkey has been searched many times in the 1900's. There have been dozens and dozens of search efforts including ground, helicopter and plane expeditions to Mount Ararat. Some of these efforts have used professional aerial mapping photos from 2000 feet, satellite images, ground-penetrating radar (GPR), and other innovative techniques. Considering the large estimated size of the Ark, no expeditions have yielded conclusive evidence for the remains of Noah's Ark.

What can we assess from this? If the remains of Noah's Ark are indeed on Mount Ararat, they are buried or hidden from plain view. The good news is that we live at a time when we have the technology to answer the question as to the Ark's existence on Mount Ararat or any other mountain. The bad news is that all sites of interest lie near hostile borders and in an area PKK separatist activity.

You can put all of claimed sightings of Noah's Ark on Mount Ararat into two separate groups, which are below or above the permanent ice cap.

Below the Ice Cap

There are several accounts that clearly place the remains of Noah's Ark in a remote canyon below the permanent ice cap between 13,000 and 14,000 feet. A few such accounts are Ed Davis, Ed Behling and Jacob Chuchian.

We are fortunate with the Jacob Chuchian account in that we have very detailed testimony given by his son Arthur Chuchian, which includes precise maps of how to find the location on Mount Ararat. Stuart Brassie and Thomas Sass conducted the original interviews and research regarding the Chuchian account. The site is clearly on the northwest side of Ararat below the ice cap. Using helicopter photos, I may have found the location described by Arthur Chuchian. There are approximately 10 or so specific details given that are all matched exactly in the photo that I have. Based on the testimony of Ed Behling, it seems likely that he was also in this northwest section of the mountain. The only question is Ed Davis, where researchers place him in the Ahora Gorge. Ed Davis does mention chimney or pinnacle peaks as one of the predominant landmarks in his testimony, which also matches the northwest site.

The other main area of interest below the permanent ice cap is the Ahora Gorge on the northeast side of Mount Ararat. Both Dr. Bill Shea and Ed Crawford share interests in inscriptions found in and around caves in the gorge area. Many people claim that in 1840, a violent explosion created the Ahora Gorge and destroyed the village of Ahora and the St. Jacob monastery. Several Ark researchers, including John McIntosh, Dick Bright and Ken Long have "objects of interest" in the Ahora Gorge. Another consideration with searching in this area beyond the physical dangers, is the fact that it faces the Armenian border and currently the Turkish military does not allow anyone in this area.

Above the Ice Cap

For explanatory purposes, I will divide the Ararat ice cap into four sections:

Eastern summit plateau (16,800 feet)

Saddle between two peaks, Abich II glacier, and Ahora
    Gorge (14,000-16,000) feet

Western summit plateau (15,000 feet)

Upper Parrot Glacier and Abich I (14,000 feet)

In 1988, Dr. Charles Willis of Fresno, California using ground-penetrating radar (GPR) successfully surveyed and profiled the ice under the eastern summit plateau and over the high ridge into the saddle between the two summit peaks. No evidence of Noah's Ark was found, but good science prevailed, and another area was eliminated.

In 1989, Chuck Aaron, Bob Garbe and B.J. Corbin attempted to use GPR on the western summit plateau, but were limited by ice conditions and a GPR unit that could not continuously profile under the ice. The team was successful in determining the depth of the ice to be over 250 feet thick in some areas, thus giving credence to those that believe the western plateau is a caldera or sunken volcanic cone. This is interesting in lieu of accounts that claim the Ark is on the edge of a lake high on Mount Ararat. An unintended bonus of this expedition was a good scale of Noah's Ark on Ararat, where markers were set on the plateau at 50' intervals up to 500 feet. David Montgomery photographed the camp from a helicopter, allowing us a good estimate of the size of Noah's Ark on the western plateau.

In 1990, Dr. Don Shockey and team focused on the Abich II glacier area, based on confidential satellite sensing information that there were two unnatural objects under the ice in the Abich II glacier. They also had a photo taken of an object in the Abich II glacier the year before by Ahmet Arslan. Close range photos and video were taken of the Abich II and the mountain in general. Several objects of interest were discovered from this expedition that need to be checked out.

This means that there are only a few places left to search under the ice on Mount Ararat.

Abich II glacier & Ahora Gorge (northeast 14,000-16,500 feet)

Western summit plateau (15,000 feet)

Upper Parrot Glacier and Abich I (northwest 14,000 feet)

Most experts agree given the temperate and fractured ice conditions of Mount Ararat that ground-penetrating radar would yield the best results over air and satellite techniques. The problem here is the lack of permission to climb and search all areas of interest on Mount Ararat. All available technology for peering under the ice on Ararat should be investigated.

There are several interesting ruins on and near Mount Ararat that should also be investigated with equal fervor:

Korhan (northwest)
Eli (southeast)
St. Jacob's Monastery (northeast)
Caves on Ararat (northeast & others)
Stones at Kazan (west-southwest)

Top of Ahora Gorge and Abich II Glacier in 1978
Courtesy of John McIntosh

Mount Cudi

An excellent book by Dr. Lloyd Bailey entitled *Noah: The Person and the Story in History and Tradition* provides modern-day Ark researchers some food-for-thought. Using ancient texts and sources, Bailey describes several alternatives to Mount Ararat and gives compelling evidence as to why one should consider Mount Cudi or Cudi Dagh a more likely candidate for the Ark's landfall based on historical accounts. Mount Cudi (pronounced Judi in Turkish) is approximately 200 miles south of Ararat near the Iraqi/Syrian borders and the Tigris River. Mount Cudi is a considerably smaller mountain than Ararat, and one could only expect to find fragments and other evidences to substantiate this mountain as the landing site for Noah's Ark.

There is a note in the reference section of the NIV Study Bible, stating the Ark probably landed in southern Urartu. Mount Cudi would fall into this general proximity, where Mount Ararat would be considered in northern Urartu.

Bill Crouse has a good web article on the subject at http://www.noahsarksearch.com/noah.htm

Dr. Charles Willis, a veteran of several expeditions to Ararat in the 1980's, now believes that Mount Cudi is the correct mountain for the Ark's landfall. He has made a couple of exploratory trips in the 1995 and 1996 to the Mount Cudi region in hopes of mounting a more formal expedition in 1999 or 2000.

Durupinar

This boat-shaped formation gained prominence with media attention of expeditions by Ron Wyatt and the late David Fasold. Though the site was regarded by many early on, as only a natural formation, it still holds the interest of several individuals and groups today. Salih Bayraktutan and Robert Michelson are still actively engaged in researching the Durupinar site. David Deal, a friend and colleague of the late David Fasold, is also in this camp, though he openly admits his bias that the Durupinar site is indeed the footprint remains of Noah's Ark. He also calls the area above Durupinar Naxuan. To be charitable, these types of declarations are premature at best. They feel that the criticisms of the site are not grounded in good science and they hope to conduct in-depth experiments before making a final determination.

Keys points by those that favor the Durupinar site:

The shape is a "boat" exactly 300 Egyptian (20.6") cubits long (Moses was trained in the court of the Pharaoh and would likely have used Egyptian units, not the later Hebrew cubit (18")). Babylonian documents place the deck area at 1 IKU. Dividing the length of the boat into the area gives right at 50 (Egyptian) cubits average width. Certainly a most intriguing coincidence if it is not related in some way to the biblical Ark.

The "boat shape" is in the mountains of Urartu and is on one of three mountains in Turkiye named Cudi. The Quran is specific that the Ark came to rest on "al Cudi."

The places surrounding the Durupinar site bear names such as Kargakonmaz ("the crow won't land"), Masher ("Judgement Day"), Yigityatagi ("hero's anchorage"), Ziaret ("to make a voluntary pilgrimage"— what Josephus said people did during his day (meaning that it was accessible to the common man)), and Nasar ("to make a sacrifice"—what Noah did upon leaving the Ark. Note: The Babylonians refer to Utnapishtim (Noah) being in "Nasir"), etc. etc.

Unlike the Ararat volcano for which unquestionable evidence has not been substantiated that it was under water (no pillow lava, no marine sediment, no fossils), the Durupinar site is littered with fossils and marine sediments which prove that this area was at one time inundated by an ocean.

Ancient writings speak of the Ark's place of "first decent" (thereby implying a place of second decent). Aerial photographs from 1959 show a boat shaped impression located around 7,300 ft at the top of a large ever-moving mudflow. At around 6,200 ft down the same mudflow is the Durupinar boat-shape which exactly fits the impression at the top of the mudflow. At these altitudes, organic materials would have rotted or been used for fuel and building materials long ago. If it is at all related to the Ark, the Durupinar site is probably the compression footprint in the natural material.

I have now been to the Durupinar site on three separate occasions and agree that an archeological dig would answer the question once and for all. Just looking and walking around the Durupinar site, it appears to be totally natural and consistent with the surrounding landscape and material. My concern is, why after all these years of controversy has the site not been excavated and the final question answered?

Reference: http://www.noahsarksearch.com/durupinr.htm

USING TOPOGRAPHY IN THE SEARCH

By Researcher John Comber

Imagine the excitement onboard Noah's Ark when that awesome vessel grounded itself after being afloat for so long. Yet, despite the assured jubilation of the crew, we're told that seventy-four days passed from the time the Ark came to rest until Noah saw the tops of mountains. Scripture is clear and very detailed in the account of the great deluge. In fact, the details are what seem odd. Why are they included? What purpose would they serve but to assist in locating it? This is where my search for the legendary vessel of antiquity begins–in the detailed pages of Genesis.

> Then God remembered Noah, and every living thing, and all the animals that were with him in the Ark. And God made a wind to pass over the earth, and the waters subsided. The fountains of the deep and the windows of heaven were also stopped, and the rain from heaven was restrained. And the waters receded continually from the earth. At the end of the hundred and fifty days the waters decreased. Then the Ark rested in the seventh month, the seventeenth day of the month, on the mountains of Ararat. And the waters decreased continually until the tenth month. In the tenth month, on the first day of the month, the tops of the mountains were seen. [Genesis 8:1-5]

Several things ought to catch one's attention in the above scripture passages. Besides the more obvious mileposts of the passage of time, we're told the manner in which the flood decreased—"continually until the tenth month." We're also given the information that more than one mountain was seen on the first day of the tenth month. "On the mountains of Ararat" narrows the search to the ancient Urartu mountain range, in eastern Turkey, but not necessarily to the single mountain bearing the name "Mt. Ararat." From the information in this portion of scripture alone, I believe the search for the notorious wooden vessel can be narrowed down considerably from the numerous mountains in that region. Using topographical maps of the area, elevation data was gathered and placed into a table. Beginning with the highest peak and following the decreasing water level, every mountain (or "target" site) over 10,000 feet was systematically evaluated as a potential landing place of the Ark. For each possible target mountain, the next two smaller mountains (deemed "remote mountains" – "R1," "R2," etc...) were determined as well as their respective distances from the target site. Provided that the elevations of the mountains have remained somewhat constant from the aftermath of the flood, this collective data gives us a snapshot of what Noah may have seen as the floodwaters decreased. This prerequisite condition becomes the first criterion for considering a mountain of the identified region as a target site. A target site must be within the "mountains of Ararat" region and have a minimum of two other mountains within view that have not changed significantly in elevation since the landing of the Ark.

Since I am not a geologist and have no intentions of traveling to every mountain of the region in consideration, I chose not to eliminate any target sites based on this criterion. This by no means diminishes the validity of the criterion, but for completeness it has been included. The second criterion is also based on the above passage of scripture. A target site must be of sufficient height to accommodate a given constant water receding rate, whereby 74 days after the Ark came to rest at least two other mountains of lower elevation would have been seen.

Target	Loc	T. Elev	R2 Elev	≥R2	R1 Loc	~R1 Dist	R2 Loc	~R2 Dist	R3 Loc	~R3 Dist	9	11	13	15	17	19	21
T1	M4	18,481	17,064	2	O4	57.0	O5	66.9	Q11	270.2	P	P	P	P	P	P	F
T4	Q11	16,946	15,919	2	R5	211.9	N4	259.5	Q5	210.0	P	P	P	F	F	F	F
T5	R5	16,558	15,669	2	N4	119.3	Q5	28.5	P5	57.0	P	P	F	F	F	F	F
T6	N4	15,919	15,243	2	Q5	92.4	P5	66.9	X8	317.5	P	F	F	F	F	F	F
T7	Q5	15,669	14,714	2	P5	28.5	X8	225.4	S5	57.0	P	P	F	F	F	F	F
T9	X8	14,714	14,048	2	S5	177.0	T5	155.0	Y8	28.5	P	F	F	F	F	F	F
T10	S5	14,681	13,947	2	T5	28.5	Y8	200.7	U6	66.9	P	F	F	F	F	F	F
											7	4	2	1	1	1	0

Table 1—Target Table

The fact that so many days passed between the time the Ark rested and when mountaintops were seen necessitates that the ship must have landed on one of the taller mountains in "the mountains of Ararat." The alternative is that a dense fog might have covered the earth until it was lifted on the seventy-fourth day, but scripture doesn't mention anything along these lines. The systematic approach of considering each peak in the area, from the tallest to the lower ones, allows us to determine whether 74 days would be sufficient to spot two remote mountains from each target site. Remembering that Noah saw at least two mountains on that day, we can utilize the following equation to determine if each target site passes or fails.

R2 elevation + (est. receding rate * 74) ≤ target elevation =>
"Pass"

"Failing" simply means that the lower of these two remote mountains ("R2") would not have been seen on the seventy-fourth day (or that the Ark would still be afloat if working in a reverse order). This requires one important bit of information that scripture does not provide, but one that can been estimated – the rate of receding water. For my calculations, I began with the estimate of 15 feet/day as put forth in J. Whitcomb/H. Morris' *The Genesis Flood* and included estimates both greater than and less than his estimate. As seen in the Table 1 below, this turns out to be a fairly accurate median rate when considering the ten highest peaks in the region. At the rate of 21 feet/day, none of the target sites pass, while at 9 feet/day seven of the target sites pass. Of the one hundred mountains with an elevation over 10,000 feet, only these seven mountains passed one or more of the seven water receding rates (9' – 21'/day). "T1" is located at "M4" in the Map Data Table, which falls outside of the region believed to be "the mountains of Ararat" and therefore is not a possible landing site. Likewise, "T5," "T6," "T7," "T9" and "T10" are dismissed as possible landing sites since they lie outside of this region. "T4" is Mt. Ararat, the only mountain that clearly falls within the designated region (location = "Q11") and passes the water receding calculation. Although Mt. Ararat failed at the receding rate of Morris' 15'/day, it passed at a close rate of 13'/day. At the rate of 13'/day, the approximate landing elevation of the Ark on Mt. Ararat would be 15,919 + (13'/day * 74) = 16,881'. At the receding rates of 9' and 11'/day, the resting elevation of the Ark figures out to be 16,585' and 16,733' respectively.

The "Loc" columns of the Target Table cross-reference the columns and rows on the Map Data Table below. "R1," "R2" and "R3" represent the three

Table 2—Map Data Table

remote mountains of progressively lesser elevation than the Target Mountain and their respective distances from the Target Mountain are also listed. The column "≥R2" provides a sum of mountain peaks greater than or equal to the R2 elevation and less than the target elevation. Each cell of the Map Data Table represents 997.5 square miles, the vertical side being 35 miles and the horizontal side equaling 28.5 miles. The values contained in the Map Data Table represent the highest elevation in the regional section bounded by the latitude and longitude coordinates listed alongside the table. The inset map in the bottom-right corner corresponds roughly to the shaded area of the Map Data Table, which is the region believed to be "the mountains of Ararat."

HIGH RESOLUTION

REMOTE SENSING SATELLITES

Commercial & Declassified Satellite Imagery with 1-5 Meter Resolution

By Jim Hays - June 1999

Introduction

For many years, Mt. Ararat has been off-limits to Ark researchers because of the conflict between the Turkish military and the PKK. Until researchers gain access once again to the mountain, high-resolution satellite imagery may be the best research option available. Unlike ground or airborne research, satellite remote sensing does not require permission from the Turkish government or military. At least four commercial companies are planning to offer one-meter resolution satellite imagery in the near future.

The main advantages of satellite remote sensing over airborne remote sensing for Ark research are availability, lower cost, and no need for research permits. However, airborne remote sensing offers multiple sensors with better spectral coverage at sub-meter resolution. Commercial remote sensing aircraft are available with hyperspectral and thermal infrared sensors, as well as synthetic aperture radar (SAR). Satellite remote sensing has other limitations too. Ground and airborne research teams are absolutely necessary for accomplishing certain types of research. Any anomalies discovered in satellite imagery would need to be investigated close-up. Validation of the discovery of Noah's Ark would ultimately require on-site research by a ground team.

This report includes information about commercial remote sensing satellites that will offer 1-5 meter resolution imagery in the near future. Currently operational satellites include SPIN-2, IRS-1C, and IRS-1D. Satellites under development include IKONOS, QuickBird, OrbView-3, OrbView-4, SPOT 5, and RADARSAT-2. Also included in this summary is information about Declassified Intelligence Satellite Photographs, which were taken by CORONA and LANYARD spy satellites.

Definition of Terms

Pixel: Picture element, which is the smallest element of a digital image

Spatial resolution: Dimensions of a ground object represented by a single pixel. For example, an image with 2 meter spatial resolution is made up of many pixels, each representing a 2 meter by 2 meter square area of the earth's surface.

Panchromatic: Gray scale (black & white) image

Multispectral: Color image, typically having four spectral bands (i.e. red, green, blue, and near infrared)

Pan-sharpened multispectral: High resolution multispectral image obtained by fusing a high resolution panchromatic image with a lower resolution multispectral image

Hyperspectral: Image with a large number of spectral bands covering both visible and invisible areas of the spectrum. Each spectral band has a narrow bandwidth and represents a unique portion of the spectrum.

Orthorectification: Image processing which corrects distortions in the image due to changes in elevation; requires a Digital Elevation Model (DEM) of the imaged terrain

Positional accuracy: Accuracy of the geographical data (latitude and longitude) provided by a satellite image. For example, a positional accuracy of +/- 25 meters means the actual location of an object is within 25 meters of the coordinates provided by a satellite image of that object.

Ground control: Positional accuracy can be greatly improved by obtaining the actual coordinates of several ground control points visible in an image. Typical ground control points include road intersections, buildings, and natural formations. Ground control can be obtained using the Global Positioning System (GPS), maps, etc.

SPIN-2
Russian Federation (owner & operator)
SOVINFORMSPUTNIK (data provider)

SPIN-2 (U.S. distributor)
http://www.spin-2.com
Phone: 1-800-478-8898

KOMETA

- KOMETA images offer the highest spatial resolution currently available:
  - 2 m resolution panchromatic (1.56 m pixel size)
  - 1.2 m pixel size will be available Fall 1999 using new acquisition medium
  - 10 m resolution panchromatic also available
- KOMETA imagery provided by commercial Russian COSMOS satellites:
  - Two missions per year (typically spring & fall), lasting 45 days each
  - 2 m resolution B&W photographs taken by KVR-1000 camera
  - Film returned to Earth at end of each mission and processed
  - Digital imagery provided by scanning the KOMETA film
- Nominal 40 km x 160 km ground coverage per photograph
- Images are orthorectified and georeferenced for high spatial accuracy. Positional accuracy is +/- 20 m (+/- 3 m with ground control.)
- Images cost $25 per km^2 (100 km^2 minimum area)
- Satellite tasking is available:
  - Images will be acquired on next KOMETA mission. Orders must be received at least two months prior to launch.
  - No tasking fee, although a 25% deposit is required. Deposit is refunded if images are not acquired or are cloud covered.
  - Up to 3-4 pre-programmed imaging attempts will be made
- Images may be purchased direct from SPIN-2 or through local distributors
- Images are available in a variety of formats to be viewed on PC or work station using image processing software
- Archived KOMETA imagery cannot be previewed online (except on TerraServer)
- Small, non-orthorectified SPIN-2 images can be previewed online at http://TerraServer.com and purchased for a very low price. The largest size available (20 km^2) costs $24.95 per image. This database is growing, but currently has limited coverage.

"Alternative" Imagery

- SPIN-2 "alternative" images offer the highest spatial resolution currently available:
  - 2 m resolution panchromatic (1.56 m pixel size)
  - 1 m resolution panchromatic will be available late 1999
- "Alternative" imagery provided by Russian spy satellites:
  - Orthorectified, digital imagery rather than scanned photographic film
  - Sub-meter resolution imagery is resampled to produce commercial imagery with 1-2 m resolution

- SPIN-2 must negotiate pricing with SOVINFORMSPUTNIK for each individual order:
  - 2 m resolution panchromatic: Approximately \$35-50 per km^2 (100 km^2 minimum area). Price depends on date imagery was collected.
  - 1 m resolution panchromatic: Pricing is TBD
- Satellite tasking is available year round:
  - No tasking fee, although a 25% deposit is required. Deposit is refunded if images are not acquired or are cloud covered.
  - No limit on imaging attempts
- Images may be purchased direct from SPIN-2 or through local distributors
- Images are available in a variety of formats to be viewed on PC or work station using image processing software
- Archived "alternative" imagery cannot be previewed online

Indian Remote Sensing (IRS)

Indian Space Research Organization (ISRO) - (owner & operator)

Space Imaging (U.S. distributor)
http://www.spaceimage.com
Phone: 1-800-425-2997 or 1-800-232-9037

IRS-1C & 1D

- IRS images offer some of the highest spatial resolution currently available:
  - 5 m resolution panchromatic
  - 20 m resolution multispectral (4 bands)
  - 5 m resolution color (obtained by fusing 5 m panchromatic images with 25 m multispectral LANDSAT images)
- IRS-1C was launched in December 1995 and is currently operational
- IRS-1D (identical to IRS-1C) was launched in September 1997, but was placed in the wrong orbit. Because of this, IRS-1D imagery did not become available until October 1998, although the satellite has been taking images since December 1997.
- Positional accuracy depends on the image product:
  - System Corrected: +/- 1000 m positional accuracy
  - Standard Orthorectified: +/- 25 m positional accuracy
- Images available in 70 x 70 km or 23 x 23 km scenes:
  - Each 70 x 70 km scene is made up of nine 23 x 23 km smaller scenes arranged in a grid

- If the geographical area of interest is straddling two or more smaller scenes, it is more cost effective to purchase the larger 70 x 70 km scene
- Pricing depends on image product purchased, for example:
  - 5 m panchromatic (System Corrected): $1400 per 23 x 23 km scene
  - 5 m panchromatic (System Corrected): $3300 per 70 x 70 km scene
  - 5 m panchromatic (Std. Orthorectified): $1750 per 23 x 23 km scene
  - 5 m panchromatic (Std. Orthorectified): $3500 per 70 x 70 km scene
  - 5 m color (Standard Orthorectified): $4400 per 70 x 70 km scene
  - Above prices are for International coverage (Dubai archive), with company/agency license agreement
- Satellite tasking is available; tasking fee depends on collection time:
  - Collection 2-8 days from order: $1700
  - Collection 9+ days from order: no tasking fee
  - Satellite tasking fee is paid up-front and is non-refundable
  - One imaging attempt will be made
  - Tasking is available for 5m panchromatic imagery only
- IRS revisit occurs within 24 days using both satellites
- Space Imaging is the U.S. distributor for IRS imagery
- Images are available in a variety of formats to be viewed on PC or work station using image processing software
- Archived IRS imagery can be previewed online at: http://origin.eosat.com

IKONOS

Space Imaging
http://www.spaceimage.com
Phone: 1-800-425-2997 or 1-800-232-9037

IKONOS 1 & 2

- IKONOS images will offer very high spatial resolution:
  - 1 m resolution panchromatic
  - 1 m resolution pan-sharpened multispectral (PSM) - (4 bands)
  - 4 m resolution multispectral (4 bands)
- IKONOS 1 launch on April 27, 1999 from Vandenburg AFB was unsuccessful due to Athena II launch vehicle failure (payload fairing failed to separate properly)
- IKONOS 2 (identical to IKONOS 1) is scheduled to be launched before the end of 1999 on an Athena II from Vandenburg AFB
- IKONOS 2 will require a 2-3 month on-orbit checkout period before becoming operational
- IKONOS image products will include Original Standard, Original Precision, Master Standard, and Master Precision:

- − Master products are orthorectified, Original products are not
- − Precision products require ground control, Standard products do not
- Positional accuracy will depend on the image product:
  - − Original Standard: +/- 25 m positional accuracy
  - − Original Precision: +/- 2 m positional accuracy (flat terrain only)
  - − Master Standard: +/- 12.2 m positional accuracy
  - − Master Precision: +/- 2 m positional accuracy
- Pricing will depend on image product purchased, for example:
  - − 1 m panchromatic (Original Radiometrically Corrected): \$20 per km^2
  - − 1 m panchromatic (Original Std Geometrically Corrected): \$23 per km^2
  - − 4 m multispectral (Original Std Geometrically Corrected): \$23 per km^2
  - − 1 m PSM (Original Standard Geometrically Corrected): \$30 per km^2
  - − 1 m panchromatic (Master Precision Orthorectified): \$81 per km^2
  - − 1 m PSM (Master Precision Orthorectified): \$105 per km^2
  - − Above prices are for International coverage out of archive, 11 x 11 km (121 km^2) minimum area, with company/agency license agreement. These prices are preliminary and subject to change.
- Satellite tasking fee will depend on collection time and region to be imaged:
  - − Collection 1-3 days from order: \$3000 (International), \$1000 (North America)
  - − Collection 4-7 days from order: \$2000 (International), \$500 (North America)
  - − Collection 8+ days from order: no tasking fee
  - − Satellite tasking fee will be paid up-front and is non-refundable
  - − Up to three imaging attempts will be made
- IKONOS 2 revisit will occur once every 3 days
- Images may be purchased direct from Space Imaging or through local distributors
- Images will be available in a variety of formats to be viewed on PC or work station using image processing software

EarlyBird & QuickBird

EarthWatch, Inc.
http://www.digitalglobe.com
Phone: 1-800-496-1225

EarlyBird 1
- EarlyBird images would have offered high spatial resolution:
  - − 3 m resolution panchromatic

  –   15 m resolution multispectral
- EarlyBird 1 was launched Dec. 24, 1997 on a Russian Start-1 launch vehicle from Svobodny Cosmodrome in eastern Russia
- EarlyBird 1 experienced a low power situation and failed four days after launch
- Plans to launch EarlyBird 2 (identical to EarlyBird 1) have been canceled
- EarthWatch is now concentrating on the development of QuickBird

QuickBird 1 & 2
- QuickBird images will offer very high spatial resolution:
  –   1 m resolution panchromatic
  –   1 m resolution pan-sharpened multispectral (4 bands)
  –   4 m resolution multispectral (4 bands)
- QuickBird 1 launch is scheduled for late 1999 on a Russian Cosmos launch vehicle from Plesetsk Cosmodrome in northern Russia
- QuickBird 2 (identical to QuickBird 1) is scheduled for launch in Fall 2000 (launch vehicle and launch site are TBD)
- Positional accuracy will be +/- 23 m without ground control
- Image products and pricing scheme are not yet defined
- The following pricing examples are approximate and subject to change:
  –   1 m panchromatic (system corrected): $5 per km^2
  –   1 m panchromatic (orthorectified, low accuracy): $25 per km^2
  –   1 m panchromatic (orthorectified, high accuracy): $50 per km^2
  –   1 m pan-sharpened multispectral: ~25% more than 1 m panchromatic
- Satellite tasking will be available (tasking fee and maximum number of attempts are TBD)
- Standard image size will be 22 km x 22 km (484 km^2)
- Minimum cost and/or minimum image area per order are TBD (EarlyBird images were to have a $300 minimum per order)
- QuickBird 1 revisit will occur once every 1-4 days, depending on latitude
- Imagery will be available directly from EarthWatch or through local distributors
- Images will be available in a variety of formats to be viewed on PC or work station using image processing software

OrbView
Orbital Image Corp. (ORBIMAGE)
http://www.orbimage.com
Phone: 703-406-5800

OrbView-3
- OrbView-3 images will offer very high spatial resolution:

- 1 m resolution panchromatic
- 1 m resolution pan-sharpened multispectral (4 bands)
- 4 m resolution multispectral (4 bands)

- Launch is scheduled for Fall 1999 on a Pegasus XL launch vehicle from Vandenburg AFB
- Imagery products are not yet defined, but will include basic data-sets, precision data-sets, orthorectified images, and enhanced imagery products
- Pricing scheme for the various image products is TBD
- Satellite tasking will be available (tasking fee and maximum number of attempts are TBD)
- Standard image size will be 8 km x 8 km (64 km^2)
- OrbView-3 revisit time will be less than three days
- Imagery will be available directly from ORBIMAGE or through local distributors
- Images will be available in a variety of formats to be viewed on PC or work station using image processing software

OrbView-4

- OrbView-4 will offer all the capabilities of OrbView-3 plus hyperspectral imagery:
  - 1 m resolution panchromatic
  - 1 m resolution pan-sharpened multispectral (4 bands)
  - 4 m resolution multispectral (4 bands)
  - 8 m resolution hyperspectral (200 bands)
- Launch is scheduled for Fall 2000 on a Pegasus XL launch vehicle from Vandenburg AFB
- Imagery products are not yet defined, but will include basic data-sets, precision data-sets, orthorectified images, and enhanced imagery products
- Pricing scheme for the various image products is TBD
- Satellite tasking will be available (tasking fee and maximum number of attempts are TBD)
- Standard image size:
  - Panchromatic & multispectral: 8 km x 8 km (64 km^2)
  - Hyperspectral: 5 km x 5 km (25 km^2)
- OrbView-4 revisit time will be less than three days
- Imagery will be available directly from ORBIMAGE or through local distributors
- Images will be available in a variety of formats to be viewed on PC or work station using image processing software

SPOT

French Space Agency (CNES) - (owner & operator)

SPOT IMAGE Corporation (U.S. distributor)
http://www.spot.com
Phone: 1-800-275-7768

SPOT 5

- SPOT 5 images will offer high spatial resolution:
  - 5 m resolution panchromatic
  - 2.5 m resolution panchromatic (resampled from two 5 m panchromatic images)
  - 5 m resolution pan-sharpened multispectral (4 bands)
  - 10-20 m resolution multispectral (3 bands at 10 m resolution, 1 band at 20 m resolution)
- SPOT 5 will join the currently operational SPOT 1, SPOT 2 & SPOT 4 satellites, which offer 10 m resolution panchromatic and 20 m resolution multispectral images
- Launch is scheduled for early 2002 on an Ariane 5 launch vehicle from the Guiana Space Center near Korou, French Guiana
- Image products and pricing scheme are not yet defined
- Satellite tasking will be available (tasking fee and maximum number of attempts are TBD)
- Standard image size will be 60 km x 60 km (3600 km^2)
- SPOT 5 revisit will occur once every 2-3 days, depending on latitude
- Imagery will be available directly from SPOT IMAGE Corporation or through local distributors
- Images will be available in a variety of formats to be viewed on PC or work station using image processing software

RADARSAT

Canadian Space Agency (CSA) - (owner & operator)

RADARSAT International (worldwide distributor)
http://www.rsi.ca
Phone: 604-231-5000

RADARSAT-2

- RADARSAT-2 images will offer high spatial resolution:
  - 3 m resolution Synthetic Aperture Radar (SAR) images
- SAR offers several unique advantages over optical systems:
  - SAR cuts through clouds and rain, and can be operated day or night

- SAR can penetrate dry sand very efficiently, making it particularly useful for locating objects and features several meters beneath the surface of a desert
- SAR is very inefficient when it comes to penetrating water, snow, ice, or moist soil (only surface features would be visible)
- RADARSAT-2 will join the currently operational RADARSAT-1, which offers 10 m resolution SAR images
- Launch is scheduled for late 2001 (launch vehicle and launch site are TBD)
- Image products and pricing scheme are not yet defined
- Satellite tasking will be available (tasking fee and maximum number of attempts are TBD)
- Imagery will be available directly from RADARSAT International or through local distributors
- Images will be available in CEOS format to be viewed on PC or work station using image processing software

Declassified Intelligence Satellite Photographs (DISP)

USGS EROS Data Center
http://edcwww.cr.usgs.gov
Phone: 1-800-252-4547

Image Scans, Inc.
http://www.imagescans.com
Phone: 303-422-2227

DISP

- EROS Data Center (EDC) offers declassified B&W photographs from CORONA, ARGON and LANYARD spy satellites, some with high spatial resolution:
  - CORONA KH-4A: 3 m spatial resolution
  - CORONA KH-4B: 2 m spatial resolution
  - LANYARD KH-6: 2 m spatial resolution
- Pricing is very inexpensive - typically under $20 per photograph
- Photographs are available on paper, negative film, and positive film
- Nominal ground coverage per photograph:
  - CORONA KH-4A: 17 km x 232 km
  - CORONA KH-4B: 14 km x 188 km
  - LANYARD KH-6: 12 km x 64 km
- No satellite tasking available
- All photographs are obtained from archive

- Archived photographs can be previewed online at: http://edcwww.cr.usgs.gov/Webglis/glisbin/search.pl?DISP
- Digital imagery can be obtained by having the photographic film scanned professionally
- Image Scans, Inc. (for example) offers this type of service:
  - Scanning done typically at 3800 - 5000 dpi
  - Up to $100 for scanning
  - Approximately $200 for scanning, non-ortho rectification, and mosaicing
  - Can obtain photographs directly from EDC for customer
- Scanned images are available in a variety of formats to be viewed on PC or work station using image processing software

Ark Research Using Satellite Imagery

- Number of pixels defining a 450 x 75 ft object is highly dependent on resolution:
  - 1 m resolution: 3151 pixels (137 pixels long by 23 pixels wide)
  - 2 m resolution: 759 pixels (69 pixels long by 11 pixels wide)
  - 3 m resolution: 368 pixels (46 pixels long by 8 pixels wide)
  - 5 m resolution: 135 pixels (27 pixels long by 5 pixels wide)
- High spatial resolution is essential for visually locating "objects of interest" in an image:
  - 1 m resolution best: IKONOS, QuickBird, OrbView-3, OrbView-4, SPIN-2 (1 m "alternative")
  - 2-3 m resolution acceptable: DISP, SPIN-2, SPOT-5, RADARSAT-2
  - 5 m resolution marginal: IRS-1C & 1D
- A combination of panchromatic, multispectral, and hyperspectral satellite imagery, at the highest resolution possible, is recommended for Ark research. The imagery should be collected in late summer during the greatest glacial meltback.
- Hyperspectral imagery is especially useful for locating anomalies because it reveals the spectral signature of each object in an image. The spectral signature of the Ark should differ from that of the surrounding terrain. Hyperspectral imagery does not have to have high resolution to be effective in locating anomalies.
- Because of the large elevation changes on Mt. Ararat, orthorectified imagery is preferred (but not required). Orthorectified imagery is more expensive and requires a digital elevation model (DEM).
- Ground control would be difficult to obtain for Mt. Ararat and is probably not necessary
- The cost of high resolution images should decrease as more commercial satellites are launched

- Satellite tasking orders should be placed as early as possible to assure data acquisition and to avoid tasking fees
- Ararat coordinates for previewing archived imagery: 44° 17' 30" East, 39° 43' 00" North
- Currently available high resolution satellite imagery includes SPIN-2, IRS, and DISP:
  - SPIN-2 is operational and offers 2 m resolution. KOMETA summer imagery is limited because missions typically occur in spring and fall. "Alternative" imagery is available year-round and probably more applicable for Ark research. Currently, there are no cloud-free summer images of Mt. Ararat in the SPIN-2 archives.
  - IRS-1C & 1D are operational, but have marginal resolution (5 m) for Ark research. The IRS archives contain several good summer images of Mt. Ararat. Currently, the best image was taken on 8/15/98 by IRS-1C (path 062, row 042, scene ID: C0620420098227PANSG). IRS images can be previewed online at: http://origin.eosat.com
  - The DISP archive contains several good summer photographs of Mt. Ararat (see table). These photographs can be previewed online at: http://edcwww.cr.usgs.gov/Webglis/glisbin/search.pl?DISP

Date	Satellite Type	Photograph Entity ID	Mission/Frame
7/13/64	CORONA KH-4B	DS1008-1040DA214	1008-1 / 214
7/13/64	CORONA KH-4B	DS1008-1040DF209	1008-1 / 209
8/8/64	CORONA KH-4B	DS1009-1040DF094	1009-1 / 094
7/28/70	CORONA KH-4B	DS1111-1082AF003	1111-1 / 003
9/20/71	CORONA KH-4B	DS1115-2154DF098	1115-2 / 098

- New high resolution satellite imagery to be available for future research:
  - Summer 2000: IKONOS, QuickBird, OrbView-3
  - Summer 2001: IKONOS, QuickBird, OrbView-3, OrbView-4
  - Summer 2002: IKONOS, QuickBird, OrbView-3, OrbView-4, SPOT-5, RADARSAT-2

Conclusion

Satellite remote sensing is a promising technology for Ark research. This is especially true in light of the inaccessibility of Mt. Ararat in recent years. Although high resolution imagery is currently limited, several companies and governments around the world are pushing hard to develop new commercial remote sensing satellites. Of particular interest are several which will offer one-meter resolution imagery in the near future. These include IKONOS, QuickBird, OrbView-3, OrbView-4, and SPIN-2. For Ark research, a combination of panchromatic, multispectral, and hyperspectral satellite imagery, at the highest resolution possible, is recommended. The more channels of imagery, the better the research. OrbView-4 is the only commercial satellite currently being planned which will offer hyperspectral imagery. With one-meter resolution panchromatic, four-meter multispectral, and eight-meter hyperspectral, OrbView-4 has the potential to be a powerful resource to Ark researchers.

Because of the large elevation changes found on Mt. Ararat, orthorectification is recommended. However, this will increase the cost of satellite imagery and require a digital elevation model (DEM). Ground control would be difficult to obtain for Mt. Ararat and is probably not necessary. Less expensive imagery products (non-orthorectified with no ground control) would probably be sufficient for researchers with a limited budget.

Low frequency (200-400 MHz) ice-penetrating SAR, hyperspectral imagery, and thermal infrared imagery (8-12 μm) are considered by remote sensing experts to be the most hopeful technologies for locating the remains of Noah's Ark. Currently, airborne remote sensing is the only way to obtain low frequency SAR and hyperspectral imagery. It is also the only way to obtain high-resolution thermal IR imagery. It should be noted that Landsat-7 offers low resolution multispectral imagery, including a thermal IR band at 60 meters resolution. While very inexpensive ($600 per scene), the usefulness of low resolution Landsat imagery for Ark research is questionable.

ANOTHER IRANIAN LOCATION

Condensed Version of Albert Groebli View

The biblical Mount Ararat had to be a pre-flood mountain. That means it could not contain fossilized sedimentary layers or be a volcano. The Ararat of Turkey is a volcano that has broken through fossilized sedimentary layers. Now I knew where Noah's Ark was not.

The highest pre-flood mountain would only be about 600 feet to 800 feet high. The scripture says the mountaintops were covered to 15 cubits of water. The Ark drifted in about 15 cubits in the water when it landed on Ararat. Where is the Ark? It is safely on the top of a 700+ ft. Ararat.

The Dasht-e-Kavir region in Iran, however, rests on a stable crustal platform that was lifted about 2000+ feet straight up. The Ark would not have experienced violent shaking at this location. If the Ark is to be found it will probably be found under the sand dunes of the Dasht-e Kavir in Iran.

At the end of one year Noah, his family and the animals left the Ark. There was no steep mountain to descend only a rolling hill. Today's central desert of Iran was at that time mostly an inland sea, and it provided an entirely habitable environment. It is an interesting point that, notwithstanding the dispersion of species after the flood, Iran today claims a wider variety of birds and lizards than any other place in the world. Iran best qualifies as the location for the spread of humanity. The oldest pottery is found there. The oldest language, Proto-Elamite, is found there. Grains and domesticated animals are normally traced to Iran.

From the preceding Flood model scenario I derived two premises that were posted on the Internet at http://noahsarksearch.com.

The location of Noah's Ark for Noah's Ark would be the following. The Scripture says when men moved from the east they found a plain in Shinar, and then built Babylon (Gen. 11:2). That verse always troubled me because the traditional Ararat is north of Shinar. Secondly, the Ararat of Turkey is a volcano that has broken through fossilized sedimentary layers. Those layers had to be laid down during the flood and the Ararat of Turkey is a post-flood mountain. In searching for a region in the Middle East that was not of volcanic origin or did not contain layers with fossils, I found the central plateau of Iran to fit my criteria primarily the Dasht-e-Kavir desert. The region was lifted straight up 2000 feet after the 150th day of the flood as the surrounding area was enclosed in higher mountain ranges as the Zagros Mts. On the 150th day of the flood the Biblical Mt. Ararat was about 900 feet to 1500 feet high, the highest pre-flood mountain. The 150th day is when the Ark landed on it and then the continents were split causing the fossilized layers and the mountain ranges we see today. The Biblical Mt. Ararat would be about 3500 feet today. My best guess to its location would be about 250 miles east of Qom, Iran. 34.5N 55.5E or 34.2E 53.5E second choice.

The following is secondary evidence for this site. The oldest pottery is found in Iran west of the Dasht-e-Kavir desert. The oldest written language Proto-Elamite is found in Iran. The most species of birds and lizards are found in Iran. Grains and domestic animals originated in Iran not Turkey. Shem's first-born son Elam established Elam in Iran. The Cambridge History of Iran Vol.1 1968 The great central desert of Iran is the most inhospitable place in the world. Men had to move 100's of miles away from its location for lack of water. It was an inland sea after the flood but soon evaporated.

Today men look to the high mountains when searching for Ararat not realizing that on the 150th day of the flood the high mountains we see today did not exist. Presently there are no ground-penetrating satellite photos of the area I believe the biblical Ararat is located.

GEOLOGIC SURVEY OF MOUNT ARARAT

ARARAT--THE MOTHER OF MOUNTAINS[1]

By Clifford L. Burdick, Ph.D.

This article presents some of the observations made during an expedition to Mt Ararat sponsored by the Archeological Research Foundation of New York. Eastern Turkey consists of a relatively barren undeveloped area. Tectonically it is very active, and unstable structurally.

The region has been folded; faulted, and intruded with basic types of volcanic rock, such as andesite and basalt. Mt. Ararat is 17,000 feet high, and at its greatest height perhaps measured nearer 20,000 feet.

Evidently the cover rocks were Paleozoic and Mesozoic limestone, and in places like Mt. Ararat were domed up by rising magma which burst through channels along fault lines

During the Flood period at least three blankets of basaltic or andesitic lava were extruded over the original Ararat which may have only been about 10,000 to 12,000 feet high originally,

Much of the lava is in rounded blocks called pillow lava, having a conchoidal appearance indicating it flowed out from the fractures while under water. After subsidence of the floodwaters, almost the whole northeast side of the mountain blew up forming the Ahora gulch. Rock fragments and ash from this eruption cover about 100 square miles.

Greater Ararat is covered with an ice cap down to the 14,000-foot level. This cap is hundreds of feet thick and divides into 12 "fingers" or glaciers.

An analysis of five rock samples is given and also a list of fossils found by Abich.

Introduction

Mount Ararat is one of the best known mountains historically, but also one of the least known geologically. For some reason some scientists have shied away from that area, perhaps because of its very Biblical connection. Two German geologists have made geological observations of the Ararat area: Hermann Abich, about 1845: and M. Blumenthal some 110 years later. Abich, it appears, was not afraid to mention the Flood and the Ark of

[1] *CRSQ* Vol. 1 No. 4, June 1967. Used by Permission. Creation Research Society 3110 N. 39th Terrace, St. Joseph MO 64506.

Noah in connection with Ararat, but not so with Blumenthal. So far as I know, geological evidence concerning Mount Ararat is unavailable to American science while geological data for most other parts of the world is quite abundant.

In 1946, an archeological company was organized in California, the Sacred History Research Expedition, with the objective of helping to fill this empty void scientifically by means of archeological, geological. glaciological, and other projects planned.

Dr. Kinnaman, the famous American archeologist was to be a member of the expedition. Col. Koor, the Russian soldier-archeologist, was to lead us to some 20 archeological sites in need of investigation. But perhaps the time was not yet ripe. Twenty long years passed before this study of the Ararat area became reality. In 1966, ten scientists and mountain climbers actually arrived at camp on Mount Ararat to begin this important work.

George Vandeman was chairman of the board of the Archeological Research Foundation of New York, and a prime mover in the organization. R. E. Crawford of Washington; Drs. Calvin and Agatha Thrash of Columbus, Georgia; Wilber Bishop [who was the creator of Little Debbies] of Cleveland, Tennessee, and Sam Martz of Nashville, were directors of the Foundation.

Dr. Lawrence Hewitt of Huntsville, Alabama was leader of the expedition, assisted by Harry Crawford of Denver, who had previously scaled the mountain to its peak. Nicholas Van Arkle of Holland was in charge of the glaciological work, mapping the ice cap—some 17 square miles in extent. He was ably assisted by two Swiss mountaineers.

Alva Appel of Washington, D.C. and William Dougall of Seattle assisted Mr. Crawford in mountain climbing and recording general observations of interest, (even hoping that one such observation might happen to be some remains of Noah's Ark, as per rumors that natives from time to time had stumbled on portions of the original wood).

Dr. Hewitt, besides giving leadership to the expedition, made a botanical study of the mountain and gathered and pressed some 150 plants and flower specimens. Mr. Eryl Cummings of Farmington, New Mexico, assisted me in making geological observations and in gathering rock samples.

Although the Archeological Research Foundation was the organizational unit, it operated largely on contracts with the United States armed forces, and with the Turkish government. The Turkish military command furnished transportation, as well as an interpreter and a soldier guard. The U. S. military command furnished tents, bedding, supplies and great quantities of food (C Rations). Since the expedition operated largely in a sensitive military zone, some of the scientific data gathered were of a classified nature.

Eastern Turkey is a relatively undeveloped and semi-desert area, lying across a recognized earthquake zone, composed largely of volcanic rock. The people native to that area have to work hard to make a living, and the Turkish government welcomed this scientific expedition gathering data on biology geology, glaciology, soil chemistry and related aspects of the region. Much of our work during the summer of 1966, revolved about the Mount Ararat region, which created general interest because of its historical connection with the Ark of Noah. The Armenians, who have inhabited that area for many centuries, call the mountain, Massis; the Turks call it "Agri Dagh," or painful mountain. The Persians call it Koh-i-Nuh, that is, the "Mountain of Noah."

Geomorphology

The central backbone of Turkey between Ankara and Erzurum is composed of a treeless, barren series of mountain chains of folded and uplifted Paleozoic and Mesozoic limestone. This is the central watershed and the source of the Tigris and Euphrates rivers. This limestone has been intruded in places by volcanic rocks, as at Kayseri (Caesarea) the locale of excavations far Hittite artifacts. The Hittite museum in Ankara is well worth visiting. South of Kayseri is a multi-peaked, snow-capped mountain of some 15,000 feet elevation, known as Erciyes.

From Erzurum, east to the Russian-Iranian border, the landscape consists mainly of volcanic rocks, except for occasional outcrops of limestone. Much of this volcanic rock is on the borderline between basalt and andesite, the samples collected from Persia being the most basic (mafic) as are also the Tendurek mountains south-west of Mount Ararat, and the Hama, Kale and Pamuk mountains to the west.

The swampy plain between Dogubayazit and Ararat is same 4,500 feet above sea level, but on the north and east sides of Ararat the Aras river valley is between 2,500 and 3,000 feet above sea-level. Some 50 miles northwest of Mount Ararat along the Aras river is an extensive salt mine with a thickness of some 400 feet. South-east of Little Ararat near the Iranian border is a deep round hole in the basaltic rack about 100 feet in diameter caused by a meteorite that struck the ground in 1910, drilling a clean round hole deep into the earth.

Greater Ararat is perpetually covered with an ice capping down to the 14,000 foot level in summer. This ice cap is hundreds of feet thick and as it flows down the sides of the mountain, it divides into twelve "fingers" or glaciers, two of which are the Parrot and Abich glaciers, the latter of which tumbles down a vertical precipice thousands of feet into the Ahora gulch, with a mighty roar that can be heard for miles. Two of our mountain climbers, who were camping in the gulch, were nearly buried when 100,000 tons or so of ice and snow came roaring down the gulch.

The comparatively high snow-line is due to the light precipitation and the upward rush of from the Aras plain. This plain is the veritable bread-basket for both Turkey and Russia. Although the upper and lower zones an the mountain are sterile, the middle zone, from 5,000 to 11,500 feet, is covered with good pasture upon which the Kurdish sheep and goat herders depend.

Mount Ararat is about equidistant from the Black Sea and the Caspian, the Mediterranean and the Persian Gulf. Around Mount Ararat gather many traditions connected with the Deluge. Koor, the Russian soldier-archeologist, lists some 20 such archeological sites which should be investigated. Both the ice cap and the resulting glaciers move over rough terrain, which breaks them into segments separated by crevasses. Often new falls of snow drift over these crevasses, thus hiding them from view. Climbers sometimes fall into them. In 1965, a 21-year-old Oxford student tried to climb the mountain alone, and was never again heard from. It was presumed that he fell into a crevasse. The year before an Austrian doctor was separated from his party in a blinding snowstorm and search parties were unable to find him. It has been thought that he too suffered the same fate. Our mountain climbers never climbed the mountain in less than groups of three tied together with nylon ropes. Even so, two of them actually fell into crevasses, but were pulled free by their companions.

The dangers are many. Storms of wind of 100 miles an hour and temperatures of below zero made life disagreeable for our glaciologists. Also, our geologists were caught out on the mountain in a thunder-storm in pelting sleet and rain, and the ensuing fog made it difficult for them to find their way back to camp late at night, soaking wet, cold and exhausted. Without a good sense of direction and a flashlight, they might have been "victims" of Ararat.

Tradition places include the Garden of Eden in the valley of the Aras river; Marand is the burial place of Noah's wife; at Ahora (Aghuri) was the spot where Noah planted his first vineyard. Incidentally, we noticed this summer that a vineyard is still located there. Here was also situated the monastery of St. Jacob, until both it and the village of Ahora were destroyed in 1840 by an earthquake and resulting avalanche, which came thundering down Ahora gulch. James Bryce, the British statesman, author, and later ambassador to Washington once climbed Mount Ararat and he wrote of his experiences in a book, *Transcaucasia and Ararat*.

> I know of nothing so sublime as the general aspect of this huge yet graceful mass seen from the surrounding plains: no view which fills the beholder with a profounder sense of grandeur and space than that which is unfolded, when, on climbing its lofty side he sees the far-reaching slopes beneath, and the boundless waste of mountains beyond, spread out under his eye. Its very simplicity of both form and color increases its majesty. All lines lead straight up to the towering, snowy summit. There can be but few places in the world where so lofty a peak soars so suddenly from a plain so low, and consequently few views equally grand. The mountain raises itself solitary and solemn out of a wide sea-like plain.

Structure

The structural trends of eastern Turkey are in a northwest, southeast direction, such as the Aras river flowage, and the "lining-up" of the triple volcanic peaks, Alagoz, on the Russian side of the Aras river, and Greater Ararat and Lesser Ararat, in Turkey. These triple peaks are in a line, because that is the direction of strike of the elongated fault in the basement complex up through which the molten magma flowed.

If the fractures are shallow, as in the August 19, 1966 quake, no lava is emitted, but when the fault extends many miles deep, it taps the area where the temperature exceeds the melting point of basalt, about 1,200 degrees Centigrade. The fault or fracture relieves the surface pressure, and the hydrostatic pressure forces the liquid magma to the surface, much as oil is blown out when an oil gusher is drilled.

The Tendurek mountains to the west and southwest of Ararat are also volcanic extrusions along faults parallel to the Alagoz-Ararat fault and are part of the complex fault system which winds and twists in a generally north-south lineament through the Dead Sea in Palestine and across the Red Sea into eastern Africa, comprising what is known as the East African Rift. This fault or rift is signalized by volcanism and black-faulting, indicating tension faults.

The Dead Sea, about 1,300 feet below sea-level and the deepest land depression on earth, is a graben, or fault-block, that has dropped down when the tension drew the crust apart. I followed the most recent fault for some 50 miles from Varto, the epicenter of the August 19 quake, to a point

Tendurek mountain crater lake
Courtesy of Doris Bowers 1986

between Erzurum and Ararat. This most recent faulting, which caused the severe earthquake, which wrecked the city of Varto and caused some 2,000 deaths, was minor in displacement as compared with the scars left by the earlier faulting which took place presumably at or soon after the Flood Period. The recent rift caused a displacement of mere feet, while the "original" fracture zone was probably miles wide in places, and furnished a channel-way up through which flawed mountains of magma. This may have taken place at the time of the volcanism which formed the Alagoz-Ararat mountain chain.

Apparently the Paleozoic-Mesozoic limestone complex which covered parts of the region was severely deformed, compressed, folded, and in places like the Ararat area domed up when the rising magma burst through. This doming effect is most evident when one views the same limestone formation on all sides of Mount Ararat. The beds dip away from the mountain on the Turkish, the Russian, and the Persian (Iranian) sides.

There were several eras of volcanic events. Professor Nazmi Oruc of Ataturk University at Erzurum told me that his soil sample study from well drillings in the Aras valley showed at least three periods of volcanism, the layers of lava being interbedded with sediments.

West-southwest of Ararat and west of Diyadin occurs a thick bed of basalt overlaid with limestone, apparently conformable. A river flows through the limestone, and the latter has been folded into an anticline which has fractured along the axis. This fracture has permitted ground water to penetrate down to the lime stone-lava contact.

The lava was apparently not very cool. When the limestone was laid dawn, for it heated the water to the boiling paint, and the steam pressure has forced steady geysers to shoot from the surface. This water flows down the sides of the geyserite or tufa and is caught in pools similar to the hot water pools in Yellowstone Park. Some of these pools are just the right temperature far bathing, and are usually put to such use. This hot springs tufa is varicolored like that in Yellowstone. Local Turkish authorities hope eventually to make a park or national monument of this hot springs-geyser area.

The orogeny of the hot springs bespeaks fast tectonic activity, cataclysmic action, and does not fit long-ages geology. Seemingly, basaltic extrusion was quickly followed by deposition of limestone before the hot lava cooled. If this limestone, designated Cretaceous, was laid down some hundred million years ago, surely the lava would have lost its heat long ago, for the lime-stone covering the basalt is not very thick. In fact one wonders how it could have retained its heat this long even if the rock was formed at the time of the Flood! The Genesis record tells us that, early in Creation week, the whole earth was covered with water similar to the flooding by the Deluge: the difference being that the whole earth was originally almost a perfect globe, without mountains and ocean basins. There was less water then to cover the earth than now. Then, the record tells us, the Creator formed the ocean basins, and dry land by diastrophism or uplift. The water ran off the land into the basins; as most geologists agree that the ocean basins existed from earliest times. We are not informed how high the continental cratons or mountains were, but presumably not as high as now. Genesis mentions rivers;

among them is the Euphrates, which rises not too far from Mount Ararat. A river drainage system needs high land for its source.

Evidence gathered at Mount Ararat indicates that the original mountain was much lower than the present one and was of different composition or at least of different texture and different color. The metrological differences will be discussed later, but the original Mount Ararat apparently was not more than from 10,000 to 12,000 feet in height. The present peak is about 17,000 feet, and at its greatest height perhaps measured nearer 20,000 feet. Erosion has worn it down.

During the Flood period—in the broad sense—at least three blankets of basaltic or andesitic lava were extruded over the first Ararat. Volcanic eruptions have taken place periodically ever since, but with subsiding activity. More recent flows have been extruded from cracks lower down on the mountain as each succeeding extrusion had less force than the preceding one.

Ararat is known as a *shield* type of volcano. This section would not be complete without mentioning what was perhaps the most violent eruption associated with Ararat. This did not occur in 1840 as some have surmised, it was infinitely more terrific. Very likely some time after the floodwaters had subsided, almost the whole north-east side of the mountain blew up. A long deep gash was opened in the mountain, known now as the Ahora gulch. This is many miles long and thousands of feet deep and wide, and a conservative estimate would be that from one to two cubic miles of rock debris and volcanic ash was blown from the mountain.

Large surface fragments were hurled miles away down toward the lower slopes of the northeast side, where they are yet visible. Lighter volcanic ash was blown into the upper atmosphere and settled down as light-colored whitish tuff on the east and northeast sides of the mountain. This ash covered some 100 square miles of surface to a thickness of from hundreds of feet near the mountain to a few feet, ten miles away. Thus, a sloping pediment of some 3-5 degrees was formed, which is similar to those seen in the desert Southwest in Arizona. As a result, varied rock specimens of the whole Ararat area are found in the Ahora gulch.

This is the type of volcanic eruption that buried Pompei and Herculaneum. Presumably Noah and his family had left the area by that time. The original Ararat had been deeply blanketed before that, and the only part of the original Ararat now exposed is that at the head of the Ahora Gulch where the giant explosion opened it up.

Little Ararat and other parasite cones are of more recent origin for Little Ararat is smoother and less gullied and eroded than Greater Ararat. The only forests in the whole area are located on the eastern [and northern] slopes of Little Ararat.

Stratigraphy

Abich and others in the past have done stratigraphic studies in the limestone formations of eastern Turkey. They identified index fossils and others belonging to late Paleozoic, mainly Permian; also Triassic, Jurassic and Cretaceous of the Mesozoic, besides some of the early Tertiary. The following are Abich's classifications, taken from the Dogubayazit-Igdir area:

Devonian, gray limestone:	*Atrypa reticularis* *Atrypa aspera* *Spiriferseminai*
Mississippian, dense limestone:	*Productus auritus* *Dalamella michellini*
Pennsylvanian, dark limestone:	*Fusulina verneuili* *Productus intermedius* *Fusulinella lenicularis*

Collection of fossils found by explorers 1984
Courtesy of Doris Bowers

Permian, limestone, shale:	*Goniatities albichianus* *Reticularia* *Spirigera* *Zaphrentis lepticonica*

Triassic, limestone, dolomite:	*Xenodiscus-Arten*
	Pseudomonotis-Arten
	Paratirolites-Arten
	Goniatites abichianus

Jurassic: (Ammonites)	*Soninia sowerbyi*
	Lytoceras mediternaeum
	Sphaeroceras bullatum

Cretaceous:	*Mortoniceras texanum*
	Parapachydiscus neubergeri
	Cyclasteraturicus

Eocene:	*Discocyclina archiaeri*
	Nummulites irregularis
	Asterodiscus

Oligocene:	*Nummulites incrassatus*

Plincene:	*Planorbis*
	Clupea lanceoplata
	Cardium protractum
	Tapes greganus
	Orbicella defancei

These fossils are all invertebrates.

Petrology

As already mentioned, Eastern Turkey lithologically consists mainly of two types of rock, Paleozoic and Mesozoic limestone intruded by volcanic rock, much of it being an andesitic-basaltic complex on the borderline between andesite and basalt. For that reason it is not practicable to map off certain parts of the mountain as basaltic and other parts as andesitic, since composition varies from place to place, not permitting a mapable unit.

The central highlands of Turkey consist in large part of a whitish limestone interspersed with volcanic rocks. The eastern part of the country is mainly volcanic, interspersed with limestone. Many of the faults cutting through the mountain of Ararat have been filled with a red intrusive rock that resembles a sandstone, but strangely enough is of essentially the same composition as the black and gray basalt and andesite, the difference being that the black magnetite has been oxidized to a red geothite. Following is a typical mineralogical composition:

Sample No. 1
augite 3% rimmed with geothite
hypersthene 5% rimed with geothite
andesine (55) 52%
glass 40% partly devitrified
magnetite trace

The augite is a triclinic pyroxene, while hypersthene is orthorhombic in crystal structure. These pyroxenes are more typical of basalt than andesite, but the plagioclase is andesine, from which the rock *andesite* gets its name. The high percentage of glass indicates that the rock was quickly "frozen" or cooled, so that solidification took place quickly, too fast for crystals to form.

Sample No. 2 was a gray-black rock taken from the 12,000-foot level to the north of the Ahora Gulch. The mineral composition is strangely like sample No. 1, although macroscopically it does not much resemble it.

Sample No. 2
augite 1%
hypersthene 10%
andesine (43) 87%
magnetite 1%
apatite trace
(Apatite is a phosphorus oxide)

As alluded to in the section on Structure, the Ahora gulch exposes the inner core of the original mountain which is distinct in color and texture from the volcanic rock. It is coarse-grained porphyry with a light buff color and much pyrite. This indicates a deep-seated intrusive that cooled slowly, permitting the coarse phenocrysts to form first. Then the whole mass was uplifted through the cover-rock, allowing the remainder of the magma to cool more quickly and form fine grained crystals and glass. This inner core may represent the original mountain dating Creation.

Sample No. 3 was collected from several places in the Ahora Gulch.

Sample No. 3 Andeslte porphyry
bastite 5% (replaces a pyroxene)
glass trace (inclusions in plagioclase)
hypersthene trace (poikolitic inclusions in plagioclase)
andesine 50 94%
sphene trace
leucoxene trace
apatite trace

Sample No. 4 is also a sample from the Ahora gulch from the inner core of the mountain. Its mineralogy is similar.

Sample No. 4
augae 4%
hypersphene 10%
andesine (55) 30% (rims are andesine 50)
magnetite 2%
glass 53%
apatite trace

Sample No 5 is also from the same source as the two previous, but the rock is a basalt rather than an andesite, because the plagioclase is more basic-labradorite.

Sample No. 5 Basalt-porphyry
augite 1%
hypersthene 3%
labradorite 35%
glass 56%
hematite 5%

These samples are typical, and it would not be necessary to give details on more samples.

Cataclysmic Flood Geology

Mount Ararat is easily associated with the Ark of Noah and the Flood in the thoughts of many people. Often the question is asked, What evidences, if any, are found around the mountain to substantiate the flood concept? The answer would be that, if the flood was world-wide as we believe ample evidence indicates, then we should find such evidences not only around Mount Ararat but most anywhere. However, since this paper is an outline in brief of some of the main points of the geology of the Ararat area, I will attempt to point out a few evidences of the flood which were identified in the summer of 1966.

One such evidence has been described concerning the geysers and hot springs west of Diyadin. (See section on Structure) In time past, these geysers were apparently much more active, as volcanic activity was greater in times past. Some lava was perhaps poured out under water while the flood was at its height, for stresses were built up in the crust of the earth, as it was out of isostatic balance due to the shifting of sediments from one place to another. The Hawaiian Islands were built up from the bottom of the ocean, some 11,000 feet deep, by volcanic extrusion. When lava is extruded under water it is cooled quickly and solidifies so rapidly that crystals often have no time to

Possible "Pillow Lava" on Mount Ararat at about 14,000 feet. Notice the sun gleaming off the smooth surfaces and the density of the lava 1984
Courtesy of Doris Bowers

form. Like obsidian; or when very small crystals are formed, much of the basalt and andesite composing upper Ararat was of this type. The lava is often found in rounded blocks called pillow lava because they are of pillow-like appearance having conchoidal fractures. Much of the basalt on Ararat had semicircular fractures, typical of underwater extrusion. When did the waters reach the 11,000-foot level on Mount Ararat? There is the puzzle of the upturned limestone beds surrounding Mount Ararat, on the Turkish, Russian and Persian sides. Near the city of Dogubayazit these limestone formations, some 1,000 feet in thickness are tilted from as much as 45 degrees with respect to the horizontal to almost vertical. The true cause is apparent, although others have not apparently sensed it. The strata dip away from Mount Ararat an every side just as the surface dirt crust does when a seedling bursts up through. Evidently Mount Ararat burst up through the limestone beds to form a near 20,000-foot peak or series of them; and, thus provided shelter for the Ark from the tempestuous storm as the waters began to recede. The Genesis account says that strong winds blew to dry up the floodwaters. If the standard geologic column is right, then these limestone formations were laid down some 100,000,000 years before Mount Ararat came into existence, at a time when the greatest land inundation from the sea took place. For that reason, I wonder if perhaps the Cretaceus period and the Flood may not be synonymous? And, carrying the comparison a bit further, would that not place Creation week way back in the Precambrian? We, of course have presented our reasons for not accepting the validity of orthodox time scales, such as 100,000,000 years in earlier issues of Creation Research Society publications. According to Genesis geology, we could scarcely visualize a universal deluge between Creation and the Flood, for the Euphrates valley, we believe, was the cradle of civilization. Limestone is precipitated under water; therefore, such sedimentary rock must have been laid down during the inundation of the earth by the flood waters-the early part perhaps-since Mount Ararat was apparently elevated to its full height during the latter period of the flood, to provide the above mentioned haven for the Ark. There are small peaks on the top of Greater Ararat, which might well have provided that haven.

This may not sound so much like fanciful speculation when one reads some recent findings of the Lament geological observatory at Columbia University. The New York Times News Service for Jan. 3. 1967, reported:

> The findings also concern a layer of sediment 1,000 feet thick beneath the floor of the Atlantic. It apparently has lain undisturbed for 70 million years. The layer across the Atlantic floor appears to be a relic of a cataclysmic occurrence at the end of the Cretaceus period, 70 million years. During the Cretaceus, oceans covered much of the present-day continents. Toward the end of the period the land rose out of the sea (or the seas subsided). Water cascading off the land carried sediment that was laid down in the deep basins. This may account for the deep buried layer.

If we but substitute the word "Flood" for "Cretaceus" in the above statement, the Lamont Geological observatory has given a very graphic, and presumably accurate, picture of just what happened at the close of the flood-period. We can detect fracture patterns running across the ocean bottoms, which may have been deepened to make roam for the floodwaters "cascading" off the continents. Greater deepening of the ocean basins was probably compensated for by a corresponding rise in the height of the continental blocks. Findings of ocean floor research are described in the December 2, 1966 issue of *Science*.

As the waters further subsided, isolated epeiric-seas were formed by arms of land cutting off small bodies of water from the ocean. As the winds of hurricane force dried up these in land seas, salt was precipitated. I examined one such salt mine a few miles northwest of Mount Ararat. The salt was laid down in layers exactly as the limestone and sandstone and shale were, interbedded with thin layers of silt and dust.

After the salt was precipitated, the wind evidently blew dust over the salt layer, then a stronger gale may have caused a tidal wave to bring in a fresh flooding of the basin. Then, as the winds died down, evaporating water again precipitated a new layer of salt. I counted as many as fifteen to twenty such layers in one place. Such surges of water can be attested to by two mountaineers in the expedition. They were camping somewhat below the bottom end at the glacier that flows down the bottom of the Ahora gulch. They were rudely awakened by a terrific roar from above when the glacier above the gulch broke loose, and some 100,000 tons of ice and rock came cascading down almost to where the men were camping. Needless to say they hastily moved their camp to safer ground. The top of Mount Ararat, down to about the 14,000 feet level, is permanently ice-capped. This means the cap is a static entity: as the snow continues to fall, the ice-cap builds up. As a consequence of this buildup, Ice "flows" outward as a *Rheid*, that is, a material that under continued pressure flows like a viscous fluid. As the Ararat ice cap flows outward in all directions it divides into about a dozen fingers or glaciers flowing down various canyons. As is typical of all glaciers, the Ararat glaciers are eroding agents, carrying tremendous quantities of rock debris from higher to lower levels. This means that each year the total height of Ararat is a little bit lower than the previous year. If we knew the annual rate of erosion, we might be in a position to estimate the altitude of Ararat at the time of the Flood.

Scientists from the United States Geological Survey have found that glaciers in Alaska have no fixed rate of advance: that sudden surges cause what they call "catastrophic advances," at speeds from 10 to 100 times the normal rate. The normal now is usually stated as from one to two feet per day "The cause of these surges is not completely understood," said Dr. Mark F. Meier, research geologist at the U.S. Geological Survey office, Tacoma, Washington.

Summary

Eastern Turkey consists of a relatively barren, undeveloped area quite without tree cover. Tectonically, it is very active, and unstable structurally. The region has been folded, faulted, and intruded with basic types of volcanic rock such as andesite and basalt.

Previously the cover racks had been Paleozoic and Mesozoic limestone, but these have been eroded, folded and faulted by frequent orogenic activity, forming volcanic mountains, among which are the Tendurek range, and also the Alagoz-Ararat system. These mountains are found along fault lines which provided channels through which molten magmas hewed from deep zones in the earth's crust, or upper mantle, where the temperature is well above that of the melting point at basalt, about 1,200 degrees Centigrade at one atmosphere pressure. (At depth, the hydrostatic pressure greatly raises the melting point of rock).

On the north and east of Ararat lies the Aras River fault block, at about 2,500 feet to 3,000 feet elevation as compared with the Dogubayazit (southwest) side of Ararat at about 5,000 feet. The rim of Ararat around the mountain forms a depression ring or "moat" of marshy land, not well drained.

Perhaps this was caused by a "collapse cauldron." That is, after a volcano attains its greatest height of activity, the magma settles back into the "bowels of the earth." Leaving an empty void, which recedes to lower levels, like the terrain around Long Beach California, after Signal Hill was drained of oil. The original care of Ararat was andesitic and basalt porphyry. During and since the flood period, the total height was raised thousands of feet by successive cycles of volcanic extrusion. The Mount Ararat region contains abundant evidences of cataclysmic geologic activity, as well as signs of the complete inundation of Mount Ararat and the whole area by floodwaters.

Bibliography

Abich. H., "Die Besteigung des Ararat im Jahre 1845,' *Boitrage z. Kenntuis d. russischen Reiches*. St. Petersburg, 1849.

Blumenthal. M. "Der Vulcan Ararat," *Rev. Fac Sc* Univ. *Istanbul*, Series B. Tome XXIII. No 3-4. 1958.

Parrot, F. *Reise zum Ararat*. Berlin, 1840.

Addendum by Rex Geissler

The issue of fossils on Mount Ararat has been a hotly debated topic recently. Note that the fossils listed by Dr. Abich in the preceding article were found in the Dogubayazit and Igdir areas not on Mount Ararat. In fact, most of the explorers in this book have found many fossils near Dogubayazit. However, in regard to fossils on Ararat, no fossil evidence has ever been verified although there are several people who claim to have found them. Ahmet Arslan, who has climbed Agri Dagh about 60 times, told Rex Geissler that he had personally found hundreds of fossils on Mount Ararat, a number of which are currently in his Virginia home.

Dick Bright reported that Keban Holding Company's Nurettin Ergucu (Chairman of the Board), Cavit Kiliccote (President), and Muammer Coskun (member of Board of Directors), who personally knew the Turkish Ministers of the Interior and Defense, told him of fossil evidence such as sea horses, seashells, and other fossils of ocean origin which have been found as high as 14,000 feet on Ararat.[2] In 1969, when he was 73 years old and near the summit of Ararat, John Libi claimed that he found a layer of water-borne fossils.

Elfred Lee, put together a 360-degree view of the 1969 SEARCH team Parrot glacier area. Lee included a 1960s photo taken by Dutch glaciologist Nicholas Van Arkle of alleged fish and seashell fossils found near Ark Rock or the western rim of the Ahora Gorge. According to Lee, Van Arkle and the other members of the team could see the fish and seashell fossils with the

---

[2] Richard C. Bright, *The Ark, A Reality?* (Guilderland, New York: Ranger, 1988), p.338.

Photo showing sedimentary layers and alleged fossils on Mount Ararat
Courtesy of Nicholas Van Arkle via Elfred Lee

naked eye but could not get across the terrain to take close up photos. Although the photo below is not close enough to make a positive identification, it definitely looks like sedimentation and possibly could be fossils.

WHO CONTROLLED ARARAT WHEN?

By Researcher C. Allen Roy

Reprinted from *Ararat Report* courtesy of Bill Crouse

Mount Ararat was part of the Urartian mountain kingdom until around 600 B.C. when the Armenian people came into the area until WWI.

From the period of WWI we have several reported sightings of Noah's Ark on Ararat. The Russian aviator, the Turkish soldiers, and the American, Mr. Guillford Officer. Since the Ottoman Turks were fighting the Russians, it is highly unlikely that if one or the other side controlled Ararat that the other side would be allowed on the mountain. A quick study into the fortunes of the war in this region show some interesting possibilities.

The Russian army had been quite successful during the first four years of the war. By December 1916, the front stretched from near Samsun on the Black Sea, through Erzincan, to Mush and Bitlis near Lake Van. The Grand Duke Nicholas and General Ludenich planned for a sprint, 1917, offensive toward Constantinople.

Due to a very demoralized Turkish army, historians believe that this could have been a successful drive. However the March (February, by your calendar) Russian Revolution changed the whole complexion of the war. The Russians held the front throughout 1917 as they sued for peace with the Central Powers. But, the Bolshevik Revolution in November (October, 1917), disrupted the armies and losses occurred.

During the winter, various conferences virtually gave away all the gains of the war. Beginning in February, 1918, the Turks began an offensive that took much of Georgia and most of Armenia, including Mt. Ararat. However, by autumn Turkey was losing in the Balkans, Palestine, Iraq, and Persia. So in October, 1918, Turkey sued for peace with the allies. Turkey slowly retreated to the 1914 border, which was later redrawn in the 1919 Peace Conference in Europe.

The Russians were in control of Mt. Ararat until about April 1918. Alexander Koor said it was 1916 and 1917 that the Ark was seen and explored by the Russians. The timing appears to fit.

From about April, 1918, until the end of the war, Turkey controlled the mountain. During November 1918, Turkey withdrew from Erivan and Armenia...

The Turkish soldiers who claim to have seen the Ark could have easily climbed Ararat at the right time, whether they came from northern Iraq or northern Persia (Iran).

I have a problem in fitting Mr. Guilford Officer's flight at the end of the war. First, the war ended in November, 1918. Any flight at that time would have been late in the season for a sighting.

Second, considering the war ravished conditions of the nations, finding fuel for the plane on such a flight could not have been easy.

Third, the countries were unstable and unlikely in the mood to want joy flights across their land. However, a lot of crazy things have been done against all odds by hardy adventurers. So who knows?

NOAH'S ARK SOURCES AND ALLEGED SIGHTINGS

Compiled by Rex Geissler
Most Pre-13th Century Ancient Sources are described by Bill Crouse

The Biblical Record of Genesis 6:5-9:20 by Moses (NASB)
- 13th-15th Century B.C.

Then the Lord saw that the wickedness of man was great on the earth, and that every intent of the thoughts of his heart was only evil continually. [6] And the Lord was sorry that He had made man on the earth, and He was grieved in His heart. [7] And the Lord said, "I will blot out man whom I have created from the face of the land, from man to animals to creeping things and to birds of the sky; for I am sorry that I have made them." [8] But Noah found favor in the eyes of the Lord.

[9] These are the records of the generations of Noah. Noah was a righteous man, blameless in his time; Noah walked with God. [10] And Noah became the father of three sons: Shem, Ham, and Japheth. [11] Now the earth was corrupt in the sight of God, and the earth was filled with violence. [12] And God looked on the earth, and behold, it was corrupt; for all flesh had corrupted their way upon the earth.

[13] Then God said to Noah, "The end of all flesh has come before Me; for the earth is filled with violence because of them; and behold, I am about to destroy them with the earth. [14] "Make for yourself an Ark of gopher wood; you shall make the Ark with rooms, and shall cover it inside and out with pitch. [15] "And this is how you shall make it: the length of the Ark three hundred cubits, its breadth fifty cubits, and its height thirty cubits. [16] "You shall make a window for the Ark, and finish it to a cubit from the top; and set the door of the Ark in the side of it; you shall make it with lower, second, and third decks. [17] "And behold, I, even I am bringing the flood of water upon the earth, to destroy all flesh in which is the breath of life, from under heaven; everything that is on the earth shall perish. [18] "But I will establish My covenant with you; and you shall enter the Ark—you and your sons and your wife, and your sons' wives with you. [19] "And of every living thing of all flesh, you shall bring two of every kind into the Ark, to keep them alive with you; they shall be male and female. [20] "Of the birds after their kind, and of the animals after their kind, of every creeping thing of the ground after its kind, two of every kind shall come to you to keep them alive. [21] "And as for you, take for yourself some of all food which is edible, and gather it to

yourself; and it shall be for food for you and for them." [22] Thus Noah did; according to all that God had commanded him, so he did. [7:1] Then the Lord said to Noah, "Enter the Ark, you and all your household; for you alone I have seen to be righteous before Me in this time. [2] "You shall take with you of every clean animal by sevens, a male and his female; and of the animals that are not clean two, a male and his female; [3] also of the birds of the sky, by sevens, male and female, to keep offspring alive on the face of all the earth. [4] "For after seven more days, I will send rain on the earth forty days and forty nights; and I will blot out from the face of the land every living thing that I have made." [5] And Noah did according to all that the Lord had commanded him.

[6] Now Noah was six hundred years old when the flood of water came upon the earth. [7] Then Noah and his sons and his wife and his sons' wives with him entered the Ark because of the water of the flood. [8] Of clean animals and animals that are not clean and birds and everything that creeps on the ground, [9] there went into the Ark to Noah by twos, male and female, as God had commanded Noah. [10] And it came about after the seven days, that the water of the flood came upon the earth. [11] In the six hundredth year of Noah's life, in the second month, on the seventeenth day of the month, on the same day all the fountains of the great deep burst open, and the floodgates of the sky were opened. [12] And the rain fell upon the earth for forty days and forty nights.

[13] On the very same day Noah and Shem and Ham and Japheth, the sons of Noah, and Noah's wife and the three wives of his sons with them, entered the Ark, [14] they and every beast after its kind, and all the cattle after their kind, and every creeping thing that creeps on the earth after its kind, and every bird after its kind, all sorts of birds. [15] So they went into the Ark to Noah, by twos of all flesh in which was the breath of life. [16] And those that entered, male and female of all flesh, entered as God had commanded him; and the Lord closed it behind him. [17] Then the flood came upon the earth for forty days; and the water increased and lifted up the Ark, so that it rose above the earth. [18] And the water prevailed and increased greatly upon the earth; and the Ark floated on the surface of the water. [19] And the water prevailed more and more upon the earth, so that all the high mountains everywhere under the heavens were covered. [20] The water prevailed fifteen cubits higher, and the mountains were covered. [21] And all flesh that moved on the earth perished, birds and cattle and beasts and every swarming thing that swarms upon the earth, and all mankind; [22] of all that was on the dry land, all in whose nostrils was the breath of the spirit of life, died. [23] Thus He blotted out every living thing that was upon the face of the land, from man to animals to creeping things and to birds of the sky, and they were blotted out from the earth; and only Noah was left, together with those that were with him in the Ark. [24] And the water prevailed upon the earth one hundred and fifty days. [8:1] But God remembered Noah and all the beasts and all the

cattle that were with him in the Ark; and God caused a wind to pass over the earth, and the water subsided. [2] Also the fountains of the deep and the floodgates of the sky were closed, and the rain from the sky was restrained; [3] and the water receded steadily from the earth, and at the end of one hundred and fifty days the water decreased. [4] And in the seventh month, on the seventeenth day of the month, the Ark rested upon the mountains of Ararat. [5] And the water decreased steadily until the tenth month; in the tenth month, on the first day of the month, the tops of the mountains became visible.

[6] Then it came about at the end of forty days, that Noah opened the window of the Ark which he had made; [7] and he sent out a raven, and it flew here and there until the water was dried up from the earth. [8] Then he sent out a dove from him, to see if the water was abated from the face of the land; [9] but the dove found no resting place for the sole of her foot, so she returned to him into the Ark; for the water was on the surface of all the earth. Then he put out his hand and took her, and brought her into the Ark to himself. [10] So he waited yet another seven days; and again he sent out the dove from the Ark. [11] And the dove came to him toward evening; and behold, in her beak was a freshly picked olive leaf. So Noah knew that the water was abated from the earth. [12] Then he waited yet another seven days, and sent out the dove; but she did not return to him again.

[13] Now it came about in the six hundred and first year, in the first month, on the first of the month, the water was dried up from the earth. Then Noah removed the covering of the Ark, and looked, and behold, the surface of the ground was dried up. [14] And in the second month, on the twenty-seventh day of the month, the earth was dry. [15] Then God spoke to Noah, saying, [16] "Go out of the Ark, you and your wife and your sons and your sons' wives with you. [17] "Bring out with you every living thing of all flesh that is with you, birds and animals and every creeping thing that creeps on the earth, that they may breed abundantly on the earth, and be fruitful and multiply on the earth." [18] So Noah went out, and his sons and his wife and his sons' wives with him. [19] Every beast, every creeping thing, and every bird, everything that moves on the earth, went out by their families from the Ark.

[20] Then Noah built an altar to the Lord, and took of every clean animal and of every clean bird and offered burnt offerings on the altar. [21] And the Lord smelled the soothing aroma; and the Lord said to Himself, "I will never again curse the ground on account of man, for the intent of man's heart is evil from his youth; and I will never again destroy every living thing, as I have done. [22] "While the earth remains,
Seedtime and harvest,
And cold and heat,
And summer and winter,
And day and night
Shall not cease."

[9:1] And God blessed Noah and his sons and said to them, "Be fruitful and multiply, and fill the earth. [2] "And the fear of you and the terror of you shall be on every beast of the earth and on every bird of the sky; with everything that creeps on the ground, and all the fish of the sea, into your hand they are given. [3] "Every moving thing that is alive shall be food for you; I give all to you, as I gave the green plant. [4] "Only you shall not eat flesh with its life, that is, its blood. [5] "And surely I will require your lifeblood; from every beast I will require it. And from every man, from every man's brother I will require the life of man.

[6] "Whoever sheds man's blood,

By man his blood shall be shed,

For in the image of God

He made man.

[7] "And as for you, be fruitful and multiply;

Populate the earth abundantly and multiply in it."

[8] Then God spoke to Noah and to his sons with him, saying, [9] "Now behold, I Myself do establish My covenant with you, and with your descendants after you; [10] and with every living creature that is with you, the birds, the cattle, and every beast of the earth with you; of all that comes out of the Ark, even every beast of the earth. [11] "And I establish My covenant with you; and all flesh shall never again be cut off by the water of the flood, neither shall there again be a flood to destroy the earth." [12] And God said, "This is the sign of the covenant which I am making between Me and you and every living creature that is with you, for all successive generations; [13] I set My bow in the cloud, and it shall be for a sign of a covenant between Me and the earth. [14] "And it shall come about, when I bring a cloud over the earth, that the bow shall be seen in the cloud, [15] and I will remember My covenant, which is between Me and you and every living creature of all flesh; and never again shall the water become a flood to destroy all flesh. [16] "When the bow is in the cloud, then I will look upon it, to remember the everlasting covenant between God and every living creature of all flesh that is on the earth." [17] And God said to Noah, "This is the sign of the covenant which I have established between Me and all flesh that is on the earth."

[18] Now the sons of Noah who came out of the Ark were Shem and Ham and Japheth; and Ham was the father of Canaan. [19] These three were the sons of Noah; and from these the whole earth was populated.

[20] Then Noah began farming and planted a vineyard.

The Hebrew for the mountains where the Ark landed is "rrt." The translator has to supply the vowels. The word was initially translated "Urartu." Over the course of time this evolved to "Ararat" (note that only the vowels have changed). This is what one finds in the Greek Version of the Old Testament (Septuagint). When the King James Version (KJV) was translated around 1611 A.D., the translators updated the location to its current name (Armenia) in 2 Kings 19:37 and Isaiah 37:38 since they assumed no one would know where the kingdom of Ararat was located. However, the KJV stuck with "Ararat" in Genesis 8:4 and Jeremiah 51:27.

Other than the previously mentioned Genesis 6-9, the only other references to the Ark of Noah in the entire Bible are Matthew 24:38, Luke 17:27, Hebrews 11:7 and 1 Peter 3:30. Although those scriptures lift Noah up as a man of faith and warn people about judgment exhibited by the flood of Noah where all but eight people on Earth were destroyed, the search for Noah's Ark and other Old Testament artifacts was non-existent from a New Testament perspective. It was not until the last couple hundred years that archaeologists and Bible believers started looking for historic evidence to substantiate the Old and New Testaments in light of anti-Bible movements.

The Samaritan Pentateuch - 5th Century B.C.

This manuscript contains only the first five books of the Old Testament. It puts the landing place of Noah's Ark in the Kurdish mountains north of Assyria. The Samaritan Pentateuch was the Bible used by the Samaritans, a Jewish sect who separated from the Jews about the Fifth century B.C. They were Israelites of mixed blood dating from the time the Assyrians deported many from the Northern Kingdom. The area was then colonized with citizens from Assyria. Intermarriage that occurred when some of these Assyrian colonists married Jews who were not deported resulted in a people who became known as the Samaritans. Their version of the Pentateuch shows a definite propensity to update geographical place names and harmonize difficult passages. There is much evidence that the Samaritan Pentateuch arose during the Fifth century B.C., though the earliest manuscript extant today dates from about the Tenth century A.D.

Targums - 5th Century B.C.

The Targums are paraphrases in Aramaic which were made for the Jews after they returned from the captivity in Babylon (See Nehemiah 8:8). During their long captivity, many of the Jews forgot their native Hebrew, and only understood the language of their former captors—Aramaic.

These paraphrases were originally oral. They were rather loose paraphrases, and in some instances were more like running commentaries. These Targums later were written down and preserved. They give Bible scholars a valuable tool for textual criticism and interpretation. Three of these Targums (Onkelos, Neofiti, and pseudo-Jonathan) put the landing place of the Ark in the Qardu mountains. It should be remembered that this mountain was not far from where some of these Jews spent their captivity. They probably did not know of the kingdom of Ararat (Urartu) since this kingdom had ceased to exist around the seventh century B.C.

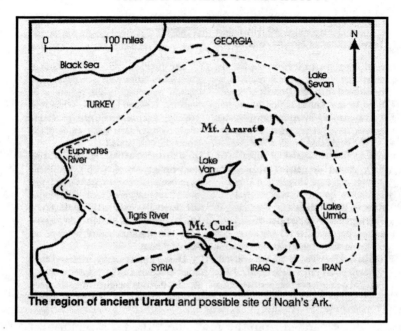

The region of ancient Urartu and possible site of Noah's Ark.

Ancient Urartu, the biblical "mountains of Ararat"
Courtesy of Bible Science Newsletter

Berossus - 275 B.C.

A Chaldean high priest and historian (third century B.C.). His writings in Greek were published about 275 B.C. but his work survived only as far as it was quoted by others, notably, Polyhistor (first century B.C.), and Josephus (first century A.D.). He is also quoted by a few others as late as the fifth century A.D. Berossus' account is basically a version of the Babylonian Flood account. He notes that the Ark "...grounded in Armenia. Some part still remains in the mountains of the Gordyaeans in Armenia, and some get pitch from the ship by scraping off, and use it for amulets."

Hieronymus - 30 B.C.

Hieronymus, an Egyptian historian, wrote about the Ark.

Nicholas of Damascus - 30 B.C.

Nicholas of Damascus, the biographer of Herod the Great and the author of a universal history, wrote about the Ark. He said in the first century A.D. that "there is in Armenia a great mountain called Baris, where many refugees found safety at the time of the flood, and one man, transported on an Ark, grounded on the summit, and relics of the timbers were long preserved."

Josephus - 75 A.D.

Living and writing during the first century A.D., Josephus was a man of Jewish birth who was loyal to the Roman Empire. He was a man of great intellect and a contemporary of the Apostle Paul. As the official historian of the Jews for the Roman Empire he had access to all the archives and libraries of the day. He mentions the remains of Noah's Ark three times. All are found in the Antiquities of the Jews. The first is found in Vol. IV on p. 43 of the Loeb edition.[1]

> Then the Ark settled on a mountain-top in Armenia. . . Noah, thus learning that the earth was delivered from the flood, waited yet seven days, and then let the animals out of the Ark, went forth himself with his family, sacrificed to God and feasted with his household. The Armenians call that spot the Landing-place, for it was there that the Ark came safe to land, and they show the relics of it to this day.

First, note that Josephus says the remains of the Ark existed in his day though he himself was not an eyewitness. Second, the mention of the Armenians assigning a name to the landing site is intriguing, even that he calls them "Armenians." They were first called "Armenians" by the Greek historian Hecataeus, who wrote of the "Armenoi" in the sixth century B.C. Josephus, who also undoubtedly used the Septuagint (the Greek version of the OT), knew that it substituted "Armenia" for "Ararat" (in the Hebrew original) where it occurs in Isaiah 37:38. At the time Josephus wrote (near the end of the first century), the Armenians were still a pagan nation. However, there is a tradition that some Armenians were being converted at this time through the missionary efforts of Bartholomew and Thaddeus. The big question is: Was Josephus quoting Christian Armenians at this early date, or, did pagan Armenians know of the flood? Regardless, it might be significant if the Armenians had this tradition at this early date. We continue to search for the evidence. Third, concerning the Armenian name for the landing place, William Whiston, in his translation of Josephus, has the following footnote:

> This *apo bah tay reon* or "Place of Descent," is the proper rendering of the Armenian name of this very city. It is called in Ptolemy, Naxuana, and Moses Chorenensis, the Armenian historian, Idsheuan; but at the place itself Nachidsheuan, which signifies "The first place of descent," and is a lasting monument of the preservation of Noah in the Ark, upon the top of the mountain, at whose foot it was built, as the first city or town after the flood. See Antiq. B. XX. ch. ii. sect. 3; and Moses Chorenensis, who also says elsewhere, that another town was related by tradition to have been called Seron, or "The Place of Dispersion," on account of the dispersion of

---

[1] The most popular translation of Josephus is by William Whiston in 1737. However, the most accurate translation is the Loeb edition from the Classical Library. We also used this edition to enable us to consult the original text. In Whiston's translation this quotation is in Book one, Chapter 3.

Xisuthrus's or Noah's sons, from thence first made. Whether any remains of this Ark be still preserved as the people of the country suppose, I cannot certainly tell. Mons. Tournefort had, not very long since, a mind to see the place himself, but met with too great dangers and difficulties to venture through them.

Whiston wants to identify "the place of descent" (*apo bah tay reon* in Greek) with the modern city of Nakhichevan situated southeast of Ararat about 65 miles inside the former USSR. Ark researchers in the past have used this footnote as an apparent early evidence for Mt. Ararat's being the site of the Ark's landing.[2] However, we must ask if this is the intent of Josephus, or the eighteenth-century interpretation of Whiston (from his footnote). There seems to be linguistic and other evidence that such is not the case.

First, to identify the current Mt. Ararat as the landing place of the Ark, as per the footnote of Whiston, is contrary to Josephus clearly identifying it as a mountain in Gordyene. Second, the early Armenian historians identified the Gordyene ("Gortuk") mountains as the landing place of Noah's Ark at least up to the eleventh and twelfth centuries.[3] Third, According to the Armenian language scholar Heinrich Hubschmann, the city of Nakhichavan, which does mean "Place of First Descent" in Armenian, was not known by that name in antiquity. Rather, he says the present-day name evolved to "Nakhichavan" from "Naxcavan." The prefix "Naxc" was a name and "avan" is Armenian for "town."[4]

The second, and perhaps most important reference is found on page 45 of the Loeb edition and is a quote from the above-mentioned Chaldean priest, Berossus.[5] We quote here the entire paragraph.

> This flood and the Ark are mentioned by all who have written histories of the barbarians. Among these is Berosus the Chaldaean, who in his description of the events of the flood writes somewhere as follows: "It is said, moreover, that a portion of the vessel still survives in Armenia on the mountain of the Cordyaeans, and that persons carry off pieces of the bitumen[6], which they use as talismans." These matters are also mentioned by Hieronymus the

---

[2] Montgomery apparently makes this assumption. See his book, *The Quest for Noah's Ark*, p.60ff.

[3] See Lloyd R. Bailey. *Where is Noah's Ark?* (Nashville, TN: Abingdon Press, 1978), p. 102ff. See also V. Kurkjian, *A History of Armenia* (New York: Armenian General Benevolent Union, 1959), p. 1-2.

[4] See the work of Heinrich Hubschmann in "Armeniaca." Strassburger Festschrift zur XLVI Versammlung Deutscher Philologen und Schulmanner (Strassburg: Verlag von Karl Tauberner, 1901), Section V. cited in Lloyd R. Bailey, *Noah* (Columbia, SC: University of South Carolina Press, 1989) p. 190ff.

[5] Found in Whiston, Book 1, Chapter 3.

[6] Bitumen is various mixtures occurring naturally or obtained by distillation from coal or petroleum, found in asphalt and tar, and used in surfacing roads and waterproofing.

Egyptian, author of the ancient history of Phoenicia, by Mnaseas and by many others. Nicolas of Damascus in his ninety-sixth book relates the story as follows: "There is above the country of Minyas in Armenia a great mountain called Baris, where, as the story goes, many refugees found safety at the time of the flood, and one man, transported upon an Ark, grounded upon the summit; and relics of the timber were for long preserved; this might well be the same man of whom Moses, the Jewish legislator, wrote."

Again, note that Josephus is not an eyewitness. Rather he is quoting all the ancient authorities he had access to. Most of these are no longer in existence, and indeed, are known only from his quotations of them. It is impressive to this researcher that Josephus seems to indicate there is a consensus among the historians of his day, not only about the remains of the Ark still existing, but also concerning their location.

Josephus also quotes the work of Nicholas of Damascus, the friend and biographer of Herod the Great. Nicholas claimed that he put great labor into his historical studies and apparently had access to many resources. It is possible he was one of Josephus' main sources. His story of the flood, however, deviates from the biblical account in that he has some surviving the flood outside the Ark. His location for the final resting-place of the Ark seems to be in harmony with the Gordyene site. He claims the Ark landed above Minyas on a great mountain in Armenia. According to ancient geographers, Minyas was a country slightly to the southeast of Armenia, below present-day Lake Urmia in Iran. The name he gives this mountain, "Baris, is a mystery. According to Bailey, the Greek word baris means "height," or "tower," and can also mean "boat!"[7] The third reference to the remains of the Ark is found in Volume XX, p. 403 of the Loeb edition.[8]

> Monobazus, being now old and seeing that he had not long to live, desired to lay eyes on his son before he died. He therefore sent for him, gave him the warmest of welcomes and presented him with a district called Carron. The land there has excellent soil for the production of amomum in the greatest of abundance; it also possesses the remains of the Ark in which report has it that Noah was saved from the flood—remains which to this day are shown to those who are curious to see them.

The context of this citation of the Ark's remains has to do with a certain royal family (King and Queen of Adiabene) who converted to Judaism. In the immediate context of the above citation, Monobazus, the man who converted,

---

[7] Lloyd R. Bailey, *Noah* (Columbia, SC: University of South Carolina Press, 1989) p. 216, see footnote #19.

[8] In Whiston it is found on Book 20, Chapter 2.

gives his son Izates the land of Carron. The clues given as to the location of the Ark's remains in this passage are not unequivocal. The remains are said to be somewhere in a country called Carron which must be found in the greater country of Adiabene. Why? Because the king could not have given what was not his, therefore, Carron must be found within Adiabene.

It is fairly certain that Adiabene is bounded by the Tigris on the West and the Upper (north) and Lower (south) Zab Rivers. Today this would be northeastern Iraq. The land of Carron presents some difficulties. It is mentioned only by Josephus. There does seem to be some doubt about the text here since the Loeb edition amends the text to read "Gordyene" where the same "Carron" is mentioned elsewhere in Antiquities.[9] If this is the case then Josephus is not giving us a second location for the remains of Noah's Ark. He may have associated Adiabene with Gordyene since they were next to each other. There is precedent for this. Pliny, a Roman author and contemporary of Josephus, places the city of Nisibis in Adiabene when it is actually located to the west of Gordyene (*Natural History*, 6.16). It is interesting to note also that Hippolytus (second century A.D.) agrees. He says, "The relics of the Ark are . . . shown to this day in the mountains called Ararat, which are situated in the direction of the country of Adiabene. This would be correct since he wrote from Rome." (*Refutation of All Heresies*, 10, Chapter 26).

From the above there seem to be grounds for arguing that Josephus pinpoints the Gordyene site as the landing place of Noah's Ark.

Theophilus of Antioch - 180 A.D.

Around 180 A.D., the sixth bishop of Syrian Antioch, Theophilus, talked briefly about the Ark of Noah. This section comes from the Marcus Dods' translation in the *Ante-Nicene Fathers* (1885, II, 117).[10]

> Moses showed that the flood lasted forty days and forty nights, torrents pouring from heaven, and from the fountains of the deep breaking up, so that the water overtopped every high hill 15 cubits. And thus the race of all the men that were was destroyed, and those only who were protected in the Ark were saved; and these, we have already said, were eight. And of the Ark, the remains are to this day to be seen in the Arabian mountains.

---

[9] The Greek is carrown. The Loeb edition suggests in a footnote that the original reading may have been cardu. This is certainly within the realm of plausibility. This, then would just be another variant spelling of Gordyene, the country of the Kurds. Interestingly enough, there is a land called "Kirruri" located southwest of Lake Urmia. See L.D. Levine, "Geographical Studies in the Neo Assyrian Zagros." Iran 11 (1973) p. 105. This land is a small district adjacent to, and north of Adiabene, just across the Little Zab River.

[10] Montgomery, John, *The Quest for Noah's Ark*. 2nd Edition. (Minneapolis: Dimension Books, 1974), pp. 64-65.

Eusebius - 3rd Century A.D.

In the third century A.D., this early church father noted that a small part of the Ark still remained in the Gordian mountains.

Faustus of Byzantium - 4th Century A.D.

Faustus was a historian of the 4th Century A.D. Very little is known about him except that he was one of the early historians of Armenia, though he was of Greek origin. His original work is lost but his writings have survived in translations.

It is from Faustus that we first hear the story of St Jacob of Nisibis, the godly monk who asks God to see the Ark.[11] After he repeatedly failed to climb the mountain an angel rewarded him with a piece of wood from the Ark. It is this story that is often quoted in succeeding centuries, and the location given for the event in these later sources is Mt. Ararat. However, please note: Faustus, the one who presumably originated the story, puts this event, not on Mt. Ararat, but in the canton of Gordukh. The St. Jacob of the story is the Bishop of Nisibis (modern Nusaybin) a city which is only about 70 miles (not quite within sight) from Cudi Dagh.[12]

To the bishop Mt. Ararat would have been near the end of the known world. If Faustus had meant this mountain he undoubtedly would have called it by its Armenian name of Masis, as he does elsewhere in his work. Armenian historians are in agreement that early Armenian traditions indicated the southern location as the landing place of the Ark. Up to the tenth century all Armenian sources support the southern location as the landing place of the Ark.[13]

Would it not be strange for the Syrian bishop to ignore what his own Syrian Bible (the Pershitta) told him was the landing place of Noah's Ark? Also, St. Jacob's own student, St. Ephraem, refers to the site of the landing as "the mountains of Qardu." It is hard to believe that one of his intimates could be that confused! The natives of the area today tell the story of St. Jacob, the Bishop, and similar traditions associated with Mt. Ararat, i.e. the city built by Noah and his grave, etc.[14]

---

[11] Montgomery, John, *The Quest for Noah's Ark*. 2nd Edition. (Minneapolis: Dimension Books, 1974), pp. 66-69. It is important to note that Faustus wrote from the same century as St. Jacob.

[12] St. Jacob of Nisibis was one of the prominent figures at the Council of Nicea (325 A.D.). He was known for his ability to perform miracles and was known as the Moses of Mesopotamia. He may also have figured in the evangelization Armenia.

[13] See endnote # 20. Also see the tenth century Armenian historian, Thomas Artsruni: Robert W. Thompson, *History of the House of the Artsrunik* (Detroit, MI: Wayne State University, 1985), p. 81.

[14] Bell, *Amurath to Amurath*, p.294.

Epiphianus - 4th Century A.D.

The Bishop of Salamis (Epiphianus) was a fierce opponent of heresy in the fourth century A.D. On two occasions he mentions that the Ark landed in the mountains of the Gordians. In fact, he says the remains are still shown and that if one looks diligently he can still find the altar of Noah.

The Pershitta - 400 A.D.

The Pershitta is a version of the entire Bible made for the Syrian Christians. Scholars are not sure when it was translated but it shows up for the first time around 400 A.D. In Genesis 8:4, it reads "mountains of Quardu" for the resting-place of Noah's Ark. This version shows a definite influence from the Targums mentioned above.

Isidore of Seville - 6th-7th Century A.D.

Isidore wrote during the sixth or seventh century A.D. from about 560 A.D. to 636 A.D. He is quoted in the sixteenth century as saying the Ark landed in the Gordyaean mountains. He states, "Ararat is a mountain in Armenia where the historians testify that the Ark came to rest after the flood. So even to this day wood remains of it are to be seen there."

The Quran - 7th Century A.D.

Written in the seventh century, the Quran says: "The Ark came to rest upon Al-Judi..." (Houd 11:44). The Modern Muslim Encyclopedia is familiar with the early traditions that the Ark came to rest on Cudi Dagh. However, the writer of the article under "Jebel Judi" believes Mohammed was referring to the Judi mountains in Saudi Arabia. This is not certain. Mohammed was very familiar with Christian and Jewish traditions, not to mention the fact that he probably traveled to this area during his days as a merchant. In the English translation of the Quran made by George Sale in 1734, a footnote concerning the landing place of the Ark states that the Quran is following an ancient tradition.[15] At least the following Muslim sources seem to agree.

Elfred Lee went to the Islamic Center in Washington, D.C. to research this issue. The curator of the center showed him a book which said that "Jebel Judi" was a peak of Mount Ararat. The curator also said that Judi results in Cudi which results in Kudi which results in Kurds. So there is a possibility that finding the Ark on Mount Ararat could substantiate Jewish, Christian and Muslim sources. This would be one area where Jews, Christians and Moslems actually agree.

---

[15] This footnote is found in the Appendix on p. 496. The footnotes were the responsibility of Frederic Mynon Cooper.

Eutychius - 9th Century A.D.

Eutychius was the Bishop of Alexandria in the ninth century. He says, "The Ark rested on the mountains of Ararat, that is Jabal Judi near Mosul." Mosul is a city near ancient Ninevah about 80 miles south of Cudi Dagh.

Al Masudi - 10th Century A.D.

Masudi, writing in the tenth century says "The Ark came to rest on Jabal Judi...8 P(F)arasangs from the Tigris. The place can still be seen." Eight P(F)arasangs is approximately 25-30 miles—the distance Cudi Dagh is from the Tigris.

Ibn Haukal - 10th Century A.D.

Also writing in the tenth century, Ibn Haukal places Al-Judi near the town of Nesbin (modern Nusaybin) and mentions that Noah built a village at the foot of the mountain.

Benjamin of Tudela - 12th Century A.D.

Benjamin of Tudela wrote that he traveled "two days to Jezireh Ben Omar, an island in the Tigris on the foot of Mt. Ararat…on which the Ark of Noah rested. Omar Ben al-Khatab removed the Ark from the summit of the two mountains and made a mosque of it." There are several things to note here: the ruins of this city, Jezireh Ben Omar, are located at the foot of *Cudi Dagh*; here is evidence that this mountain was also called "Mt. Ararat"; it does have two peaks; and remains were still there at this date.

William of Rubruck - 1254-1555 A.D.

Dr. John Warwick Montgomery recorded the following account.

In 1252, a Franciscan called William, a native of Rubruck in French Flanders, was sent by King Louis IX of France on a secret mission to the court of the Mongol Emperor. His *Itinerarium* records the experience he underwent during the next three years and 10,000 miles of journeyings. It is an account to which geographical science, natural history, ethnology, and the history of religions have subsequently been greatly indebted. Sir Henry Yule, the greatest authority on midiaeval geography of the last century, calls it "one of the best narratives of travel in existence" and its author "an honest, pious, stouthearted, acute and most intelligent observer, keen in the acquisition of knowledge."

[William of Rubrick stated the following]

Near this city [of Naxua] are mountains in which they say that Noah's Ark rests; and there are two mountains, the one greater than the other; and the Araxes flows at their base; and there is a town there called Cemanum, which interpreted means "eight," and they say that it was thus called from the eight persons who came out of the Ark, and who built it on the greater mountain.

Many have tried to climb it but none has been able. This bishop told me that there had been a monk who was most desirous (of climbing it), but that an angel appeared to him bearing a piece of the wood of the Ark, and told him to try no more. They had this piece of wood in his church, they told me [Etchmiadzin monastery of Nadjivan]. This mountain did not seem to me so very high, that men could not ascend it. An old man gave me quite a good reason why one ought not to try to climb it. They call the mountain Massis, and it is of the feminine gender in their language. "No one," he said, "ought to climb up Massis; it is the mother of the world." [...a man can no more reach its top than re-enter his mother's womb. Rubrick was misinformed about the gender of this word, as inanimate objects have no gender in Armenian.[16]

Vincent of Beauvais - 13th Century A.D.

Vincent says the following.

In Armenia there is a noble city called Ani where a thousand churches and a hundred thousand families or households are to be found. The Tartars captured this city in twelve days. Near it is Mount Ararat, where Noah's Ark rests, and at the foot of that mountain is the first city which Noah built, called Laudume. Closer by the city flows the river Ararthosi, which traverses the plane of Mongan where the Taratas winter, and empties into the Caspian Sea...

Ibn Al-Mid - 13th Century A.D.

This thirteenth century Muslim historian informs us that an emperor (Heraclius) wished to climb Jabal-Judi to see the site in the seventh century.

Zakariya ben Muhammad al Kazwine - 13th Century A.D.

A Muslim geographer of the thirteenth century also reports that wood from the Ark was used to construct a monastery. He does not, however, give a location.

Odoric of Pordenone – 1286-1331 Century A.D.

Odoric, a Bohemian of Friuli near Pordenone in northern Italy, was a Franciscan monk who is remembered chiefly for his wanderings in the Far East and returning back to Italy.

---

[16] Montgomery, John, *The Quest for Noah's Ark*. 2nd Edition. (Minneapolis: Dimension Books, 1974), pp. 81-83.

Departing thence, I came into Armenia the Greater, to a certain city which is called ARZIRON [Erzrum], which in time long past was a fine and most wealthy city...But it hath most excellent water, the reason whereof seems to be that the springs of this water are one day's journey from the city; and this city is just midway to Tauris.

Departing from it, I came to a certain hill which is called SARBISACALO; and in that country is the mountain whereon is Noah's Ark. And I would fain have ascended it, if my companions would have waited for me. But the folk of the country told us that no one ever could ascend the mountain, for this, as it is said, hat seemed not to be the pleasure of the Most High.[17]

Jordanus - 1321-1330 Century A.D.

Dr. Montgomery notes the following about Jordanus.

Friar Jordanus (fl. 1321-1330), a French Dominican missionary-explorer and bishop of Colombum in India, recorded his wide-ranging experiences in Asia in Mirabilia Descripta (ca. 1329-1338)...

[Jordanus stated the following]

In Armenia the Greater I saw one great marvel. This is it: a mountain of excessive height and immense extent, on which Noah's Ark is said to have rested. The mountain is never without snow, and seldom or never without clouds, which rarely rise higher than three parts up. The mountain is inaccessible, and there never has been anybody who could get farther than the edge of the snow. And (marvelous indeed!) even the beasts chased by the huntsmen, when they come to the snow, will liefer turn, will liefer yield them into the huntsmen's hands, than go farther up that mountain. This mountain hath a compass of more than three days journey for a man on horseback going without halt. There be serpents of a great size, which swallow hares alive and whole, as I heard from a certain trustworthy gentleman who saw the fact, and shot an arrow at a serpent with a hare in his mouth but scathed it not.[18] In a certain part of the mountain is a dwelling which Noah is said to have built on leaving the Ark; and there, too, is said to be that original vine which Noah planted, and whereby he got drunk; and it giveth such huge branches of grapes as you would scarce believe. This I heard from a certain Catholic archbishop of ours, a great man and a powerful, and trustworthy to boot, the lord of that land; and,

---

[17] Montgomery, John, *The Quest for Noah's Ark*. 2nd Edition. (Minneapolis: Dimension Books, 1974), pp. 85-86.

[18] Stories of serpents seem to be rife in Armenia. On the Araxes, south of Nakhchevan, is a mountain called the Serpent Mountain, where serpents are said to collect in such numbers at certain times, that no man or beast dare approach (See Haxthausen's *Transcaucasia*, pp. 144, 181, 353, etc.)

indeed, I believe I have been at the place myself, but it was in the winter season.[19]

Marco Polo - 14th Century A.D.

Marco Polo traveled near Mount Ararat and stated in *The Travels*:

> In the heart of Greater Armenia is a very high mountain, shaped like a cube, on which Noah's Ark is said to have rested, whence it is called the Mountain of Noah's Ark. It is so broad and long that it takes more than two days to go round it. On the summit the snow lies so deep all the year round that no one can ever climb it; this snow never entirely melts, but new snow is for ever [sic] falling on the old.

Pegolotti - 1340 A.D.

Francesco Balducci Pegolotti was a merchant in the service of the Company of the Bardi in Florence. He prepared a handbook of international trade and commerce in about 1340 A.D. Dr. Montgomery notes that "It shows that the Ark's presence on Ararat was a matter of such common opinion in the medieval period that merchants could use the expression 'under Noah's Ark' as a synonym for Ararat, without even mentioning the latter."

> Under Noah's Ark,   for duty 3
>   Ditto   ditto   for tant 0   ½
>
> And you may reckon that the exactions of the Moccols or Tartar troopers along the road, will amount to something like fifty aspers a load. So that the cost on account of a load of merchandize going by land from Ajazzo of Armenia to Tauris in Cataria will be, as appears by the above details, 209 aspers a load, and the same back again.[20]

---

[19] The name of the province and town of *Nakhchevan*, east of Ararat, signifies "first place of desent, or of lodging." The antiquity of the tradition is proved by the fact, that Josephus affirms that the Armenians call the place where the Ark rested "*the place of descent;*" whilst Ptolemy supplied the name of *Naxuana*.

The place alluded to by Jordanus appears to be Arguri, the only village upon Ararat. Here Noah is said to have built his altar on the exact spot now occupied by the church, and it is of the vineyards of Arguri that the Scripture is believed to speak when it is said that "Noah began to be an husbandman, and planted a vineyard." The church is of unascertained but remote date; and the name of the place signifies (*Argh-urri*) "He planted the vine." At Nakhchevan "the grapes were almost unequalled in excellence, and seemed to deserve the honour of growing on the spot." (Smith and Dwight, *Researches in Armenia*, p. 256.) Arguri was buried by an earthquake, accompanied by volcanic indications, July 2nd, 1840 [June 20th, Old Style].

[20] Montgomery, John, *The Quest for Noah's Ark*. 2nd Edition. (Minneapolis: Dimension Books, 1974), pp. 86-88.

Sir John Mandeville - 1372 A.D.

John Mandeville, an English Knight, wrote a debated account of his alleged world travels between 1322 and 1356. He is identified with Jean de Bourgogne or Jean à la Barbe who lived in Liège, France.

> From that city of Artyroun [Erzerum] men go to a mountain called Sabissocolle; and there beside is another mountain called Ararat, but the Jews call it Taneez, where Noah's ship rested, and still is upon that mountain; and men may see it afar in clear weather. That mountain is full seven miles high; and some men say that they have seen and touched the ship, and put their fingers in the parts where the devil went out, when Noah said "Benedicte." But they that say so speak without knowledge; for no one can go up the mountain for the great abundance of snow which is always on the mountain, both summer and winter, so that no man ever went up since the time of Noah, except a monk, who, by God's grace, brought one of the planks down, which is yet in the monastery at the foot of the mountain. And beside is the city of Dayne, which was founded by Noah, near which is the city of Any, in which were one thousand churches.[21]

Gonzalez de Clavijo - 1412 A.D.

This is the account of the embassy of Ruy Gonzalez de Clavijo to the court of Timour started Spanish travel literature.

> On Saturday, the 13th of May, the road led along the foot of the mountain of the Ark of Noah. It was very high, and the summit was covered with snow, and it was without woods; but there was much herbage upon it, and many streams. Near the road there were many edifices, and foundations of houses, of stone; and great quantities of rye was growing, as if it had been sown by man, but it was useless, and did not come to grain; and there was also plenty of water cresses. At the foot of this mountain they came to the ruins of a town long since deserted, which was a league in length; and the people of the country said that it was the first town that was built in the world, after the flood, and that it was founded by Noah and his sons.
>
> After leaving these ruins, they came to a great plain, in which there were many streams of water, and trees, and rose gardens, and fountains. The mountain had a very sharp peak, which was covered with snow, and they say that the snow never leaves this peak all the year round, either in winter or summer, and this is on account of its great height.

---

[21] Montgomery, John, *The Quest for Noah's Ark*. 2nd Edition. (Minneapolis: Dimension Books, 1974), pp. 89-90.

On this day the ambassadors took their siesta by a beautiful fountain, near a stone arch; and while they were there, the clouds moved away, and the peak of the mountain appeared, but they suddenly returned, and the people said that it was very seldom visible.

Next to this mountain, there was another, which also had a sharp peak, but not so high as the first, and between these two peaks there is one like a saddle, and they were all very high, and their summits were all covered with snow.[22]

John Heywood - 1520s A.D.[23]

In his play titled *The Four PP*, a playwright in the 1520s by the name of John Heywood mentions the fact that Armenia was considered to be the location of Noah's Ark and a place of pilgrimage.

The Two Ararats, by Boulé Legouze. This French traveler sketched this crude rendering in 1647. His numbered locations represent: (1) the resting place of the Ark, (2) snow, (3) fog, (4) the mountains of Ararat, (5) St. Jacob himself, (6) the voice that speaks, and (7) foothills. From *Penashkharik Pararan*.

Boulé Legouze - 1647 A.D.

French Traveler Boulé Legouze sketched a representation of several Ararat features including his view of the Ark's resting place, snow, fog, Little and Greater Ararat, St. Jacob and the foothills.

---

[22] Montgomery, John, *The Quest for Noah's Ark*. 2nd Edition. (Minneapolis: Dimension Books, 1974), pp. 91-93.

[23] Tim LaHaye and John Morris, *The Ark on Ararat* (Nashville: Thomas Nelson Publishers, 1976.

Adam Olearius - 1647 A.D.

Adam Olearius published *The Voyagers and Travels of the Ambassadors*. He states the following:

> [24]Mount Ararat, upon which Noah's Ark rested after the deluge, and which the Armenians call Messina, the Persions, Agri, and the Arabians Subeilah, is without comparison much higher than the Caucasus, and is indeed but a great black Rock, without any Verduere, and cover'd with Snow on the top, as well in Summer as Winter…The *Armenians*, and the *Persians* themselves, are of opinion, that there are still upon the said Mountain some remainders of the Ark, but that Time hath so hardened them, that they seem absolutely petrify'd. At *Schamachy* in *Media* Persia, we were shewn a Crosse of a black and hard Wood, which the Inhabitants affirmed to have been made of the Wood of the Ark: and upon that accompt [sic] it was look'd upon as a most precious Relick, and, as such, was wrapp'd in Crimson Taffata. The Mountain is now inaccessible, by reason of the precipes whereby it is encompass'd of all sides.[25]

Jans Janszoon Struys - 1694 A.D.

A monastic friend told Dutch traveler Jan Janszoon Struys that "[because of the weather on the mountain] the Ark is not decayed, and that it is after so many centuries as complete as the first day it came here."

Woodcut showing Echmiadzin and Ararat with Ark on side 1711
Sir John Chardin

Doc.62: Engraving of Mt. Ararat showing reported resting place of the Ark. From *Travels in Persia* by *Sir John Chardin. -1711-*

After the vulcan explosion 1840 A.D. the Ahora Gorge became bigger.

---

[24] Tim LaHaye and John Morris, *The Ark on Ararat* (Nashville: Thomas Nelson Publishers, 1976.

Sir John Chardin - 1711 A.D.

Sir John Chardin created a woodcut of Echmiadzin with Ararat and the Ark on top in 1711 A.D.

Pierre Daniel Huet - 1722 A.D.

Pierre Daniel Huet created a conception map entitled "Terrestrial Paradise" which placed the Ark on top of another traditional "Mount Ararat" in Iran, "Kuh e Alvand." The map was placed in Calmet's *Dictionnaire historique del la Bible*.[26]

Map 10. Map showing Noah's ark atop Alwand Kuh (?) in modern Iran. From A. Calmet's Dictionnaire historique, critique, chronologique, géographique et littéral de la Bible, Vol. A–D, 1730.

Pierre Daniel Huet conception map entitled "Terrestrial Paradise"
Courtesy of Dr. John Warwick Montgomery book *The Quest for Noah's Ark*

---

[25] ibid.

[26] Montgomery, John, *The Quest for Noah's Ark*. 2nd Edition. (Minneapolis: Dimension Books, 1974), Preface.

Some researchers have also suggested that this or another Iranian mountain (perhaps in the Zagros Mountain range) may have been the mountain that Ed Davis was taken to rather than today's Mount Ararat and that it should be checked out. Of course, it should be noted that "Kuh e Alvand" is outside the traditional boundaries of the biblical "mountains of Ararat."

Sketch of St. Jacob Monastery at Ahora and Mount Ararat 1829
Detailed sketch by Dr. Friedrich Parrot

Dr. J. J. Friedrich Parrot - 1829 A.D.

Dr. Parrot visited St. Jacob monastery at Ahora eleven years before the entire village disappeared in a massive earthquake in 1840 A.D. At the monastery (located at an elevation 6,394 feet), David Balsiger in *The Incredible Discovery of Noah's Ark* claimed Parrot saw Ark artifacts although he did not specify what the articles were. Parrot was the first foreigner in modern times to climb to the summit of Ararat. He also visited the Armenian Echmiadzin Monastery where an alleged Ark wood cross is located.

Parrot never did claim to see the Ark himself but he wrote, "They are all firmly persuaded that the Ark remains to this day on the top of Mount Ararat, and that in order to ensure its preservation no human being is allowed to approach it."

The Parrot glacier on the northwest side of the mountain was named after him. Dr. Parrot wrote about his adventure in *Journey to Ararat*.

Karl Behrens - 1835 A.D.

Karl Behrens reached the summit of Ararat and confirmed seeing the cross that was planted by Parrot at the summit. Behrens' ascent was confirmed by the Imperial Russian Geographical Society.

Devastating Earthquake - 1840 A.D.

In 1840, an earthquake, subterranean roar, terrific blast of wind, rocks and ice from the Ahora Gorge area killed 2,000 people in Aghuri (later Ahora) and buried the St. Jacob Monastery that Dr. Parrot had visited eleven years earlier.

Thirty-six years later, James Bryce discussed the 1840 explosion of Ararat in his book *Transcaucasia and Ararat*:

> There formerly stood a pleasant little Armenian village of some 200 houses, named Arghuri, or Aghuri...Not far above the village...stood the little monastery of St. Jacob, eight centuries old. Towards sunset in the evening of the 20th of June, 1840, the sudden shock of an earthquake, accompanied by a subterranean roar, and followed by a terrific blast of wind, threw down the houses of Arghuri, and at the same moment detached enormous masses of rock with their superjacent ice from the cliffs that surround the chasm.
>
> A shower of falling rocks overwhelmed in an instant the village, the monastery, and a Kurdish encampment on the pastures above. Not a soul survived to tell the tale...
>
> The little monastery, where Parrot lived so happily among the few old monks...is gone forever.

Civil engineer, Grand Canyon tour guide and weather history researcher Allen Roy has some interesting comments about the 1840 earthquake.

> It has been argued that the catastrophe that destroyed the village of Ahora and the nearby monastery in the 1840s was of such magnitude that the entire Ahora Gorge was created at that time. It is also proposed that the Ark was broken in two pieces or sections.
>
> However, according to geologist Clifford Burdick, "This did not occur in 1840 as some have surmised, it was infinitely more terrific. Very likely some time after the flood-waters had subsided, almost the whole north-east side of the mountain blew up." (See the Geologic Review appendix from *Ararat: The Mother of Mountains* by Clifford L. Burdick, Ph.D., CRSQ Volume 4, p. 9)
>
> We can confirm that the canyon was formed long before the 1840s by comparing the only visual record we have of the Monastery and the mountain—Parrot's lithograph. In that drawing the Ahora Gorge is plainly visible in it's full extent. If you look at any photograph of the gorge taken from the vicinity of the old

village of Ahora you will see on the far back wall of the gorge a waterfall. Deep in the farthest reaches of the canyon, adjacent to the waterfall is a large triangular feature on the canyon wall. That same triangular area is plainly depicted in Parrot's lithograph.

What likely happened at Ahora in the 1840s was an earthquake, an ice fall and avalanche out the mouth of the gorge. It was big enough to destroy the village and monastery but it did not cause the Ahora Gorge.

It is likely that it did not contain enough energy to cause the Ark to break apart. This is a silly idea anyway. We know that the unbroken Ark was visible after 1840 per Haji Yearam, Georgie Hagopian, the Russian account via Ray Lubeck, etc. so the avalanche likely had very little effect on the Ark.

The only logical way for the Ark to have existed this long after the Flood is for it to be in a completely stationary ice or snow pack. If it had been in any glacier, not only would it have been shredded, but all the fractured pieces would be scattered in the rocky end moraines of the mountain's glaciers hundreds or thousands of years ago.

German Dr. Herman von Abich - 1845 A.D.

German geologist Dr. Herman von Abich reached the Ararat summit on July 29, 1845, after three frustrating attempts. The eastern summit as well as Abich I and Abich II glaciers are named after him.

Dr. Abich apparently was not looking for the Ark but rather climbed Ararat to see whether or not the stars and planets were visible during the day from extremely high mountaintops.

Russian Colonel Khodzko - 1850 A.D.

A Russian army officer, Colonel Khodzko, put together an organized team of sixty men to search for Ark but was hampered by poor weather. Their goal was to systematically search the mountain until the Ark was found.

British Major Robert Stuart - 1856 A.D.

British Major Robert Stuart led an expedition of four other British climbers that successfully reached the summit of Mount Ararat and created a sensation with the Kurds. Stuart's group did not claim to see the Ark.

Armenian Haji Yearam and the English Scientists - About 1856 A.D.

Haji Yearam was an Armenian Seventh-Day Adventist whose family lived at the foot of Mount Ararat. This man's name Yearam in Armenian is Jeremiah when translated into English. He made a pilgrimage to Jerusalem and thus gained the title of Haji, Haji Yearam, or Jeremiah the Pilgrim.

When Haji was a large boy but not fully grown, his father was supposedly hired by scientists as their guide to find the Ark. It was an unusually hot summer and the snow and glaciers had melted more than normal. When his father allegedly found the Ark, they went inside and explored the structure which was covered with a strong, thick varnish or lacquer both inside and outside. There were many floors and compartments with bars like animal cages. Despite the purported discovery, the scientists tried to destroy it and took an oath to never let the Ark discovery be known. The scientists had no tools strong enough to destroy the Ark. They pulled out some timbers but they were so hard that they were impossible to burn. The scientists took an oath and threatened everyone present with torture and murder if anyone discussed the incident.

Haji's story was retold second-hand according to his minister, a Rev. Williams of Brockton, Mass. According to Williams, Haji's story was confirmed by an elderly scientist on his deathbed in London. As he was dying, the scientist is said to have changed his attitude about the threats on Ararat and the Ark story. The article was published around 1918 in a Brockton or Boston newspaper which has never been found to confirm the story. Yearam also died in 1920 at the age of 82.

Violet Cummings notes the following in her book.[27]

> Haji Yearam's parents and family lived at the foot of Greater Mount Ararat in Armenia. According to their traditions, they were descended directly from those who had come out of the Ark, but who had never migrated from that country. The descendants of Ham and his sympathizers had migrated over into the land of Shinar and built the tower of Babel. And others had migrated to various countries. But Haji's forebearers had always remained near the mount where the Ark came to rest in a little valley surrounded by some small peaks about three-quarters or more up on the mountain.
>
> For several hundreds of years after the flood his forebears had made yearly pilgrimages up to the Ark to make sacrifices and to worship there. They had a good trail and steps in the steep places. Finally the enemies of God undertook to go to Ararat and destroy the Ark, but as they neared the location there came a terrible storm that washed away the trail, and the lighting blasted the rocks. From that time on, even the pilgrimages ceased, because they feared to betray the way to the ungodly, and they feared God's wrath. They took that terrible storm to be a token that God did not want the Ark disturbed until near the end of the world, when they believed that is presence would be revealed to the whole world. However, the tribesman there handed down the legends from generation to generation, and from time to time lonely shepherds or hunters in very hot summers came back with stories that they had reached the

---

[27] Violet M. Cummings, *Noah's Ark: Fable or Fact* (San Diego: Creation Science Research Center), pp. 119-125.

little valley and had actually seen one end of the Ark where it had been made visible by the melting snow and ice.

When Haji was a large boy, but not yet a man fully grown, there came to his home some strangers. If I remember correctly there were three vile men who did not believe the Bible and did not believe in the existence of a personal God. They were scientists and evolutionists. They were on this expedition specifically to proved the legend of Noah's Ark to be a fraud and a fake. They hired the father of young Haji Yearam as their official guide. (Haji at that time had not yet become a Haji, and was just a large boy.) They hired the boy to assist his father as guide.

It was an unusually hot summer, so the snow and glaciers had melted more than usual. The Armenians were very reticent to undertake any expedition to the Ark because they feared God's displeasure, but the father of Haji thought that possibly the time had come when God wanted the world to know the Ark was still there and he wanted to prove to those atheists that the Bible story of the flood and the Ark is true.

After extreme hardship and peril the party came to the little valley way up on Greater Ararat, not on the very top, but a little down from the top. This little valley is surrounded by a number of small peaks. There the Ark came to rest in a little lake, and the peaks protected it from the tidal waves that rushed back and forth as the flood subsided. On one side of the valley the water from the melting snows and glacier spills over in a little river that runs down the mountain. As they reached this spot, there they found the prow of a mighty ship protruding out of the ice. They went inside the Ark and did considerable exploring. It had bars like animal cages of today. The whole structure was covered with a varnish or lacquer that was very thick and strong, both outside and inside the ship. The ship was built more like a great and mighty house on the hull of a ship, but without any windows. There was a great doorway of immense size, but the door was missing. The scientists were appalled and dumbfounded and went into a Satanic rage at finding what they hoped to prove nonexistent. They were so angry and mad that they said they would destroy the ship, but the wood was more like stone than any wood we have now. They did not have tools or means to wreck so mighty a ship and had to give up. They did tear out some timbers and tried to burn the wood, but it was so hard it was almost impossible to burn it.

They held a council, and then took a solemn and fearful death oath. Any man present who would ever breathe a word about what they had found would be tortured and murdered.

They told their guide and his son that they would keep tabs on them and that if they ever told anyone and they found it out they would surely be tortured and murdered. For fear of their lives, Haji and his father had never told what they found except to their best trusted and closest relatives.

In the year 1918 we moved to Brockton, Massachusetts, where I took the position of Supervisor of Manual Arts in the High School of that city. I was soon put on permanent tenure by the State Board of Education and held that position for nearly eight years until I entered the gospel ministry.

Now, if some atheistic scientist had found an elephant's knee cap that looked something like a skull bone, they would have proclaimed it a missing link and it would have been printer in large letters across the top of the daily newspapers, but any news that would support the Bible is largely ignored.

One evening (I am pretty sure it was in 1918) I sat reading the daily paper in our apartment in Brockton. Suddenly I saw in very small print a short story of a dying man's confession. It was a news item one column wide and, as I remembered it, not more than two inches deep. It stated that an elderly scientist on his deathbed in London was afraid to die before making a terrible confession. It gave briefly the very date and facts that Haji Yearam had related to us in his story. I got out the composition book containing the story he had me write. It was identical in every detail. Haji Yearam had died in my parent's home in Oakland, California, about the same time that the old scientist had died in London. We had never for one moment doubted Haji's story, but when this scientist on his deathbed on the other side of the world confessed the same story in every detail, we knew positively that the story was true in every detail...

At that time there were two daily papers in Brockton. I do not remember whether it was one of these or a Boston paper, in which we found the story, as I used to buy first one and then another. But this I feel sure of—Noah's Ark is still on Mount Ararat, and when it pleases God, some expedition will give the news and facts to the world so that skeptics will have no excuse.

During the same year Harold Williams had also written.

Certain facts stand out so strongly that I have no hesitancy at all in what I have given you previously: Haji was born about 1840 because he was 75 years old when he had me write the story in 1915-1916. He was a lad of about 15 years of age or a little less when they made the expedition. My memory and impression says between 13 and 15, so they made the expedition about 1853 or 1854...

Haji lived with us and with my parents for several years before he died in my parents' home. His word was absolutely reliable. He would have no reason to concoct the story...Evidently Haji's father had previously seen the Ark or knew from others exactly where to find it because he took the scientist directly to it—BUT IT WAS A

VERY EXHAUSTING AND PERILOUS EXPEDITION, high up on the mountain...

The great door was removed from the Ark and was lying up on rocks forming a sort of roof under which was an ancient altar and smoke from the altar was on the rocks and underside of the great door...It is my strong impression from memory that Haji believed that Ararat is about 16,000 feet high, but I know that he said it (the Ark) rests in a glacier and that only in a very hot summer could its prow be seen protruding from the melting end of the glacier where it feeds a stream that flows down the mountain...Haji was not a large man, perhaps 5 feet seven inches in height, and only weighing about 150 pounds when well. But he was broadshouldered and muscular, with typical Armenian features and gestures, and straight, fine hair. Although grave, earnest and sincere, his brilliantly smiling eyes lent animation to his features. He was deeply religious, but never fanatical, and because of his many excellent qualities, soon became a beloved member of the Williams family.

The composition book and the article including everything that we owned were burned up in a butane explosion. Later, as Violet Cummings checked Haji's death certificate, it stated by Mrs. Williams that he was 82 when he died on May 3, 1920 and that he was born in 1838.

During the period around 1856 there may have been other expeditions to Ararat about which nothing definite is known. Perhaps the atheists' expedition was one of these. It seems there was some debate going about the Ark and Ararat in the Royal Geographical Society with a Henry Danby Seymour, brother-in-law of noted Assyiologist Sir Henry Rawlinson and James Bryce. It seems Seymour did climb the mountain in 1845 or 1846 and may have again in 1856. Some have theorized that Seymour may have been one of the scientists, but other than his liberal views, there is nothing to validate that theory.

The search for the missing column has gone far and wide without any result. Dr. Lawrence B. Hewitt, a physician in Huntsville, Alabama, was one of the individuals who remembered the story well. As a teen-age boy, Hewitt remembered the small article with the bold header "Scientist Makes Deathbed Confession."

Lloyd Bailey notes some questions:

The following curiosities about this story should be noted: (a) Williams apparently made little mention of Yearam's adventure until 1952—remarkable in view of the sensational nature of the case. (b) Williams' report is prefaced by a troublesome "If I remember correctly...." (c) Where would the "vile" scientist have learned of the Ark's location?... (d) The reason for guiding the Westerners up the mountain, put in the mouth of Yearam's father, sounds precisely, and surprisingly, like the thought of modern Ark-searchers...[28]

British Viscount James Bryce - 1876 A.D.

In the late 1870s, Viscount James Bryce, a respected British statesman and author, conducted extensive field and library research and became thoroughly convinced of the historical accuracy of the Bible. Persuaded that the Ark was on Mount Ararat, he set out to disprove the prevailing winds of atheism. In 1876, Bryce climbed Ararat alone after his guides left him at the ice cap. He then wrote an intriguing and well-researched book of his experiences called *Transcaucasian and Ararat* as well as another article for the *Journal of the Royal Geographical Society* in London titled "The Ascent of Mount Ararat in 1876."

Bryce was the first person in modern times who claimed to find wood higher than 13,000-foot mark. He stated:

> Mounting steadily along the same ridge, I saw at a height of over 13,000 feet, lying on the loose rocks, a piece of wood about four feet long and five inches thick, evidently cut by some tool, and so far above the limit of trees that it could by no possibility be a natural fragment of one...I am, however, bound to admit that another explanation of the presence of this piece of timber...did occur to me. But as no man is bound to discredit his own relic,...I will not disturb my readers' minds, or yield to the rationalizing tendencies of the age by suggesting it.

It should be noted that Dr. Parrot (1829 on the summit), German Dr. Herman Abich (1845 on Western Slope) and Russian Colonel Khodzko (1850 on the summit) planted wooden crosses on the mountain earlier. Parrot's largest piece of wood was five feet long and two inches wide. Khodzko's cross of seven feet could have fallen or been moved down to lower elevations where Bryce found it.

Turkish Commissioners and British Captain Gascoyne - 1883 A.D.

A May 2, 1883 earthquake buried mountain villages with rock and ice. After the violent earthquake, Turkish commissioners and British Captain Gascoyne (an English attaché of the British Embassy) claimed to have seen the Ark and to have taken detailed measurements and notes on the ship sticking out from a glacier. The local people said that the Ark had been visible for the past six years.

After announcing the find to the world, they were ridiculed and the Turkish government did not follow up on the find. The *New York WORLD*

---

[28] Lloyd Bailey, *Noah* (Columbia, South Carolina: University of South Carolina Press, 1989), pp.83-84.

published the following statement, "An extraordinary spell of hot weather had melted away a great portion of the Araxes glacier, and they were surprised to see sticking out of the ice what at first appeared to be the rude façade of an ancient dwelling."[29] The original press release from Constantinople has never been found but an article that was probably changed from the original story was found in the British *Prophetic Messenger* stated:

> The expedition was fortunate in making a discovery that cannot fail to be of interest to the whole civilized world, for among the vastnesses of one of the glens of Mount Ararat, they came upon a gigantic structure of very dark wood, embedded at the foot of one of the glaciers, with one end protruding, and which they believe to be none other than the old Ark in which Noah and his family navigated the waters of the Deluge...
>
> At last they were rewarded by the sight of a huge dark mass, protruding 20 or 30 feet from the glacier, on the left side of the ravine...It was in a good state of preservation, being painted on the outside with a dark brown pigment, and constructed of great strength...
>
> The projected portion seemed about 40 or 50 feet in height, but to what length it penetrated into the glacier they could not estimate.
>
> Effecting an entrance through one of the broken corners, the explorers found it filled for the greater part with ice, the interior being partitioned off into compartments about 12 or 15 feet high, into three of which only they were able to make their way, owing to the mass of frozen substance with which these were filled, and also because of their fear of the structure collapsing with the overhanging mass of the huge glacier.

Embarrassed by the reaction of the world's press, the Turkish government did not follow up the report with another expedition.

Again, Lloyd Bailey makes some interesting points to consider:

> The report is remarkable for at least the following reasons. (a) In order to reach the heights of the mountain, the groups went through a "dense forest." This is in absolute contrast to many detailed descriptions of the mountain, which report that there are no trees at all—to say nothing of a dense forest. (b) The group also encountered a stream on the mountain, "wading sometimes waist high in water." Other accounts mention occasional streams from the melting snow of the glacier, but otherwise there is usually no flowing water on the mountain...(d) The original news release, cited by the *Prophetic Messenger*, has never been produced. (e) The story seems to have

---

[29] Violet M. Cummings, *Noah's Ark: Fable or Fact?* (Old Tappan, NJ: Spire Books, 1975), p. 77.

gathered additional details as it spread from newspaper, with the *Prophetic Messenger* version representing a late stage of development...[30]

There does happen to be a forest on the north and east sides of Little Ararat.

Nestorian Archdeacon John Joseph Nouri - 1887 A.D.

John Joseph Nouri (born in 1864), who claimed to be a Nestorian Prince, also stated he saw the Ark from within rifle shot on his third attempt to climb Ararat on April 25, 1887, when he was in his early twenties. He purported to speak ten languages as well as attributed to himself a mountain of important-sounding titles. Here is the account of his sighting that was published in the *Zion's Watch Tower* of August 15, 1894.

> His expedition up the Euphrates and over to Ararat was an expensive affair, but he got there, camped on the plateau and climbed the two peaks. Between them there is a valley, and from each side of it rise the peaks—one 16,000 and the other nearly 18,000 feet high. Starting in March, they found the snow-drifts impassible, and waited another month. Then they climbed to within sight of a narrow plateau almost on the summit, and on that plateau they saw the Ark.
>
> The bow and stern were clearly in view but the center was buried in snow, and one end of it had fallen off and decayed.
>
> It stood more than 100 feet high and was over 300 yards long [an estimate; without any ability to measure the vessel, Nouri has overestimated the size compared to biblical dimensions]. The wood was peculiar, dark reddish in color, almost iron colored in fact, and seemed very thick...
>
> Though within rifle shot, they could not reach it, the slope from the bench on which it rested being a glare of ice and snow, and they could not remain till the midsummer thaw.[31]

Other accounts say the Prince actually entered the structure and took careful measurements. Nouri attempted to find financial support to no avail in order to recover the Ark and take it to the Chicago Exhibition at the 1893 World's Fair. Nouri died suddenly from pneumonia a few years later.

There are a number of problems with Nouri's account. First, the other alleged sightings tend to discourage the possibility of an April viewing because the annual recession of the glaciers does not peak until the later summer months.

---

[30] Lloyd Bailey, *Noah* (Columbia, South Carolina: University of South Carolina Press, 1989), p.85.

[31] *A Remarkable Narrative* (Allegheny, PA: Zions Watch Tower August 15, 1894 Vol. XV No. 16.) p. 1689.

Another problem is Nouri's tendency to seemingly exaggerate details. It is difficult to verify many of his numerous titles. From friends' accounts, Nouri was extremely bright, was stunningly handsome (looking like the Renaissance Christ), was extremely articulate and had captivating speech but had no hard evidence as backup to what he claimed.

According to friends in the United States, Nouri also had a problem near San Francisco and was said to have been placed in the Napa Insane Asylum. Although Nouri claimed that he was beaten and robbed of everything, his fascinating stories and lack of financial support in America could give one the sense that he was less than completely balanced mentally.

Lloyd Bailey notes the following:

John Joseph Nouri

John Joseph Nouri
Courtesy of Eryl Cummings

> The problems with this account include: (a) He reported that the beams of the structure were joined "with long nails." This detail is emphatically denied by others who claim to have been inside the same Ark (Hagopian). (b) He was, it seems, unable to verify any of his pretentious titles…(c) At public lectures he was unable to convince others of the truth of his claim (even his close friends said that he "almost convinced others")…(e)…In any case, since the structure was not totally exposed ("wedged in the rocks and half-filled with snow and ice"), one wonders how the measurements were possible.[32]

Russian E. de Markoff - 1888 A.D.

A member of the Russian Imperial Geographical Society, E. de Markoff claimed to find wood above timberline near 14,000 feet. The wood was carved with two previous Russian explorers' initials, C.B.

Markoff believed that the stick may have been the one that Dr. Parrot originally planted on the summit and however unlikely, was possibly carried down by avalanches to the spot it was found.

---

[32] Lloyd Bailey, *Noah* (Columbia, South Carolina: University of South Carolina Press, 1989), p.86.

British Merchant H.F.B. Lynch - 1893 A.D.

H.F.B. Lynch was a British merchant who was listed in *Who's Who* and climbed the mountain in 1893 although. Although Lynch never claimed to see the Ark, his lasting legacy is the two-volume set of detailed information and careful accounts in *Armenia: Travels and Studies*. He spent three years editing the set to make sure they were accurate. He also reconnoitered the mid-east on horseback, sailed the Tigris to Baghdad on a raft, surveyed the great crater of Nimrud and mapped the country of Armenia.

Armenian Jacob Chuchian - 1890s, 1914, 1915 A.D.

Arthur Chuchian, an Armenian born around 1915 and a lifelong resident of St. Louis, claimed that his father Jacob Chuchian saw the Ark a number of times between the ages of nine and nineteen. He stated that his father happened upon the Ark as a young boy while chasing a wild goat up the mountain. In fact, Arthur claimed that entire villages would climb to the Ark in the summer for worship services, beginning from the village of Ortulu (southwest side). Arthur also claimed that Jacob had been on the Ark. In a 1975 interview with minister Stuart Brassie, Arthur discussed the path to the Ark:

> To reach the site where the Ark is, one must follow a narrow goat trail beginning on the west side of the peak, approximately 4 feet wide, which starts out of nowhere and runs for about three miles. Near the clear spring well not far from the village they took a goat path that traversed the grasslands on the western side of the mountain. The goat path took them in the direction of the snow-fingers and led them in a north east direction around the mountain.
>
> He says that one can avoid the tremendous winds by taking the path. They passed Lake Kop on the left. Chuchian says his father told him that he could see where the Ark is from the rim of the crater of Lake Kop. However, he says that you would have to know exactly where it is or you would not see it.
>
> From this point the directions are more obscure. He says that after passing Lake Kop, they continued in a north-easterly direction around the mountain. In doing so, the path led through small valleys and along rock walls. Sometimes they had to climb almost on their hands and knees as they gained altitude.
>
> The goat trail branches off in several directions at various times. Armenians knew which path to take to the Ark because of [the] special insignia marking the path. From his father's directions, he says it is approximately two canyons to the east of Lake Kop. This isolated canyon that the Ark is in is very difficult to locate. Is supposedly within a larger canyon.
>
> Once the right canyon is located, the goat trail will continue on the right side of the canyon up a slight grade. The path then

separates at some point. The left branch takes you to below the cliff on which the Ark rests. The right branch will take you up and around to a cliff over-looking a bowl or cove. The entire hike on this goat trail is about three miles, and takes about three hours according to Chuchian.

The path will dead-end at a rock wall. At this point, if one looks to the left and down, one can see the Ark which is about 100 feet down from that vantage point. The canyon is surrounded by small peaks especially on the left side. At one time, his father says, another trail led down from the top right to the Ark...

The Ark rests in a large body of water about three to four times the size of the boat, and except for one time when the front third of the boat was plainly visible, the boat was completely covered by a shimmering, very clear covering of ice, so that only the huge, but clear outline of the Ark could be seen. The front 40 feet was exposed above the water which covered another 30 to 50 feet. The rest is encased in ice.

The canyon is about two canyons east of Lake Kop.[33]

The *Ararat Report* also reported the following account of Jacob and Arthur Chuchian's story.

The boat has a reddish brown wood appearance and is similar to a houseboat with a flat deck surface. The Ark rests on a type of cleft or ledge and is accessible only by the goat's trail. The ledge on which the Ark rests drops off very rapidly from the front side, and is surrounded by the other three sides by walls of rock.

Chuchian says the Ark is wedged between large rocks. The Ark is lying roughly in a north-south direction and just a little to the west. It is slightly tilted to the left side with the front slightly raised. The right side is exposed and the left side is against the rocks. Parts of the front side are missing as well as parts of the bottom.

Only the front 40 feet was exposed at the time but this varies according to the time of the year and previous precipitation. Another 30 to 50 feet could be seen in water and ice. The water from the melting ice formed a little pool. This run-off formed a little waterfall. He says the water is very clear as well as the ice.

He also notes that there is definitely a catwalk on top of the Ark. He remembered that the wood of the Ark had a reddish-brown appearance.

Arthur Chuchian shared with Stuart Brassie that his father brought a large steamer trunk with him when they escaped. In this

---

[33] Interview with Arthur Chuchian conducted in St. Louis, MO, on June 24, 1975 by Rev. Stuart Brassie and Thomas Sass of the Arkfact Research Association. Also used the *Ararat Report*.

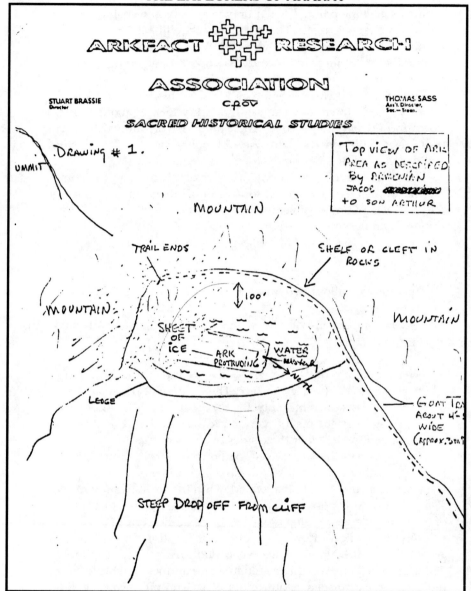

Arthur Chuchian drawing of alleged sighting
Courtesy of B.J. Corbin

trunk was a piece of the Ark and piece of the rock the Ark rests on, as well as other documents and artifacts.

He acknowledged the trunk during my visit, but did not know what happened to it.

Crouse went on to critique the Chuchian account.

Whenever we hear stories like this we propose that certain procedures are necessary to be able to judge the truthfulness of the account...

How does Chuchian's story hold up?...

We found that he was rather cynical and had a paranoid view of life.

For example, he believed the government was suppressing a lot of news. He claimed he saw many items come over the wire service that never made the news. He believed the government was responsible for flu outbreaks, and was involved in altering the weather.

He also related to this editor that he believed there was a civilization of small beings living inside the earth. They were discovered by Admiral Byrd [sic] in the '30's when he visited the North Pole. He believes the government squelched the story by confining Byrd and his crew to a mental institution...

I have reason to believe he was also interested in and a participant in the occult practice of "remote viewing" (by traveling out of body). When I related to him about my intention of returning to Mt. Ararat the summer of '85 he wished for me to keep him informed as to the exact dates we would be there because it was possible that he would "join" us.

Chuchian informed us that his mother had seen the Ark as well, and that she recounts an experience whereby the groups journeying to see the Ark would be transported down to the base of the mountain during the night as they slept.

This is reminiscent of the Armenian tradition concerning St. Hagop (Jacob) who also continually found himself at the base of the mountain in the morning as he tried to climb the mountain to get wood from the Ark...

Upon returning home from the visit with Chuchian, we contacted his employer for his impression. The man was blunt and to the point: "The man does his job faithfully, otherwise he ought to be in a mental institution." At the time we took this comment to mean that Chuchian was somewhat of an eccentric and not actually mentally impaired...

(1) ...One almost gets the impression he is an eyewitness and not his father...
(2) When all the reports are compared we are left with a great deal of contradiction. He told Stuart Brassie his father last saw the Ark in 1933 whereas to us he said 1914 or '15...
(3) Chuchian says the canyon in which the Ark is located is just above the ancient timberline. We also find no reference to there ever being trees on Ararat. It's possible he meant the grassline...

Conclusion: It is another tantalizing story! Perhaps Chuchian's father saw something as a child. We will never know. However, we have ample reason to doubt the facticity of this report. Even if it has a grain of truth we cannot be sure what it is, nor can we put any stock in any of the detail.

There does happen to be a forest on the north and eastern slopes of Little Ararat though it does not go up very high. Some researchers have proposed that Chuchian's Jacob's Well may be named after his father Jacob rather than the more well known Jacob's Well near Ahora Village. According to B.J. Corbin, "The Chuchian drawings show an intersect between Ortulu and Lake Kop, which would place the location on the northwest." Corbin has a helicopter photo of what he believes could be the site described in the account.

Armenian Shepherds George Hagopian and His Uncle - 1900-1906 A.D.

In 1970, George Hagopian, a seventy to eighty-year-old Armenian, claimed to walk on the Ark at about age 10 while shepherding sheep with his uncle. Hagopian and his uncle took an eight-day trip from Van to reach near the summit of Ararat, to reach the high grazing areas and glaciers of Ararat. Their primary reason to travel to Ararat was a four-year drought and the sheep were dying in the Lake Van area.

Hagopian's early years were challenging. Hagopian was about 5'4" or 5'5" but appeared to be a stout man as he was enlisted in the Turkish army. He was assigned as part of the guard for the Sultan. He actually witnessed three assassinations of the Sultan since the Sultan regularly had stand-ins. When the Armenian persecution broke out, George witnessed the massacre of his entire family and fled out of the country. Hagopian was caught by Russian border agents with a false passport. He was sentenced to eighteen months of hard labor in the Siberian coalmines. After his imprisonment in Russia, he weighed 97 pounds. Hagopian came back to Armenia and Yerevan (within the shadow of Mount Ararat). He sold hot water and bread on the streets of Yerevan for 25 cents each day before saving enough money to relocate to the "holy land" of America (Hagopian figured that anywhere he was not a slave must have been the "holy land").

George Hagopian took a photographer to Turkey in 1922 to photograph the Ark on Ararat. Because of the fighting between the Turks, Greeks and Armenians, he was stuck in Ismir and not allowed to travel to eastern Turkey. After returning to the United States, Hagopian ran a carpet company on the East Coast from Easton, Maryland. He never married.

The following 1970 statement was put together by Elfred Lee. Lee met with Hagopian numerous times over a two-year period from 1970 until Hagopian's death in 1972. Hagopian seemed to trust Lee more than other researchers because Lee had been on Masis (Armenian for Mount Ararat meaning "mother Earth of life"), Lee was used to speaking with foreigners with heavy accents (Lee was brought up in a Japanese prisoner of war camp and lived in several non-English speaking nations), would patiently repeat his questions which is laborious, and was an artist which helped Hagopian put his mental thoughts onto paper. Lee checked out Hagopian's stories by bringing in hard-nosed reporters to check out his story, by looking at his bank account for money received from Ark publicity, by trying to trick Hagopian with his questions to see if he would stick to his story and by traveling to Ararat and the Armenian church building on the Lake Van island to confirm

Elfred Lee painting of George Hagopian sighting
Courtesy of Elfred Lee 1972

specific details of Hagopian's background such as the church cemetery he discusses in the tapings.

In 1970, Hagopian had never heard of Fernand Navarra and insisted that Navarra and the SEARCH Foundation's wood was not from the petrified stone Ark he had seen. Sadly, Lee notes that Fernand Navarra and Ralph Crawford (President of SEARCH) were upset that Hagopian had been found and wanted to suppress Hagopian's speaking out.

George Hagopian discussed his alleged sightings of the Ark around 1904 and 1906 when he was an Armenian boy of age 10 and 12 and talked about specific Ararat features and close villages such as Bayazit. This is a summary of the two years of interviews that Lee completed with Hagopian. Hagopian's taped account is long and choppy because of his Armenian accent so the summary is provided instead. Elfred Lee has released the Hagopian tapes and they are available from the publisher in CD and cassette formats (check the back page order form or the website http://greatcommission.com).

> My grandfather was the minister of the big Armenian Orthodox Church in Van (near Lake Van), and he always told me stories about the holy ship on the mountain.
> And then one day my uncle said, "Georgie, I'm going to take you to see the holy Ark." We packed supplies on his donkey, and together we started our trek toward Mount Ararat.
> My feet were getting sore, and the donkey kept wanting to go in the wrong direction, but we continued climbing until we got about

halfway up. Then Uncle took both supplies and me on his back, and we climbed and climbed.

It took us almost eight days from the time we left Van to the

moment we got to the place on the holy mountain where both my grandfather and my uncle had said the holy ship had come to rest.

I guess my uncle took me there that year because it was a year without much snow—a "smooth year" or "no snow year" we called it.

Elfred Lee painting of Hagopian sighting 1972
Courtesy of Elfred Lee

There's one of those about every twenty years.

And then we got to the Ark. It was getting dark and misty around us. My uncle dropped his pack, and together we began to haul stones to the side of the ship. Within a short time we had stacked a high pile of rocks against the side of the ship.

"Georgie, come here," he said, grabbing me by the arm. "You are going on top of the holy Ark." He lifted me up and put me on his shoulders, and together we climbed the pile of rocks. When he had reached the top of the rocks, his hands grabbed my ankles and he began to push me up toward the stairs that someone had added to the Ark.

"Reach for the top, Georgie," he yelled. "Grab the edge and pull yourself up!"

I stood up straight and looked all over the ship. It was long. The height was about forty feet.

"Look inside the Ark," my uncle called up to me. "Look for the holes. Look for the big one. Look inside and tell me what you see."

I shivered from the cold and from fear and glanced around me. Yes, there was the hole, big and gaping. I peeked into the blackness of the hole, but saw nothing. Then I knelt down and kissed the holy Ark.

When we were there, the top of the Ark was covered with a very thin coat of fresh fallen snow. But when I brushed some of it away I could see a green moss growing right on top. When I pulled a piece off...it was made of wood. The grain was right there. This green moss made the Ark feel soft and moldy.

On the roof, besides one large hole, I remember small holes running all the way from the front to the back. I don't know exactly how many, but there must have been at least fifty of them running down the middle with small intervals in between. My uncle told me these holes were for air.

George Hagopian and Elfred Lee with Ararat painting in Easton, Maryland 1970
Courtesy of Elfred Lee

That roof was flat with the exception of the narrow raised section running all the way from the bow to the stern with all those holes in it.

I remember, my uncle took his gun and shot into the side of the Ark, but the bullet wouldn't penetrate. Uncle then pulled his long hunting knife from hi belt, and with the heavy handle he chipped a piece from the side of the Ark. Then we went down the mountainside and returned to Van.

Bill Crouse gave the following critique of the Hagopian story in the *Ararat Report*.

Hagopian's story is difficult to falsify. As he told and retold his story he never deviated from his original account. The fact that he is no longer with us makes it difficult to render any kind of judgement.

His knowledge of the Ararat area as he describes it is accurate and detailed. Other aspects of his story given to researchers seem to substantiate his credibility. For instance, he claimed that at the time he was taken to the Ark the region had experienced several consecutive years of drought. Weather records are something that can be checked, so in 1987, we commissioned Allen Roy to tap the databases for the weather information at the time Hagopian claimed he saw the Ark. What he found was astounding! For four straight years (1901-1904) the temperature and precipitation were so abnormal they were off the charts.

Hagopian was not very helpful with regard to location...

The most fascinating part of his story was the description of the Ark itself, wholly petrified with green moss growing on the top. He depicted it as barge-like with no visible doors or windows, and totally intact sitting on a huge ledge over-looking a deep drop off...

He also says that he later discovered that other Armenian boys had seen the Ark. This point interested me. In 1985, I traveled to Washington, D.C. for the 70th Commemoration of the Armenian Holocaust. While there, I chatted with an elderly Armenian survivor in his 80s. He related that as an orphan he roamed the streets of Yerevan and often listened to the stories of the older boys. Once, he recalled, some were telling about visiting the Ark on Masis!

Do I have any problems with the Hagopian story? Some, but they are not enough to dismiss the story...Some things that trouble me are the fact that the testimony itself is secondhand.

From experience, I am skeptical of the way testimony has been elicited from alleged witnesses by Ark researchers in the past. When one wants to believe a story, as Ark researchers desperately want to do, it is often difficult to maintain the proper neutrality. Often words are put into their informants' mouths.

Negative, or contradictory facts are simply ignored. I am also troubled by the great length of time from Hagopian's boyhood until the time of his testimony (70 years). The years can really dim the details. But on the other hand, some elderly people have vivid memories of their early years.

Another matter hard to dismiss is Hagopian's social situation. He was apparently a lonely man with no relatives and few friends. With this condition it is easy for someone needing to feel important to embellish their past! Ask any psychiatrist.

Some researchers are troubled by Hagopian's description of the size of the Ark. He says it was 1,000 feet long and 600 feet wide. This is at odds with the Biblical dimensions (450' by 70' approximately). However, you have to remember that Hagopian probably saw things in terms of meters, and to a small boy it must have looked huge. I'm personally not bothered by this. The George Hagopian story remains an interesting, but unverifiable story.

If Hagopian truly saw an unbroken Ark, another question that should be asked is how did the Ark split in two between 1906 and 1943. Some researchers claim there was an earthquake. Others say that glacial activity broke the Ark. It would appear disconcerting that from 2500 B.C. or earlier until 1906 A.D., the Ark remained complete and then was suddenly broken in two in the next 37 years. However, perhaps Hagopian stood on the larger portion of the Ark and simply did not see the broken portion from his vantagepoint. Note that unlike Hagopian the other eyewitnesses who claimed to see a broken Ark indicated that the

Elfred Lee Painting of Hagopian reaching stairs
Courtesy of Elfred Lee 1972

smaller portion was about one-half mile from the larger portion, that they were not standing on top of the larger portion when they saw it, and that they were not boys.

The reader should note that two tapings of the first 1970 Hagopian meetings are available to the public on the last page of this book although there are at least three more. Although Hagopian's Armenian accent and broken English make it difficult to understand him, Elfred Lee's communication abilities with non-English speakers and patience elicited the basic facts of the encapsulated statement. Over the two-year period of conversations, Lee said that he attempted to occasionally test Hagopian to see if he would stick to his original statements but Hagopian never deviated from his main tenants. Also, Hagopian's lonely demeanor can be attributed to the 1922 incident at the Mayflower Hotel where uniformed American officers and Turkish embassy agents threatened and silenced Hagopian if he talked anymore about his other experiences.

Note that there are discrepancies between Hagopian's statements and Lee's statements with regard to the actual years that Hagopian saw the structure, the year that he was born, and the ages he was when he saw the structure. Note also that in many foreign countries, birth certificates and birth years are not tracked accurately which may also account for the confusion. To the publisher, these discrepancies are irreconcilable and thus the range of years that the sightings occurred should be considered 1900-1908.

Armenian Shepherd George Hagopian - 1902-1908 A.D.

George Hagopian again made trek up Ararat at age twelve to see the Ark.

> I saw the Ark a second time. I think it was in 1904. We were on the mountain looking for holy flowers, and I went back to the Ark and it still looked the same. Nothing had changed. I didn't really get a good look at it. It was resting on a steep ledge of bluish-green rock about 3,000 feet wide.
>
> Another thing I noticed was that I didn't see any nails at all. It seemed that the whole ship was made of one piece of petrified wood.
>
> There was definitely no door in the side of the ship that I could see. No opening of any kind. There may have been one in the part I couldn't see, but that I don't know. That side was practically inaccessible. I could only see my side and part of the bow.
>
> The sides were slanting outward to the top and the front was flat. I didn't see any real curves. It was unlike any other boat I have ever seen. It looked more like a flat-bottomed barge.

Turkish Soldiers - 1916 A.D.

Five or six Turkish soldiers returning from the Baghdad area 450 miles from Mount Ararat claimed to find the Ark resting against a mountain. Since they could not read or write, they told their story to a learned friend, Duran Ayranci of Adana, Turkey. The men asked him to write a letter in 1946 to the American Embassy in Turkey offering their services as guides to any Americans looking for the Ark. The letter stated:

> When returning from World War 1, I and five or six of my friends passed by the Ararat. We saw Noah's Ark leaning against the mountain. I measured the length of the boat. It was 150 paces long. It had three stories. I read in the papers that an American group is looking for this boat. I wish to inform you that I shall personally show this boat and I request your intervention so that I may show the boat.[34]

Ayranci also recalled his friends' claimed that the Ark was resting on a rock in a north-south direction near the top of Aghri Dagh. Wooden pegs held it together. Portions were decayed and broken, he remembered, but most of it was preserved in the glacial ice.

Later, Ayranci thought that the mountain was called "cudi," a hill very close to the mountain of Ararat. According to Sakir, Ayranci's late friend,

---

[34] Tim LaHaye and John Morris, *The Ark on Ararat* (Nashville: Thomas Nelson Publishers, 1976), pp. 90-91.

"The Ark is on that hill, facing north-south, and the body is on the west side of the hill."

Bill Crouse notes in *The Ararat Report* that it would be strange for the returning soldiers to go to Mount Ararat on their way back home, let alone to climb the intimidating peak. However, their route could easily have taken them up the Tigris very near Mount Cudi. Also, the statements that portions have decayed and that it was on the west side of the hill seems contradictory to other alleged eyewitnesses. Another interesting fact is that the Turkish soldiers' friend lived in southwestern Turkey, possibly near the soldiers, again away from Mount Ararat (Aghri Dagh).

In regard to trying to figure out the relationship between Mount Ararat and Al-Cudi, Violet Cummings notes the following.

> One day, while searching for a tantalizing, only half-remembered quotation long hidden in the file, an unexpected and astonishing discovery relating to the mystery suddenly leaped, full-blown, from the page. Buried in the heart of an ancient and yellowed clipping entitled "Ararat," taken from an encyclopedia with the pencilled dates of 1830-31 in the margin, and on loan from Col. Alexander A. Koor, the following words finally closed the gap between conjecture and fact:
>
> "Ararat, a mountain of Asia, in Armenia, on which the Ark of Noah rested after the cessation of the deluge. Concerning the etymology of the name Dr. Bryan observes that it is a compound of Ar-Ararat, and signifies 'the mountain of descent'...*it is called by the Arabs Al-Judi*, and also Thaminin..." (emphasis supplied).
> "Ararat—called by the Arabs Al-Judi..."
>
> What a simple solution to a problem that had seemed so complex! Ararat...had been Al-Judi all the time.[35]

The problem with this line of thinking is that other mountains throughout history are also considered a "Mount Ararat" and an "Al-Judi" but this does show that at an earlier date, modern day Mount Ararat was also considered Al-Judi.

"Vladimir Roskovitsky" / Russian Lt. Zabolotsky & the Czar's Expedition - 1916-1917 A.D.

A 1940 issue of *The New Eden Magazine* reported that Russian pilot "Vladimir Roskovitsky" saw the Ark while flying a plane around Ararat in 1916 A.D. and that the Czar sent a detachment of men who found and

---

[35] Violet M. Cummings, *Noah's Ark: Fable or Fact* (San Diego: Creation Science Research Center), pp. 176-177.

photographed the Ark in 1917. The fictitious nature of the story was confirmed to Bill Crouse and the *Ararat Report* in a personal letter from the author in 1986. Other researchers discovered that while the article's details were made up by Floyd M. Gurley, it appeared to be based on actual reports that a Russian aviator had seen a boat-like structure on Ararat that same year. Gurley's neighbor, a retired lawyer named Benjamin Allen, claimed he had heard from other sources about a story of an alleged Russian discovery. Eryl Cummings (who searched for Noah's Ark for over 40 years beginning in 1945) also alleged that Gurley admitted to him that he received other facts about the story from a Russian immigrant living in one of his apartments. Also, Cummings claimed a British subject preserved in hand-copied form an account (plagiarized almost word-for-word to Gurley's account) from a religious publication dated 1920.

Cummings also quoted James Frazier whose father-in-law John Schilleroff and friend John Georgeson separately talked about the same expedition. During the summer of 1917, the Czar is said to have sent two research divisions with a total of 150 infantrymen (groups of 50 and 100 going up two sides of the mountain), army engineers and scientists on a ground expedition to find the Ark. It supposedly took them a month to reach the site because of the difficulties in scaling the mountain and carving out a path. They are said to have made it in the treacherous month of December.

Soon after the *New Eden* article, Benjamin Franklin Allen, a retired Army officer and creation geologist, stated that the publication was a "most exaggerated account" with Gurley's imagination running wild on only the "basic facts" Allen had given Gurley. According to Allen, these "basic facts" included:

> the few details originating from two soldiers in the Czarist Russian Army during the First World War, deceased many years ago. The story of these soldiers came to me from their relatives of how a Russian aviator had sighted a suspicious looking structure in one of Ararat's obscure canyons. Infantrymen were sent on foot to investigate and their officers and they decided it must be Noah's Ark, with one end sunk in a small swamp.

On October 6, 1945, a former Four-Star White Russian General Alexander Jacob Elshin and former White Russian Colonel Alexander A. Koor confirmed Allen's "basic facts" that there was a Russian aviator sighting as well as an expedition sent by the Russian Czar to investigate the report just before the Czar was exiled and murdered during the Communist revolution. Colonel Koor was a friend of some of the soldiers involved in the aerial expedition that spotted the Ark and also had discussed the alleged ground expedition as well. He had been stationed at the base of Ararat for several years before the Bolshevik Revolution. Koor wrote an article in the

White Russian publication *Rosseya* which was a 4,000 word, more detailed accounting of the *New Eden* story. When questioned about the *New Eden* story, Colonel Koor stated that he had never heard of or read Gurley's story.

In 1915, the Colonel also discovered the ancient Sumerian inscription at Karada near Greater Ararat, on the Araratsky Pass, which tells about the great flood of the Bible. Regarding the authenticity of the remarkable inscription's translation, Dr. J.O. Kinnamman wrote on August 2nd, 1946: "I have received two letters from Col. Koor...and have read and surveyed them critically... Col. Koor proves himself a scholar of high degree of attainment. Being familiar with Babylonian cuneiform, Egyptian hieroglyphics, Hebrew, etc., I would say that Col. Koor has made very accurate translations of the inscriptions he has set out to interpret. 'God sowed the seeds of the word into the waters...the waters filled the earth, descending from above...his children came to rest on the mountain or peak.'" Koor also detailed 20 archaeological sites to be examined in the Ararat region, one of which was found in 1969 by Eryl Cummings and Dr. Lawrence B. Hewitt.[36]

Koor said the group of soldiers came from the Russian Caucasian Army, 1914-1917, directed by General E.B. Mavlovsky and revealed the following.

> The headquarters of the 11th Railroad Battalion was at Bayazit, just southwest of Greater Ararat, with Brigade Headquarters at Maku, southeast of Lesser Ararat, commanded by Col. Sverczkoff. The 14th Battalion came to the front in the summer of 1916, from Russia. I understand that the discovery of Noah's Ark was in the end of 1916, with the scouting parties having to wait until the summer of 1917...1st Lt. Zabolotsky is the man you are looking for, for he, from an airplane, sighted the Ark and started the investigation. Captain Koorbatoff was his supervisor.
>
> I was in the Ararat region in November, 1915, during the war between Turkey and Russia. The general headquarters of the Caucasian Army sent me and other officers in command of emergency forces from Barzem and Pytergorsky for protection of the Araratsky Pass, just northwest of the peak of Greater Ararat and Zorsky Pass a few miles to the northwest, from the imminent Turkish attack.[37]
>
> About July or August, 1921, I and Lt. Leslin met 1st Lt. Rujansky in Harbin [Manchuria]. During one of our conversations, Lt. Rujansky told me about the discovery of Noah's Ark. He (1st Lt. Rujansky) didn't know about the details because he was wounded and sent to Russia, but he knew because his brother, Boris Vasilivich Rujansky, Sergeant of the Military Railroad Battalion, was a member

---

[36] Violet M. Cummings, *Noah's Ark: Fable or Fact?* (San Diego: Spire Books, 1975), p. 63-68

[37] Violet M. Cummings, *Noah's Ark: Fable or Fact* (San Diego: Creation Science Research Center), *p. 62-63.*

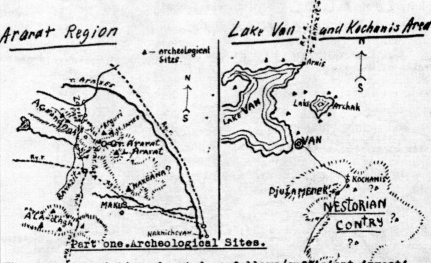

Archeology of Ararats and Vicinity Still Untouched by Investigation

Archeological Sites and Data on Mt.Ararat and the surrounding
region.
by Col. Alexander A. Koor.

Ararat Region   *Lake Van and Kochanis Area*

Part one. Archeological Sites.

There are inscriptions located as follows/sufficient investigation would reveal many more than these/:
1.On the Araratsky Pass/just north west of Greater Ararat/high
on the eastern wall, there are several inscriptions.
2.On the summit of Lesser Ararat there are several tombs and
some inscriptions on the stones/2'x3'/,not yet deciphered.
3.On the Ala-dagh/mountain/south west from Bayazit.
4.At the lake Archak.
5.North and North-East of the lake Van.
6.In the Nestorian Country/posterity of ancient Assyrians/.
7.Close to Maku city,on the southern slope of the Lesser Ararat
thereare the ruins of the ancient town Naxuana,here is tomb of
Patriarch Noah,according to Armenin historian Vartan.
8.On the North Eastern slope of Greater Ararat there is the ruin
of the ancient site Ar-Guri.
9.Not far from Ar-Guri there is the ruin of the St. James monas-
tary,destroyed by an earthquake in 1840/Many ancient books and
relics of Noah's epoch were lost here.
10.On Agri- dagh/mountain N-E.of Greater Ararat/there is a very
old road/called Colchis Road/.This area should be searched.

The inscriptions are in the following languages: Hettit,Assi-
ro-Babilonian/Cuneiform/and Arabic-Tartar.There are some Sumerian Cuneiform inscriptions around Lake Van.

Then there are perhaps 50 or more other archeological sites in
the Ararat region which have never been investigated-the ruins
of ancient villages,towns,buildings,tombs,caves,etc.

Russian Colonel Alexander Koor Map and unexplored archeological sites

of the investigating party which was sent to Mount Ararat to corroborate the discovery of Noah's Ark.

Lieutenant Leslin admitted he had also heard about the discovery of Noah's Ark, not as a rumor, but as news, from the Senior Adjutant of his division, who had told him that Noah's Ark was found in the saddle of two peaks of Mount Ararat.

This is all I heard from these two officers, and I am sure both told me the truth.

(signed) Col. Alexander A. Koor[38]

Violet Cummings stated about the alleged discovery.

The Russian investigators claim to have taken measurements of the Ark. It was supposedly 500 feet long, about 83 feet wide at the widest place, and about 50 feet high. These measurements, when compared with a 20-inch cubit, fitted proportionately with the size of Noah's Ark as described in Genesis 6:15. The entire rear end of the ship was in ice. But through the broken hatchway near the front of the boat, the investigating party were [Sic.] able to enter first the upper room, a "very narrow one with a high ceiling." From here, "side by side to it, stretched rooms of various size: small and large ones."

There was also "a very large room, separated as if by a great fence of huge trunks of trees," possibly "stables for the huge animals," such as elephants, hippopotami, and others. On the walls of the rooms were cages, "arranged in the lines all the way from the floor to the ceiling, and they had marks of rust from the iron rods which were there before. There were very many various rooms, similar to these, apparently several hundreds of them. It was not possible to count them, because the lower rooms and even a part of the upper ones—all of this was filled with hard ice. In the middle of the ship there was a corridor." The end of this corridor was "overloaded with broken partitions."

"The Ark was covered from inside as well as from outside," the story went on, "with some kind of a dark brown color" resembling "wax and varnish." The wood of which the Ark was built was excellently preserved except 1) at the hole in the front of the ship, and 2) at the door-hole at the side of the ship; there was the wood porous and it broke easily.

The analysis of the wood showed it to be similar to the cedar and larch tree, which are related to the family of the cypress trees "which cannot decay."

---

[38] Richard C. Bright, *The Ark, A Reality?* (Guilderland, New York: Ranger Associates Inc., 1989), p. 45.

"During the examination of the surroundings around the lake...there were found on one of the mountaintops the remains of some burn wood 'and a structure put together of stones,' resembling an altar. The pieces of wood found around this structure were of the same kind of wood as the Ark." Was this the "altar of Noah." Asked the author of the article, or was it built later by some other people...? This question no one can answer.

As in the Roskovitsky story which had first come to hand, this very similar but far more detailed account stated that the description and measurements of the Ark, both inside and out, together with photos, plans, samples of wood, were sent at once by special courier to the office of the chief commandant of the Army—"as the Emperor had ordered."[39]

An eyewitness is said to have stated:

As the huge ship at last loomed before them, an awed silence descended, and "without a word of command everyone took off his hat, looking reverently toward the Ark; everybody knew, feeling it in his heart and soul," that they were in the actual presence of the Ark. Many "crossed themselves and whispered a prayer." It was like being in a church, and the hands of the archaeologist trembled as he snapped the shutter of the camera and took a picture of the old boat as if she were "on parade."[40]

The Russians were in control of Mt. Ararat until about April 1918. Alexander Koor said it was 1916 and 1917 that the Ark was seen and explored by the Russians. The timing appears to fit.

The *Ararat Report* states the following about the story.

That the story may have been based on a Real Russian discovery was given a boost when I first visited Ararat in 1984. Our guide, Yavuz Konca, reported that an elderly Kurdish tribal chief living north of Lake Van, remembered just such a Russian discovery in the summer of 1917. At the time, he was a young man of 18 years of age. And was employed by the Russians who were building a railroad around the western pass of Ararat. He recalled an unusual event that summer in which returning Russian soldiers came into the village throwing their hats in the air and shooting their rifles. When he inquired as to the celebration, he was informed that they had discovered Noah's Ark on Mt. Ararat. I have my doubts that

---

[39] Violet M. Cummings, *Noah's Ark: Fable or Fact?* (San Diego: Creation Science Research Center, 1973), p. 57-58.

[40] Ibid, *p. 136.*

this elderly Kurdish man ever read any Ark books much less Gurley's tale. Gunnar Smars tells of hearing a similar story from Kurdish natives living in the village of Aralik on the Soviet Armenia border...

Cummings also claims to have found another source who verifies the Russian discovery. Col. Alexander Koor, an officer in the Czar's army, was stationed in this region during the time of the discovery...He claimed to be personally acquainted with relatives of some of the soldiers of the land expedition and with the brother of the pilot who made the flight. He gives his name as well as specific details about the military attachments which took part in the discovery. Koor claims the Ark was found in the saddle of the two peaks of Ararat. Koor was the anonymous author of the story about the Russian discovery which appeared in the Russian language newspaper, Rosseya, in 1945.

This account is similar to Gurley's account but is much more detailed. Noorbergen concludes that Koor used Gurley's story as his outline and questions why he waited till 1945 to recount one of the world's greatest discoveries. Cummings, however, claims Koor never heard of the New Eden story. Professor John Warwick Montgomery visited Koor just before he died (d. 1971) and was impressed by the man's integrity and scholarly ability. Koor believed the true name of the Russian pilot who made the discovery while flying over Ararat was Lt. Zabolotsky.

It is hard to fault the Koor account as it stands. We can see nothing in the story which is easily discountable. On the other hand, since we are so far removed from the man and his claims, it is almost impossible to corroborate the facts. It is interesting, however, that he claims the military detachment (14th Railroad Battalion) involved in the land search was building a railroad. This is also what we were told by the elderly Kurdish leader in 1984.

(3) Montgomery quotes an article which appeared in the Chicago Sunday Tribune in which the author claims the report made by this Russian expedition fell into the hands of Gen. Dimitri Osnobichine, an aide to the Grand Duke Cyril. He further states that the General's papers were later donated to a library in Geneva. Montgomery found that all facts in this newspaper article proved to be true, but nothing was turned up in the archives about the discovery of Noah's Ark...

First of all, it does not appear to us to be a hoax entirely perpetrated by an eccentric Floyd Gurley. Something, either a real discovery, or some false rumor seems to have preceded Gurley's account.

It is interesting to note the statement by Koor about the Ark location being at about the saddle of the Ararat peaks. This is also the location of the 1989 George Stephen III/Shockey/Simmons site.

Other relatives and friends of the alleged Russian discoverers such as Mrs. Gladys Evans have claimed that this incident was based in reality and have retold the stories as follows. Evans said that her father entertained three former Russian flyers who were part of the search team. They left her father a document (which has now been destroyed in cleaning) which stated the men's names, birth places, ages, ranks in the Air Force, name of the airfield where they were stationed, their commanding officer, and name of their plane. Mrs. Evans continued below.[41]

> They told how the Ark was "half in and half out of a lake like a log floating in water. It was an immense thing, and it had cages— some with metal on them. It had a catwalk on top and the door was off. The door was nearby and had apparently been struck by lightning because it was partly burnt. The Ark was just as good as the day it was built." The wood reminded them of oleander.
>
> When they first saw the Ark from the air, they thought it was a submarine, but couldn't figure out why someone would be building it on a mountain. On the later reconnaissance expedition, these three airmen actually got inside the Ark where they took pictures and measurements. The film was turned over to the Russian

Armanaff photo sketch of the alleged 1917 Russian expedition
Courtesy of Don Shockey via B.J. Corbin

---

[41] Richard C. Bright, *The Ark, A Reality?* (Guilderland, New York: Ranger Associates Inc., 1989), p. 40.

government.[42]

Minnesota resident Alvin Holderbecker, nephew of a czarist expedition eyewitness, stated the following.

> My Aunt Eva worked in the Czar's palace as a housemaid during World War I when she was about nineteen or twenty years old. Her father was a medical officer in the White Russian Army and a highly respected friend of the Czar and his family. He was the chief medical officer on the expedition that found Noah's Ark. When he came back from the expedition, he showed my Aunt Eva the photographs and reports.
>
> Then, the Bolsheviks took over and confiscated all of the photographs and reports and killed as many of the men from the expedition as they could find. My aunt Eva was the only one from her family who escaped. She was sent by the Czar to Kaiser Wilhelm in Germany.
>
> My Aunt, having seen the pictures, told me the Ark was three decks high, and on top of the roof there was a catwalk that was about knee-high with openings underneath to provide ventilation or light.[43]

Note that the Armanaff photo showed three Russians standing in the doorway of the Ark.

Despite the possible allusive evidence, many researchers find the Russian accounts difficult to believe because there is so little back up from Russian archives. Ahmet Arslan went to Moscow for one month and could find no evidence of a Russian expedition. Arslan also interviewed the former chief of the KGB who denied any existence of an Ark expedition.

However, the Ray Lubeck/Russian film shown in World War II in 1942 places fresh interest on the Russian expedition. See the Ray Lubeck 1942 section below.

U.S. Air Force's Guillford Officer - 1918 A.D.

Guillford Officer claimed that he was taken on a flight by a casual acquaintance.

> As the men crossed the Ahora Gorge at approximately 14,000 feet and turned south, they were surprised to find themselves nearly level with a great ship in a small lake valley, half-exposed and

---

[42] David Balsiger and Charles E. Sellier, *In Search of Noah's Ark* (Los Angeles: Sun Classic Books, 1976), pp. 108-109. Cited interview with Gladys Evans in February, 1976, El Cajon, CA.

[43] Violet M. Cummings, *Noah's Ark: Fable or Fact?* (San Diego: Creation Science Research Center, 1973), p. 56.

protruding from a melting glacier, with deep snow still piled on the back. It was about noon on a hot July day, and the ship stood out clearly in the bright sunlight.

The vessel resembled a submarine, listing to one side, with a superstructure (or deck-house) on top. As they passed, the men noted a door on one side, as well as openings for windows around the top.[44]

The *Ararat Report* stated the following about Guillford Officer.

An American pilot named Guillford Officer claimed to have seen Noah's Ark while flying over Ararat in 1918! His description sounds very much like the one in Gurley's story. His testimony was given to Eryl Cummings in 1972. Nothing about this story seems credible. For instance, the war ended in November, 1918. I can't imagine he and his buddy taking a joy ride over Ararat during war. If he indeed flew over Ararat after the war, i.e. November and December, it would have been covered with snow.

Russian Chief of Russian Camouflage Major Jasper Maskelyn - circa 1920 A.D.

Jasper Maskelyn, wartime Chief of Russian Camouflage claimed the following.

Fernand Navarra reported a Russian Major Jasper Maskelyn claimed one of his men was instructed to fly over Ararat to verify the rumour that Noah's Ark had been sighted by one of their pilots in WWI. He claimed they did indeed found Noah's Ark partially submerged in a lake of ice. Later climbers undertook an exploration of the area and found the remains of an ancient vessel, badly rotten about 400 feet long!! They said the wood was "very rotted" and composed of a fossilized wood which looked like coal.

The *Ararat Report* stated the following about Jasper Maskelyn.

Frankly, this account resembles the kind of thing we see on a regular basis in the tabloids at grocery checkouts! Would Russian pilots fly over Turkish territory? Would Russian climbers be allowed on Ararat? If you think so, you don't know Turks, nor their attitude about Russians.

---

[44] Violet M. Cummings, *Has Anybody Really Seen Noah's Ark?* (San Diego, CA: Creation-Life Publishers, 1982), p. 62-66.

American Radio Talk Show Host Carveth Wells - 1932 A.D.

Carveth Wells, a radio talk show host and traveler from Los Angeles, toured the U.S.S.R. in 1932. He visited Soviet Armenia and was shown the wooden cross at the Echmiadzin Monastery by Archbishop Mesrob, which he captured on film. In his book on the trip to the Soviet Union, *Kapoot!*, Wells placed a photo of Ararat from Yerevan which said the natives claimed that the base of the mountain was where the Garden of Eden was situated. Note that Ed Davis was also told about the Garden of Eden by the natives eleven

Archbishop Mesrob with ornamented cross laid in alleged "Ark Wood"
Courtesy of Carveth Wells 1932

years later, although Davis appeared to be talking about a location south of Hamadan, Iran.

Carveth Wells with Armenian Archbishop Mesrob 1932
Courtesy of Carveth Wells

"We have come all the way from Chicago on purpose to visit Echmiazin. We are looking for Noah's Ark or what is left of it!" I continued with a smile.

The old man's eyes twinkled. "We have the remains of the Ark here in the church!"...

"May we see it?" we all said eagerly.

..."I must explain to you, that it is the most prized possession of the monastery. Do not misunderstand me; we do not class it as merely a relic. We have many relics; we even have the iron spear which was thrust into the side of Jesus at his crucifixion; we have the nails and a piece of the Cross, but," he continued with a merry twinkle in his eye, "there are many such relics in other churches. This piece of Noah's Ark is in quite a different category, and no other church in the world possesses or even claims to possess such a thing…"

He then introduced himself to us.

"I am Archbishop Mesrop. Our Katholikos has recently died and until his successor is elected, I am in charge of Echmiazin!"

The archbishop…told us that, although he himself would have no objection to our seeing and photographing the portion of the Ark which had been in the church for centuries, it had never been shown to a layman…

I opened the last casket, which looked very much like an ordinary ikon from the outside, but on opening the two doors of the casket, instead of finding the usual painting of Jesus or the Holy Family, there was a piece of reddish-colored petrified wood, measuring about twelve inches by nine and about an inch thick.

"You may examine it as much as you like," said the Archbishop. "This is the portion of Noah's Ark which was brought down from Ararat by one of our monks named Jacob, St. Jacob."

It was obviously petrified wood, as the grain was clearly visible, but having expected to see a piece of wood that was curved like the side of a boat, I remarked that I was surprised to find it was flat.

Archbishop Mesrop had a sense of humor. He instantly remarked, "You have forgotten the rudder, Mr. Wells!"

So this was the piece of wood I had come so far to see, and the thing that so many other travelers, including Lord Bryce, had been unsuccessful in seeing.[45]

In 1970, Dr. John Millish, a friend of Wells and research astronomer at Yerkes Observatory for two years, stated that he had examined a piece of very hard wood, purported to have been brought out of Russia by Wells bribing a government inspector. Millish said that some shepherds had been involved in the transaction.[46] This second-hand account is typical of the lack of primary source details that are often rumored in the Ark search. Also, if the photo of Mount Ararat from Yerevan was taken at the time Wells was near Ararat, no one was climbing it as both Little Ararat and Greater Ararat were immersed in snow.

American Sister Bertha Davis - 1935-1941 A.D.

Sister Bertha Davis, a Bible teacher in Holtville, California would show photographs in Bible schools that she claimed was Noah's Ark. Those who saw the photos claimed they were actual photographs, not sketches or

---

[45] Wells, Carveth, *Kapoot: The Narrative of a Journey from Leningrad to Mount Ararat in Search of Noah's Ark* (New York: Robert M. McBride & Co., 1934), pp. 223-229.

[46] Violet M. Cummings, *Noah's Ark: Fable or Fact?* (Old Tappan, NJ: Spire Books, 1975), p. 71.

paintings. One person who saw the photos was Joe Bosse. Another was his brother-in-law, Walter Hefner, who stated the following.

> Only part of the boat was sticking out. The rest was covered with debris. It didn't look like an ordinary boat, like the pictures of the Ark we see today. It was more like a barge, with a house on top. It looked sort of as if it was made to wallow in the water. You could even see where the timbers jointed...I used to talk about the pictures a lot when I was young...Even got into a lot of fights over it...Could I draw a sketch of the way it looked? Sure. Just hand me that piece of paper and a pencil. Now, like I explained, it didn't look like an ordinary boat. The timbers appeared to be hand-hewn, and running horizontally around the ship...

Walter's sister Maurine also remembered the pictures.

> The pictures were old, very old. They were on heavy cardboard—sort of faded and gray. I've held them in my hands many times. The photos were kept with other pictures in a portfolio about 12 x 14 inches in size that had a pocket in one side...There was another picture, too, that went with the picture of the Ark. It was old and faded, too, and was of a stone bench, or maybe it was an altar, with a roof or cover of some kind over it. The roof was partly burned and black. Yes, Sister Davis sincerely believed they were pictures of Noah's Ark and the altar he had built.[47]

Note that the "remains of some burned wood" and a stone structure "resembling an altar" matches the *Rosseya* story by White Russian Colonel Alexander Koor (1917) and the story of Haji Yearam told by Harold Williams (1856). Fred Drake, who saw the George Greene photos (1953), also noticed horizontal timbers.

New Zealand Archaeologist Hardwicke Knight - 1936 A.D.

Hardwicke Knight was a New Zealander who claimed to find waterlogged rectangular timbers nine inches to a foot square which formed a rectangular structure pointing out of the snow. The wood was very dark in color but extremely soft and soggy as if it had been submerged in water for a long period of time. Knight originally thought the wood was the remains of a gun carriage or a heavy wagon. He had ascended past Lake Kop and a couple ice fields when he found the wood. Knight is a traditional archaeologist who does not believe in a worldwide flood.

---

[47] Violet M. Cummings, *Noah's Ark: Fable or Fact?* (San Diego: Creation Science Research Center, 1973), p. 146-148.

Australian Serviceman "Aussie" R. Taylor, U.S. Seabees Dale Nice and Roy Tibbetts - 1940-1945 A.D.

Dick Bright reports the following in *The Ark, A Reality?*

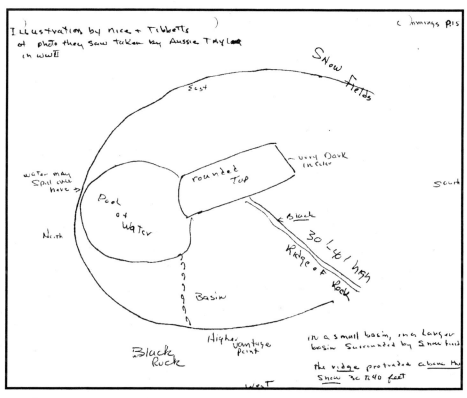

Dale Nice and Roy Tibbetts sketch of R. "Aussie" Taylor Ark photo 1977
Courtesy of Dr. John Morris

Another strange but convincing story came to light in late June and early July of 1977. Following a "Noah's Ark" presentation in...Durango, Colorado, Dale Nice, a businessman from Cortez, Colorado, announced that he had seen a picture of the Ark in World War II. Not only that, but his wartime buddy, Roy Tibbetts, who had served with him in the Seabees in New Guinea, also lived in the area, and he too had seen this picture...

On July 4th, the two men drove to Farmington, New Mexico, for a taped interview, from which the following story was gleaned.

It seems that an Australian whom they remembered only as R. Taylor, had come to their tent to look up one of their platoon members, a Wes Taylor, to learn if there might possibly be any relation between them. It was during his brief visit that the Aussie, as they called him, had shown them several pictures that he carried in the breast pocket of his battle jacket, along with his can of Sir Walter Raleigh tobacco. Nice remembers looking at only one, but

Roy Tibbetts recalls seeing at least two pictures, not exactly identical, but very similar.

The photo was very clear, and the men recalled it distinctly, although they had not been particularly interested in hearing about the Ark at the time. As they put it, they were more interested in passing around pictures of their wives and sweethearts than looking at snowfields and a purported ship on an icy mountain in a remote part of the world.

"What with war and Japs on their minds," said Tibbetts, "the average person wouldn't remember such things, but for some reason I've kept track of a lot of things."

Taylor, as they recalled, had been called back from Europe when the Australians had entered the war—around 1940-1941, they believed. He had been sent to New Guinea to train convicted but rehabilitated headhunters, as native police. It was probably during his European tour of duty that Taylor, described as an adventurous type, had made his Journey to Ararat, where he told them head had climbed the mountain and photographed the Ark...

The object, which Taylor had assured them was Noah's Ark, appears to sit in a small basin which was situated in a larger basin, surrounded by snowfields. It looked to be slightly tilted to one side, also possibly slanting a bit downhill and grounded on the shore of a small pool of water at one end. Both ends were still buried in snow, and the object leaned against a dike, or hogback, or ridge, producing some thirty to forty feet above the snow.

Taylor had pointed out footprints, plainly visible in the snow, that led across the base to the ship. They were his own footsteps, he declared, from boots especially made-to-fit in Turkey, from goatskin with the hair turned inside. It was obvious he had somehow managed to climb to a higher vantage point above the ship, and from there the pictures were taken.

The Ark, the man said, was very dark, but not as black in color as the rocky ridge it was leaning against, and it seemed to be sitting at an angle, kind of on its side. Right at the end of it, recalled Nice, was what he took to be ice water. Neither Dale Nice or Roy Tibbetts recalled seeing a door. Perhaps it was still hidden under the snow. The top appeared to be slightly rounded but, perhaps because of the tilt, no catwalk or windows were visible in the photos. Said Nice, the thing that impressed me was that there was a little pond of water there—I couldn't figure that out, at that altitude...Was the ship quite close to the hogback? Yes, replied Tibbetts, right at the base of it. Pointing to the sketch, Nice added, it was lying right in here, and apparently right against it. [48]

The Ark lying on its side sounds similar to Ed Davis description in 1943.

---

[48] Richard C. Bright, *The Ark, A Reality?* (Guilderland, New York: Ranger, 1988), p.81-82.

U.S. Navy Machinist Mate 1st Class Ray Lubeck - 1942 A.D.

In 1942, Ray Lubeck became an alleged eyewitness to a silent film of 50 Russian soldiers marching past Noah's Ark near the top of Mount Ararat. Ray was a Machinist Mate 1st Class in the U.S. Navy on Midway Island in 1942. Later, Lubeck was trained to be a Deep Sea Diver for the Navy and dug submarine torpedoes from the mud underneath harbors and bays. To keep up the morale of the Navy, Marines, and Air Force stationed on the island, movies would occasionally be shown. One film clip of between 30 seconds and a couple minutes showed 50 Russian soldiers marching single file down a ridge and past Noah's Ark. Since the film was silent, black and white, and older quality, there was an American commentator describing the scene in English. He stated that the Russians were going on a campaign to fight the Turks although Lubeck did not notice any guns since he was stunned to see Noah's Ark in one piece.

Lubeck attended a seminar on Noah's Ark in his former hometown of Desert Hot Springs, CA taught by Elfred Lee in the 80s. He gave the attached map to Elfred Lee after the seminar. Lubeck told Lee and Rex Geissler that he could not believe he was looking at Noah's Ark and that the image was burned into his mind to the point that every boat he saw since then he compared to Noah's Ark. He also said that as a machinist, he was used to constantly looking at blueprints which helped him memorize the dimensions of drawings better than most people. Lee then moved to Mexico and the map

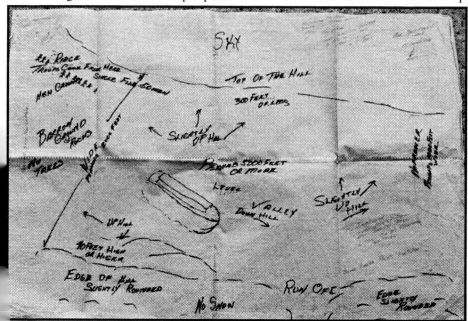

Ray Lubeck sketch of Russian film of 50 soldiers and Noah's Ark near the top of Mount Ararat
Courtesy of Ray Lubeck via Elfred Lee via Rex Geissler

was forgotten until Lee and Geissler were pilfering though Lee's Noah's Ark paraphernalia. There were 30 or more people who witnessed the film. Lubeck only knew one of them and he already died.

Lubeck stated that the location of the film was near the top of Mount Ararat on the border of Turkey and Russia. He said it appeared to be within a few hundred feet or a thousand feet of the summit of the mountain. This and the map he drew may indicate the saddle area which is where Russian Colonel Koor stated the ark was located by the Russians and there was a group of 50 Russian soldiers on one side of the mountain and 100 on another side of the mountain.

Lubeck stated that the dimensions of the ark appeared to be about 75 feet wide by 50 feet high by several hundred feet long and that it was completely intact with no damage at that time, possibly World War I judging by the olive, drab uniforms they were wearing and the poor quality and silence of the film. He said there was a superstructure that ran all the way from the front to back and was about 6-8 feet high with a roof on top that was pointed at about a 20-degree angle. Lubeck stated there was a keel perhaps 18-24 inches wide that appeared to run under the ship all of its length and up to a point on the bow. The bow was rounded and pointed like a boat not a barge. There was also a solid wood railing around the edge of Noah's Ark that extended up about 3 feet. Note that William Todd mentioned a similar railing, "The upper part had additions that looked like a railing or a roof that was in extreme disrepair." There is also a lip but not a high railing on the Hagopian/Lee Ark sketch. Lubeck said that there was a hill on one side and a drop-off on another side. He stated the Ark was on a precipice and about 75 feet from the drop off. It was in a little valley.

Note that Lubeck stated that the video showed no snow although there was a run off area apparently from snow or rain similar to the Ed Davis/Elfred Lee sketch. Also note that on the backside of the saddle, there is no snow in an area almost up to the Eastern Summit at 16,800 feet. Perhaps with low snowfall and warm weather, that area of no snow perhaps extended over the northern side of the saddle down the mountain some distance.

One may notice that some words are misspelled as Lubeck readily states that he is not an educated man although he does have an impressive vocabulary. Also, note Lubeck's impression of North in the upper right corner of the map. Lubeck went to Washington to begin looking for the Russian film in July 1999. Lubeck is also coming to southern California for two professional artists to sketch his view in more detail and to be interviewed in depth. The first professional artist will be one that is not familiar with the search for Noah's Ark. After that, the second professional artist will be Elfred Lee while Robin Simmons, Doris Bowers, David Montgomery and Rex Geissler are present to interview him.

U.S. Army Corps of Engineers Sergeant Ed Davis - 1943 A.D.

Sergeant Ed Davis claimed to see the Ark in 1943 while working for the Army Corps of Engineers. He was brought to an Ark-a-thon meeting by Dr. Don Shockey in June 1986 where he was questioned and videotaped by several Ark researchers including Bob Stuplich, John McIntosh, Elfred Lee, Eryl Cummings, Al Jenny and Bill Crouse. Davis passed a two-hour lie detector test and the questioner said that Davis definitely saw a boat-like structure on a mountain although he could not be positive which mountain. Ray Anderson says Davis told him that it was an exceptionally hot summer

Elfred Lee painted the Ed Davis account 1986-87. Doris Bowers pointed out that the superstructure was enhanced from the 1986 Ark-a-thon drawing to include windows. However, Ed Davis did sign his OK on the enhancements in 1987 even though he was previously chastised for not seeing any windows on the Ark.
Courtesy of Elfred Lee

which helped uncover the Ark and was the reason that the Lors came to get him. Anderson also said the Lors stated that the Ark could be seen many summers because of the prevailing hot winds coming off the plain and sweeping up the mountain through the Ahora Gorge.

Ed Davis stated at the Ark-a-thon in 1986 that the superstructure or catwalk was knee-high, about 20 feet wide (one-third the total width) and that the keel on the bottom of the boat was 18-20 inches wide. He said that there was water standing everywhere along the trail. Davis also stated that he was not on the icecap and that it was above them for most of the trip, "We wasn't ever on the ice cap." He said that snow and ice were in the canyons but that they did not cross much of it. Abas Abas also told Davis that "many years the entire Ark canyon is completely covered with ice and snow and will never come out." Ed said there were three or four floors to the structure.

Day 1 was spent driving the Army truck from Ed Davis' base in Hamadan along the border (Russian or Iraqi?) to Casbeen and Abas Abas' little village (Casbeen and the village have not been identified as Robin Simmons checked two earlier Iranian maps and Rex Geissler checked the Microsoft Virtual Globe and the latest Iranian map). Note that Ahmet Arslan showed a village named Tarlabas (which Davis seemed to recognize by describing the large rocks to Arslan and he said that was the location that he used dynamite to get the well water flowing again although Davis did not recognize a tree that Ahmet talked about) near Ahora village on his map on the inside cover of *The Lost Ship of Noah* by Charles Berlitz. Also, this village next to Ahora would not make sense if Davis was driven through the night for several hours by 4-Wheel Drive from Tarlabas to Ahora. Therefore, Abas Abas' village appears to have been in Iran. Arslan confirmed this in a phone call with Rex Geissler, saying that he had gone door to door through Ahora Village and Tarlabas looking for anyone who knew Abas Abas but it was to no avail. Arslan concluded that Abas Abas was an Iranian, smuggler or nomad. Davis left his Army truck in Abas Abas' compound.

On Day 2, Abas Abas' sons and relatives arrived right after they went to sleep at the end of Day 1. They drove them through the night in a British Lori from Abas Abas' village to a primitive village in the foothills of Ararat (some think Ahora), arriving at breakfast. After driving through the night to begin Day 2, they spent the day getting horses ready and looking at artifacts.

On Day 3, they rode the small, wiry horses the rest of the day from the small village up a canyon past Jacob's Well. At a meeting on December 29th, 1987, Arslan questioned Davis if he saw the white rocks of Jacob's Graveyard. According to Davis, they ate at a "hidden cave deep in the foothills of Greater Ararat, possibly a little over 8,000 feet elevation on the western wall of the Ahora Gorge. They say it's where T. E. Lawrence (of Arabia) hid when he was doing reconnaissance." Ahmet Arslan marked the T. E. Lawrence cave on the inside cover map of *The Lost Ship of Noah* just west of St. Jacob's Well across the Black or Ahora Glacier. Dr. John Morris said that they saw the cave and tried to get to it but it was too dangerous to climb up the embankment of rocks that guarded it.

On Day 4, they hiked all-day and stayed in another hidden cave higher in the gorge. Again, Arslan marked two rock caves on his *The Lost Ship of Noah* map which may correspond to the Davis Day 4 cave. Arslan also stated that the Doomsday Peak is the triangular peak in the Ahora Gorge to the west a couple formations from Avalanche Canyon and just below the opening to the Cehennem Dere. Although Ahmet Arslan probably knows Mount Ararat better than any other known explorer, no one else has corroborated Doomsday Peak. Arlsan says that Doomsday Peak is at the end of Camel's Back Trail, which he claimed Hagopian used on one of his trips. Also, explorer Ray Anderson points out that Ahmet's "Doomsday Peak" and Ed Davis' "Doomsday Rock" may be different formations. Note that Davis seemed to indicate that "Doomsday Rock" was rounded off whereas "Doomsday Peak" is triangular. From the Ark-a-thon tapes, Davis stated that the final cave was still several kilometers and a steep climb away from the "Ark cove."

On Day 5, they waited until afternoon for the rain to stop and then climbed steeply several kilometers to see the broken pieces of the Ark in a canyon after going around "Doomsday Rock." Davis stated repeatedly that many people would go higher along a ridge which led over the top back into Turkey and would thus miss the Ark cove completely.

Only three of the eight natives went to the Ark with Davis as Abas Abas had the other five working on some project. On that final morning of the trip going up, Abas Abas pointed out a cross in the mountainside in the distance. Davis also stated in the Ark-a-thon tapes that the Kurds tried to protect the Ark by digging diversionary routes for water to go around it rather than cutting underneath it. The Kurds also tried to cover the Ark with rocks to hide it from the Turks. They move rocks and cause rockslides to accomplish these purposes. It is interesting to think of the Kurds as preservationists.

After Davis began discussing his experience, he began receiving bizarre phone threats warning him that he had betrayed an Abas family secret and that as a result "the Black Hand of Allah was upon him." Ed Davis died on November 17th, 1998.

The following was his testimony.

Something happened to me in '43 that's haunted me all my life. I'm in the 363rd Army Corps of Engineers working out of a base in Hamadan (ancient Ekbatan or Ecbatane), Iran. We're building a Way Station into Russia from Turkey. A supply route.

My driver's a young man named Badi Abas. One day while we're at a quarry site loading rock, he points to a distant peak and says, "Agri Dagh, my home."

We can see it clearly on the horizon with its year-round snowcap. "Mt. Ararat, that's where the Ark landed?" I say. He nods. "My grandfather knows where it is and has gone up there," he says matter-of-factly. I thought, boy would I like to see that...

One day in July, his grandfather, Abas-Abas, visits our base and tells Badi the ice on Ararat is melting to where you can see part of the Ark. Badi tells me if I want to see it they will take me there. I had done a favor for their village that put me in good stead with the Abas family. In fact, they now have water, where before they had to walk two miles to get it.

So I go to my commanding officer and ask for a leave. He says, "It's dangerous, you'll get killed." I tell him how much I want to go.

Ed Davis and Ahmet Ali Arslan with Elfred Lee sketch 1987
Courtesy of Don Shockey

He says, "I can give you R&R in Tehran and you could take the long way." I stock up on extra gasoline, oil and tires.

A few days later, we get up early and Badi, Abas and I drive down along the border as far as Casbeen until we get to his little village (this was the settlement I had helped get water). We spend the night there.

At dawn the next day, we reach the foothills of Ararat and arrive at another primitive village. Abas tells me the name of the village means, "Where Noah Planted The Vine." I see grapevines so big at their trunk you can't reach around them. Very, very old.

Abas says they have a cave filled with artifacts that came from the Ark. They find them strewn in a canyon below the Ark, collect them to keep from outsiders who, they think, would profane them. It's all sacred to them. That night, they show me the artifacts. Oil lamps, clay vats, old style tools, things like that. I see a cage-like door, maybe thirty by forty inches, made of woven branches. It's hard as stone, looks petrified. It has a hand-carved lock or latch on it. I could even see the wood grain.

We sleep. At first light, we put on mountain clothes and they bring up a string of horses. I leave with seven male members of the Abas family and we ride—seems like an awful long time.

Finally we come to a hidden cave deep in the foothills of Greater Ararat. [Note: this cave is probably a little over 8,000 feet elevation on the western wall of the Ahora Gorge.] They say it's where T. E. Lawrence (of Arabia) hid when he was doing reconnaissance. There's a huge pot of hot food waiting for us. There's fungus there that glows in the dark. And they say Lawrence put it on his face to convince the Kurds he was a god and get them to join him in his war against the Turks.

We eat and then climb back on our horses and continue riding higher on the narrow trail. They tell me we're going through the "Back Door." It's a secret route used by smugglers or bandits. Along the way, they point out a pair of human legs sticking out of the ice and tell me he shouldn't have been up there. I believe them.

I don't know how the horses are able to follow the route. In some places you can tell we were riding along a high cliff but most of the time it's hard to see because of the rain and fog. A freezing wind is blowing and it feels like it's going right through me. Soon, Abas tells me to be quiet because we're at a place where Russian sentries, stationed below, might hear us.

We ride in silence for the rest of the day. Sometimes they'd communicate in their own private code by short whistles. Eventually we run out of trail. Someone from the Abas family is waiting for us, takes our horses and we are roped together and climb on foot much higher to another cave. I can't tell where we are. The rain never lets up...

After three days of climbing we come to the last cave. Inside, there's strange writing, it looked beautiful and old, on the rock walls and a kind of natural rock bed or outcropping near the back of the cavern. Another pot of food is waiting for us. Everything's prepared for my visit by the Abas family. It rains hard all night.

The next morning we get up and wait. The rain lets up and we walk along a narrow trail behind a dangerous outcropping called "Doomsday Rock". I guess it's called that because it's a place you could easily die, and many have. Some not of their own doing. We doubled back around behind the imposing rock formation and come to a ledge. We are enveloped by fog.

Suddenly the fog lifts and the sun breaks through a hole in the clouds. It's a very mystical sight as the light shimmers on the wet canyon. My Moslem friends pray to Allah. They speak quietly and are very subdued...

After they finish praying, Badi Abas points down into a kind of horseshoe crevasse and says, "That's Noah's Ark." But I can't see anything. Everything's the same color and texture. Then I see it—a huge, rectangular, man-made structure partly covered by a talus of ice and rock, lying on its side. At least a hundred feet are clearly visible. I can even see inside it, into the end where it's been broken off, timbers are sticking out, kind of twisted and gnarled, water's cascading out from under it.

Abas points down the canyon and I can make out another portion of it. I can see how the two pieces were once joined—the torn timbers kind of match. They told me the Ark is broken into three or four big pieces. Inside the broken end of the biggest piece, I can see at least three floors and Abas says there's a living space near the top with forty-eight rooms. He says there are cages inside as small as my hand, others big enough to hold a family of elephants.

I can see what looks like remains of partitions and walkways inside the bigger piece. I really want to touch it—it's hard to explain the feeling. Abas says we can go down on ropes in the morning. It begins to rain and we go back to the cave...

Next morning when we get up, it's snowing. It had snowed all night and it's at least belt deep on me. I can't see anything down in the canyon. The Ark is no longer visible. Abas says, "We have to leave—it's too dangerous."

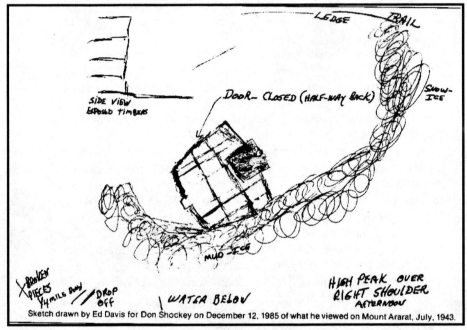

Sketch drawn by Ed Davis for Don Shockey on December 12, 1985 of what he viewed on Mount Ararat, July, 1943.

Sketch drawn by Ed Davis for Don Shockey on December 12th, 1985 of what he viewed on Mount Ararat in July, 1943
Courtesy of Dr. Don Shockey from *The Painful Mountain*

It takes five days to get off the mountain and back to my base. I smell so bad when I get back, they burn my clothes. And no one seems interested in what I saw, so I quit talking about it. But I dream about it every night for twenty years.

There's something up there...[49]

Bill Crouse notes the following concerns he has about Ed Davis' testimony in the *Ararat Report*.

---

[49] Ed Davis statement courtesy of Robin Simmons, FindTheArk@aol.com

Davis's story may very well be true. However, there are some things in his story that we know are impossible and so may cast a shadow on his testimony.

(1) If Davis maintains he was at Hamadan when he saw Mt. Ararat, there is a big problem. Hamadan is over 400 miles from Mt. Ararat of Turkey as the crow flies. It is impossible to have seen Ararat from that distance. The curvature of the earth does not permit it.

(2) Davis also claims they drove to Abas's village in a little over half a day. This again is impossible if they were starting from Hamadan. To travel 400 miles in a truck in a half-day would be difficult even on our modern interstate roads. Not much existed in the way of roads in Iran in 1943.

(3) In Shockey's book, one is led to believe that Abas is a Kurd. These are of course the people who make their home on the foothills of Ararat. However, at other times Davis has referred to Abas as a Lourd. He has also confirmed this in a phone conversation. The Lourds inhabit the area around Hamadan, and it is highly unlikely (if indeed this is the case) that Abas would be a tribal leader in an area inhabited by Kurds!...

(4) If the Ark is in the area that Davis indicate, it would be visible every summer for several months as the altitude in this area is barely above 13,000 feet. The local tradition goes against this. Many believe that the Ark is buried under ice and is visible only two or three times a century during unusual weather patterns.

(5) The details of what the natives found in the Ark as related to Davis are absolutely incredible. Davis shares that Abas told him they found honey still in jars, feathers in cages, fish remains, and beans that were still edible! Now we reiterate, that this is what Davis said he was told.

(6) Davis mentioned at the Ark-a-thon in Farmington in June, 1986, that he was also privileged to see the Garden of Eden. This is also mentioned in the written account. We find it very curious that there is not only a traditional Garden of Eden near Hamadan where Davis was stationed, but also near the traditional resting place of Noah's Ark!

This site is approximately 50 or more miles from Hamadan. This mountain is known as "Kuh e Alvand." Its altitude is 11,700 feet. For a good part of the year it is snowcapped. A French Bible Encyclopedia contains a map of the area with the Ark on top of this mountain.

Questions: Is it possible that this is the mountain that Davis saw that day in Hamadan?

Was Davis on this mountain?

Do we have any definitive evidence that Davis was actually in Turkey on Mt. Ararat?...

We don't know the answer to these questions, and they are troubling.

Mr. Ed Davis is a kind old gentleman...He claims to be in his eighties. We wish to give him the benefit of the doubt. Perhaps he is just confused about the details of events which occurred so long ago.

After a year, Bill Crouse and the *Ararat Report* added an addendum to the Ed Davis story that follows.

Mr. Davis...was considerably upset because he feared we were leaving our readers with the impression that he was just a senile old man. If other readers were left with this impression, we apologize to Mr. Davis...Mr. Davis, for his age, (he says he is in his eighties) is quite clear-headed...

Since our published report, several things have been brought to our attention which warrant an update and additional reflection on this matter. Personally, I believe Ed Davis had some kind of experience. He either truly saw Noah's Ark; OR he was led to believe that he had seen it.

I believe this to be the case for two reasons: (1) the notation in his Bible does not seem to be something that he wrote recently (see p. 51, *The Painful Mountain*). (2) He was given a polygraph exam (6/1/88) in which he did quite well. We have been privileged to see the results. Prior to the aforementioned exam Davis was approached several times about taking the polygraph. In each case he responded negatively. Several Ark researchers then became very skeptical about his story.

It is to his credit, we believe, that Mr. Davis finally agreed to such a test. It was administered by P.G.P. Polygraph of Albuquerque, NM. It was the examiner's conclusion that Davis was being truthful to the target issue of having been shown Noah's Ark...

We heartily commend Davis for being willing to take a polygraph exam. His refusal would not have meant he was lying, but the natural reaction most of us have in this kind of a situation is suspicion...

Another matter that we bring up here with regards to Ed Davis' testimony, is the apparent negative result of last summer's helicopter search...

As far as we are concerned the Ed Davis file is still open.

To be fair, a few things must be added to the review of the Ed Davis testimony. In another interview with Dr. Don Shockey and Howard Davis, Ed Davis stated that from Mt. Ararat, "The Lur told me if it were clear they could see into Iran and Russia." Note that it was raining or snowing most of the time Davis was on the mountain. The poor weather factor and forty-four years of time may be why he did not appear to readily recognize clear photos of Ararat. Other indications that Davis was on Turkish Mt. Ararat included the party's repeated avoidance of Russian sentries and the Russian border (for some researchers, this confirms that he was on modern day Mount Ararat), his visits to Jacob's Altar (where the Lurs placed a rock on top of it just like Dr. Howard Davis said the Kurds do as well), Jacob's Well, Jacob's Graveyard, Doomsday Rock and Camel's Back Pass which are known features on Turkish Mount Ararat. Note that Davis stated the only water they did not need to boil during the trip was from St. Jacob's Well which again Ahmet Arslan notes as spring water. Dr. Parrot confirmed that Jacob's Well contained pure water in 1829, writing the following from Dr. John Warwick Montgomery's book *The Quest for Noah's Ark*.

> [Parrot, the first explorer in modern times to reach the summit of Ararat (1829), saw this well near a little deserted chapel some two thousand feet above the monastery of St. James (i.e. St Jacob)...]
>
> The fountain which springs out of a rock, at this spot, affords a clear drinkable water, of a pure natural taste, and is therefore an object deserving of general estimation: as I have proved to my vexation; since, in all my excursions upon it, I never either found or heard of any other...
>
> [The blowout which destroyed the town of Arguri in 1840 did not affect St. Jacob's well; Lynch saw it in 1893 (*Armenia: Travels and Studies*-1901, I, 194)]...

Elfred Lee also stated that both George Hagopian and Ed Davis talked about a tree on Mt. Ararat which native women would tie rags on and pray at in order to have children. Ed also talked about seeing Lesser Ararat when the clouds would occasionally part. Davis indicated that the natives claimed that a glow above the lights in Tehran, Iran could be seen on a very clear night from the mountain's summit which could be for or against the Turkish Ararat. Also, note that because of the ice and snow on the mountain in July, it appears doubtful that Davis was on a lower 11,000 to 12,000-foot mountain.

Badi Abas may have pointed out Mount Ararat from a certain quarry they were using that day. Also, since Badi Abas was Davis' driver that means he was driving Davis somewhere, possibly outside Hamadan and closer to Ararat. Davis simply said he was stationed in Hamadan. Since Davis' particular duty was to build a Way Station or Supply Depot to help transfer supplies from Iran to Russia, he was probably working north of Hamadan closer to the Turkish Mount Ararat and perhaps it was visible from his workplace. In the book, *The Painful Mountain*, there is a purported photo of the end of the road Davis was building which went through a tunnel into Russia. Other Ark researchers have serious concerns about some of the photos in the book. The Iranian border with Russia is bisected by the Caspian Sea. Since Hamadan is on the western side of Iran, it is probable that the route to Russia went on the western side of the Caspian Sea. In this case, the furthest one can get from Mount Ararat on the Iranian/Russian border is 270 miles. A more reasonable assumption may be that the route went near the Iranian city of Tabriz and thus could have been only 125-150 miles from Ararat. However, since Davis mentioned going through Casbeen along the border on the way to Ararat, if Casbeen were found, Davis' Ararat would also be close. Despite these possible scenarios, Davis maintained that Badi pointed out Ararat on an ideal clear morning from Hamadan.

If Davis were working away from Hamadan (as his testimony seemed to indicate since he said they were "loading rock one day") and closer to Mount Ararat on the Turkey to Russia route then it may have been easy for him to get to the Turkish Mount Ararat in less than a day as he stated. Also, Davis described in minute detail unique conditions on Ararat as well as cultural details of the interaction of his mountain guides—things like "urinating on your hands to prevent chapping and wind-burns." It would be difficult to make-up this accurate minutia and these details which were not readily available in print. Davis later acknowledged that Shockey accidentally called Abas a Kurd in his book. Davis maintained that Abas was a Lor but that he was "kissing cousins" with his Kurdish relatives around Mount Ararat and thus the Lor/Kurd confusion might be solved.

Another issue that has confused researchers is the elevation that Davis finished his ascent. Perhaps the ice cap was higher at that time which would more easily revealed the Ark. This is what the natives actually told Davis who stated at the 1986 Ark-a-thon, "Many times, the whole canyon is one complete ice cap, I mean, snow and ice." Perhaps, today, the real Ed Davis Canyon or "Ark cove" is part of the "ice cap." Note also that the several kilometers they traveled "way up high" on the last day from the last cave could have placed them above the Gorge in the upper Abich II/Stephen Site/Anderson area. Abas Abas also told Davis that the Ark used to be even higher on the mountain but had come down a hundred or more feet when it broke.

Ed Davis also discussed and showed a keel at the bottom of the boat in his sketch and Elfred Lee's drawings. This keel boat design is exactly the way that David Duckworth described the boat he had seen in the Smithsonian Institution photographs to Rex Geissler. In fact, after meeting with Ed Davis at the June 1986 Ark-a-thon, artist Elfred Lee and Eryl Cummings met with David Duckworth in Farmington, New Mexico. Lee stated that Ed Davis' and David Duckworth's Ark descriptions were one and the same.

Another concern about Davis is that the photo given by Abas-Abas to Davis shown in *The Painful Mountain* that illustrated the difficulty of climbing Mount Ararat in wintertime does not appear to be a picture of Mount Ararat. The photo caption in the book does not make it clear that Abas-Abas or Davis believed the photo was actually of Ararat but it definitely does not look like Ararat. Rather, it appears to be a valley in a mountain range. Also, according to Ark researcher Bob Cornuke who has photos to prove it, another photo in the book allegedly shows "Mount Ararat viewed from the Iranian side" but is really Kūh-e-Damāvand, also a strato-volcano with a permanent snow cap which is the highest mountain in Iran, west Asia and Europe at 18,602 feet and is a popular tourist destination just northeast of Tehran. Rex Geissler found two photos on the Internet that confirmed Cornuke's statement   about   Kūh-e-Damāvand   at http://itto.org/attract/damavand/index.htm. Cornuke also stated that the photo labeled "Street scene of the village of Abas Abas in 1943" is really downtown Hamadan.

This brings up the idea that Davis may have been in Iranian Mountains (the Lur or Lor live in the Zagros Mountains of western Iran called Luristan or Lorestan) rather than in Turkey. Partially because of some historical references, partially because researchers have given up hope on Turkish Mount Ararat, and because of reasoning based on Genesis 11:1-2, Ed Davis' Lur and Iranian connections, the oldest pottery found is in Iran, the oldest written language Proto-Elamite is found in Iran, and other non-biblical documents, there is a growing trend to study possible sites in Iran. Bob Cornuke, Larry Williams, Bob Stuplich, Kevin Kluetz, Albert Groebli and others are interested in possible Iranian sites. Bob Cornuke toured Iran in 1998 and plans to return again.

Researcher Kevin Kluetz notes the following.

> Ed told me that from his viewpoint of the Ark, the mountain summit was to his back, the morning sun would have risen from his right-front, and the evening sun would have set to his left-rear. If he turned around to face the summit, the evening sun would have set to the right of the summit. If he turned back around and directly faced the Ark at night, he could see the glow of the lights of Teheran reflecting off the clouds to his front, approximately 10 degrees to the left of the Ark. Most Ark researchers assume that Ed had been on Mount Ararat, so I asked Ed if perhaps the glow he saw was from the lights of Erivan, Armenia, to the northeast of Mount Ararat, Turkey. Ed adamantly said, "No, it was Teheran."…

A clue that may help identify the location of the region of Ararat is in the following Bible passage:

"So Sennacherib king of Assyria departed and went away, returned home, and remained at Nineveh. Now it came to pass, as he was worshiping in the temple of Nisroch his god, that his sons Adrammelech and Sharezer struck him down with the sword; and they escaped into the land of Ararat. Then Esarhaddon his son reigned in his place." (this passage is found in both 2 Kings 19:36-37 and Isaiah 37:37-38 [New King James version])

The above passage indicates that these men escaped from Nineveh, Assyria to Ararat. Nineveh was in modern day Iraq. Based on the Flood account and Genesis 8:4, quoted above, Ararat has a mountainous region. If the men in the above passage escaped from [Iraq] to a nearby region that had mountains, they may have escaped eastward into modern, mountainous Iran.

Another clue that may help identify the Ark's landing spot is in the passage below.

These were the families of the sons of Noah, according to their generations, in their nations; and from these the nations were divided on the earth after the flood. Now the whole earth had one language and one speech. And it came to pass, *as they journeyed from the east*, that they found a plain in the land of Shinar, and they dwelt there. Then they said to one another, "Come, let us make bricks and bake them thoroughly." They had brick for stone, and they had asphalt for mortar. And they said, "Come, let us build ourselves a city, and a tower whose top is in the heavens; let us make a name for ourselves, lest we be scattered abroad over the face of the whole earth." (Genesis 10:32-11:4 [New King James Version])

The passage above transitions from the end of the Flood account to mankind's activities after the Flood, beginning with the Tower of Babel. Interestingly, after the Flood, the passage above indicates that men migrated from the east and then found a plain in Shinar (the Mesopotamian vicinity of the Tigris and Euphrates Rivers: modern Iraq). Based on this passage, it appears that men lived in modern Iran after the Flood and then migrated to modern Iraq, where they built the Tower of Babel. Based on this passage, perhaps the Ark landed east of Iraq, in the mountains of Iran.

The only other Bible passage that mentions Ararat is quoted below.

Set up a banner in the land, Blow the trumpet among the nations! Prepare the nations against her, Call the kingdoms together against her: Ararat, Minni, and Ashkenaz. Appoint a general against her; Cause the horses to come up like the bristling locusts. (Jeremiah 51:27 [New King James Version])

The name "Minni" in the Bible is only used to describe a nation once in the Bible: in the passage above. Elsewhere, the word "minni" generally means "from" in the Bible. *Unger's Bible Dictionary* (Chicago, USA: Moody Press, 1966) suggests that "Minni" was in the region that is now Armenia. The name "Ashkenaz" in Modern Hebrew means "Germany" (Kolatch, Alfred J., *The Second Jewish Book of Why*, Middle Village, NY, USA: Jonathan David Publishers, 1985). Interestingly, both the Iranians and the Germans claim to be of Aryan descent. [50]

Also, in regard to Davis claiming to see the Garden of Eden, Carveth Wells states in the caption about his picture of Erivan and Mount Ararat in his book *Kapoot!*, "The plain at the base of the mountain is said to be the site of the Garden of Eden." It is interesting to note that Wells wrote that only eleven years before Davis claimed to have been shown the Garden of Eden by the natives although he indicated in the first Ark-a-thon session that the Garden of Eden location was south of Hamadan, Iran. Davis appears to have accepted what he was told by the natives and one wonders how much he was

Alleged Ark Eyewitness Vince Will being interviewed by Matthew Kneisler
Courtesy of Jonathan Brisbin

tainted by what Ark researchers told him as well. However, Davis' basic story appears to have stayed consistent throughout the thirteen years he told it until his death.

U.S. Air Force Sergeant Vince Will, *Stars and Stripes* 1943-1945 A.D.

Vince Will, now a minister in Springfield, Missouri saw a front page *Stars and Stripes* Ark photograph looking into an opening of the Ark. His brother also saw a different version of the *Stars and Stripes* photo while in Europe (possibly a North Africa edition of the paper).

According to Ark researcher Cliff Moody, "The *Stars and Stripes* alone published forty-nine articles dealing with Noah's Ark from September 1949, through August 1984. Unfortunately, the particular 1943-1945 European issues containing actual Ark photos has not yet been located."

According to Violet Cummings, one of the earliest confirmations of the story comes through two southern California physicians, Dr. Chaunceford Mounce and a Dr. Connor, both of whom served in Algeria during the first 6 months of 1943, and in Tunisia in the last 6 months of 43. "If you could get the *Stars and Stripes* of the 12th and 15th Air Force, I'm certain you'd find the story about the ship on Ararat...I saw the report on the front page of *Stars and Stripes*...Mediterranean copy sometime during the summer of 43," stated Mounce.

Vince Will also talked to three flyers in an Italian officers' mess hall who

were looking at several Ark photos. They showed him the photos while Will was serving as a Technical Sergeant for the Air Force during World War II. He also claimed to fly up the Ahora Gorge in a C-47 and saw the structure for 15-20 seconds.

In World War II, I was stationed in North Africa with the signal installation battalion that was attached to the Army Air Force. We put up electronic beacons that airplanes would fly on...

Sketch of alleged Ark photos Vince Will saw in W.W. II 1943
Courtesy of Vince Will via Michael Castellano, Cliff Moody and Robin Simmons

---

[50] Kevin Kluetz has more information about Ed Davis and other issues at http://www.geocities.com/Athens/Parthenon/3021

One time, I was in the airport in Naples, Italy, with a buddy of mine and we went over to the officer's mess to have a cup of coffee. Our guys had been flying supplies over Turkey to the back part of Russia to Yerevan, and one of the pilots had taken some pictures. Three officers were looking at the four or five pictures of Mount Ararat and a boat-like object on it, and we looked too.

Some of them thought it was Noah's Ark. Two of the pictures were hazy, but one of them was clear. A section of the Ark was sticking out of the snow and ice 40 to 50 feet on a ledge without anything underneath it. The wood was darker than the rocks around it. The wood was in pretty good shape. I couldn't see any holes on the top. There was a hole on the right side where you could see the different levels and structural beams. I could see two decks through the hole.

As we looked at these photos, there was no question in the minds of these flyers that this was Noah's Ark. I'm convinced that I was looking at Noah's Ark, and a similar picture was put into the *Stars and Stripes* in about 1944. It was a front-page photo that looked like the one I saw in the officer's mess. I was upset that *Stars and Stripes* selected that photo since some of the others were much clearer.

Another time, we flew over Ararat toward the east and came around the mountain another time. The rumble of our C-47 aircraft started several avalanches on the mountain. We went up the Ahora Gorge around 4PM in the afternoon and saw the structure for about 10-15 seconds. The Ark was not as clear from my position in the air as the photos were since the updraft pushed the plane up so high on the second pass. The thing that impressed me most though was the size of the huge girders in the Ark. What I saw in person was the same as the Ark in the photos. I think it is a little above 14,000 feet up the mountain.

When I told my company commander that I had seen Noah's Ark in person, he exclaimed "Hell, man. We're fighting a war not looking for Noah's Ark!"[51]

Vince Will drew this on 3/7/99

Vince Will drawing of his sighting of Noah's Ark
Courtesy of Matthew Kneisler

---

[51] Rex Geissler conversation with Vince Will on March 25th, 1999.

U.S. Army Air Forces Corporal Lester Walton - 1945 A.D.

Lester Walton, an Army Air Forces Corporal stationed at Wright Patterson Air Force Base in Dayton, Ohio during World War II, claims to have seen photographs of a structure on Ararat. He was assigned to testing a new Fairchild camera that gave better resolution of Norton bombsites. During the winter of 1945/1946, he and others were taken into a theater and shown three or four minutes worth of black and white footage (film or photos) that had been taken only months previously on a bombing mission. In early fall, a seven-plane squadron of B-24s from their base in North Africa to a target in eastern Europe when they flew over Mount Ararat and accidentally

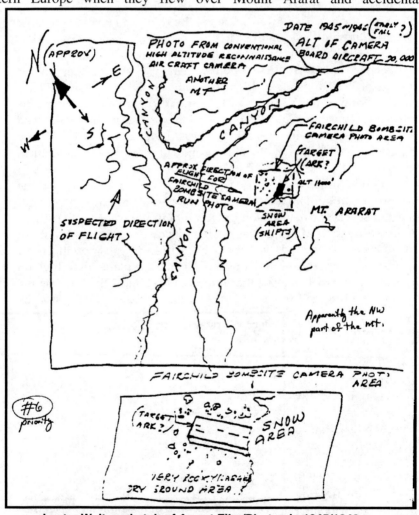

Lester Walton sketch of Ararat Film/Photos in 1945/1946
Courtesy of Lester Walton via John Morris and B.J. Corbin

photographed the Ark from 20,000 feet altitude.

Walton remembers, "When they flew over Mount Ararat, a structure was seen and the speculation was that it was the Ark. There were those present who felt merely a large rectangular rock was photographed but others believed it was quite possibly Noah's Ark," remembers Walton. "The pilot of the plane banked sharply to position the camera to get a good shot, and then proceeded on to our objective."

Walton recalled a large canyon on the north side of the mountain and a "box-shaped structure protruding out from the ice or rock debris. The north end of the structure was higher than the south end and the entire thing was tilted about thirty degrees. It was darker than the surrounding rock. At the time, an expeditionary effort was ruled out due to lingering instability of that area," said Walton. Soon word came that the documentation would be carried out by the National Geographic Society.

U.S. Air Force Personnel Andy Anderson - 1948 A.D.

Andy Anderson claimed to see a photo of Noah's Ark from an Air Force source after World War II. On February 8, 1984, Anderson signed an official document for Elfred Lee saying that he saw an Ark photo taken on Turkish Mount Ararat by an Air Force reconnaissance plane. Anderson stated that the Ark looked like the Hagopian Ark that Lee showed him. Anderson lived in Las Vegas at the time and he attended the Elfred Lee talk in Scottsdale, Arizona.

Kurdish Farmer Reshit as told by Shakru Asena - 1948 A.D.

The Reshit story was announced to the Associated Press by Shakru Asena, a 69-year-old farmer who owned large acreage in the Eastern frontier district and claimed that Reshit said, "I climbed down to it and with my dagger tried to break off a piece of the prow. It was so hard it would not break. It was blackened with age." Reshit insisted it was not a simple rock formation, "I know a ship when I see one. This is a ship."

Lloyd Bailey writes the following about a Kurdish farmer Reshit who claimed to see the Ark.

A Kurdish farmer named Reshit is reported to have discovered the Ark in 1948. The prow, "about the size of a house," was projecting from beneath the ice "about 2/3 of the way up" the mountain. Its wood, blackened with age, was so hard that a piece of it could not be severed with a knife. Reshit's fellow villagers, upon hearing his account, climbed to the site and agreed that it was unmistakably a boat.

The account, reportedly carried by the Associated Press, motivated A. J. Smith, dean of a small Bible college in North Carolina, to journey to the mountain in 1949. His goal was to locate Reshit, hire him to serve as a guide, and verify that the Ark had at least been discovered. Unfortunately, however, Reshit could not be found. A search of villages "for 100 miles around failed to produce anyone who claimed ever to have seen the Ark or even anyone who had heard the story."

LaHaye and Morris are so predisposed to believe such secondhand hearsay that they seek to explain away Smith's on-the-spot evidence (or lack of it). They propose that since Reshit was a Muslim (a fact that they do not verify), he would not have wanted to cooperate with the Christian Ark-searchers, nor would any of the persons for miles around—despite the fact that Smith offered a reward for information. No concrete evidence for such local hostility is offered.

One must be even less charitable toward Balsiger and Sellier, who, thirty years later, still repeat the Reshit story as valid evidence for the Ark's survival, not even mentioning the fact of Smith's unsuccessful expedition.[52]

It should be noted that the Smith party included the Turkish military brandishing machine guns and scouts which could have easily intimidated the villagers (especially the Kurds) from being more forthright.

U2 Photos and Other Flights - 1950s - 1970s

Some U2 pilots have claimed they photographed the Ark on Mount Ararat. As with other eyewitness accounts, although some of these alleged sightings are intriguing, they are typically based on second-hand information that is difficult to verify.

Apache Jim Wilson of Oden, Arkansas, claimed to see U2 photos of the Ark in 1973.

The object looked as though it was broken into two pieces—the ends were jagged. The pieces were separated, being some distance apart and partially covered with ice and snow. The parts sticking out of the snow looked to be 20 to 50 feet long. I saw six to eight

Apache Jim Wilson sketch of alleged Ark
Courtesy of Dr. John Morris

---

[52] Lloyd Bailey, *Noah* (Columbia, South Carolina: University of South Carolina Press, 1989), p.88.

windows on the top. I don't know where it was on the mountain, but the enlarged pictures were very clear.[53]

Notice that the sketch shows a little more rounded end coming to a point similar to the Ray Lubeck/Russian, David Duckworth/Smithsonian, George Greene photo eyewitness and Colonel Walter D. Hunter accounts. However, Dr. Don Shockey, who is a friend of Wilson, stated that Apache Jim is not always trustworthy.

Other flights that claimed to see something were the flying ace Major Bong who showed C. Craig Griswold of Lockheed a picture of an object the major told him was Noah's Ark. The photograph had been taken at an elevation of 13,000 feet or more over Mount Ararat and the object appeared to be sitting on the edge of a ledge and mostly covered with snow.[54]

In 1983, explorer Ray Anderson received a telephone call from an old climbing companion, Jerry Williams, an Adventist minister. In a conversation with a high official of his church, the subject of his involvement in the Ark search arose. This official told him that he was working with a new member of their lay-missionaries who was a former U-2 pilot but was now out of the service. He had shared some of his experiences as a pilot during the 1960's with this official. Some of it was still classified but he felt he could tell him about seeing what he believed was a section of Noah's Ark. He had been flying a very low-level photographic mission along the border of Turkey near Mt. Ararat. A U-2 was flying a very high flight to decoy radar away from him. Before heading back to his base in Turkey, he made a low sweep up the north side of Ararat, just to the right of the Ahora Gorge. As he swept across the mouth of the gorge at a very low level, he looked out of the left side of his cockpit and saw at the top of the ridge, a bowl shaped formation which he also described as an inverted fish hook. Inside this, against the wall, he saw protruding from the glacier, about 20-25 ft. of what he believed to be a man made structure. It was rectangular in shape and had some damage. He made a quick turn and flew over it again, getting his left wing tip within 200-300 ft. of it. He was convinced it was man made and being a religious man, concluded it had to be Noah's Ark.

Through church connections, Ray's friend Williams was able to contact the man who confirmed the story. Anderson traced the pilot to his hometown in Louisiana and located his father who confirmed that his son had been a U-2 pilot but had given him orders to not reveal his name or location. The father thought it was something about security and classified information. Ray believed the pilot's story because several years later, Ed Davis told him the object the Kurds/Lor showed him was resting against a wall of a bowl or horseshoe shaped formation just above the mouth of the Ahora Gorge at the

---

[53] Charles E. Sellier & David W. Balsiger, *The Incredible Discovery of Noah's Ark* (New York: Dell Publishing, 1995), p. 211.

[54] Richard C. Bright, *The Ark, A Reality?* (Guilderland, New York: Ranger, 1988), p.85.

top of a ridge just as the pilot described it and as the 1973 Hewitt picture shows.[55]

However, one concern that researcher Jonathan Brisbin had with the preceding account beside than the account's anonymity is that:

> U2's don't make a "quick turn." They are very fragile and can't withstand more than 4-5 G's of force (pretty sure that's right). The wingtips rip off if you dive too fast at altitude... How in the world are you supposed to make a 'quick turn' at 14,000 ft.? The wings would pop right off. We designed turns measured in tens of miles.

Anderson responded that the author of the statement was a U2 pilot, not that the lower plane was necessarily a U2. The U2 pilot could have been flying another type of plane.

Another researcher, Dave Larsen had an opportunity to speak a couple times about the search for Noah's Ark. In one small group, before he had even had an opportunity to say anything, a man approached Dave.

> A man, Patrick G., approached me before the start of my talk and said, "I've seen photos of Noah's Ark." At first, I was not quite sure what to make of him and, I must confess, only listened with one ear as I tried to organize my material. Since that time, I have had an opportunity to become friends with Patrick and spent several hours discussing his recollections (sometimes of many things besides the Ark). His story, in simple form, is that his father was in the Air Force while doing photo analysis for the CIA. Sometime in 1974, his father called him into his office in order to show him some photos. In one of the photos of Mount Ararat, he could see the prow of a large wooden ship jutting out of the ice. Snow and ice came down at an angle and covered a portion of it. His immediate response was "That's Noah's Ark!" "Sure is," said his father. The photos were then destroyed.
>
> He told me that the photos were taken from the SR-71 Blackbird and, to the best of his knowledge, were on the Russian side of the mountain (which would be basically northeast or upper Ahora Gorge). I found it very interesting when later leafing through John Morris' book, *Noah's Ark and the Ararat Adventure*, to come across a sketch at the bottom of page 30 purported to be from someone who had seen "spy plane photos." His sketch was virtually identical to the one my friend drew for me. Same basic shape. Same basic snow coverage. Same angle. Everything. When I eventually spoke to John by phone, he admitted that he did not personally know the man who claimed to have seen the photo, and there was apparently, then, no possibility of comparing notes firsthand. So, it seemed once

---

[55] Well-known researcher's email correspondence with Rex Geissler.

again, that intriguing possibilities were short-circuited just prior to a major breakthrough.

At this point, Patrick G. is not willing to have his full name released, and his father is not willing to discuss it or release any file-location information. As I understand it, files are coded in such a way that anyone releasing such information—even anonymously—leaves a trail clearly back to himself or herself. I have asked my friend to see if his father is willing to put information in a sealed envelope to be released to me after he has passed away. As morbid as that may sound, it may be the only way to uncover such information without jeopardizing someone involved. In any case, I believe my friend to be completely honest in his appraisal of what he saw in 1974. Neither he nor his father had any doubt in their minds that what they saw was a large wooden boat. Neither of them has sought to publish his account or gain anything from the telling. Whether anything further comes of this remains to be seen.

Note that Patrick G.'s sketch, which was a reverse angle view of the alleged spy plane's photo on the bottom of page 30 in Dr. John Morris' book *Noah's Ark and the Ararat Adventure* is the Apache Jim Wilson sketch above in this section. Note also that 1974 was the year of U.S. Navy Lieutenant Al Shappell's photographic mission for the intelligence community of the boat-like structure on Mount Ararat.

French Explorer Fernand Navarra - 1952, 1953, 1955, 1968, 1969

Fernand Navarra wrote about his 1952 climb of Ararat in *The Forbidden Mountain*.

[There was] an astonishing patch of blackness within the ice, its outlines sharply defined. Fascinated and intrigued we began straightway to trace out its shape, mapping out its limit foot by foot: two progressively incurving lines were revealed which were clearly defined for a distance of three hundred cubits before meeting in the heart of the glacier. The shape was unmistakably that of a ship's hull: on either side the edges of the patch curved like the gunwales of a great boat. As for the central part, it merged into a black mass the details of which were not discernable. Conviction burned in our eyes: no more than a few yards separated us from the extraordinary discovery which the world no longer believed possible. We had just found the Ark...The evidence must be acknowledged: the remains are those of the Ark, if only because it cannot be anything else.

The type of thinking that says "the remains are those of the Ark, if only because it cannot be anything else" must be seriously questioned. Not only that, but to state that the structure was uniformly visible through ice high on a mountain for a distance of "three hundred cubits" (about one and a half football fields) defies logic. Also, if Navarra really saw something, why did he describe in a biblical term "cubits" rather than his frame of reference which was "meters?" Possibly because he did not want to make a commitment in a standard measurement but would rather use a term that is not known for sure.

A year later, in 1953, Navarra went back again. Once again, he claimed to see the outline of what appeared to be a great ship embedded in the ice. This time, a sudden and overpowering illness forced him and his companion to abandon their plans and return to camp.

In his 1955 climb with his son Raphael, he claimed to find a beam of Ark wood near the Parrot Glacier which was later Carbon-14 dated along with the SEARCH Foundation wood to 1300-1900 years old, far younger than a possible Ark age. Note that this age could be in accordance with possibly an old monastery. According to the *Ararat Report*, since the climb his son has refused to talk to anyone about the discovery. However, when asked about the results, Carbon-14 dating method inventor Wilbur F. Libby stated that contaminated wood or wood soaked in water could yield unreliable

Parrot Glacier with SEARCH Team including Fernand Navarra, Bud Crawford, Hugo Neuburg just prior to ice bridge collapse 1969
Courtesy of Elfred Lee

Carbon-14 results.

Over the years, Navarra has given conflicting maps and information about the locations of his wood finds. Even more concerning, J.A. de Riquier, Navarra's friend and climbing partner in 1952, accused Navarra of attempting to purchase a piece of timber from an ancient structure in a nearby city in 1952, implying that the wood had been planted and was not found on Ararat at all. When Riquier sent the letter accusing Navarra to the SEARCH

Foundation, Elfred Lee and Hugo Neuberg read the letter. Then they took the letter to SEARCH's President, Ralph Crawford, who immediately destroyed it and called Navarra to let him know that SEARCH supported him completely against Riquier's claims.

Navarra went on his final expedition in 1969 with the SEARCH Foundation group that also found traces of wood. A very serious accusation (although there is some doubt) came from Navarra's 1952 climbing partner, Turkish Lt. Sahap Atalay. Navarra does not mention climbing with Atalay in 1952 (perhaps it was 1953) but the announcement which reached the press shortly after the 1969 expedition indicated that Atalay did climb with Navarra in 1952. Atalay indicated that Navarra had planted the wood in order to make money on photos and books. However, at least in the 1969 SEARCH discovery of wood, several different men found wood although some have wondered if Navarra planted the wood in the 1968 SEARCH mission before it was canceled because Navarra twisted his ankle.

U.S. Navy Photographer&Chief Petty Officer William Todd - 1953-1955

At age 27, William Todd of Yuma, Arizona, was a Photographer's Mate Chief who joined the U.S. Navy on June 24th 1944 and retired after 21 years in 1965. The Navy Hydrographic Office in Washington, D.C. and the Army Map Service combined with the Turkish Air Force in Diyarbakir to give the first accurate topographic maps of Turkey. Todd's account is another aerial sighting with some amazing claims about photographing the object but without any photographs to show. Note that 1953 was the same summer that George Greene claimed to see the Ark which again might confirm the theory that in better weather conditions, the structure becomes visible.

> My U.S. Navy squadron V.J. 62 was attached to the Turkish Air Force in both Ismir and Diyarbakir, Turkey. In Diyarbakir the dust and flies tested the spirit as the summer temperatures reached 120 degrees.
>
> We were flying U.S. Naval AJ2P photographic-configured Savage aircraft. Our coverage was three 6-inch focal length aerial cameras, mounted in a trimetrogon mounting to ensure vertical and 30-degree obliques, which give a 1:60,000 ratio. This is a standard configuration for horizon to horizon coverage. We had a 6-inch focal length in the prime vertical gyro stabilized mount. Our other prime vertical was a 12-inch focal length in a static mount, which give a 1:30,000 ratio. The aircraft was the steadiest platform that the Armed Forces had at that time. Along with the navigation I was also one of two camera repairmen on the detachment. Our mapping altitude was 30,000 feet (true altitude) and remained the same for four years to get a 1:30,000 ratio. I won't go in detail about confirming "true altitude" over "indicated altitude" at this time, but I will add that daily flights must use true altitude or the flight lines

will not match when laid as a mosaic. In order to re-set their altimeters perfectly, we would fly our AJ2P aircraft over the Black Sea otherwise our true altitude was typically off some.

Between 1951 and 1955, the Navy was in charge of mapping the entire nation of Turkey because most of Turkey's maps were outdated and incorrect. We mapped over the borders up to 250 miles. Since there were no markings on our aircraft because we didn't want the U.S.S.R. or Iran to know that we were U.S. airplanes, it was dangerous to fly into other countries' airspace but we did it anyway.

That afternoon we spotted the anomaly while we were descending to Diyarbakir. It was interesting and we had plenty of fuel, so we descended and took a long look-see. When we flew over the summit, we noticed an object above the gorge (their maps did not have the name Ahora on it at that time) sticking out of the ice at a true altitude of 14,500 to 16,000 feet.

The very thought of the Ark would have been ridiculous, as there was no reason to believe that it existed to modern times. But there appeared this structure lying on a little shelf protruding from ice and snow. At the base were snow patches and large to small rocks. The upper part had additions that looked like a railing or a roof that was in extreme disrepair. The color was about the same as the ground.

We witnessed the structure from about 2,000 feet above the object. However, once it was spotted, we flew around the mountain a number of times along the side of the object. It was a rectangular, slate-colored boat that we all claimed was Noah's Ark.

The object appeared to be of huge size and was surrounded by ice and snow. This anomaly looked like a craft of some sort. The ground around the structure was broken up and ice was all around the area. As a Naval Photographer and Chief Petty Officer, it did not look like a typical boat and was completely out of place. It appeared more like a barge.

I shot one roll of aerial film 400 feet long by 9 inches wide. Since we wanted to use all the film, we had to make a number of passes.

We proceeded to Diyarbakir where I personally processed the film and made prints. In the Navy it's said if you need to do something of extreme importance, "Process it yourself." Otherwise, someone else invariably causes a mishap and ruins the film.

Rails or openings ran all the way from the bow to the ice. About 35 feet of the structure was sticking out of the ice. As we were professional photographers, we measured the photos to determine the width and height of the object using the formula Scale = Focal Length / (12 * Altitude). It turned out to be exactly 75 feet wide by 45 feet high. When we found that it precisely matched the description in Genesis 6:15 using an 18-inch cubit, we were running around with chills down our back.

I noted that the Tigris River was running high that year because of the extreme heat melting snow in the mountains. After a few months, I gave my photos to a Baptist minister (perhaps named Grant?) in Sanford, Florida who kept them and then died. Later attempts to get them back were never successful. The Naval Photographic Science Center Archives in Washington D.C. should have the negatives but claimed that they could not find them.

We gave four or five copies of the pictures to all of our crew. The whole squadron of six mapping planes was abuzz about Noah's Ark and everyday some plane "accidentally" went by Ararat to see it. You practically needed a control tower around Ararat that summer. After seeing the photos, we were convinced that the structure was Noah's Ark.

Others in my group who were eyewitnesses included an Uncle Joe Gorsky (a retired U.S. Naval pilot and Lt./Commander of Russian decent), Ensign Glacow (navigator who later flew for United Airlines and supposedly found several million dollars of gold in the Amazon River mud), Mr. Trent and Mr. Finkbiner who were stationed for a time in Sanford, Florida. I have lost track of them all as the Navy moves you around constantly. I am confident that the set of photos still exist if we could just track them down. I highly regret my having given them to my minister.

Although I have read Bill Shea's articles and have conversed with James Irwin, Barry Setterfield, and John McIntosh, I have attempted to write this without being influenced by their views.[56]

Bill Todd's elevation would indicate that the Ark-like structure could easily be in the traditional ice cap. Barry Setterfield, one of the earliest interviewers of Todd who also sent him Bob Garbe photos of the mountain, stated, "Bill was categorical when I interviewed him that the boat he saw was in the depressed region to the right of and above the Red Gorge as seen from the air. There is a ridge of rock that marks the upper side of that depression." However, the south side of Ararat may have the least likely chance of being the location of Noah's Ark since it is also the most heavily traveled since it is the tourist route and almost every expedition is now forced to begin on the south side. Note also that Todd's elevation could easily place the structure near the Stephen Site objects in the upper Abich II above the Ahora Gorge. The best way to find an exact location for all anomalies would be to fly a remote sensing plane over the mountain.

American Helicopter Pilot George Greene - 1953 A.D.

George Greene took several pictures of a boat-like structure on Ararat. He then failed to get funding for a ground expedition. Greene was murdered in 1962 and his photos were never found although numerous witnesses

---

[56] Bill Todd statement to Rex Geissler on March 27, 1999.

acknowledged seeing them and a barge-like structure on a mountain. There were 30 confirmations of individuals who saw George Greene's photos.[57]

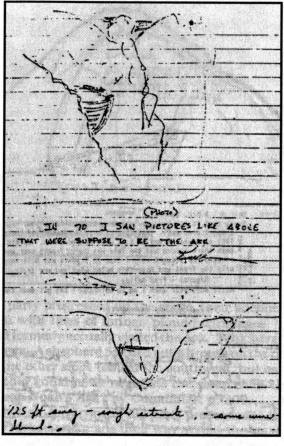

IN 70 I SAW PICTURES LIKE ABOVE THAT WERE SUPPOSE TO BE THE ARK

125 ft away - rough estimate

Family member sketch of Greene photos
Courtesy of Richard Bright 1970

Luckily, the finest of company camera equipment was within reach. Directing the pilot to maneuver the craft as closely as possible to the huge wooden object below, the excited engineer clicked the shutter again and again. Close and closer the whirly-bird edged, while Greene recorded his discovery on film. Side-wise, head-on, from as close as 90 feet away— the thrilling moment was preserved to be taken home as incontrovertible proof of the gigantic, ancient artifact he had just found!

When Greene returned to civilization and the priceless film was processed, he found to his delight that he possessed some half dozen clear black and white pictures of the object he had photographed on the remote peak in far-off Turkey. Elated with the possibilities of his discovery, and armed with a convincing portfolio of 8 x 10 enlargements, he tried again and again to interest friends in forming an expedition to return with him to the mountain for further investigation from the ground...

Fred Drake, who saw the photos, stated:

"As he circled the north and northeast side of the mountain Greene was startled to spot a strange anomaly, an object protruding

---

[57] Violet M. Cummings, *Noah's Ark: Fable or Fact?* (San Diego: Creation Science Research Center, 1973), p. 144.

from rock debris on a mountain ledge, with the striking similitude of the prow of a great ship, parallel wooden side planking and all.

There were six clear photographs, taken from different angles as they flew around the ship...

I will admit that I had never been much of a Bible believer, but these pictures sure made a believer out of me!"[58]

Dick Bright notes that Greene was "above the Ahora Gorge in an inaccessible area...On a shelf cliff with glacier and snowfields around." Dr. John Warwick Montgomery also noted that the Greene photos revealed other details as well—the boat was situated on a "fault" on the mountainside and a sheer drop-off on the other.[59] This "fault" and the sheer drop-off are reminiscent of the satellite remote sensing analyst George Stephen's description, "They're sitting in a fault on a ledge. The upper one is hanging. They are both in a glacier. Last time I looked there was about 70 foot of ice over the upper object."

Bill Crouse disputes the Greene sighting in the *Ararat Report.*

For two very good reasons we are now 99% convinced that what George Greene saw was a large rock formation that is known to most Ark researchers. The particular formation we refer to came to light in the mid-seventies as result of an expedition led by Tom Crotser of the Holy Ground Mission. The movie, *In Search of Noah's Ark,* which we refer to elsewhere in this issue, zooms in on the Crotser photograph and shows an object with planking clearly visible. Ark researchers have looked this photo over and have questioned its authenticity. It appeared to have been retouched. We now know for a fact that it was indeed retouched, but not with any fraudulent intent, so says Mr. David Fry of Cleburne, TX a former acquaintance of Crotser's...

The object in question is positively located on the eastern rim of the Ahora Gorge at approximately 12,000 feet. It was photographed by Bob Stuplich from the air in 1983 and by expeditions on the ground.

There are two reasons to link the Greene and Crotser sightings. Our first reason for concluding the two objects are one and the same is their similarity to the sketch made by Fred Drake who claimed to have viewed Greene's photographs...

To us the similarity is striking! The object lies almost due north and south exactly as Green described it. The object is on a kind of rock shelf over-looking a shear drop-off...

---

[58] Violet M. Cummings, *Noah's Ark: Fable or Fact?* (San Diego: Creation Science Research Center, 1973), p. 140.

[59] Montgomery, John, *The Quest for Noah's Ark.* 2nd Edition. (Minneapolis: Dimension Books, 1974), pp. 121.

The fact that the object is at about 12,000 feet also supports our contention. This is about the ceiling for a helicopter in the early '50s. We did some checking on this awhile back and found that there was a high performance French helicopter that could have flown to the summit of the mountain, but it is doubtful that Greene would have had one of these at his disposal.

This of course does not seal the case in concrete. We will never know for certain until we actually see Greene's photos...

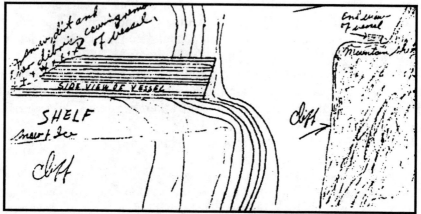

Fred Drake sketched this object in the Greene photos
Courtesy of John McIntosh via B.J. Corbin

Rod Youngquist, engineer and veteran of several trips to Ararat, related to *AR* that he one met members of Crotser's expedition who informed him that they had shown their photographs to people who had also viewed Greene's missing photographs. Upon viewing the Holy Ground Mission photographs, their response was: "Oh, where did you get George Greene's photographs?" Hence our second reason is the fact that Greene's friends mistakenly identified the Crotser photographs as Greene's.

Note that Greene's 1953 sighting was also the same year that the William Todd mapping crew claimed to see the Ark. Todd said that the unseasonably hot temperatures may have contributed to a reduction in the Ararat ice around the structure.

Another important statement about Greene is recorded in *The Ark on Ararat* by LaHaye and Morris, "he detoured from his major area of interest on the northern flank to the high elevation above the Ahora Gorge." This again could easily be the Stephen site in the upper Abich II glacier.

One final thought is that since George Greene worked for an American oil company, they might be able to afford a French high-performance helicopter for his research.

Explorer John Libi - 1954-1969 A.D.

John Libi attempted unsuccessfully to find the Ark eight times in fifteen years. He did not claim to see the Ark but encountered many interesting problems while searching the mountain. During his eight searches of Ararat Libi was chased by two bears near the ice cap, got seriously ill during the run away from the bears, fell thirty feet to a rock ledge and was carried off the mountain, acquired pneumonia and required hospitalization, was robbed of all finances, and weather claimed the life of a Belgian climber who joined Libi's team.

Libi concentrated his search about 500 feet below the summit. When little snow was present on the summit in 1969, he claimed to have discovered three huge stone "corrals" with high walls that appear to him to have been used to house animals.[60] This type of meltback is difficult to conceive for many researchers who have never been fortunate to see conditions like that.

U.S. Air Force Pilot Captain Gregor Schwinghammer - 1959 A.D.

A fighter pilot, Captain Gregor Schwinghammer (then a Second Lieutenant) saw a structure on Ararat from his F-100 cockpit.

> In 1959 we were flying fighters over Mount Ararat when we spotted what looked like a large, rectangular, barge-like structure sticking out of the side of the mountain. It was in kind of a horseshoe-like depression and it definitely appeared to be man-made. I didn't think of Noah's Ark at the time because, frankly, I wasn't aware of a biblical story placing Noah's Ark on Mount Ararat.

Bill Crouse in the *Ararat Report* interviewed Schwinghammer several times. He concluded the following.

1. According to Schwinghammer there is definitely a structure of some kind up there…
2. He says the "ark" looked accessible…
3. I found it odd that he did not remember either the gorge or Little Ararat. But one has to remember he was only there for seconds—enough to see the object and make an exit.
4. He indicates, like others, that the object is pointing north-northwest.
5. Schwinghammer may have been trying to tell me that there is some sort of lake around the Ark…

Schwinghammer had a recollection of the U-2 pilots also seeing something in photos. They flew out of the same base in Adana. As

---

[60] Tim LaHaye and John Morris, *The Ark on Ararat* (Nashville: Thomas Nelson Publishers, 1976), pp. 139-142.

you will recall from the Gary Powers' incident the Americans were flying reconnaissance missions deep into the heart of the Soviet Union. On many occasions this took them right over Ararat...

After his basic training, this man spent most of his four years in the Air Force in top security work at a large Midwest base. His job was to process film as it was brought into the lab from around the world...Our man remembers film coming in from eastern Turkey...After processing the film, he turned it over to analysts. It seems they could not figure out what the Turks could have built of that size at that extreme altitude. What could it be? Finally, he recalled hearing one of them jokingly exclaim: "It must be Noah's Ark!" He went over for a closer look. Basically, what he remembers is a barge-like object sticking out of the ice with most of it still buried...

Upon discharge from the Air Force this gentleman enrolled in a Baptist college near this Air Force base to prepare for the ministry...To his surprise he noticed on the bulletin board a photo cut out of a newspaper with the caption "Could this be Noah's Ark?" He did a double take when he realized it was from the roll he had processed only a few years previously in the lab. He wondered who dared disclose the photograph because he remembered how his superiors drilled into them the subject of secrecy and the penalty involved.

It is interesting to note that on the Tom Pickett Corona Satellite picture in the Introduction, there is a horseshoe-shaped valley in the Abich II glacier below the saddle of the peaks in the George Stephen III site area.

Turkish Captain Ilhan Durupinar and Ron Wyatt - 1959, 1984 A.D.

Bill Crouse reports the following in the *Ararat Report* about the Durupinar site.

In 1959 a pilot in the Turkish Air Force flying on a NATO mapping mission near Ararat photographed an unusual ship-shaped object near Mt. Ararat. Later when the aerial photographs were viewed stereoscopically by Captain Durupinar, he noticed that the object appeared even more like a ship.

Photographs of the strange formation appeared in the world press and created a sensation and speculations abounded that it was Noah's Ark. This editor remembers well seeing the photo in *Life* magazine (9/5/60) as a teenager. The location was fifteen miles away from Mount Ararat.

A group, calling themselves the Archaeological Research Foundation (ARF), investigated the "ship" with the full cooperation of the Turkish government in the summer of 1960. After doing preliminary excavation and dynamiting one of the sides, they concluded that the formation was only a freak of nature, a clay upthrust in a lava field. No artifacts or petrified wood were found.

For the next 24 years the Ark search was concentrated on Mt. Ararat itself. From 1960 till 1984 nothing was heard of the "ship" formation. Attention again focused on the Durupinar site (which is what we have been calling it in this report) in the summer of '84 when Ron Wyatt convinced Col. Jim Irwin, Dr. John Morris, and Marvin Steffins to take a look at the site.

Ron, who can be a very persuasive fellow, succeeded in convincing Steffins it was the Ark. Steffins immediately flew to Ankara to hold a news conference and announced the discovery. The next day the news was broadcast throughout the world.

Some Christian radio and TV stations played it up pretty big. This editor was in Denver at the time, and one radio station was reporting that the explorers had succeeded in getting inside the Ark and that wood was being flown back to the states for testing...

It is safe to say that without Ron Wyatt's efforts there still would be no interest in the "ship" discovered in 1959 by Durupinar. With varying degrees the following men have either advocated the site as the authentic Ark of Noah, or feel that it deserves further inquiry: David Fasold, Marvin Steffins, Dr. William Shea, René Noorbergen, and Dr. John Baumgardner. All of them owe their initial interest in this site to Ron Wyatt.

"Who is Ron Wyatt?" is certainly a legitimate question...Wyatt is a nurse anesthetist (a CRNA) from Madison, Tenn., who claims he has been searching for Noah's Ark for 25 years, and believes he deserves most of the credit for its discovery...

Without any big money behind him, Ron traveled to turkey in 1977 with his two sons to investigate for himself the formation he believed could be Noah's Ark.

This was to be the first of many trips. The experiences that he claims he had on this trip with the local criminal element could easily be made into a thriller of an adventure movie. The story is told in a self-published, 36-page booklet, authored by Wyatt and entitled *Noah's Ark Found*.

When Ron arrived in eastern Turkey in the Ararat area, he did not know immediately where to locate the ship-shape. Ron's procedure for finding the location of what he believed to be the Ark was to hire a cab (at night) to drive around the area on the outskirts of Dogubayazit.

He then prayed that God would stall the taxi in the areas where he was to look. Each time the cab stalled, Ron jumped out of the cab and made a pile of stones (see Wyatt, p. 44). The next day the Wyatts located the stones and walked perpendicular to the road to see what it was God wanted him to find.

During this first trip, according to his written account, he did not actually get to the site to do any investigation. However, he did manage to turn up a good number of artifacts that he associates with Noah.

Among these are: (1) stone sea anchors that he believes were used by Noah to steer the vessel into the wind, (2) petrified timbers from the Ark that were used as memorials in an Armenian graveyard, (3) a house that Noah built, and (4) on this house, stones containing inscriptions which recorded details about the Deluge, (5) a pictograph depicting eight people leaving a large wave of water with a boat perched above it, and (6) the burial place of Noah.

Wyatt says he arrived at the latter conclusion after close study, prayer, and reflection (p. 9).

Durupinar with Buelent Atalay, Ron Wyatt. Notice the other ridges in the area which look similar to the site itself 1984
Courtesy of John McIntosh

Ron returned to Ararat for the second time in 1979, but prior to going he prayed that an earthquake would split the Ark so he could investigate the interior. Sure enough, according to Wyatt, before he departed he heard on the news that an earthquake had struck eastern Turkey.

When he arrived there, it was split down the middle from bow to stern. When Ron peered into the crack he claimed he saw petrified timbers...

It is probable that this ship-shape is a purely natural phenomenon...

Rock specimens and soil samples were also tested by geologists Clifford Burdick and John Morris on separate occasions. Thin sections of rock samples were examined with petrographic microscopes, and in no case was there any hint of decayed or petrified wood.

They concluded that the elevated elemental carbon levels were due to the presence of calcium carbonate in some of the rocks. The metallic levels were consistent with the ores found in the region.

When in our office several weeks ago—at which time we extensively questioned Ron about his claims—he produced a black rock which he claimed was a ballast stone taken from the formation. According to tests, the rock was manganese dioxide. This again is a mineral fairly common to the region.

Ron suggested that there were trainloads of this inside the formation, and that this was probably tailings from Noah's production of aluminum. Noah simply used the tailings for ballast!

Durupinar
Courtesy of Bob Stuplich

Our question here is why would there be a need for ballast on the Ark? It seems the load on the Ark would be sufficient...

Both Wyatt and Fasold claim to have found metal readings at regular intervals on the formation...We have the following objections and observations:

(a) At least one of the detection devices used in his survey is certainly not scientifically valid, and is forbidden in the Bible (Deut. 18:10) as a tool of divination. This device is given the high-sounding name of molecular frequency generator, but in reality is nothing more than brass welding rods used as divining rods. Advertising for such gadgets can be seen in the back of any treasure-hunting magazine...We consulted four qualified scientists about this gadget, and they were unanimous that there were no scientific principles being

employed. Two of these scientists built and tested working
models...

(b) We think a perfectly valid natural explanation exists for the
regular metal readings. This type of volcanic rock, as it cools
and contracts, typically fractures into perpendicular joint
sets, based on regional stress orientation. The metal readings
can then be accounted for as ground water laden with
metallic minerals which over the years has been deposited
into the cracks...

However, Ron does not seem to understand scientific protocol.
He consistently violates the procedures for verification...

Dr. John Baumgardner, Dr. John Morris, Dr. Clifford Burdick,
and a Turkish geologist have examined the site and have not seen
any evidence of petrified wood. Wyatt, however, claims there is a
train load of it there...

We also have several reasons for disagreeing with the idea that
these were anchors or *drogue* stones used in the Ark:

(a) Our impression from Scripture is that Noah had no kind of
mechanism to steer the ship; he could not even close the
door himself...When I asked Wyatt why the anchor stones
were found so far away from the site, his reply was that one
day when Noah was looking out the window he discovered
that the Ark was heading in the direction of dry land so he
cut the anchor stones. But this means Noah had something to
do with the destiny and direction of the Ark!

Durupinar site with Ron Wyatt markings
Courtesy of John McIntosh

Dr. Terian is fairly certain that these stones were originally pre-Christian Armenian *stelae* containing pagan inscriptions. Armenian historians note that immediately after their conversion, in their zeal for Christ, they removed all remnants of paganism from such *stelae* and replaced them with crosses. According to those who have examined these *stelae* closely there is evidence of an earlier defacement...The holes in these *stelae* were put there by the pre-Christian Armenians according to Terian, and had occultic significance, possibly as the "eye of the dragon." The theory that these are Armenian *stelae* is also supported by the fact that the stones are located in an ancient Armenian graveyard...

Who is Ron Wyatt? Would you not question someone who not only claims to have found Noah's Ark, but also every archaeological site of interest to Christians?

- Ron Wyatt has made such claims. We have him saying it on tape.
- Ron claims that on January 6, 1982 at 2:00 P.M. he found the Ark of the Covenant under the escarpment of Calvary.
- We heard him say to a Nashville newsman that he held in his hands the stone tablets of the ten commandments and that they were fastened with golden hinges!
- He claims he found the Ark of the Covenant under the exact spot where Jesus was crucified. He found the stone socket in which the cross of Christ was placed. When pierced by the sword, Ron believes the blood dripped down into the socket and dripped through a crack caused by the earthquake and landed on the mercy seat 60 feet down in a subterranean chamber.
- He also found the mountain that is the biblical Mt. Sinai where God dispensed the law to His people. This mountain is located in Saudi Arabia (Jabal Al Lawz), and is strangely enough, one of the legendary places for the mountain. Dr. Frank Cross of Harvard thinks it is a good candidate, but admits there is as of now no evidence to confirm it. [The recently published *The Gold of Exodus* propagates this view as well.]
- Ron believes he has located the 12 altars built by Moses in Exodus 24. This strains credulity again since Moses built these in one day and the rocks were not to be hand-hewn. How could they possibly be recognizable today? Ron is undaunted.
- He also found the spot where the ground swallowed up Korah and his followers.
- Ron also knows exactly where the Israelites crossed the Red Sea...
- Ron claims that he has solved the problem of the construction of the pyramids, and the problems in Egyptian chronology...

- Ron knows how the Shroud of Turin was forged; he has cracked the code of the Copper Scroll; in fact he has claimed to mutual acquaintances that he can read any ancient inscription.

Is Ron Wyatt the greatest archaeologist who ever lived? Or is there a better explanation?...

His brochure lists Ron as graduating from the University of Michigan with honors in Pre-med and as having finished all the requirements for both M.A. and Ph.D. in antiquities. It also lists him as being a Korean war veteran.

We found none of the above to be true. When we called the P.R. firm [who produced the brochure], they admitted that the document needed to be re-written, but they did not know who was to blame for the inaccuracies...

To us it seems incredible that Ron could have found and solved problems that have baffled professional archaeologists for more than a century. We think Ron missed his calling. He could be a "can't lose" writer for episodes of "Indiana Jones" movies...

In the pass between greater and lesser Ararat, there are numerous phantom Ark shapes like the famous one at Durupinar 17 miles south of Ararat. How many more can you find?
Photo courtesy of US Army Colonel stationed in Izmir
via Dr. Charles Willis via Robin Simmons

Dr. John Morris added the following.

There are other "ship-shaped" formations in the immediate area as well as on the slopes of little Ararat (See Photo)...In our minds these other geologically-formed "ships" are devastating to the Wyatt-Fasold thesis.

Wyatt seemed to realize this since he immediately claimed to *Ararat Report* via a letter that the photograph of the Little Ararat foothills was doctored. We understand he is now telling audiences that Elfred Lee doctored the photograph, a charge Lee categorically denied in a recent phone conversation. The source of the photograph, by the way, is the Turkish Air Force...

Unfortunately, these two individuals [Wyatt and Fasold] have convinced some Turkish officials to promote this site as the Ark. A "visitor's center" has been constructed nearby and a road sign directing travelers off the road has been erected...

We must keep in mind that the Bible does not prophesy that the Ark will be found in these latter days...The Bible does not even specify a particular mountain...

The only reason to be looking at all is that eyewitnesses claim to have seen the Ark, and while none of them are able to pinpoint the location, the consensus is that the remains were seen on the huge mountain known today as Greater Ararat...

Elfred Lee stated in an interview with Rex Geissler that Ron Wyatt asked him to retouch Durupinar photographs. In the Doris Bowers videotape, one can also see a clear phantom ark shape next to the Durupinar depression which Bowers is standing on. David Fasold publicly renounced the Durupinar sight before his death on 4/26/98. However, his renouncement was supposedly to benefit his court case against Allen Roberts in Australia. Robert Michelson told John McIntosh that he talked with Fasold shortly before his death and that Fasold still privately thought the site was the Ark.

Dr. Salih Bayraktutan of Erzurum and Professor Robert Michelson of Georgia Tech University are still actively engaged in researching the Durupinar site. David Deal, a friend and colleague of the late David Fasold, is also in this camp.

U.S. Air Force Pilot Gus Pipkin - 1963 A.D.

As a C54 (DC-4) pilot for the Joint United States Military Mission Aid to Turkey, Gus Pipkin of Rocklyn, California flew service men from Ankara to a Turkish base in Erzurum and from Erzurum to Diyarbakir in southeastern Turkey and back again to visit their families. One day in late June or July, their plane gained altitude as it took off toward the east from Erzurum and banked toward a southerly course over the northwestern slopes of Ararat. Pipkin glanced down and saw what looked like a portion of a boat sitting on the mountain with rocks around. The time of day was just past noon. The weather and visibility were exceptional for the Ararat area as there were no clouds and no haze.

Pipkin maintained that there was no point or bow shape to the boat-like object. He was looking straight down on the dark gray object which had a whitish outline or railing and simply saw the form of it in the rocks. Pipkin saw colors of browns, tans and oranges. There was no visible ice or snow which may correspond to a possible location of the object below the ice cap. He believed that he was a couple thousand feet above the object at the time. Since he was flying the plane on a mission, he knew it was proper to circle around and see the object again or attempt to take a photo. He only saw the object for a couple seconds before he was past it.

It does seem strange that a C54 would continue going east from Erzurum 160 miles to Ararat and wait until a minute or two before entering Soviet airspace before turning back to the southwest to go another 250 miles to Diyarbakir. It is also interesting to note that Diyarbakir is the base where another alleged eyewitness, Ed Behling, was stationed.

National Geographic Society, Smithsonian Institution & David Duckworth - 1958, 1964, 1968 A.D.

Some people have alleged that the National Geographic Society, Smithsonian Institution or organizations working on their behalf have searched for the Ark, found it, taken photographs of it as well as brought back artifacts from it. In 1968, infrared photography of the structure was supposedly done. Thermite bombs were used to burn down into portions of the hull. Part of the deck near the bow was blown out and possibly a tunnel was burn into the side in order to remove artifacts. Heavy black wood with wooden pegs was allegedly brought back to the Smithsonian.

The Smithsonian Institution and the National Geographic Society have denied any involvement or funding in a search for Noah's Ark. However, Ralph Crawford, President of the SEARCH Foundation, disputed the National Geographic Society's claim by stating that the Society gave thousands of dollars worth of film to the 1968 SEARCH Foundation expedition and that the National Geographic Society reserved first rights to the photographs in the event of a possible discovery.[61]

Also, Rene Noorbergen, a tough veteran newsman and war correspondent, stated that he met one individual in Washington who confirmed he was involved in the 1968 expedition. He also learned of a man who had allegedly sat in on a meeting between the Smithsonian and National Geographic Society where they discussed a joint expedition and discovery and decided not to reveal it.

---

[61] Charles E. Sellier and David W. Balsiger, *The Incredible Discovery of Noah's Ark* (New York: Dell Publishing, 1995), p. 238 and Elfred Lee statement.

Additional corroborating information came from two chaplains in the U.S. Air Force in Turkey and three other officers. During Autumn of 1964, a group "identifying themselves as members of a National Geographic expedition returning from Mount Ararat" stopped at the U.S. Air Force base in Trabzon, Turkey. Chaplain (Lt. Col.) Roger H. Pearson stated the following in a letter to Dr. Charles Willis.

> Sometime in late 1964 a group of people stopped at Trabzon [Turkey] and asked for overnight lodging. They drove a Land Rover and I believe there were four individuals in the group...They identified themselves as members of a National Geographic expedition from Mount Ararat...When I asked him almost jokingly if they had discovered the Ark, he said, "Chaplain, you wouldn't believe what we found!" He went on to explain that he couldn't talk about what they had found, but gave the impression that they had made a discovery of tremendous significance. I was impressed so much that for about a year I kept checking issues of *National Geographic* for information.

In another letter noted by Cummings from Chaplain (Capt.) Clair Shaffer to Dr. Willis dated September 4th, 1973, he wrote the following.

> A team had stopped and spent the night at our base [Samsun, Turkey]. This was a National Geographic expedition which had been to eastern Turkey and to Mount Ararat and was on their way home. When asked the expected question, "Did you find the Ark?" they answered, "We cannot answer that question now, but may we say that we have made the greatest discovery in the history of man!"

David Duckworth, now a security guard in Farmington, New Mexico, stated the following.

> I was working at the Smithsonian Institution in Washington, D.C., in the fall of 1968 as a volunteer in the vertebrate paleontology section. When I went to get some acetone to clean up a specimen I was working on one day, I noticed my immediate supervisor Al Merrick with a visiting scientist named Dr. Robert Geist. They were both bending over a magnification tripod viewer looking at some photographs. I wandered over there and just asked what they were doing. They told me to take a look myself, so I did.
>
> What I saw was a composition picture of like four photographs put together to make one whole picture. In the picture, there was an oblong object resembling a ship that wasn't under the ice and snow but was semi-covered with it. This object appeared to be broken in the middle with several feet separating the two halves and one end definitely appeared to be smashed.

I asked my supervisor some more questions and he said the photos had been taken on a mountain named Ararat in Turkey and that the photos had been taken from a balloon suspended by cables with an airborne camera package. You could see the shadow of the balloon on some of the pictures.

He said the film that I was looking at was a composite of infrared photographs. So I looked at it and browsed through the pile of pictures next to it. Some of them were just taken from different angles at different altitudes and some showed people on the ground looking at the ship.

There were also some pieces of fossilized wood. It was heavy black wood, like stone, but it was wood. You could see where it had been chopped and drilled—where it had been worked and the remains of wooden-like pegs in it.[62]

After we had been there about a month, several crates were delivered to our section which seemed to cause quite a bit of interest among the directors.

So they went ahead and opened them up and took out several artifacts like old wood and some old style tools and things like that. And they had some photographs, which I went over and looked at, arranged on a table which had been taken from a balloon, they told me. Showing a ship like object down in some ice.

So I took a look at them, and talked some, and I was told by Geist that it was Noah's Ark. And I looked at the artifacts and that was the general impression I got at the time—that they'd found it. The fractures, Geist said, had been caused as the ground gradually gave way beneath its great weight over the years.

They said they used thermite bombs and actually burned down into portions of the hull. One hole was made through the deck and one where it was broken. The holes were plainly visible on the photos. A four-man team went down into the burned out portion and had taken another infrared photo from deep inside the ship. An obviously fascinated Geist pointed to an outline revealing what he believed could be a stall, or a cage, and a box that might have served as a feeding trough, and slide bards. The floors were slightly slanted and there was a drainage trough. Dr. Geist showed what was thought to be "a long hall...with a lot of rooms on the side with small apertures...for air, you know, and feeding troughs set up for the animals." Geist was a typically professional, confident, live-for-science type who stated that "the reason he finally accepted it [as the Ark] was the fact of the way the sanitation was set up. He said that's the only way it could have had a centralized gather place to get rid of it [the waste] if they sailed around as long it said it did.

---

[62] Charles E. Sellier & David W. Balsiger, *The Incredible Discovery of Noah's Ark* (New York: Dell Publishing, 1995), p. 235.

After a careful study of the photo, there was found an area on the deck that looked like it was an uprising about six feet maybe. Geist called my attention to a few wooden or stone huts down farther on the slope.

Later, a friend and I were going to lunch and we passed the loading dock on our way to the cafeteria and we saw a couple crates marked: "MT ARARAT—National Geographic / Smithsonian Expedition." And that's what everybody was talking about for three or four days. That's all you heard—was about this thing they found, you know, Noah's Ark, they'd identified! There was quite a bit of excitement about it.

One day he noticed a coffin-shaped alabaster box which had been transferred to the Department of Physical Anthropology. His friend from that department told him, "they thought it was Noah's based on something they had told him." Supposedly the body was preserved and a tablet was with him. He was not sure if it was a mummy or preserved human remains because of the coldness of Mount Ararat.

After about five days, though, it started changing a little bit. They didn't talk anymore. They started taking the stuff out and placing it under lock and key. The questions we'd ask, they just kind of ignore us, and finally they pretty well came out and told everybody to just keep their mouth shut. There was a sudden pall of gloom that had fallen over the normally pleasant department. From that time on, an air of "extreme secrecy" prevailed.

Because they were having some problems at the time with some 'religious' groups. Geist said, "If the religious fanatics ever found out who was in that box, it would really cause trouble." This was about the same time that the Department of Natural History was preparing a circular wall exhibit called the "Evolutionary Time Clock." It started with molecules in the water that would work up through fish and amphibians through millions of years. This is what was being protected from the "religious fanatics" according to his advisors.

Frankly, I didn't think much more about it until I came out to Farmington, New Mexico, where a fellow named Eryl Cummings called me about his book, *Noah's Ark:: Fable or Fact?* I said, "Fable? Well, that's a strange title for the book since I'd seen it [the Ark] four years before."

After some of my comments were published in Violet Cummings' book *Has Anyone Really Seen Noah's Ark?* I was visited at work by two men who identified themselves as FBI agents (even though I was called Daryl Davis in her book). They told me my statements were making waves at the Smithsonian. And that I had been somewhere where I should not have and seen something that did not concern me. They didn't threaten me, exactly.

Later I phoned Al Merrick and asked him if he remembered me. He said he didn't. When I described him as the guy who often wore a little red bow tie and pedaled his three-speed bike to work, he suddenly remembered me. I asked him some questions about all that stuff from Ararat and the Ark. He said, "You know, I really can't talk about it," and kind of laughed.[63]

Rene Noorbergen analyzed a tape of Duckworth which he claimed revealed high stress levels that might indicate deceit. However, it appeared that Duckworth was agitated at the time because he was being accused of lying about his experience so the stress analysis may not be fair. Also, Rene had a falling out with Eryl Cummings which may have influenced his view of Eryl's friend, Duckworth.

In a phone interview with Rex Geissler, David Duckworth added more information. He stated that the boat was like a gigantic keel boat that was used on canals with a half-size cabin on top with openings on the superstructure and one large opening or door in the side of the boat. Duckworth also stated that the structure was hanging on a ledge or promontory over a valley and that the broken section was below it in the valley. He stated that the holes which held the wooden pegs in the boat were created by burning them out in some manner. Other notable things in the photos were dark shapes (possibly rocks), people, a tripod arrangement of poles over the center of the boat, cylinders on the ground (possibly to inflate the helium balloon taking the photos from 100 feet overhead or oxygen for the people), a horsehoe-shaped building or corral, crude tools such as a wooden triangle with a slant base with a marked angle for a type of plum. Duckworth's father (retired Army Colonel) and mother corroborated his story which he told them immediately after the incidents and he responded that he was open to taking a lie detector test. Elfred Lee called Dr. Geist and Al Myrick in the 1980s. Although Dr. Geist was never successfully contacted, Dr. Myrick was cordial but stated that he had no comment on the subject. To many, "no comment" in this issue indicates that there could easily be some validity to the story.

Note that the pointed, broken stern in the sketch does not match the Hagopian account of a rectangular box-like structure. However, it does match Air Force Lt. Colonel Walter Hunter's description of the photos he saw in 1969 or 1970 as well as the Ray Lubeck/Russian film of the alleged Ark. Elfred Lee said that Duckworth's drawing of the Smithsonian photos matched Ed Davis' almost exactly. The pointed stern might be part of the debris trail of the object's broken off section that Ed Davis (1943), Al Shappell (1974), and George Stephen III (1989) discussed.

---

[63] David Duckworth statement to Robin Simmons, 1998.

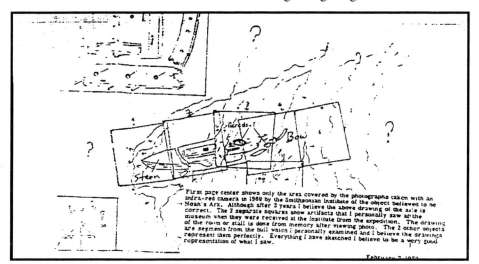

Within the sketch:
?
?
?
?
Bow
Stern

First page center shows only the area covered by the photographs taken with an
infra-red camera in 1969 by the Smithsonian Institute of the object believed to be
Noah's Ark. Although after 3 years I believe the above drawing of the scale is
correct. The 2 separate squares show artifacts that I personally saw at the
museum when they were received at the Institute from the expedition. The drawing
of the room or stall is done from memory after viewing photo. The 2 other objects
are segments from the hull which I personally examined and I believe the drawings
represent them perfectly. Everything I have sketched I believe to be a very good
representation of what I saw.

February 7, 1972

**David Duckworth sketch of alleged Smithsonian Institution composite
photograph and objects. Note that the stern appears to have been broken off
in the picture. 1968**
Courtesy of David Duckworth

Recently, the secretive and somewhat bizarre nature of the Smithsonian
came to light. In three separate but related 1999 articles, the *Los Angeles
Times* printed accounts of Ishi, the famous Yahi Indian who was the last of
his tribe and who stumbled out of the California wilderness into civilization
in 1911. Ishi died in 1916. His brain was removed and added to a
Smithsonian Institution collection of 300 human brains which have been kept
in a climate-controlled warehouse in Suitland, Maryland. Quoting from the
Los Angeles Times, "The anthropologist, Frank Norick, told [researcher]
Rockafellar that a colleague at the Smithsonian Institution had told him years
ago that the brain was there. But the Smithsonian dismissed the reports as
gossip when Rockafellar called. 'I just hit a brick wall,' she said." Later, the
LA Times wrote about statements by Thomas W. Killion (the Smithsonian's
director of repatriation), "The museum always knew it had the brain and
scoffs at the notion that it has been 'discovered.' The museum never said
anything about the brain because it was never asked."

Now who is bringing hidden information into the light and educating the
public, the Smithsonian or the researchers? One has to wonder what else
might be stored in the Smithsonian's Suitland, Maryland, climate-controlled
warehouse or in other locations.

SEARCH Foundation - 1968, 1969 A.D.

In 1968, Fernand Navarra led the SEARCH group before breaking his
foot, when the expedition was cancelled. It was estimated that some 900,000
cubic meters of ice and moraine would need to be shifted in order to reach the
lake and access Navarra's alleged object.

**Fernand Navarra, Elfred Lee and Hugo
Neuburg on Parrot Glacier in 1969**
Courtesy of Ralph Lenton via Elfred Lee

In 1969, the SEARCH Foundation discovered wood on Ararat under the guiding hand of Navarra. But once again cries of fraud went up from the expedition's team members. Navarra had led them to a completely different location than the previous year although several individuals on the team verified finding wood.

As with the 1955 Navarra wood, the results from Carbon-14 dating came back with an age of 1300-1900 years. However, when asked about the results, Carbon-14 dating method inventor Wilbur F. Libby stated that contaminated wood or wood soaked in water could yield unreliable Carbon-14 results.

The age of Navarra's and the SEARCH team's wood is not the only issue with the wood find that have been questioned. Navarra had apparently become lost for a day and shortly after his return, a few pieces of wood suddenly appeared. Bud Crawford, a member of the expedition, put it this way, "It was strange that only a day or so after Navarra had become lost, we found the wood." Elfred Lee, the photographer and archaeological illustrator, raised another question, "Why such 'shingles' when Navarra had reported 150-foot beams in 1955?" On the way to Ararat, Navarra also got out of the van and refused to go on because of an argument with Hugo. Hagopian refused to believe that Navarra's wood was the petrified wood of Noah's Ark that he claimed to have walked on, "It was absolutely petrified, pure stone."[64]

The location itself of the wood in the Parrot Glacier has raised suspicions of it not being from other possible Ark locations around the mountain and not in the line of gravity falling down compared with the Stephen site, etc. However, Navarra, Cummings and glaciologist Van Arkle disputed this point.

---

[64] Richard C. Bright, *The Ark, A Reality?* (Guilderland, New York: Ranger Associates Inc., 1989), p. 95.

In a personal letter to Eryl Cummings, Pat Frost (who visited the Navarra glacier next to the Parrot glacier in 1979) wrote the following.

> Navarra's glacier is also not the resting-place of the Ark. In 1969, this glacier or ice pack extending back in the mountain might have looked like a good place for the Ark to be hidden. Today, this ice pack is melted, filled with very deep crevasses, and is only about 150 feet long. It is not large enough to be the resting-place of the ark. Also, the mountain has carved in on a lot of the ice pack. The glacier that runs beside the ice pack has melted down 50 to 75 feet since 1969. The water is rushing down this glacier and disappears into big holes in the mountain, making a loud noise as it goes into the mountain.
>
> My guide and I were eating our lunch on a big flat rock overlooking the millpond at Navarra's glacier the other day, when the whole side of the area started sliding into the water. We grabbed our cameras, food and equipment, and go out of the way as fast as we could By the time I finally got my movie camera going, everything had disappeared into the water. The water was still boiling form the rockslide.[65]

U.S. Air Force Lieutenant Colonel Walter D. Hunter - 1969-1970 A.D.
(Memo from Dr. Walt Brown follows)

Memorandum of Phone Conversation with Lt. Col. Walter D. Hunter 24 June 1975

About 5 or 6 years ago, Lieutenant Colonel Walter Hunter saw two photos of what allegedly was Noah's Ark. These photos (either 5" x 7" or 8" x 11") were in the possession of "two guys" who were standing in Base Operations at Beale Air Force Base in California.

An object in the photos, which looked like a boat, was encased in a glacier on an unrecognizable mountain. Lt. Col. Hunter did not know who took the photos or where they were taken but felt that they probably were taken from a U-2 aircraft. He thought they had been taken in November but did not say why. He also recalled that the photos were oblique shots. In further describing the photo(s) he said:

> It looked like a glacier with an object buried in it [which was] obviously underneath ice. The photo had red caliper marks on it which were used in determining its length of 450 feet. It [the object] was pointed on both ends...They [the photos] had no edges on them, they just had been run off on photo paper...The first photo was a 'pan shot' of a large glacier.

---

[65] Richard C. Bright, *The Ark, A Reality?* (Guilderland, New York: Ranger Associates Inc., 1989), p. 98.

Lt. Col. Hunter described this experience in Base Operations as a "passing thing," lasting no more than the minutes while he filed his flight plan. When I asked how he would recommend tracing these photos, he said that the only thing he could think of was to see if the Unit Historian at Beale Air Force Base could find them in his files.

(end Walt Brown memo)

Note that the structure's shape with pointed ends appears similar to the David Duckworth sketch and description of the Smithsonian photographs he allegedly saw near the same time in the fall of 1968 as well as the Russian Ark/Ray Lubeck film, the U2/Apache Jim Wilson sketch and one George Greene eyewitness sketch. A structure with pointed ends appears to be contradictory to the Hagopian structure and other accounts which appeared to have a rectangular box-like shape. However, if the structure is now broken into pieces, some of the pieces may have a box-like shape caused by a fairly clean break.

"Dr. Donald Liedmann" Hoax - 1969-1978 A.D.
This supposed eyewitness account was thoroughly debunked by Bill Crouse in the *Ararat Report*.

> This story was first reported by Violet Cummings, and for more details see her book *Noah's Ark: Fable or Fact* (page 328 ff.). "Liedmann" was originally discovered by James M. Lee, a missionary to Korea, and a former officer of Search Foundation.
> In 1969, a man identifying himself as "Dr. Donald M. Liedmann" approached Lee at a Christian businessmen's convention in Chicago where he was maintaining a booth on Noah's Ark set up by the Search Foundation. "Liedmann" proceeded to relate to Lee that he had seen actual photographs of Noah's Ark taken by Russian pilots. "Liedmann" maintained he had been a squadron leader in the Royal Air Force at the time, and that he had been shot down twice by the Germans within a space of six months! He also claimed to have a medical degree in neurosurgery from the University of Upsala in Sweden and a Ph.D. from another university...
> *AR* picked up his trail in Lubbock, TX where we had heard that he attended church for a short period in the late '70s.
> What he discovered is that "Liedmann" has indeed had a colorful past, almost the kind Hollywood would like to make a movie about. Unfortunately, we also discovered that "Liedmann," according to his own confession was not who he said he was. While at Trinity Church in Lubbock he was using the name "Jacob Liedmann." The people at the church there were awed by the stories he told...The

reasons were not revealed to us but something must have been said in a lecture which led to his being called before the elders of the church. During this and subsequent sessions "Liedmann" admitted that his past was a lie and that he had problems. He made this confession before the whole church body. We talked with members who remembered the incident clearly.

We were also told that a pilot in the church took "Liedmann" up in his private plane and discovered that he did not know the first thing about flying an aircraft.

Since the church sincerely wanted to help "Liedmann" in a healing way he agreed to receive their counsel for a period of one year. However, he disappeared after about three months.

U.S. Air Force Personnel Ed Behling - 1973 A.D.

In 1981, Ed Behling told Bob Stuplich that he was shown the Ark by an old Kurd on Ararat while working for the Air Force in 1973. Behling was assigned to Diyarbakir, about 250 miles southwest of Mount Ararat. The following is the transcript of Behling's 1982 description of his experience in the Oklahoma City-based *Prophecy in the News* program hosted by J.R. Church. At the initial printing of this book in 1999, Ed Behling was the only known ground-based eyewitness who claimed to see Noah's Ark and was still alive.

Church: We have a rare privilege on today's *Prophecy in the News*. We have a gentleman with us who has seen the Ark of Noah. Now this is not the Ark of the covenant which we have been speaking about on previous broadcasts. This is the Ark, the huge boat, that Noah saved the human race back about 4,500 years ago. And this gentleman Mr. Ed Behling, originally from Michigan, now living in Gunnison, Colorado, has been to the mountain and he has seen the Ark of Noah. And he is here today to tell us about it. Ed, thank you for coming to be with us today on Prophecy in the News.

Behling: Thank you.

Church: I'd like to ask you about your discovery, if we could call it that, you were on the mountain in 1973. What were doing in Turkey, could you tell us?

Behling: I was in the Air Force in Turkey and really as far as a discovery, I had no idea it was a discovery until eight years later [1981] until some people started talking to me and asking me questions about it. Like I was saying, I was in the Air Force and I was assigned there in a little station of 250 Americans called Diyarbakir Common Defense Installation (CDI).

Church: Now this is about southwest of Ararat. Do you know about how many miles?

Behling: Oh, I'd say about 100 miles. I've never really looked you know. The car that we drove in to go up there was in kilometers and I realized the metric system was coming in but I had no idea what a kilometer was then. I knew we'd say we were going about a hundred miles an hour as far as I was concerned but it was actually about sixty miles an hour. So I don't know exactly how far it was.

Church: While you were there you met a friend, a Turkish army soldier?

Behling: Yes, it was a Turkish *abi*, that was our term for them. His name was Mustafa. He was in the army at that time about a year. And I was in the Air Force at that time about a couple years. And I probably would have never met him. However, I wanted to see how the people operated, who the people were, what feelings they had. This was a rare experience for me to be in a foreign country. I'd lived my life in the United States kind of sheltered by the U.S. environment and I wanted to see how they operated, how they felt, their feelings, who they were. And in doing so, I met Mustafa who was the Turkish soldier who eventually took me up to the Ark.

Church: OK, now you arrived in Diyarbakir in November of 1972?

Behling: Yes.

Church: About six months later, in late May, you had met Mustafa and you had asked him to take you to Mount Ararat.

Behling: Well, almost. After I had arrived in Diyarbakir, I met him shortly afterward because I was roaming around trying to find my way to Diyarbakir because we were stationed outside Diyarbakir and asking people and trying to talk to the guards because they were on the same installation we were. And I met him and we kind of hit it off in the sense of the word. And I was learning my Turkish and he wanted to learn the American dialect. And we were having a good time and he took me to places in Diyarbakir and showed me places and helped me buy some Turkish memorabilia. So we started meeting and knowing one another and we had known each other for about five months and I started talking to him about historic sites.

Church: And you were about twenty-three years old?

Behling: Yes, about that.

Church: And today you are a clinical psychologist, is that right? Established a practice in Gunnison, Colorado, is that right?

Behling: Yes.

Church: So you wanted to see Mount Ararat. Was there any particular reason? Did you specifically want to see the Ark of Noah?

Behling: It wasn't so much the Ark of Noah. I made it a goal when I left the United States to go to Turkey to see as much I could. I had read about Paul's journeys through Turkey through Antioch, Iconium, Lystra, Darbe—his three missionary journeys basically. And I've read about the seven churches of Revelation and that had always fascinated me that in Revelation something could actually be real. And these seven churches were real. And to see that and to see the holy lands and to see Egypt; all that was basically free. I could travel anywhere I wanted. I wanted to see the Bible for real. We were stationed on the Tigris River. The Euphrates was down the road a little bit. A hundred miles away was Mount Ararat. For a young

Christian, a babe in the woods, what better place could you be? So I was really excited and I wanted to see everything. And the Ark and Mount Ararat were just another part of the whole scope.

Church: OK, now, when you asked to go see the Ark of Noah, you were 23 years old, you were somewhat naïve about the subject. You, what, thought that everyone knew about the Ark?

Behling: Yes, you know, if Israel was discovered and the seven churches of Revelation were discovered and in the sense of the word I grew knowing that the Ark was on Mount Ararat. Well then, that was discovered too. And I was just one of many going up there to look at it and in the sense of the word felt privileged because there I was. I was able to do it and not very many people could travel all the way across Turkey to see it.

Church: Little did you know that nobody else had been up there to see it.

Behling: I had no idea, no idea that nobody else had seen it until last year when people started asking me questions about it.

Church: Could you tell us briefly what was the occasion of your finding out? How did you find that you were among the privileged few among the world's population to have seen the Ark?

Behling: Well, it was, we were in church and it was just after fellowship and I was talking about the Ark or something else...Somebody says there is another fellow [Bob Stuplich] who...had seen the Ark too..."Isn't that incredible to have such a large ship up in the side of such an incredible mountain?"..."What are you talking about?...I've been looking for it but we've never found it"..."Oh, I'm sorry about that. I thought that you had seen it"...I never thought anything about it until Bob and his friend Scott Van Dyke, who were trying to get over here this last summer, tried to get up this way.

Church: Alright, now let's go back to 1973 late May that year, spring. Tell us about the trip?

Behling: ...The process of going to see the Ark took about a month...I was telling him [Mustafa] about how I was going to try to get up there and he said, "I can take you."...I asked him to a take a camera but he preferred that I didn't "because number one, Ararat is near the Russian border, if you have a camera you're American and I'm Turkish, and it's not going to look good..." He said that he had a great-uncle who knew where the Ark was and his great-uncle was going to take us up to it. So it was kind of exciting, you know. Boy, I'm on an adventure. And we avoided most of the villages that we went by because we wanted to stay as low-level as possible. We didn't want to gather any attention...Whenever you went off our base you dressed as non-attentive [non-attention grabbing] as possible...So we got to some old set of ruins where we finally parked...

Church: OK, now what side of the mountain were you on?

Behling: Well, see that's hard to say because it was cloudy while we were there and basically the whole mountain was in a cloud. That was a big

disappointment to me. I wanted to see Mount Ararat. I had seen it from a
distance from where we were stationed. But now that we got there, the whole
thing was in a cloud. You know, you could see maybe a couple thousand feet
up on the side of it but that was it. And it kind of a disappointment to me.

Church: Would you say you were basically on the west side of the
mountain?

Behling: I would say basically that we were on the north side. North,
northwest. I guess that's from talking to Mr. Cummings, and talking to Pat
Frost, trying to remember and relocate myself and that's where the ruins are.
So we took off from the ruins and about three hours later, hiking, we found
ourselves at this old tent, this old camp of four, three plus Mustafa's great-
uncle. Three other shepherds. He was the master-shepherd I guess would be
the term. He knew it all basically. He was the elder of all. He looked like an
elder of all too. He looked like he had been dead three years and just didn't
know enough to drop over. His skin looked like very, very old tanned
leather…So I sat in the camp and tried to understand because his great-uncle
spoke Kurdish…The next morning, just before light…we started out on our
journey. His uncle seemed kind of reluctant to take us up there. Mustafa said
that he had convinced him to take us up there…

Church: Would you say that most of the shepherds around the mountain
know where the Ark is located?

Behling: I had that impression—at least the older ones.

Church: It is amazing that so many groups have gone to the mountain
and none of them have been able to find it. All of their guides seem to be
taking them off into another part of the mountain. Do you have any thoughts
on that?

Behling: Yes, I do. And it is pure speculation on my part. However, I
know how the system works in Turkey. Being with the people, trying to
understand their customs and their traditions, their rituals and that they hold a
lot of weight with the old Turks, the old Kurds. They are the masters. They
are the ultimate authority. And you don't go against anything they say. I mean
not even the soldiers go against the old men, the wise, the sages. You don't go
against their word. What they say goes. And I see a lot of people going over
searching for the Ark and they're using younger guides. Well, these younger
guides, the younger Turks, they're kind of spunky. They are like a banty
rooster. They think they can whip the world. And they get these spunky
guides. And they say, "Lead us to the Ark." "Oh, yeah,…we can lead you to
the Ark. No trouble." And they don't lead them anywhere because the old
men say and I'm speculating now, "No, you're not going to take those people
anywhere." If you were to contact the really old men and ask them to take you
to the Ark and win over their confidence and allow them to respect them a
little bit by your humbleness, I think you might find one that would take you
to the Ark. But the younger men, they might know where the Ark is but the

old men say, "You will not take them to the Ark." And you better believe those young men will not go against the ruling of an older man.

Church: Do you suppose that it could also be that once the Ark has been located that groups will stop coming to the mountain and stop paying the guides to take them and possibly be a loss of income?

Behling: No, I feel just the opposite.

Church: Do you think they hold the Ark so sacred that they just don't want outside people there?

Behling: Exactly...And as far as the Koran goes, Noah and the Ark is very sacred to them. I mean, they are very privileged people to have the Ark of Noah on their mountain. That is very sacred to them. Nobody touches that Ark. Nobody goes to the Ark without the elders' permission.

Church: Now the morning comes when you are ready to make the ascent. Can you describe it for us and tell us what the Ark looked like?

Behling: ...I have no idea how high we were when we started out. Because I really wasn't paying attention to specifics. I wasn't making a journal and not being very scientific about it because it was just another thing in my repertoire of events in my year and a half in Turkey...We took off to find the Ark. It was a little before daylight. I had my arctic suit on...a big huge coat. [Mustafa's great-uncle] took us right up the side of the mountain. We were going around rocks and above cliffs and below cliffs—it was like a trail. There was a lot of snow on the mountain at this time, but it wasn't that uncomfortable. It was a hard snow; it wasn't very slippery. He was like a guide; he knew exactly where he was going...

Church: How many hours of walking before you came upon the Ark?

Behling: Oh, boy, we started out before light. I don't remember what time light was at that time. And we got there in late afternoon. It was kind of funny.

Church: Three or four o'clock in the afternoon.

Behling: Yeah, something like that. Because we were walking and I was tired. Not being a mountain man at that time. Never being ever in the mountains and here we've got this 17,000-footer. And I'm tire and I'm winded and it's like, "Oh boy, when is this ever going to end. Mustafa, I am tired. When are we going to see the Ark? You know, if we don't see it pretty soon, I want to go back." So Mustafa talks to his great-uncle saying that "Hey, Ed here is complaining. We'd better get to the Ark pretty quick." His uncle turns around and laughs at me and he points down. And I thought that was a gesture that I wasn't a very nice guy or this guy's no good. But Mustafa then turns around to me and says, "Do you want to see the Ark?" I said, "Yeah." And he points down. And I look over this cliff. We were walking on this, well, it's not really, yeah it was a cliff down to it but we're walking on the side of this mountain...It was a fairly wide trail, maybe fifteen feet wide. And I walk over to the edge and look down and here is this massive black thing just sitting there on this shelf of rock and it kind of fades off into a snow bank. It's obviously 100-150 feet long. And I look at this thing and it is so large and so big sitting in the side of this mountain. It's kind of eerie. Now here we are standing on the side of the mountain. There's clouds all around us. We can only see 300-400 feet at the maximum, about the length of a football field. And that's hazy. And you're kind of walking through. And it's mysterious. The mountain is incredible because number one, it is hard walking. And there's always these old rocks and everything around. And you can always hear rocks falling. You can hear landslides, avalanches, whatever. And you get this mystical sense about you. And you kind of soaking all of this in. And then all of the sudden you look down and here's this huge, awesome ship standing or sitting below you in this fog. It's almost like you picture a dream. There it is.

Church: But it was no dream, right?

Behling: No it wasn't. It was not.

Church: It was real?

Behling: It was very real.

Church: How high above the Ark were you standing when you saw it?

Behling: I would say someplace around fifty feet, sixty feet, seventy feet. I don't know exactly.

Church: Tell us about the roof.

Behling: From where I was standing, you could tell the roof sloped very gradually, maybe a 10-degree slope, 15-degree slope to it. And then it had a wide spot in the center of it that went the length of it. Now this was maybe 10 feet wide—like a catwalk...I noticed from where I was standing that the front was chopped off or broken off or something. How much of the front was broken off, I had no idea, but it was broken off.

Church: The whole front end of the boat or back end, whichever you were looking at, was broken and it was just jutting out or sticking out with a big gaping hole in the end of it.

Behling: Which I found out later when we walked down below the Ark where we camped that night.

Church: You went down below then and looked back up at it?

Behling: Yes, after we looked at it a little bit his uncle, Mustafa's uncle motioned to us to come on so we followed down around and then below it. We couldn't jump down on it because it was too far to jump and we didn't have any ropes or anything. I kind of wanted to walk on it but we didn't get a chance. We walked down below it and there was about a hundred-foot cliff or something like this, the shelf that it was on, a big table and it was cliff all the way around.

Church: And you spent the night there?

Behling: Yeah, underneath.

Church: And then went back down the next day?

Behling: Yeah.

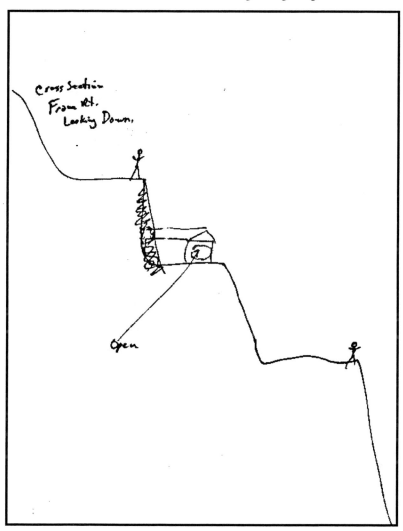

Ed Behling sketch of Noah's Ark
Courtesy of Ed Behling via John Morris via Dick Bright

Church: I want to thank you for coming and telling us about this unusual experience to see the Ark of Noah. Perhaps one of these days somebody's going to go up there and take a picture of it.

Behling: We have.

Church: Then we'll be able to see and let all the world see what it really looks like. Thank you again for coming and being with us on today's Prophecy in the News.

Behling: Thank you.

Behling spoke again with J.R. Church the next day on *Prophecy in the News* and stated the following.

I saw the Ark from two points. We saw it from the upper point looking down on it and I would say it's maybe 150 to 200 feet and then it vanished into the snow. It was all foggy around so hard to get very precise. Then we walked down around and beneath it and wound up 75 to 100 feet below it because it was resting on a shelf or a cliff. It was on a table and we camped underneath it.

Basically, the mouth of it (we were looking at it from the end) was square. However it was wider than it was tall. It was 40 to 50 feet tall and there was a thing on the top of it 10 to 15 feet wide. It was something like a catwalk six or eight feet high. The roof and catwalk were slightly sloped. It was broken off in the front, 60 to 70 feet wide and 40 to 50 feet high. The roof and catwalk were slightly sloped, perhaps for water to run off. I'm looking at this from 75 to 100 feet below it and compared to the hill or cliff that it was on, it still looked enormous. I mean, here is this huge, gaping hole in this ship that is incredibly large and I think about it in my mind's eye and it's still hard to imagine...The ship was very black. The sides were jagged or ripped up a little. I could see what resembled planks but they were all in one big piece...I trust that it will be photographed. It's there. All people have to do is go up and look at it.

John Morris added the following quote from Behling in his book.

The walls must have been 18 inches thick...The walls were straight up and down on each side and the base, which I couldn't see because of the angle, looked fairly flat.[66]

An interesting thing to note in the Behling account compared to the Davis account of a three-day ascent is the indication that the group ascended the mountain to the Ark in one day. It is unclear where Behling and the Kurds started from and it could have been up to thirteen hours of hiking at the most (figuring leaving before sunrise at 4AM and arriving in the late afternoon at about 5PM) and the weather was much better than the Davis trip's rain and snow.

Pat Frost taped Ed Behling speaking at an Oklahoma church. Frost, who explored Mount Ararat nine times, said that Behling sketched a picture of what he saw which looked like an "exact replica" of the Hagopian/Lee drawings. Also note that the shelf and canyon that Behling describe sound similar to some of the other eyewitness accounts. One would think that the ground-based eyewitnesses would be more trustworthy than the air-based eyewitnesses since they tend to be so much closer to the Ark (dozens of feet

---

[66] Tim LaHaye and John Morris, *The Ark on Ararat* (Nashville: Thomas Nelson Publishers, 1976), pp. 302-306.

away in this case) compared with the air-based eyewitnesses (hundreds or thousands of feet away) as well as the ground-based eyewitnesses are stationary rather than constantly moving in different directions.

Dick Bright reports the following from Eryl Cummings' interview.

> The ruins that they began at could have been Karada on the west side of the mountain, although that is not certain. The town of Igdir is mentioned, and this does give us another clue as to where he might have started his climb, and that's on the northwest side of the mountain.
>
> They walked on a plain, plateau, or pasture for a time, and keeping the mountain summit to their right, they walked up and across the face in a north and east direction...
>
> After the pasture, plain, or plateau, they walked on a lot of rocks which were partly covered in about a foot of packed snow...Apparently, they followed the edge of the ice, and [Behling] estimated his altitude to be as high as 15,000 feet, but he wasn't sure.

As a matter of record, according to Microsoft's Virtual Globe, Diyarbakir is 404 kilometers or about 249 miles as the crow flies from Mount Ararat and more by road.

From a more critical perspective, Bill Crouse wrote the following about Behling in the *Ararat Report*.

> Since the early '80s, he has not wanted to talk about his experience. He talked with us only reluctantly when we called his home in 1985. He took great offense when asked about certain questionable aspects of his testimony.
>
> For instance, he says they built a campfire just below the Ark and then spent the night there. When I questioned him about the nature of their campfire there was silence and reluctance to continue the interview. Any mountain climber knows that to build a campfire above 13,000 feet requires some pretty good fuel!
>
> Many hours were spent examining this testimony and this man's character. The people we interviewed who know Behling, spoke of him as a sincere Christian but one who embellishes for effect. We think this is a story that grew out of hand each time it was told.
>
> I have two great problems with the Ed Behling story:
>
> Again, as with the Davis story, you have to give credence to the conspiracy theory.
>
> If he really saw the Ark his behavior is difficult to explain. If I had seen the Ark, I would not have lost contact with the people who revealed it to me, nor would I cease trying to go back for a second look. Would I be quiet about it? No way.

In regard to the fire, many times the Kurds bring dung chips or gasoline with them to create fires high on the mountain. Also, it should be remembered that the Kurds created a blazing "campfire" at 13,000 feet of the 1985 Crouse expedition tents and equipment that burned pretty well and was even visible from Dogubayazit.

Scott Van Dyke, an early interviewer of Behling in 1981, said that when he and Bob Stuplich showed Ararat photographs to Behling, he attempted to test Behling several times by inverting the slides. Every time a slide was inverted, Behling said that the slide was familiar but that there was something wrong with it, which would indicate familiarity with Mount Ararat geographic features. Van Dyke also said that Behling talked about pinnacle peaks near the alleged Ark and wolf dogs as well. However, Bob Stuplich who originally met Behling, does not remember this meeting or these statements from Behling.

If George Stephen III is correct with his Satellite Remote Sensing view of the two pieces being under the ice cap near the Abich II glacier between 15,000 and 16,000 feet, then perhaps the weather occasionally allows the horseshoe-shaped valley to be uncovered of ice and the structure becomes visible. Since researchers have been concentrating looking in the Ahora Gorge below the Abich II glacier and the photos of the ice cap recently show more snow and ice in this area, this might explain why researchers have not been able to see the structure since 1973. If the Abich II depression were opened up, perhaps it was considered part of the Ahora Gorge in other accounts. In regard to weather, another thought is that if the structure is black as several accounts indicate, perhaps when the ice is cleared away from a portion of the object, then the direct sun light hitting the black surface makes it warmer and actually speeds the thawing process on the top. However, Ed Behling might have been in that area only 10-12 weeks before the 1973 Dr. Lawrence Hewitt slide was taken. Despite the Hewitt slide showing apparent fresh snow, it is difficult to believe that most of that Abich II depression would be melted away 10-12 weeks earlier in the summer to allow Behling to walk up and around one (possibly the lower) of the two Stephen objects and then camp below it. Another question is that if the two objects in the Stephen site are accurate, how in the world did hikers like Behling and Ed Davis actually get to it without going over the ice cap?

The publisher made a call recently to Ed Behling as follow up with him. Unfortunately, Behling did not want to discuss the experience since he felt that he had already talked with others about it and was sick and tired of answering the same questions all over again. He appeared to feel that others (perhaps Sun's and CBS's video *The Incredible Discovery of Noah's Ark*) took advantage of his previous video taping without getting permission from him.[67] Pat Frost also said that in regard to Behling not talking extensively about his

---

[67] Rex Geissler conversation with Ed Behling in January, 1999.

experience between 1973 and 1981 he was afraid that Noah's Ark might become an idol to some people like the "shroud of Turin." Pat Frost stated the following.

> His fear is that people would be tempted to worship the Ark rather than the Lord. So that was the reason that Ed hasn't said much about it the last few years because of thinking possibly that many people would worship the object rather than the Jesus Christ.
>
> Ed has been asked to go back to Mount Ararat by Eryl Cummings and by myself. We decided that he would need to pray about it...
>
> He was also asked if he could retrace his steps on Mount Ararat back to the Ark. Ed responded, "Yes, I definitely could."

Behling may be also protecting his family because of Crouse's straightforward investigative reporting into his personal life as "Many hours were spent examining this testimony and this man's character." However, Bob Stuplich believes that Behling is simply tired of taking time to reiterate his story to dozens of researchers, especially because the cloud cover on the mountain was thick which caused Behling to not recognize photos and know where to lead researchers (similar to the issue with the poor weather on the Ed Davis trip).

As the only known living ground-based eyewitness who claimed to see the Ark from 75 to 100 feet away, it would be helpful if Ed Behling would consider answering a few more questions in the future simply to accurately document Behling's experience. Rex Geissler (the publisher) put together 33 questions which were forwarded to Behling via Bob Stuplich. In July 1999, Stuplich talked with Ed Behling who confirmed that the basic story recited in the pages of this book above was an accurate portrayal of what he saw and experienced. However, in July 1999, Behling decided to not answer Geissler's 33 questions to finish documenting his experience.

U.S. Navy Lieutenant JG Al Shappell - 1974

In 1974, Al Shappell stated that he saw a boat-like structure while flying over Mount Ararat on a Top Secret mission to photograph the object. Shappell's mission may have had something to do with the statement made to David Montgomery in 1989 later in this appendix. This is his statement.

> In June, 1974, a Navy pilot and I were assigned a mission from the higher ups to fly a highly secret reconnaissance trip over Mount Ararat to photograph something that they thought might be a Soviet-made defense installation or radar station with a black tarp over it. Others in "the land of Oz," as we called the unknown location where our orders would come from, had recently obtained a satellite photo of a foreign object toward the summit of Ararat.

Since it was a secret mission and that corner of the world was a strategic area with several nations and the Soviets nearby, there was no identification on the plane or on us.

We placed Sponset [sp.] mounted cameras on the belly and the two wings of our F-4 plane by pulling out other panels and replacing them. I was responsible for connecting together all the flight systems of the aircraft, so I was taken along on an F-4

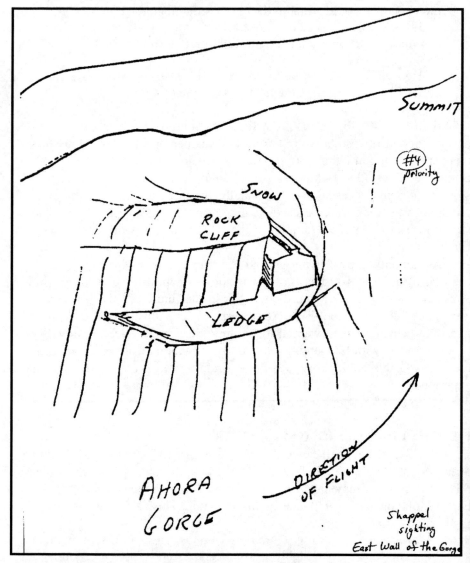

Al Shappell sketch of the object he saw on Mount Ararat 1974
Courtesy of Al Shappell via John McIntosh

Phantom fighter to monitor the plane and take pictures of the object. We flew over it at a low altitude, less than 1,000 feet from the surface of the mountain while I took the photos.

The film was turned over to the Air Force and classified "Top Secret." We photographed Mount Ararat for 35-40 seconds and the structure for 5-10 seconds and then headed back to the Aegean Sea. We never saw the film as it was unloaded from the aircraft before we got out of the plane. Once the film was viewed and they realized it was not a threat, the film was probably destroyed. I believe that Kevin Kluetz, John Morris, and Walt Brown have done some checking into this but have not been able to find anything, probably because there is no documentation left.

I am not sure what they did with it, but I can tell you what I saw with my own eyes. It was a coal-black foreign object about two-thirds of the way up the mountain near a gorge. It was oblong and partially buried in ice, overhanging a cliff. The terrain around it was brownish along with ice and snow. To me, it certainly looked similar to a boat-like object, definitely manmade. It also appeared as though it did not belong on the mountain. It was just totally out of place.

You could tell that there was a big meltback of the ice cap for two reasons. First, there was a tremendous amount of water rushing down the mountain from the ice cap. Second, the intelligence community had military satellites photographing this area for years before but it wasn't until 1974 that they noticed this object and had us go check it out. I believe this is because it was recently uncovered from the glacier and they recently spotted it.

Flying in the plane, the structure appeared to be about 300 feet long until snow and ice covered it. It was square on the end and I would guess it might be 100 to 200 feet in width and height. There is another ledge with an icepack 30 to 50 feet below the main structure with a littering of debris underneath the main structure. The end of the upper structure had broken off and I could see the broken off piece in the snow pack at the bottom of the ledge.

They probably had the Navy check it out because the ship was in the Aegean Sea at the time. Our F-4 refueled from tanker planes (one was an A-6) both directions in and out of Ararat. I had never met the pilot before and don't think he gave me his real name, which was typical for top-secret missions, where we did not even carry identification. I never saw the pilot again. He was a top-notch pilot because we had to fly extremely low through the mountain ranges to avoid radar on the way to Ararat and several times I thought we were going to crash along the flight route. As soon as we came over the Ararat summit, three Russian MIGs were scrambled and chased us a long way back through eastern Turkey. They were only fifteen miles out from us. The Turkish Air Force did not even know we were there until we identified ourselves on the way back.

My beginning in the Navy was as follows. Before I even took the oath, the Department of Defense and Navy interviewed me. They already had a game plan. Three days after I began the service, I had an in-depth interview at Great Lakes. They gave me 8-9 hours of tests. Then I received my clearance.

The Navy trained me as an F-4 flight control and electronics system technician. When you were initially trained by the Navy as a maintenance person, you were given a maintenance level to learn. I was given the level of "S," which stands for system maintenance. My responsibilities were top level security computer systems and flight control. I knew exactly how the entire F-4 aircraft fit together electronically and could dissect it and put it back together to make sure the pilots were always taken care of. I was in school constantly. I studied six days a week 10-12 hours per day for over two years. Saturday or Sunday was dedicated to survival and flight training.

On the aircraft carriers, we had to do basic flight tests and make planes operational before they went back to the pilots. I would take planes up and run them through a series of tests. These tests would check the plane limits and include things like doing a 32-degree bank to see if the ACS system went off-line, G-forces, gyros, altitude tests, altimeters, fire control, etc. Then I was working with vendors constantly. I trained in two years rather than the typical 6-8 years to get pilot carrier-qualified so I had a jump on the pilots. Plus I knew all the internal electronics. I had to fix the aircraft, know how to fly the aircraft and how to keep the aircraft flying. They liked people like myself because I had one year of electronics training without going to a college. If you went to college or university, they said they had to deprogram you. I was thrown out of my A School after two weeks and placed in secured room alone with a military guard. They gave me 8-9 hours of tests each day for three weeks. I thought that I was in trouble but they graduated me to B School. Then they sent me to C school. I was escorted by a marine to my first class but was immediately thrown out by the teacher because I had a blue suit on. The head of the school and the teacher had an argument. Then I was told to put khakis on and received bars as an officer Lieutenant JG. The big problem with me not being an officer was that the pilots would never respect me so they made me an officer. So that is the unceremonious way that I became an officer. I finished up my training at Pensacola.

Because of security concerns and because it was an "unauthorized flight," if you go to the Department of Navy, they will tell you that the flight did not occur and that I am lying. In fact, I was with my home squadron for only three days before leaving on special assignments for the rest of my tour. I would typically be on a carrier for only 3-5 days (TAD or Temporarily Assigned) or so and then my group would be transferred to another carrier for another few days. It was rare to be on a carrier more than three weeks. I worked on nine different carriers although only six were the normal ones rotating watches in the Mediterranean. A few of the carriers I worked on were the Independence (my home ship although I was on it seldom), the America (my second home ship when the Independence was off watch), the Saratoga, the Franklin D. Roosevelt, the Forestal, the Kitty Hawk, the Enterprise, and the Hornet.

Since I was trained for such a specialized assignment (there were only seven of us in the entire military), I was in constant demand. The admirals, ship captains, and CAGs (Commander of Air Wing's) were judged by their ship's battle readiness which meant the percentage of planes that could fly safely. If the reports always showed a close to 100% flight readiness for their planes, then they might get a bar some year. This 100% airplane readiness was especially important in the hotspot of the eastern Med. The western Mediterranean was not as bad because of the stability of the nations surrounding it. Since I was the main aircraft systems technician, I was in constant demand. And believe me, when an admiral screamed for something, he got what he wanted. Typically, I would check a plane over, correct or change something, and then fly it off the ship to do our standard series of tests. If it worked fine, then I would bring it back and move on to the next plane. If it didn't react correctly in every area, I would change it again and take it back up in the air to test it again. This meant that I was flying 4-5 hours in multiple flights every day whereas the pilots themselves were only flying one flight 1-2 hours a day. If the plane was a two-seater, I would be in the back seat with a pilot. The younger pilots had to get hours so they would ride along with me while I ran the plane through the series of tests. I had to train new pilots to trust the system on automatic landings because the nose was up and they couldn't see the ship while we were coming in. The new pilots would constantly get concerned because they didn't have control on the automatic landings. As soon as they touched the stick or the pedals, the plane reverted from automatic to manual and they had to immediately abort the landing. I finally got in the habit of telling the new pilots to leave there hands above along the railing so they wouldn't touch the stick.

Because I went through so many landings, I now have a bad neck. In an aircraft landing, there was no way to hold your helmet and head from going forward. A landing on an aircraft carrier is really a controlled crash. The G-force tears up your body. If I landed more than once a day, I would have bruises where the straps were located. After my two years of training, I was in active duty about seventeen months. But in that time period, I had 273 carrier landings and 2003 hours logged in the air which was more than most pilots get in a six-year slot.

Even after my training, I still had to learn constantly. Rather than just work with the Navy technicians, I worked directly with vendors who supplied the Navy with hardware. For example, I worked extensively with Honeywell to enhance and perfect automatic landing systems. I worked on multiple types of aircraft including F-4s, A-6s, A-7s and a few F-14s as well as Sea King and Sea Nook helicopters. That's why I moved around so much. There were only a few people that were systems people.

Because of the stress level of my job and because there were only a few people trained for it, I was getting run ragged. We had monthly physicals. The flight surgeon and psychiatrist said that the physical and mental stress was eating me up. The surgeon gave me three weeks off to rest up. When the Admiral found out, he went straight to the sickbay. He told the surgeon that I couldn't take three weeks but only three days. I guess that tells you how important the percentage of readiness was to the Admiral and how important my job was in making the percentage of readiness happen. At the same time, my dad had gotten pushed off a contracting site and fell 30 feet down a cement elevator shaft. The first report I received from the Department of Defense said that my dad was dead. The second report three hours later said that he was in critical condition and the doctors said he would never walk again. Dad had bones broke in about ten locations. Despite that, I was not allowed to go visit him for nine months. I couldn't tell my parents where I was or what I did for that three and a half-year period of time which was also stressful.

When the Department of Defense finally gave me my first leave after being in the Navy three and one-half years, my admiral hid the letter for 30 days because he didn't want to lose me. Finally, someone called him and ordered him to get me to the states by the next day. He called me and said, "You've got 20 minutes to get off this ship or you're not going."

The Navy will tell you that I had family problems and that is why they let me out of the service. The reality is that this was my first leave ever and that I had always planned to make a career of the Navy. But many military people were running for holes to hide in because the Department of Defense did not know about programs like the one I was in. And when Nixon went down, they were afraid that they might as well. My program was simply implemented by those commanders in the field to help out the battle readiness. The other six guys who also did my job were also let out and the program has changed since then.

When I arrived in the U.S., they placed me alone in a barracks (BOQ) under the 24-hour guard of two marines. I went through three entire weeks of debriefing from the CIA, FBI and the Department of Navy. For many people, debriefing is simply a formality with a warning or a 10-20 minute interview. The first person that interviewed me said that if he could do it, he would throw me in Leavenworth for ten years so I couldn't talk to anybody. The day I got out, an agent from Langley had me watch as he placed my service record and flight log in a cross-grain shredder.

He did it on purpose so that I would know those records were gone and that their would be nothing to substantiate my testimony of this unauthorized program. Again, it seemed like after Nixon was impeached, I got the sense that more documentation was destroyed and stories fabricated rather than being saved or archived.

After they released me from the service, the Department of Defense preferred that I disappear and go to an obscure college which they helped me pick. In 1981 FBI agents were still checking up on me. They gave me advice to find a job where there was no public exposure and preferred that I disappear completely.[68]

Prior to the Shappell mission, Dr. Walter Brown, a retired U.S. Air Force colonel was asked to CIA headquarters and debriefed by someone who worked for the director on all he knew about Noah's Ark. Some researchers have suspected that the debriefing had something to do with the Shappell mission. However, according to Kluetz this was not the case and the two incidents were completely unrelated. In this Kluetz account, "Navy" is U.S. Navy Lieutenant JG Al Shappell.

Walt Brown told me that he had spoken with a woman named Charlotte Cherry, a former administrative assistant to a 1970's ranking former U.S. government top secret official named Roland Inlow. Ms. Cherry had seen a top-secret file labeled "Noah's Ark" on Roland Inlow's desk. She was unable to view the contents of the file, though, because her security clearance did not allow her to do so. Walt Brown also knew that in the early 1970's, a U.S. government top secret contract employee who I'll call "Secret" had been given authorization to search for Noah's Ark on Mount Ararat. "Secret" was not able to say how he conducted his search. Walt Brown hypothesized that perhaps "Secret" had compiled the file that Ms. Cherry had seen on Roland Inlow's desk, and that perhaps the file contained photographs taken by "Navy" that "Secret" had ordered. I interviewed "Navy" in person in 1994 and 1995 for a total of approximately 14 hours. I also interviewed him for several hours over the phone alone and also in a three-way phone conversation that included Dr. Walt Brown. Additionally, Dr. Walt Brown obtained copies of "Navy's" military records and historical information that gave the location of the aircraft carrier on which "Navy" said he had been assigned. Based on all the evidence, Dr. Walt Brown and I concluded that "Navy's" account was not reliable. The aircraft carrier had not been where "Navy" said it had been on the dates he gave us. I found no evidence to indicate that the type of aircraft "Navy" said he had been flying (generally a supersonic fighter) has ever been mission-configured to take aerial

---

[68] Al Shappell statement to Rex Geissler on May 5th, 1999.

reconnaissance photographs, as "Navy" said. According to "Navy's" military records, he was not qualified to fly an aircraft. "Navy" had pointed to a rock in the upper Ahora Gorge on Mount Ararat, claiming he had seen the Ark behind that rock. That rock, only a few feet wide and tall, turned out to be much too small to hide the Ark, which, based on the Biblical dimensions, is approximately 450 feet long, 75 feet wide, and 45 feet tall. Based on these and many other observations, I quit pursuing "Navy's" account.

Based on the research and concerns of Kevin Kluetz, Rex Geissler asked Al Shappell to respond to a few questions.

Rex Geissler: Kevin told me that when the Radar identified the Russian MIGs, the sound you said it made was different than what F-4 pilots stated it should be. Can you explain that discrepancy?

Al Shappell: First, there are several different kinds of Radar equipment. There is coverage or wide band radar, weather Doppler Radar (weapons systems use), etc. In fact, I worked with literally hundreds of different radar systems from four separate manufactures. They were updated on a monthly basis with service changes and defense sweeps for detecting other types of aircraft. Again, I personally worked with these vendors on many prototypes from Grumman, Dialogic (integrated circuit boards), Honeywell, and McDonald Douglas. We used different Radar systems on each plane and each mission. In fact, most planes would have three different radar systems and some would have five to eight. So a person should not box me into one particular type of Radar that some pilots used in F-4s. That is a misunderstanding of the nature of Radar systems and how maintenance technicians like myself would change them. Yes, they are all Radar. However, many pilots did not understand how they worked on different frequencies so they did not overlap, how many were not connected, etc.

Also, going into Ararat, most of our radar systems were off and we were flying by the seat of our pants. On the way out, I turned the Radar systems on. I told the pilot that we had been "lit up." Kevin did not like that terminology but some pilots did use those words. In fact, terminology would even differ from squadron to squadron just like local dialects or a family's use of certain words.

Rex Geissler: Why did Kevin or Walt Brown discover that the aircraft carrier Independence was in Norfolk, Virginia when you claimed that you were in the Mediterranean?

Al Shappell: Each ship was typically out to sea for nine months and then returned to its home port for three months while other carriers rotated in its place. As I stated before, my average assignment was 3-5 days on each carrier. Since I never received a leave, I had simply been transferred to other carriers while the Independence was off watch. Although there was no animosity between Kevin and myself, I did feel like his style was similar to other military officers who sometimes are a little close-minded. When we were trained in the military, we were trained that there was typically one way to do things. Some people transfer that into their thinking. If a new idea or concept does not fit into their box of "the way it ought to be according to the way I was taught," then the other person is labeled unreliable and wrong. Although I told him I was based on the Independence, I did not volunteer the information that I had been constantly transferred to other carriers in the Mediterranean during the time it went to port so I did not correct his assumption that I was still on the Independence.

Rex Geissler: It has also been alleged that there is no way to fit the Ark behind the rock you specified on Mount Ararat. Can you explain that?

Al Shappell: I was never shown any photos that I thought was the actual outcropping of rock so I don't think that statement is fair to say. I also say that because if you see the rock, you will probably also see the object. It should be remembered that I sketched the rock and the object in the drawings but never identified the rock specifically in the photos. Perhaps snow and ice had covered the object when the researcher photos were taken. In fact, this is why I think that the satellite spotted the black structure to begin with. The satellite had gone over the same area numerous times but never picked up this object. The satellite may have noticed it when the ice cap receded.

The Shappell incident sounds amazingly similar to the David Montgomery intelligence agency account recounted in 1989 during Montgomery's trip to Ararat. Note that Shappell's drawing appears very much like Ed Behling's 1973 Ark description one year earlier and like the Armenian man's sketch from about 1973 (Robin Simmon's chapter). It also may be the same object as the box-like structure in the 1973 Dr. Lawrence Hewitt/Ray Anderson slide and the 1989 Ahmet Arslan/Don Shockey/Robin Simmons photograph. The 1973 photos and connections are especially important because of the one-year differential in the sightings. If the weather truly plays a large role in revealing the object, it is possible that the structure is visible for several consecutive warmer years. The reader should also note that since 1974, there have not been any similar sightings (except for possibly General Ralph Havens' Air Force pilots and the Arslan photo in 1989). Once again, perhaps this points to the ice cap deepening in thickness over the object.

Another Shappell drawing shows a trail of debris in the ravine underneath the ledge that the anomaly is sitting on. This matches the trail of debris that Ed Davis (1943) discussed and Satellite Remote Sensing expert George Stephen III (1989) described between the first and the second objects. The reader should also compare the Shappell drawing to the George Hagopian Ark (1900-1908) and George Greene's structure in 1953. Unless some of the witnesses are lying or some are copying other reports, the first portion of the object appears to have a similar structural shape and be located on a similar ledge.

There may also be occasional confusion between sightings of the first object and the second object. Discrepancies may also arise because of the pieces being viewed from different locations. Some of the photos and sketches themselves were in slide format or negatives that have been reproduced. If the slide or negative was accidentally inverted, they will cause an erroneous, backward view of the object which may also be confusing.

U.S. Air Force General Ralph Havens Confirmation of the Structure on Ararat – 1985

Elfred Lee showing paintings to Two-Star Air Force General Havens
Courtesy of Elfred Lee

In 1985, Elfred Lee went to Turkey with Jim Irwin and Eryl Cummings. While they were in Ankara, former astronaut Jim Irwin with the help of the U.S. Ambassador was able to secure a meeting with U.S. Two-Star General Ralph Havens of TUSLOG, the Turkish U.S. Logistical Command. At the U.S. and NATO Defense Installation, Lee showed drawings of alleged Ark sightings to General Havens. When the General saw the George Hagopian drawings he stated, "We've seen that. We have photos of that. Our pilots have photographed that very object. It looks just like that. It is on a ledge. In fact, I was shown two slides of this object at Fort Leavenworth in a presentation for people assigned to Turkey." General Havens told Lee and Irwin that his flyers had seen the similar structure on the north side of Mount Ararat.

When the General checked on the two slides, they were missing from the presentation. Despite not having the slides and after 40 years of Ark study, this confirmation from an American General caused Eryl Cummings to exclaim with tears in his eyes, "This is the *greatest day* in all the years of Ark research!"

One must admit that the confirmation of an American Air Force General about the structure high on the north side of Ararat similar to the Hagopian Ark is intriguing.

"George Jammal" Hoax - 1985-1993 A.D.

From 1985 to 1993, George Jammal and Gerald Larue maintained a hoax that Jammal and a friend were eyewitnesses to the Ark and Ararat. Jammal was used as a purported eyewitness in the 1993 video airing of *The Incredible Discovery of Noah's Ark.*

Jammal originally wrote to creationist Duane Gish that he had searched for the Ark in 1972, 1980 and 1984. In the 1984 trip, he claimed to crawl in a cave on Ararat which turned out to be Noah's Ark. Jammal's companion fell to his death in a crevasse.

With a mixture of profane names for fictitious friends, Jammal continued the practical joke, being interviewed by John Morris, Bill Crouse and others who had their doubts about the veracity of the story.

However, Sun went ahead with the 1993 video including Jammal. The Sun researcher, David Balsiger, accepted Jammal's claims and the hoax was propagated worldwide. Balsiger was accused of discovery bias, token skeptics, misrepresented credentials, misleading statements and sensationalism for profit.[69] CBS attorneys were even notified by Robin Simmons about the Jammal issue prior to the airing but the broadcast went ahead anyway.

Neither Jammal's deceit nor Balsiger's sensationalism should be condoned. However, simply because Jammal and Larue were able to continue this hoax over a period of years and received a national audience does not diminish the possibility that other eyewitnesses could be authentic. On the other hand, it also shows the desperate need for researchers to think more critically, objectively and to not lead those they are "interviewing."

---

[69] Jim Lippard, *Skeptic* (Altadena, CA: Skeptics Society, 1994), vol. 2 no. 3, *Sun Goes Down in Flames: The Jammal Ark Hoax* p. 22-33.

Canadian Ed Crawford - 1987 A.D.

The *Ararat Report* stated that Ed Crawford mad another claim for sighting Noah's Ark. The latitude/longitude grid position is about 3946 9650 and Site-map PvB2C3. This time, though, it was not a ground-based or aerial sighting but based on satellite information. However, the Landsat satellite photo which was used and that was taken on July 13, 1973, located at http://www.vonbora.com, appears to have fresh snow or does not appear to be conditions of high meltback as purported. Also, one can easily see that the lines in the snow are located perfectly at the top and in line with the downward flowing Parrot glacier area. Crawford's area intersects the Abich I and upper Parrot glaciers. One may also note that the American explorer Bob Stuplich in 1974 saw a "dark spot" in the ice near this location as well as it is one of Italian explorer Angelo Palego's three alleged sites.

> An apparently solitary effort was carried out by Rev. Ed Crawford, a Bible Presbyterian minister from Edmonton, Canada. According to his news releases. He is now claiming to have found the location of the Ark with the aid of satellite photos.
>
> The Religious News Service reports that he climbed Ararat in September, but was unable to get to the site.
>
> We did quite a bit of checking on this story. It is our conclusion that his claims are greatly overstated. We feel this principally because Crawford claims his photographs are old *Landsat* photos. We are confident that technology could not produce this kind of information.
>
> We also know the Turkish government was not allowing expeditions on the mountain last summer. We feel he probably climbed the tourist route up the south side. The site he identifies lies somewhat north and east of the summit at about 16,000 ft. It is strange that Crawford did not have a camera!

This account and the 1973 Behling and 1974 Shappell sighting raise some interesting questions. Who thought that 1973 was a "good meltback" year? Why did they think 1973 was a "good meltback" year? What does the meteorological records for 1972, 1973 and 1974 show? On July 13th, 1973, does the Landsat photo simply show new snow or ice cap glaciers as well? New snow on Ararat could easily deceive a person when there really is good meltback from the ice-based glaciers.

Snow Tiger Team - 1988 A.D.

This group of explorers headed by Dr. Charles Willis eliminated the Eastern Plateau of Mount Ararat as a possible resting-place for the Ark by using underground radar sensors to see what was under the ice. Although the Ararat ice cap was discovered to be over 90 feet thick in places, there was no trace of any wood.

American Journalist Bill Crouse - 1989 A.D.

Since American journalist Bill Crouse climbed the Armenian holy mountain of Ararat, he was allowed to view the Echmiadzin Monastery wooden cross forty miles from Ararat in 1989. Crouse states:

Echmiadzin Monastery "Ark Wood" Cross with Corner Missing
which was given to Russia's Catherine the Great 1989
Courtesy of Habib Alajaji and Bill Crouse

They say the Ark relic was brought to Armenia by Saint Jacob in A.D. 318, and finally found its way to the Etchmiadzin Cathedral in A.D. 678, where it has been kept locked in an elaborate silver case since 1698.

I was only the second Westerner this century allowed to view and examine the bejeweled cross up close. The relic looked like petrified wood. It was grayish brown with some dark markings. To me, its size was about 8 inches by 5 inches—it seemed smaller than Wells's estimate. When I noticed one of the corners was broken off, I was told that in the eighteenth century a piece was sent as a gift to Catherine the Great of Russia.

American Scott Van Dyke - 1989 A.D.

Scott Van Dyke from the Houston, Texas-based Mount Ararat Research Foundation succeeded in hiring a professional Turkish mapping company to completely map Mount Ararat with a high-resolution Zeiss mapping camera. Four types of film were used, including infrared. In all, 910 overlapping photos (in stereo pairs) were made, covering approximately 50 square miles and the entire mountain above 10,000 feet. The resolution was so good that sheep on the mountain are clearly visible and Kurdish residents could be seen near their tents. A volcanologist from the Lunar & Planetary Institute in Houston, Texas studied the nine-inch by nine-inch photos and detected a number of objects that could be man made but nothing was concrete. This research is very important because along with the numerous airplane and helicopter flights by researchers around Mount Ararat, it helps show that the alleged Ark is probably not below the ice cap unless it is covered by debris.

Matthew Kneisler studying Scott Van Dyke photos 1999
Courtesy of Jonathan Brisbin

U.S. Remote Sensing Specialist George Stephen III - 1989 A.D.

George Stephen III claimed to be a military-trained remote sensing photo interpreter. Dr. Don Shockey met George Stephen III in a Truth or Consequences, New Mexico restaurant. Stephen told Shockey, Robin Simmons, and George Adams that he was 100% sure there were two man-made, rectangular objects on the upper north glaciers of Ararat. One object is said to be 1,200 feet above the other object and both objects appear to have been joined at one time. This is compelling evidence given that Shockey did not tell Stephen about the Davis sighting in which there were two objects several hundred yards apart. Stephen said that the objects are not metal nor are they rock. Stephen stated that there was 30-70 feet of ice on the structures at different times of the year depending on the weather. Stephen also stated that the structures were not built on the top of the mountain but were placed there somehow. Simmons, Adams and Shockey told Ahmet Arslan about the area. Arslan took a photo of a possible object that needs to be scrutinized more closely before making any determination. Carl Baugh referred to this location as the Shockey Site but it may be more aptly named the Stephen/Shockey/Simmons/Adams/Arslan Site since they were all involved in this site. To see maps of the George Stephen III site in the upper Abich II area, please refer to the Robin Simmons chapter.

I looked at the mountain from the 10,000-foot altitude to the top. I'm a hundred percent sure there's two man-made objects up there on the north side of the mountain above the 13,000-foot elevation. What amazes me is a structure at this altitude. The terrain is just treacherous! And the amount of ice on it...

It's definitely not a military object or device because it couldn't be used since it's under ice almost all the time.

The process I use is a Photo Analysis Material Spectra (PAMS). We pull up a photo from a satellite, I can't tell you which one, but it's available. The photograph is put into one of our own processes which is a laser process that takes a spectra reading. We work with 64 different shades of *every* color. Each one of those shades means something that is going on with that anomaly or target. Then we use "perforation" in which we take "plugs" out of that area. In other words, instead of looking for the needle in the haystack, we remove the haystack. We perforate the area and pull those plugs until we come up with an "image" of whatever is in the target area.

On that mountain (Ararat) is the rectangular shape of two man-made organic objects. One above the other. Looks like maybe 1,200-foot difference. Both objects look like they were joined at one time because there's a spectral trail going down from one to the other. They're sitting in a fault on a ledge. The upper one is hanging. They are both in a glacier. Last time I looked there was about 70 foot of ice over the upper object. The lower one I can't tell because it's at too steep of an angle.

I can't tell you what it's made of, but it's not metal and it's not rock. It would have to be organic, perhaps wood. It's ancient but I'm not saying it's the Ark because I haven't "seen" it. All I can say is that I'm a hundred percent sure it's a man-made object. But for somebody to take something up there, to haul it up there, to build a thing of this size would be an amazing feet.

The most peculiar thing about this anomaly is that there are no trails to it that indicate it was constructed on this site. I don't know if this is the original location of this object. Maybe it's been raised up from a lower elevation. Or maybe it was higher and slid down throughout the centuries. It's almost like it crashed or landed there...

Perhaps this glacier melts back and this object being hollow, up there on this ledge like it is, with thousands of tons of ice in it and around it, breaks off and takes part of it on down the canyon.

Personally, I don't believe in Noah's Ark. And frankly, I've no idea what it is.[70]

It is very interesting that Stephen stated the objects did not originate in that spot on Mount Ararat but were "raised up from a lower elevation...It's almost like to crashed or landed there." Of course, this is what one would expect of Noah's Ark and a worldwide flood.

Tom Pickett has worked in the Remote Sensing field for 25 years. Tom is a former Lockheed Martin Skunk Works employee. Currently, Tom is the Remote Sensing Team Lead for the ARP expedition to locate Noah's Ark. He analyzed George Stephens' account and stated the following.

I find the George Stephen III account fascinating and to be an excellent technical description of an eye witness Ark sighting. I can find nothing flawed in his account. Although I cannot say it is true, I am willing to consider its importance in the search for Noah's Ark. As part of our remote sensing efforts, we plan to try to duplicate what Stephen saw.

"On that mountain (Ararat) is the rectangular shape of two man-made organic objects. One above the other. Looks like maybe 1,200-foot difference. Both objects look like they were joined at one time because there's a spectral trail going down from one to the other. They're sitting in a fault on a ledge. The upper one is hanging. They are both in a glacier. Last time I looked there was about 70 foot of ice over the upper object."

---

[70] George Stephen III quote received while Robin Simmons and George Adams were filming the video *Riddle of Ararat*.

One of the problems in looking for Noah's Ark is the possibility that it could be invisible to the naked eye. Mount Ararat is a mountain of volcanic origin. If the mountain erupted in the past after the Ark landed, it could have deposited a layer (or multiple layers) of ash on it. This would cause the Ark to appear to be camouflaged (as well as to protect it from decomposing). If this were the case, it would be very difficult to locate the Ark with the naked eye. However, remote sensor systems could "see" the Ark.

Our plan is to use a hyperspectral camera (HSI) to attempt to find this spectral trail that Stephen speaks of. If the Ark did break in half and one of the sections moved down hill, it would have deposited a trail as pieces which would have been split loose from inside the Ark. We know the location of where Stephen sighted the Ark (according to information he has supplied to Robin Simmons and Don Shockey). We also plan to use a thermal IR camera that will measure the heat radiated from different objects on the mountain (an Ark structure would radiate much differently than a rock, thus yielding different temperature characteristics. A Synthetic Aperture Radar (SAR) will be used for ice penetration. This will allow us to look under the ice to some extent.[71]

George Stephen III was also used as a remote-sensing source to supposedly identify the alleged location of Israel's crossing of the Red Sea in the book *The Gold of Exodus*. Although Stephen's statement is tantalizing and may be the best evidence to date of a specific Ark location, it should be readily stated that there is absolutely no proof to back up his statement. Stephen has been asked numerous times for proof. He has been unable to provide it because the information is supposedly classified. Until the site is studied in more detail or other satellite/plane/helicopter remote sensing information and qualified remote-sensing experts come forward to back him up with actual data, Stephen's tantalizing statement will remain simply that.

In regard to the Stephen site location, Doris Bowers confirms that some researchers believe that because of the eyewitness sightings, the Ark would have to be above the Ahora Gorge since that section of the mountain has experienced tremendous destruction, the last time in the 1840 incident. Unless the Ark had fallen into the Gorge since 1840 or was buried in the Gorge, a more likely scenario would be the eyewitnesses were above the Gorge which could correspond to the Stephen site. Based on the Stephen information given to Shockey and Simmons, the following is Shockey's words about the 1989 expedition with Simmons and Arslan.

---

[71] Tom Pickett statement made to Rex Geissler June 14th, 1999.

We've been given new information about the possible real locations of the Ark on Mount Ararat. Through a meeting with a government official who analyzes information, he gave us some information on two objects located in the ice cap high on the northeast side of Mount Ararat. He told us the depth, how far apart they were, and the size. He described it as rectangular with one piece being 1,000 feet below the other.

In 1989 I went to Turkey on my second trip to Mount Ararat. We hired two Turkish guides and climbed the mountain. Since Americans weren't allowed to go around to the north side we sent them. I marked for them a map exactly where the satellite information said to look.

The Turks went, and one of them [Dr. Ahmet Ali Arslan], took a photograph from a distance and came back all excited and said, "It's a coop. It looks like a chicken coop. There's something man-made there and I think it's the Ark...[72] It was something that shouldn't be there—just a few thousand feet below the summit.

It almost looked like kind of a captain's cabin. You could look in and see beams and things like that. I immediately took my camera and shot three pictures—one wide-angle, one regular, and one close-up. In the pictures you can see flat beams and such, in what appears to definitely be a man-made structure.

My belief is that what I saw and what is in the photographs I took was without question Noah's Ark.[73]

It is interesting to note that Ahmet appeared to be shocked that this Ark-like structure was there. Arslan says that he has been on the mountain close to sixty times and never noticed this structure in the upper Abich II, probably because of the good meltback in 1989. Although the Arslan photo does not show a lot of the object's exposure on top, it would be very interesting to look at the Scott Van Dyke high resolution photograph of the same area which was taken within a couple weeks from the shooting of the Arslan photo.

American David Montgomery - 1989 A.D.

Two days before leaving for Mount Ararat with B.J. Corbin and other explorers, a wealthy family friend who was in the intelligence community and shook the hands of U.S. Presidents approached David Montgomery. He told Montgomery that he had read a classified report about a satellite which went off course in the early to mid 1970s. The satellite mapped the Mount Ararat region and observed a structure on top. According to the intelligence source who had read the classified report, a National Security meeting was called

---

[72] Charles E. Sellier & David W. Balsiger, *The Incredible Discovery of Noah's Ark* (New York: Dell Publishing, 1995), p. 247-248.
[73] Ibid., p. 307.

since the American officials were concerned that the location might be a new Russian missile installation or other Russian construction.

A plane was immediately sent to Mount Ararat to photograph the structure. The plane photographed the site and the Americans allegedly identified the structure as Noah's Ark but because of the concern of Holy Wars, etc. the files were simply kept classified. The friend warned David to be careful because whoever found the Ark might be killed for discovering it. The intelligence person told Montgomery that if he persisted in searching, to look for the object in multiple pieces because it was broken and at least one portion was wedged in a crevasse under ice. Again, the anonymity of intelligence agency source casts questions on the account's credibility. However, it is interesting that the early 1970s keep popping up with this similarity of the U.S. Navy Al Shappell Top Secret flight based on an intelligence agency sighting from a satellite as well as the SR-71 account.

Italian Angelo Palego - 1990 A.D.

Italian researcher Angelo Palego claimed to see the outline of the Ark under ice on Mount Ararat. He alleged that the Ark has split into three pieces traveling different directions down the ice cap. Parts of his assertions are dependent upon Fernand Navarra, whose experience also may be problematic. Palego produced a small booklet *The Way I Found Noah's Ark* about his research that is not convincing and appears premature at best. Interestingly, one of his objects appears to be a continuation or source of Navarra's original discovery on or near Ed Crawford's upper Parrot Glacier and Abich I site. This area is also where American explorer Bob Stuplich and Turkish guide Gazi saw a "black spot" in 1974, a "good meltback" year.

1990s A.D.

Permission to climb the mountain has been denied every year in the 1990s up to 1999. Permission for helicopter flights was given in 1990, which is where the *Visions of Ararat* video was created by George Adams and Robin Simmons. There were a couple August 1999 permits that had yet to be accepted or denied. Those planning to go to Ararat in 1999 included the Ark Research Project for flying a helicopter or remote sensing plane to identify objects under the ice. Ahmet Arslan who is still interested in the upper Abich II area where he took the 1989 photo of the upper Stephen Site object, and the Tom Hayek/Palego expedition to film the search for Noah's Ark on Mount Ararat. Dr. Robert Ballard (Titanic) who heads the Institute of Exploration of Massachusetts Institute of Technology has arrived Turkey to search for Noah's Flood. He mentioned Noah's Ark by the thesis of Bill Ryan/Walter Pittman from Columbia Univ. Dr. Ballard said that this research is made with the sponsorships of the National Geographic Society and J.M. Kaplan Foundation. Some of Ballard's group was reportedly in Dogubayazit.

SUMMARY OF EYEWITNESSES

By Rex Geissler

Summary of Eye Witness Accounts

Year	Account	Location	In Ice	Shape	Valley/Depression	Catwalk	Ledge	Cliff	Broken	Water
1856	Haji Yearam	Mt. Ararat a little down from summit	Yes	Box/barge	Yes		Yes	Yes		Lake spills into river
1883	Turkish Commission	Mt. Ararat foot of glacier	Yes	Box/barge	Yes					
1887	John Nouri	Mt. Ararat narrow plateau almost on the summit								
1890-1915	Arthur Chuchian	Mt. Ararat up goat path	Yes							Waterfall spills over ledge
1900-1908	George Hagopian	Mt. Ararat top on blue rock	Yes	Box/barge			Yes	Yes	No	
1916	Turkish Soldiers	Mt. Ararat top of Mt. Cudi	Yes							
1917-1918	Russian Soldiers		Yes	Box/barge					Yes	
1916	USAF Guilford Officer	Mt. Ararat saddle	Yes	Submarine	Yes					
1920	Russian Major Jasper Maskelyn	Mt. Ararat about 14,000 ft.	Yes		Yes					
1935-1945	Bertha Davis	Mt. Ararat	Yes	Box/barge						
1940-1941	WWII "Aussie" R. Taylor/Nice/Tibbets	Mt. Ararat basin next to hogback ridge	Yes	Box/barge	Yes		Yes	Yes		Pool of water may spill over
1942	US Navy Machinist Mate Ray Lubeck	Mt. Ararat on Russian/Turkish Border	No	Box/Points	Yes		Yes		No	Water run off area
1943	US Army Sergeant Ed Davis	Mt. Ararat north side on blue rock or Zagros	Yes	Box/barge	Yes		Yes		Yes	Water cascading out of ark
1943	US Air Force Sergeant Vince Will	Mt. Ararat north side about 14,500 ft.	Yes	Box/barge	Yes		Yes			
1948	US Army AF Corporal Lester Walton	Mt. Ararat on Russian/Turkish Border	Yes	Box/barge			Yes			
1953	US Navy Photographer Andy Anderson	Mt. Ararat on Russian/Turkish Border	Yes	Box/barge	Yes		Yes			
1953	US Navy Photographer William Todd	Mt. Ararat above Ahora Gorge 14,500-16,000 ft.	Yes	Box/barge		Yes	Yes			
1959	George Greene	Mt. Ararat on Russian/Turkish Border	Yes	Box/barge	Yes, fault		Yes			
1969	US AF Captain Gregor Schwinghammer	Mt. Ararat on Russian/Turkish Border	Yes	Box/barge	Yes, horseshoe		Yes			
1968	David Duckworth	Mt. Ararat	Yes	Box/Points			Yes			
1968-1972	US Air Force Colonel Walter Hunter	Mountain with glaciers	Yes	Box/Points			Yes			
1973	US Air Force Personnel Ed Behling	Mt. Ararat on Russian/Turkish Border	Yes	Box/barge	Yes, horseshoe		Yes			
1974	US Navy Lieutenant JG Al Shappell	Mt. Ararat top of Ahora Gorge 14,500-16,000 ft.	Yes	Box/barge	Yes		Yes			
1985	US Air Force/NATO General Ralph Havens	Mt. Ararat above Ahora Gorge near cliff	Yes	Box/barge	Yes		Yes			
1989	US Military Pi George Stephen III	Mt. Ararat Abich II fault 15,000-16,000 ft.	Yes	Box/barge	Yes, fault		Yes			Yes

Year	Account	Length	Width	Height	Burnt Altar	Catwalk	Debris	Pinnacles	Levels	Cages
1856	Haji Yearam					Knee high				Yes
1883	Turkish Commission	900 ft.		40-80 ft.	Yes			Yes		Yes
1887	John Nouri	40-60 ft.		100 ft.						
1890-1915	Arthur Chuchian							Yes		
1900-1908	George Hagopian	1000 ft.	600 ft.	40 ft.						
1916	Turkish Soldiers	450 ft.								
1917-1918	Russian Soldiers	500 ft.	83 ft.	60 ft.	Yes		Door		3	Yes
1920	USAF Guilford Officer	400+ ft.								
1920	Russian Major Jasper Maskelyn	400+ ft.		Yes	Yes	Yes, windows			3	
1935-1945	Bertha Davis									
1940-1941	WWII "Aussie" R. Taylor/Nice/Tibbets	400+ ft.		60 ft.		6-8 ft. high, 20 ft. wide	No		3	
1942	US Navy Machinist Mate Ray Lubeck	200 ft.	60-100 ft.	60-100 ft.		20 ft. wide, knee high	Yes		3-4	Yes
1943	US Army Sergeant Ed Davis	40-50 ft.	45-50 ft.	75 ft.		Yes				Yes
1945	US Air Force Sergeant Vince Will	15 ft.								
1948	US Army AF Corporal Lester Walton									
1953	US Navy Personnel Andy Anderson	35 ft.	75 ft.	Yes/45 ft.		Yes			3	Yes
1953	George Greene									
1959	US AF Captain Gregor Schwinghammer	450 ft.	60-70 ft.	6 ft. high			Yes		2+	Yes
1968	David Duckworth	480 ft.					Yes			
1973	US Air Force Personnel Ed Behling		8-3 ft. high	8-3 ft. high						
1974	US Navy Lieutenant JG Al Shappell	160-200 ft.								Yes
1985	US Air Force/NATO General Ralph Havens	300 ft.	100-200 ft.	40-50 ft.		Yes				
1989	US Military Pi George Stephen III						Yes			

HISTORICAL RESEARCH STILL NEEDED

By Rex Geissler

If you have a photograph that shows Mount Ararat or other interesting areas, let us know by contacting us at research@greatcommission.com. Also, most people do not have the "primary objective" knowledge of access to Remote Sensing technology via flying a plane, helicopter or satellite around 17,000-foot Mount Ararat to specifically identify a possible location. If you still want to help, you can help research historical topics such as those missing items listed below. Please let us know so that we can coordinate the activities and refer the following topics to the details in the previous appendix to get started.

1) There is an alleged black and white Russian silent film showing 50 Russian soldiers marching past Noah's Ark on the top of Mount Ararat that is missing. The film clip was shown to 30 service men on Midway Island in World War II between March and November of 1942, probably in April. Ray Lubeck was in the audience of the 30 U.S. Navy, Marines and Air Force servicemen. The film clip was only about 30 seconds to several minutes long and had an American announcer documenting the Russian campaign to fight the Turks and passing Noah's Ark on Mount Ararat on the way. The Russian uniforms appeared to be World War I vintage and the silent nature of the film might corroborate that early date.

2) There are allegedly missing U.S. Navy photographs from the William Todd Turkish mapping expedition between 1953-1955. Contact Navy airmen Uncle Joe Gorsky, Ensign Glacow, Mr. Trent and Mr. Finkbiner or Navy Hydrographic Office in Washington, D.C. or Army Map Service to find and analyze the photos. Todd says that since they crossed the borders of several countries up to 300 miles, these photographs were classified. The following map which Ed Crawford used may be the one that Todd helped create, *The Topographical Map of Reference*, Title: Igdir, 1952, U.S. Army, No. NJ38-2, Series K502, Edition 1.

3) There are at least two missing *Stars and Stripes* issues that supposedly have Noah's Ark photos in them. At least one of the

photos is on the front cover. Both issues were distributed in Europe or North Africa around 1943-1945.

4) If George Stephen III is correct with his Satellite Remote Sensing view of the two structures being under the ice cap near the Abich II glacier between 15,000 and 16,000 feet, then perhaps the weather occasionally allows the horseshoe-shaped valley to be uncovered of ice and the structure becomes visible. Since the researchers have been concentrating looking in the Ahora Gorge below the Abich II glacier and the photos of the ice cap recently show more snow and ice in this area, this might explain why the researchers have not been able to see the structure since 1973. It would be helpful to have photos (possibly aerial) of the Abich II glacier disruption area from 1953 (William Todd and George Greene), 1973-1974 (Ed Behling, Dr. Lawrence Hewitt, Al Shappell) or other years when the ice meltback might have been less. The 1973 Dr. Lawrence Hewitt/Ray Anderson slide appears to show this object more distinctly than current photos as if the meltback were better although it has fresh snow on it as does the 1989 Ahmet Arslan/Don Shockey/Robin Simmons photo. It is interesting to note that Ahmet appeared to be shocked that this Ark-like structure was there. Arslan says that he has been on the mountain close to sixty times and never noticed this in the upper Abich II, probably because of the good meltback in 1989. Although the Arslan photo does not show a lot of the object's exposure on top, it would be very interesting to look at the Scott Van Dyke high resolution photograph of the same area which was taken within a couple weeks from the shooting of the Arslan photo.

5) Find "Casbeen" the village that Ed Davis claimed to have gone to on the way to Mount Ararat, which is probably on the Iranian border with either Russia or Iraq. This may point to the mountain that Davis climbed as Mount Ararat. "A few days later, we get up early and Badi, Abas and I drive down along the border as far as Casbeen until we get to his little village. This was the settlement I had helped them get water. We spend the night there... At dawn the next day, we reach the foothills of Ararat and arrive at another primitive village. Abas tells me the name of the village means 'Where Noah Planted The Vine.' I see grapevines so big at their trunk you can't reach around them. Very, very old."

6) In 1989, Robin Simmons and Dr. Don Shockey talked with an Iranian man near Mount Ararat. Since then, Dr. Shockey has kept in correspondence with the man. The man stated that there was a large photo of Turkey's Mount Ararat with Noah's Ark exposed in one of the main hallways of a Teheran museum from at least the 1970's through the 1980's if not still there now. Bob Cornuke checked at the

main archaeological museum in Teheran but there was no photo although the supposed picture could be in another museum.

7) There are no known ancient writings that undeniably refer to modern-day Mount Ararat/Lesser Ararat (biblical "mountains of Ararat") as the final resting-place of Noah's Ark. Since few Armenian writings have been translated into English, it is difficult to know whether there is any ancient Armenian references or not. Again, this is important because pre-1300 A.D. Noah's Ark sources do not definitively point toward today's Mount Ararat as the correct mountain for the landing.

8) The supposed deathbed confession obituary of the London scientist who threatened Haji Yearam and his father if he told anyone about finding the Ark has never been located. It was supposedly in a 1918 Brockton, Mass. newspaper, possibly in November at the end of W.W.I up to 1922. It was probably reprinted in other newspapers and would be an original story in a London paper.

9) The original press release of the Turkish commissioners report about discovering the Ark is missing. In Ankara, they supposedly reported the discovery of the Ark after evaluating the damage from a May 2, 1883 earthquake which buried mountain villages with rock and ice. Turkish commissioners and British Captain Gascoyne (an English attaché of the British Embassy) climbed the mountain to look at the damage. The possibly later version appeared in the London *Prophetic Messenger.*

10) The alleged photos and documentation of the Czar's army expedition to the Ark are missing. Also, the Russian Armanaff photos have been missing since he died.

11) There are a host of purported Air Force U2, SR-71 and other photographs that should be researched. Unfortunately it is difficult to know where to begin unless you have a precise date, service, flight, storage location and photo location available.

12) The 1953 George Greene photos have been missing since he was murdered in South America.

13) The alleged 1968 Smithsonian Noah's Ark photos and artifacts are missing. Locate David Duckworth's supervisor, Dr. Albert Merrick (Myrick?) 1969-1974 Vertebrate Paleontology Wing. Find out what else is stored in the Smithsonian climate-controlled Suitland, Maryland warehouse and other locations.

14) The Fort Leavenworth slides of the Ararat structure that two-star Air Force General Ralph Havens was shown in preparation for service in Turkey have been missing since 1985.

15) The exact location of the St. Jacob Monastery is unknown. It would be interesting to excavate the St. Jacob monastery in Ahora at the foot of Mount Ararat since Dr. Friedrich Parrot claimed there were

artifacts from Noah's Ark in the monastery. Since the 1840 A.D. earthquake which killed most of the inhabitants and covered the village with rock, the exact location of the monastery has been lost. In 1983, Doris Bowers and the Irwin team was told that the monastery foundations were visible. They attempted to go to the location with Irwin's group but landslides narrowly missed them and they decided to turn back. Ahmet Arslan says that he knows the location as well.

16) If it is a deep desire to help out financially with the Ark Research Project efforts which B.J. Corbin, John McIntosh and others are involved in, then send your tax deductible contribution to Ark Research Project, PO Box 4312, Lynchburg, VA 24502.

THE U.S. GOVERNMENT AND NOAH'S ARK

By Kevin Kluetz[1]

This article has more details and context at Kevin's website footnoted below.

Many in the Ark research community have been skeptical of U.S. government top-secret organizations, believing that the government is hiding photographic evidence of Noah's Ark. This belief is unreasonable, since the U.S. government has no security reason to withhold photographs of the Ark, and since many individuals with top secret clearances are Christians and Jews who would probably have a difficult time keeping such information secret. In 1995, I contacted several public affairs organizations of U.S. government top secret agencies. None claimed to have any photographic or any other type of evidence of the Ark. The Defense Intelligence Agency claimed to have a number of aerial photographs of anomalies on Mount Ararat. I looked at two of these "Ararat anomaly" photographs and saw only what appeared to be rocks and cliff-overhangs. One public affairs representative told me that he wished that he did have photographs of the Ark so that he could give them to the public and his agency would no longer have to deal with requests from Ark researchers.

I searched for the roots of the thought that the U.S. government has photographs of Noah's Ark and found that this thought probably originated in the early 1970's when a man working on a U.S. government top secret contract was given authorization to search for Noah's Ark on Mount Ararat. I tracked this man down and spoke with him. I will not release his name, but I will say that he was a former military officer who had left the U.S. military and then worked on this contract. I'll call him "Secret". He could not say how he searched for the Ark, but he did say that he found nothing on Mount Ararat except rocks. He suggested that if the Ark is on Mount Ararat, that it could only be located under the ice cap, completely buried. I asked him about the file that Ms. Cherry had seen on Roland Inlow's desk, labeled "Noah's Ark." "Secret" said that that file was probably his file (the file he had compiled). I asked him whether a navy flier had taken any pictures for him,

---

[1] Kevin Kluetz has more information about the search for Noah's Ark and other issues at http://www.geocities.com/Athens/Parthenon/3021

and I briefly related the story of "Navy" (above in the "eyewitness" appendix). "Secret" said, "No."

In late 1997 or early 1998, the Washington Times printed an article about Noah's Ark research performed by a man named Porcher Taylor, a lawyer who has been working for years to get the U.S. government to release any photographs related to anomalies on Mount Ararat. The U.S. government has been slow to release such photographs, but Porcher's relentless requests have resulted in a number of photographs being released. These photographs generally show pictures of anomalies on Mount Ararat that appear to be rocks or ledges. The government has not yet declassified many of its top-secret photographs, however, probably to keep enemies of the United States from learning the quality of U.S. spy technology and/or intelligence-gathering capabilities. Porcher became interested in Noah's Ark research in the 1970's when he heard rumors that the U.S. launched a secret search for the Ark (that secret search is discussed in the previous paragraph). I spoke with Porcher at least twice in the summer of 1995. In our last conversation, I suggested to him that he contact "Secret", the former contract employee mentioned in the previous paragraph. I don't know whether Porcher did this.

In summary, I am convinced that the U.S. government has no photographs of Noah's Ark, has no reason to hide such photographs, but that the U.S. government would release such photographs if it had them. The rumors that the U.S. government has secret photographs of the Ark probably began in the early 1970's, when the U.S. unsuccessfully searched for the Ark.

Publisher's Note:

Many U.S. government officials and workers are normal, middle-class Americans. They have a job to do just like everyone else. Sometimes, these elaborate schemes attributed to the government in some conspiracy theories show overconfidence in how smoothly the political and military entities really work. Also, these jobs have a turnover rate just like regular companies, which makes it difficult to have an accurate, continuous view of governmental affairs and history. This is especially true in the military where Armed Forces personnel are physically moved constantly and entire bases are even shut down.

It is possible that there might be photographic evidence that has been archived and will never be found. In order to properly request photographic evidence from the military, the exact source, dates, and mission number are needed. There must be thousands of government information repositories around the earth with no global search engine which further complicates the possibility of finding any alleged photographs.

WHAT IF NOAH'S ARK IS FOUND OR NOT FOUND?

By Rex Geissler

Does the fruitless search to date for Noah's Ark diminish the need to do more research on the subject? No, of course not. People searched many years before finding hundreds of historical and biblical sites such as Troy, Jericho, etc. Just because Noah's Ark has not been found does not mean that it never existed. There is also the possibility today that the Ark might be in a recognizable but dilapidated state.

In fact, it would be interesting to evaluate how people would react if Noah's Ark was found or if it was not found on Mount Ararat. Would such an Ark discovery further separate Bible believers from non-believers as both camps might get further entrenched in their views? Here are some thoughts to consider on the matter.

What if Noah's Ark is shown to not be on Mount Ararat?

1. The young-earth creationists and Ark explorers will search for the Ark on other mountains within Turkey, Iran (primarily because of the Ed Davis testimony and Pierre Daniel Huet map) and throughout the historic and biblical "mountains of Ararat."
2. Some young-earth creationists will revert to old-earth views but might still reject evolution.
3. Skeptics of the Bible will press their case and scoff at young-earth creationists.
4. The alleged eyewitnesses of Noah's Ark (the best evidence of the Ark's existence thus far) will be scrutinized even more. More theories will arise as to what the eyewitnesses "really" saw.
5. The Turkish, American and other governments might suppress any information that they currently know about the supposed structure.

What if Noah's Ark is discovered?

1. The first question is how could a person conclusively prove that a boat or barge-like structure on a mountain was Noah's Ark?
2. Samples of the structure will be immediately submitted for Carbon-14 testing and other high-tech date testing techniques to multiple respected institutions.

3. The explorers will attempt to make scientific information known to convince people that the structure is not a hoax or mistake (as in the past) and that this Ark is the real McCoy. Without many trained archaeologists and scientists on their teams, the documentation quality may be poor and rushed. Because of the biblical and religious ramifications, the announcements and documentation may also be rushed and unprofessional.

4. Bible believers will push with renewed fervor their case that the Bible is historically accurate even to the earliest chapters.

5. Because there have been so many false alarms of claimed discoveries of Noah's Ark in the past, more documentation, details and proof will be demanded by the scientific world.

6. Since many of the explorers tend to be spiritually motivated, an unbiased on-site international expedition will be required to document the artifact. Because of climatic, political and security conditions, it will take years or decades to get this team to the site to properly document it. Then the analysis and release of the official document will take even longer while "press leaks" occur.

7. The Turkish government will possibly decide what direction to push this archaeological site, possibly toward tourism or else toward suppression. If governments or institutions attempted to suppress the information, Bible believers, the press and other rights activists would be up in arms about their lack of openness and truthfulness.

8. Some of those people who have been burned by previous premature announcements will disregard this announcement without any serious investigation.

9. Some researchers and opportunists will attempt to make money off the discovery through books, appearances, videos, tapes, photos, real or fake pieces of the structure, and real or fake rocks from the structure or from Mount Ararat.

10. If one explorer or group finds the Ark, others may begin jockeying to announce it in a more scientifically or financially opportune time revealing an unhealthy desire for money or fame. To not be self-serving in the announcement, there will need to be much collaboration, cooperation and trust between the explorers and a full, free disclosure of all information including photos and other documentation, preferably on a Website for worldwide access.

11. The researchers and other Bible believers will start mixing religious and scientific views as well as accusations against the scientific world. Critics in the academic and scientific world will seize upon the sensational pseudo-scientific statements to promote their view of the researchers' bias and lack of formal scientific training and documentation.

12. Life for most people will not change as stated in Matthew 24:35-42.

13. It might affect the world social and political systems in that all people would be descended from one ancestor Noah and would all be family members.

14. The traditional view of the geologic sedimentary rock layers and the time scale involved will be challenged. Instead of millions of years for these layers to be formed, young-earth creationists will push harder than ever for the biblical global cataclysmic flood. This might imply that much of the sedimentary rock record could have been created within the one-year flood period. This would challenge many aspects of evolutionary theory, including the interpretation of the fossil record, long geologic ages, etc. The potential for rewriting some of the world's geology textbooks might exist.

15. Some scientific, academic or anti-Bible individuals will immediately propose alternative explanations for the structure such as:

   A. The structure may appear to be a seaworthy barge but it is not Noah's Ark. How can it ever be proven that it is Noah's Ark?

   B. Even if a person assumes that the structure is Noah's Ark, how can one prove that there was a worldwide flood which supposedly created most or all of the sedimentary layers? Mount Ararat is a young mountain and is probably of post-"flood" origin so the Ark could have been pushed up with the mountain from a lower flood-originating elevation consistent with regional floods.

   C. Since the structure appears to be petrified wood, the structure is simply another rock formation that researches mistook for Noah's Ark as in the past. Also, ancient wood may have been substituted in the age tests as has been alleged with Navarra's wood.

16. Some people basing their religious convictions on scientific and evolutionary views rather than the Bible will get off the fence and begin believing the Bible and perhaps start following the Bible.

Although it is interesting to play these "What if?" games, until the opportunities arise to rule out possible locations or identify a possible object, people will keep waiting and asking questions. In the meantime, since most explorers already have a search plan, they should also take note and make sure they have a well thought-out plan in the case that a discovery might occur.

BIBLIOGRAPHY

Many of the books were compiled by Bill Crouse in *Ararat Report #22*

Suggested Reading (Note that most of the reference books are out of print but can be found through Interlibrary Loan or Rare Book Stores)

Bailey, Lloyd R., *Noah—the Person and the Story in History and Tradition*, (Columbia, SC: University of South Carolina Press, 1989).

Bailey, Lloyd R., *Where is Noah's Ark?* (Nashville, TN; Abingdon, 1978).

Baring-Gould, S. *Legends of the Patriarchs and Prophets* (New York, NY; Hurst, no date).

Bell, Gertrude, *Amurath to Amurath* (London; William Heinemann, 1911; MacMillan, 2nd Edition, 1924).

Berlitz, Charles, *Doomsday 1999 A.D.*, (Garden City, NY: Doubleday, 1981).

Berlitz, Charles, *The Lost Ship of Noah* (New York: G .P. Putnam's Sons, 1987).

Bright, Richard, *The Ark, A Reality?* (Guilderland, NY: Ranger Assoc., 1989).

Brown, Walt, *In The Beginning*. 6th Edition (Phoenix, AZ: Center for Scientific Creation, 1995).

Bryce, James, *Armenia and Mount Ararat* (London: MacMillan, 1878).

Bryce, James, *Transcaucasia and Ararat*, 4th Edition (London: MacMillan, 1877).

Budge, E. A. Wallis, *The Babylonian Story of the Deluge* (London: 1920).

Bueler, William, *Mountains of the World: A Handbook for Climbers and Hikers* (Seattle, WA: The Mountaineers, 1970).

Burdick, Clifford L., *The Geological, Glaciological and Botanical Reports Taken During the 1964 and 1966 Expeditions to Eastern Turkey and Mount Ararat*. Edited by Lawrence Hewitt (New York: The Archaeological Research Foundation, 1967).

Burney, Charles and Lang, David Marshall, *The Peoples of the Hills*. (New York: Praeger, 1972).

Chantre, Madame B., *A Travers L' Armenie Russe* (Paris: Librairie hachetteet, c. 1893). (French but interesting photos)

Church, J.R., *I Saw Noah's Ark* (Oklahoma City: Prophecy in the News, 1983). Radio interview with eyewitness Ed Behling.

Coan, Frederick B., *Yesterdays in Persia and Kurdistan* (Claremont, CA: Saunders Studio Press, 1939). (Chapter XVI)

Crouse, Bill, (*Ararat Report*. Richardson, TX: Christian Information Ministries, 1986-1993). (Newsletter)

Cummings, Violet M., *Has Anybody Really Seen Noah's Ark?* (San Diego: Creation-Life Publishers, 1982).

Cummings, Violet M., *Noah's Ark: Fable or Fact* (San Diego: Creation-Science Research Center, 1972).

Cummings, Violet M., *Full Circle: From the Twin Peaks of Karada To Noah's Ark* (By the author, no date).

Dodwell, Christina, *A Traveler on HorseBack in Eastern Turkey and Iran* (New York: Walker Publishing Co., 1989).

Euro Map, *Eastern Turkey GeoCenter Euro Map*. Stuttgart, (Germany: American Map Corp., 1993).

Fasold, David, *The Ark of Noah* (New York: Winwood Press, 1988).

Freely, John, *The Companion Guide to Turkey* (Englewood Cliffs, NJ: Prentice-Hall, Inc., 1984). (See Chapter 26)

Gates, Bill, *Microsoft Encarta Visual Globe 99* (Redmond, WA: Microsoft, 1998). (Mapping software)

Haxthausen, Baron Von, *Transcaucasia* (London: Chapman and Hall, 1854).

Humberd, R. I., (*Noah's Ark*. 5th Edition (Flora, IN: R. I. Humberd, no date).

Irwin, James B. with Unger, Monte, *More Than An Ark On Ararat*. (Nashville: Broadman Press, 1985).

Katz, Robert, *The Spoils of Ararat* (Boston: Houghton Mifflin Co., 1978). (A novel about the search for Noah's Ark)

Kite, L. Patricia, *Noah's Ark* (Minneapolis, MN: Greenhaven Press Inc., 1989).

Kurkjian, V., *A History of Armenia* (Amenian General Benevolent Union, 1959).

Lahaye, Tim and Morris, John, *The Ark On Ararat* (Nashville, Thomas Nelson, Inc., 1976).

LaRue, Bart, Noah's Ark Video.

Lynch, H. F. B., *Armenia:Travels and Studies*. 2 vols. (London: Longmans, Green and Co., 1901).

Meyer, Nathan M., *Noah's Ark Pitched and Parked* (Winona Lake, IN: BMH Books, 1977).

Montgomery, John, *The Quest for Noah's Ark*. 2nd Edition. (Minneapolis: Dimension Books, 1974). (Great bibliography)

Morris, Henry and Morris, John, *Acts & Facts* (El Cajon, CA: Institute of Creation Research, 1985-1998). (Newsletter)

Morris, John, *Adventure on Ararat* (San Diego, CA: Institute of Creation Research, 1973).

Morris, John, *Noah's Ark and the Lost World* (El Cajon, CA: Master Books, 1988).

Morris, John, *Noah's Ark and the Ararat Adventure* (Colorado Springs, CO: Master Books, 1994).

Navarra, Ferdinand, *Noah's Ark: I Touched It*. (Plainfield, NJ: Logos International, 1974).

Navarra, Ferdinand, *The Forbidden Mountain* (London: Macdonald and Co., 1956).

Nersessian, Sirapie Der, *The Armenians* (London: Thames & Hudson, 1969).

Noorbergen, Noor, *Noah's Ark Found* (1980).

Noorbergen, Rene, (*The Ark File*, The. New York, NY: Barnes & Noble, 1974).

Ousley, Sir W., *Travels in Persia 1810-1812*. Vol III. (London: Rodwell and Bartin, 1823).

Palego, Angelo, *The Way I Found Noah's Ark*. Self-published (Italy: 1997).

Parrot, Andre, *The Flood and Noah's Ark*. 1st English Translation. (London: SCM Press, 1955).

Parrot, J. J. Friedrich, *Journey to Ararat* (London: Longman, Brown, Green and Longmans, 1845; New York: Arno Press, 1970).

Parseghian, Masis, *Ararat Beckons* videotape (J. Michael Hagopian narrated by Mike Connors, 1996). Excellent photos (some pictures are from the explorers and in this book) and documentary of the Ararat region and history.

Petrosyan, Gavrill, *Armenia* (Moscow, Russia: Novosti Press Agency, 1981).

Piotrovsky, Boris, *The Ancient Civilization of Urartu* (New York: Cowles, 1969).

Porter, Sir Robert Ker, *Travels in Georgia, Persia, Armenia, Ancient Babylonia, during the years 1817, 1818, 1819, and 1820*. 2 volumes (London: Longman, Hurst, Rees, Orme, and Brown, 1821-1822).

Rich, Claudius James, *Narrative of a Residence in Koordistan*. (London: James Duncan, 1836).

Rutstein, Harry and Kroll, Joanne, *In the Footsteps of Marco Polo: A Twentieth Century Odyssey* (New York: Viking Press, 1980).

Seagraves, Kelly L., *Search for Noah's Ark* (San Diego: Beta Books, 1975).

Sellier, Charles E. Jr. and Balsiger, David, *In Search of Noah's Ark* (Los Angeles, CA: Sunn Classic Books, 1976).

Sellier, Charles E. Jr. and Balsiger, David, *The Incredible Discovery of Noah's Ark* (Los Angeles, CA; Sunn Classic Books, 1995).

Shockey, Don, *The Painful Mountain* (Fresno, CA: Pioneer Publishing Co., 1986).

Smith, A. J. and Fletchall, G. F., *The Reported Discovery of Noah's Ark*. Revised Edition. (Published by authors, 1944).

Smith, A. J., *On the Mountains of Ararat in Quest for Noah's Ark* (Apollo, PA: West, 1950).

Southwest Radio Church. Ed., *In Search of Noah's Ark* (Oklahoma City, OK: Southwest Radio Church, 1983). (Ed Behling story, also Dr. Edward Blick tape)

Stark, Freya, *Riding the Tigris* (New York: Harcourt, Brace, and Co., 1959).

Thomsen, Paul, *The Mystery Of The Ark* (Brentwood, TN: Wolgemuth and Hyatt, 1991).

Wells, Carveth, *Kapoot: The Narrative of a Journey from Leningrad to Mount Ararat in Search of Noah's Ark* (New York: Robert M. McBride & Co., 1934).

Wenham, Gordon J., *Word Biblical Commentary: Genesis 1:15.* Vol 1 (Waco, TX: Word Books, 1987).

Wigram, W.A. and Wigram, T.A. Edgar, *The Cradle of Mankind.* (London: 1914).

Wright, Thomas, editor, *Early Travels in Palestine* (London: 1848).

Xenophon. *The Anabasis of Xenophon* (New York: The Limited Editions Club, 1969).

Yamauchi, Edwin M., *Foes from the Northern Frontier* (Baker, 1982).

WEBSITE AND EMAIL INFORMATION

Author Website Address (URL): http://noahsarksearch.com
Author Email Address: bjcorbin@noahsarksearch.com

Publisher Website Address (URL): http://greatcommission.com
Publisher Email Address: books@greatcommission.com

The Explorers of Ararat—And the Search for Noah's Ark
Website Address (URL):
http://www.noahsarksearch.com/explorers/

A Few of the Explorers of Ararat
Courtesy of John McIntosh

Order Form
Great Commission Illustrated Books
Order On-line at http://greatcommission.com

Name_____Address_____

City_____State_____ Zip_____

Phone_____Nation_____

Email Address_____

If the order includes ten or more of an individual item, a discount of 25% applies to that item's Line Total. If you include proof of purchase of previous version of *The Explorers of Ararat*, take 25% off retail price below.

Item	Quantity	Price	Total
Explorers of Ararat: Noah's Ark Search		$24.95	
Ed Behling Interviews on Cassette		$ 8.95	
The Original Ed Davis Video		$24.95	
Riddle of Ararat: Ed Davis, Remote Sensing Expert & More on Video		$24.95	
George Hagopian Interviews on CD		$12.95	
George Hagopian Interviews on Cassette		$ 8.95	
Visions of Ararat Video of Mt. Ararat		$24.95	
The Quest for Noah's Ark Video: PAX		$24.95	
Ararat Report: All Volumes		$49.95	
Is There A God? Science & Bible		$10.95	
In the Beginning: Evolution, Flood		$17.95	
Keeping the Faith: Early Church		$14.95	
Born of Water: The Bible on Baptism		$ 8.95	
		Sub-Total	
	Postage & Handling		
CA residents add 7.25% Sales Tax			
		Total	

For U.S. orders, please include $4.00 postage and handling for the first item ordered, and 50 cents for each additional item. For other countries, add $10.00 for the first item plus $5.00 for each additional item. Orders outside USA, send money order payable in U.S. dollars on U.S. banks only.

Great Commission Illustrated Books (GCI)
4208 Stanbridge Ave.
Long Beach CA 90808-1649
http://greatcommission.com books@greatcommission.com